コンプレックス・エイジ

Complex age
Yui Sakuma

6

C O N T E N T S

Complex age

n.43 3

n.44 23

n.45 43

n.46 63

n.47 83

n.48 103

n.49 123

n.50 143

n.51 163

n.52 Bonus Original Manga 185

Cospedia: Glossary of Cosplay Terms 206

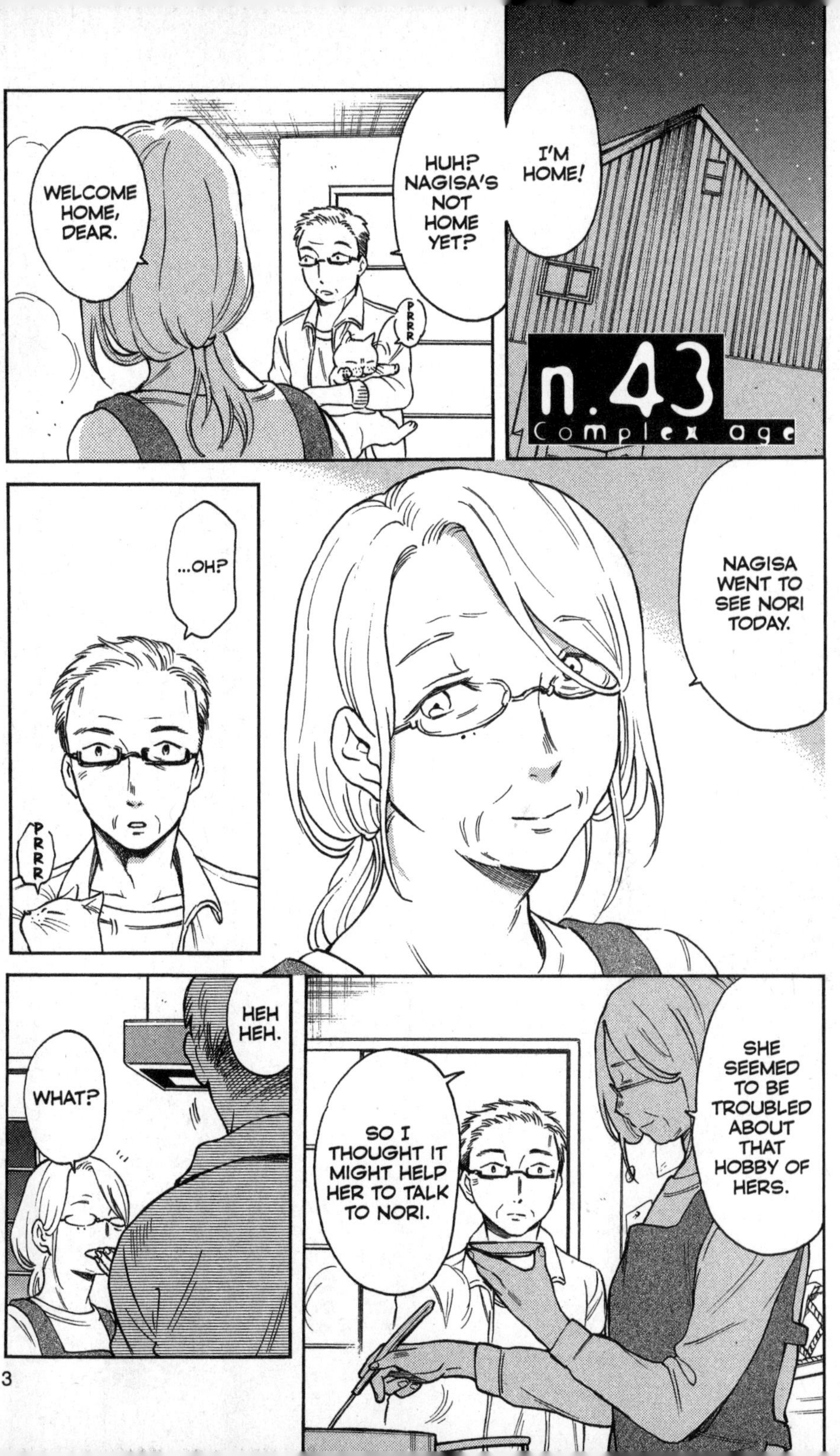
I'M HOME!
n.43
Complex age
HUH? NAGISA'S NOT HOME YET?
PRRR
WELCOME HOME, DEAR.
NAGISA WENT TO SEE NORI TODAY.
...OH?
PRRR
SHE SEEMED TO BE TROUBLED ABOUT THAT HOBBY OF HERS.
SO I THOUGHT IT MIGHT HELP HER TO TALK TO NORI.
HEH HEH.
WHAT?

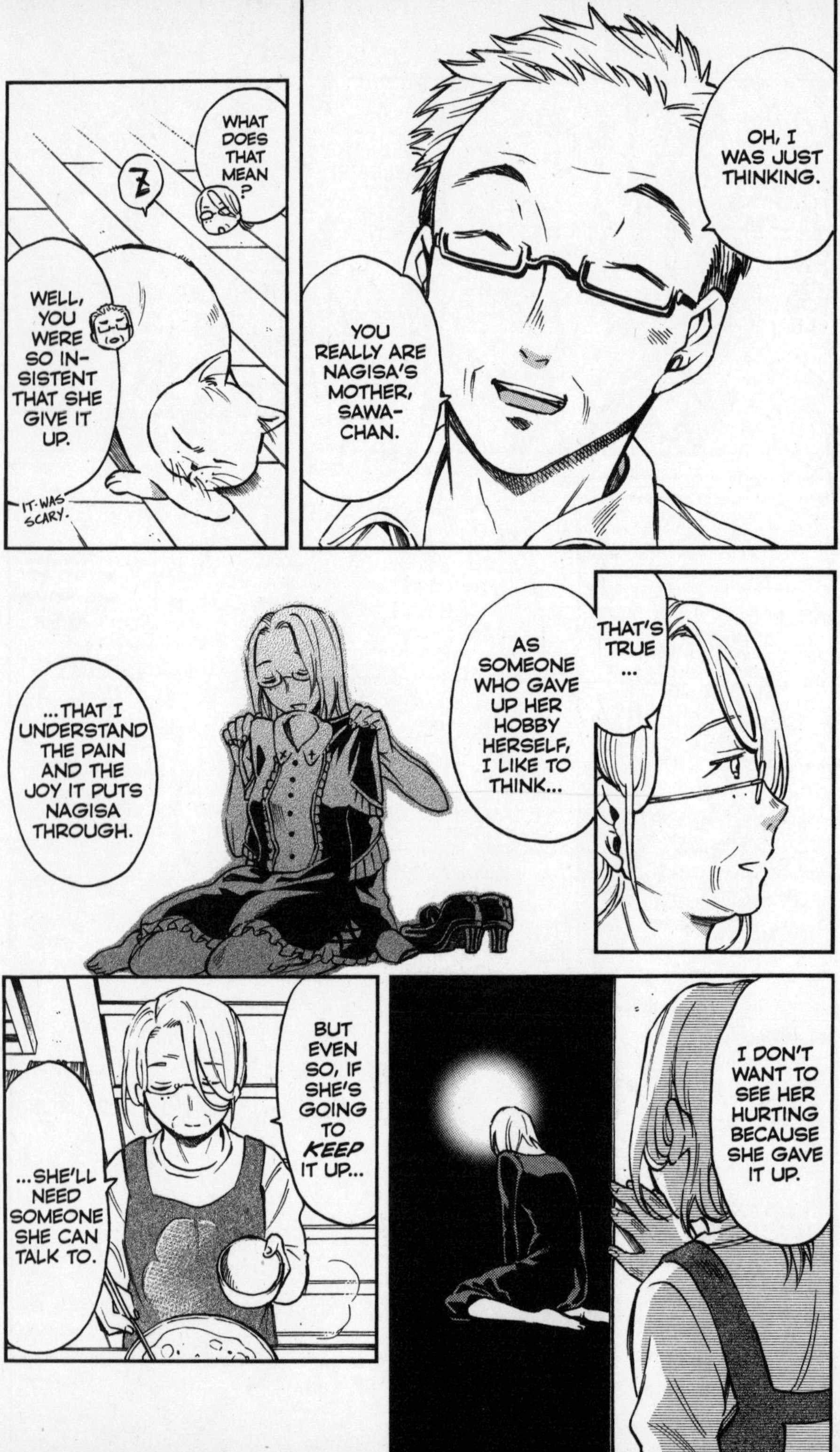
OH, I WAS JUST THINKING.
YOU REALLY ARE NAGISA'S MOTHER, SAWA-CHAN.
WHAT DOES THAT MEAN?
WELL, YOU WERE SO IN-SISTENT THAT SHE GIVE IT UP.
IT WAS SCARY.
THAT'S TRUE...
AS SOMEONE WHO GAVE UP HER HOBBY HERSELF, I LIKE TO THINK...
...THAT I UNDERSTAND THE PAIN AND THE JOY IT PUTS NAGISA THROUGH.
I DON'T WANT TO SEE HER HURTING BECAUSE SHE GAVE IT UP.
BUT EVEN SO, IF SHE'S GOING TO *KEEP* IT UP...
...SHE'LL NEED SOMEONE SHE CAN TALK TO.

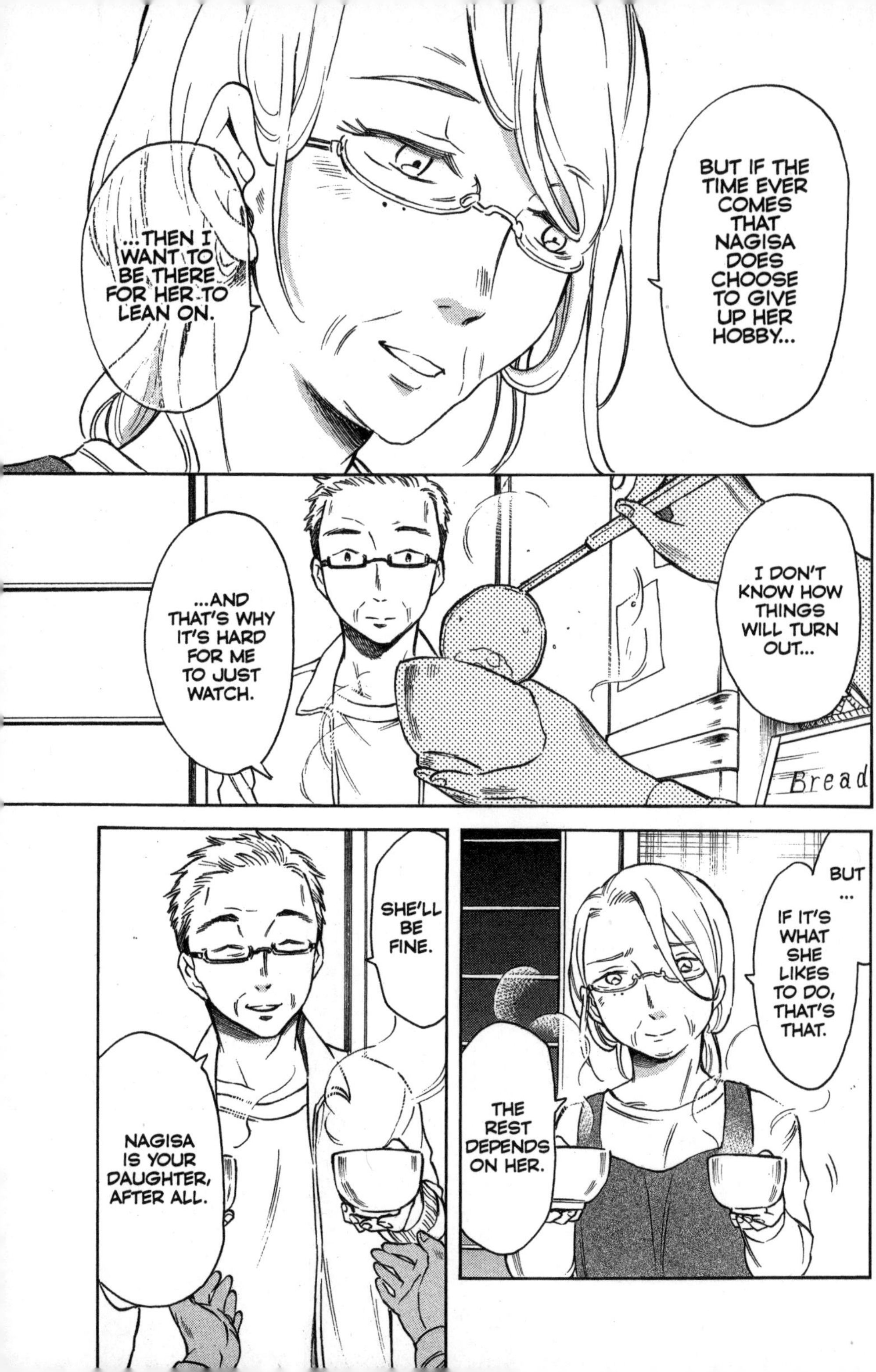
BUT IF THE TIME EVER COMES THAT NAGISA DOES CHOOSE TO GIVE UP HER HOBBY...
...THEN I WANT TO BE THERE FOR HER TO LEAN ON.
I DON'T KNOW HOW THINGS WILL TURN OUT...
...AND THAT'S WHY IT'S HARD FOR ME TO JUST WATCH.
Bread
BUT ... IF IT'S WHAT SHE LIKES TO DO, THAT'S THAT.
THE REST DEPENDS ON HER.
SHE'LL BE FINE.
NAGISA IS YOUR DAUGHTER, AFTER ALL.

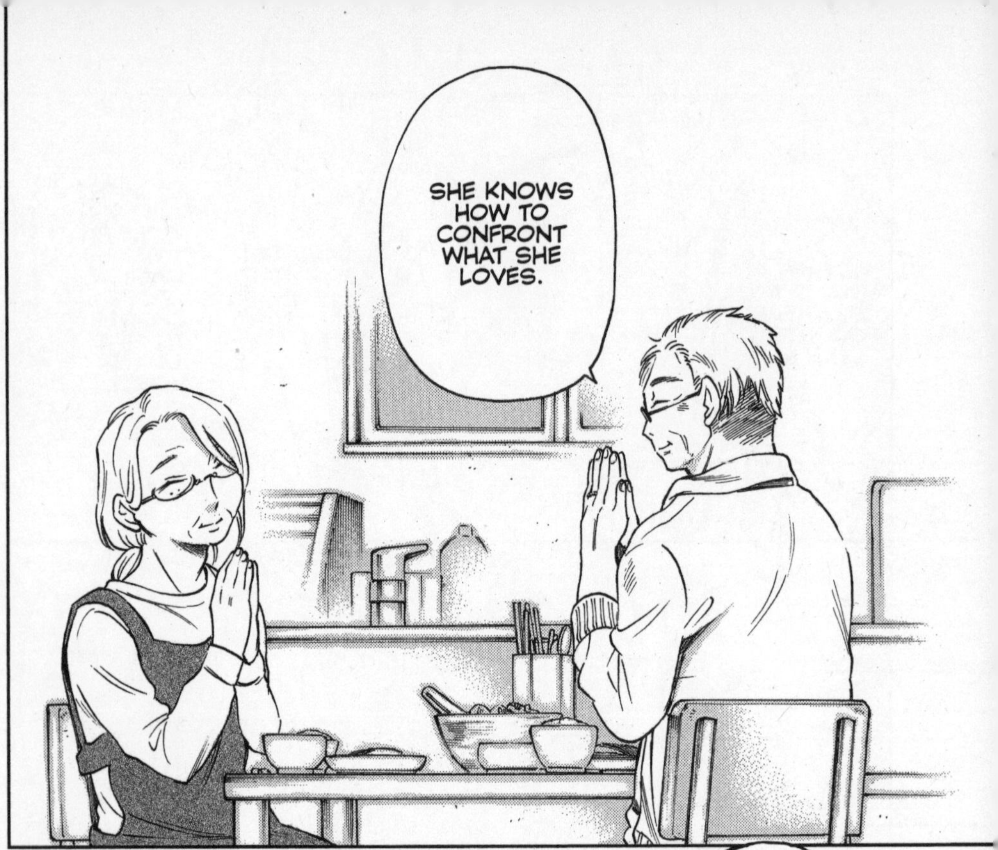
SHE KNOWS HOW TO CONFRONT WHAT SHE LOVES.
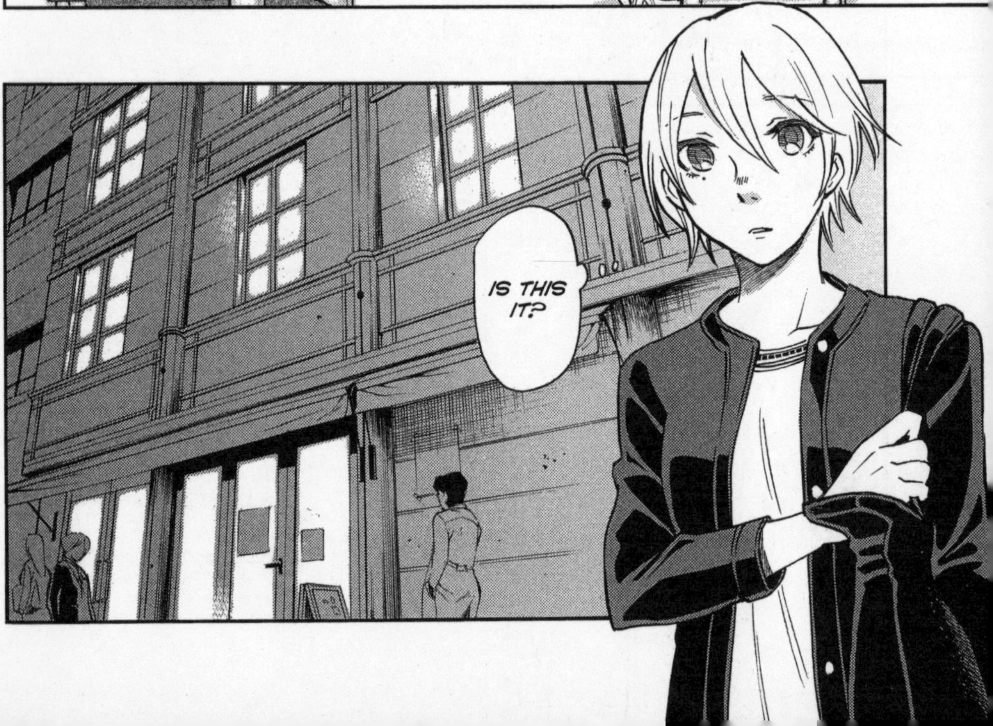
IS THIS IT?

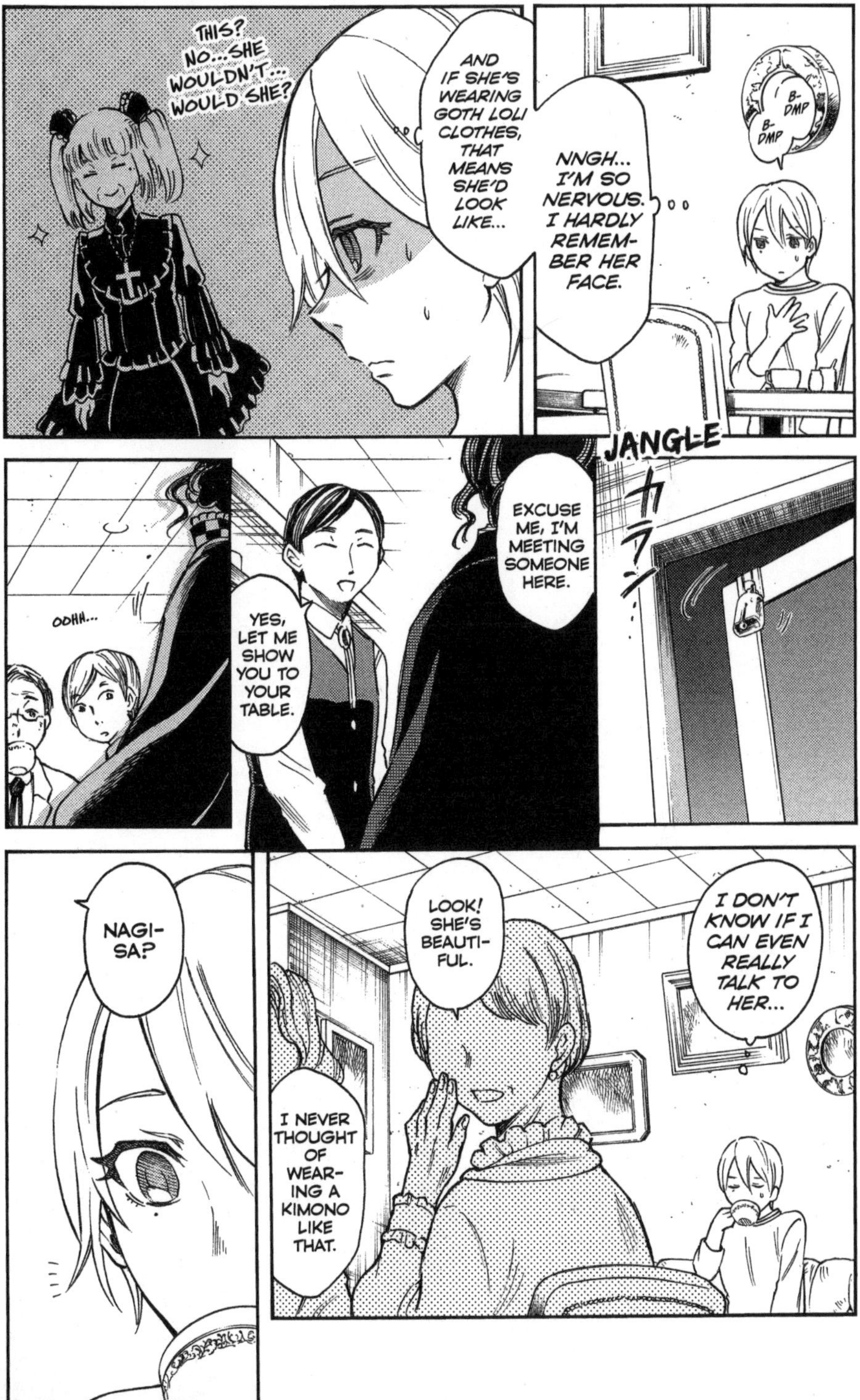
B-DMP B-DMP
NNGH... I'M SO NERVOUS. I HARDLY REMEMBER HER FACE.
AND IF SHE'S WEARING GOTH LOLI CLOTHES, THAT MEANS SHE'D LOOK LIKE...
THIS? NO...SHE WOULDN'T... WOULD SHE?
JANGLE
カラン
EXCUSE ME, I'M MEETING SOMEONE HERE.
YES, LET ME SHOW YOU TO YOUR TABLE.
OOHH...
I DON'T KNOW IF I CAN EVEN REALLY TALK TO HER...
LOOK! SHE'S BEAUTIFUL.
I NEVER THOUGHT OF WEARING A KIMONO LIKE THAT.
NAGISA?

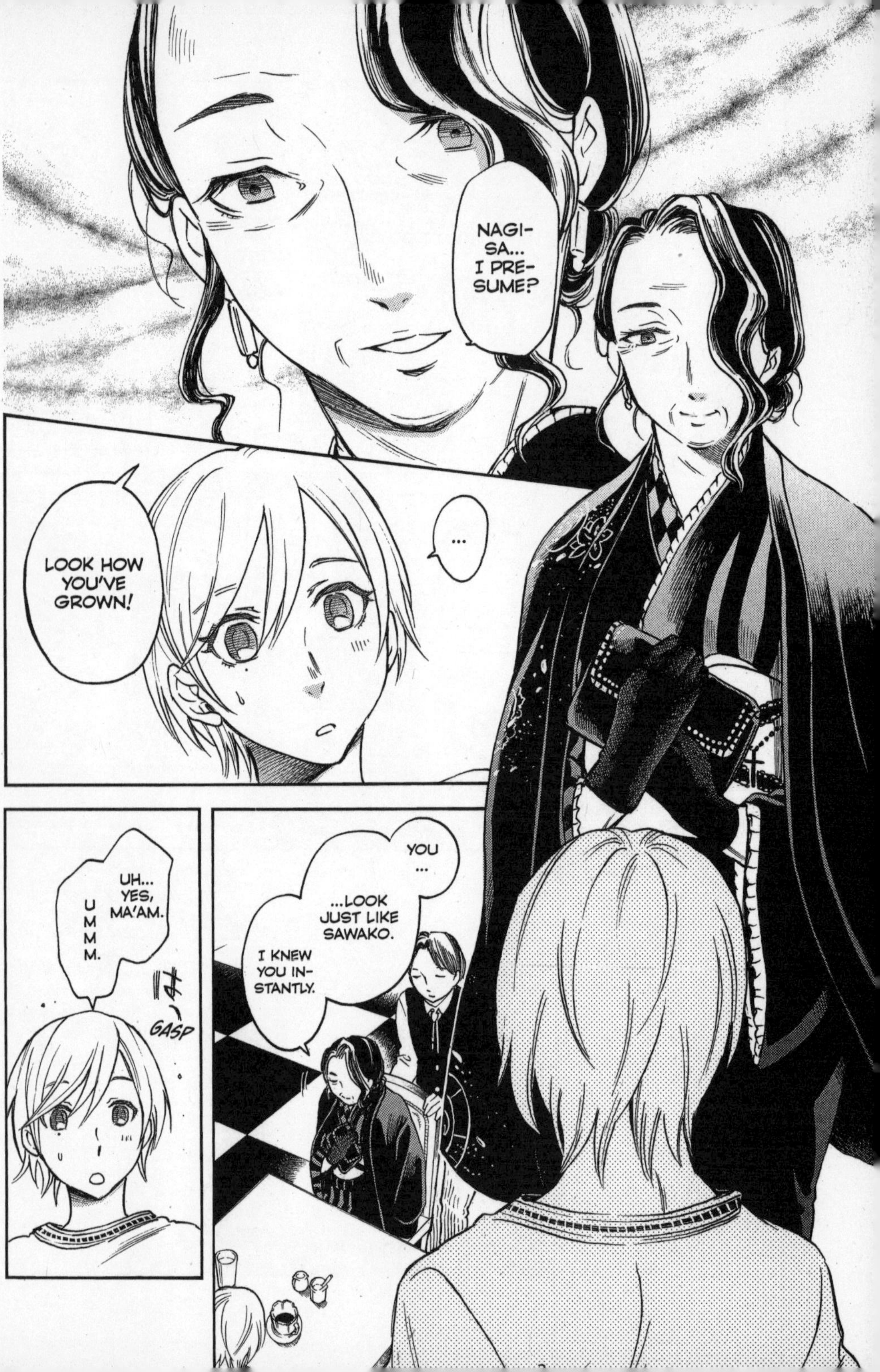
NAGI-SA... I PRE-SUME?
...
LOOK HOW YOU'VE GROWN!
YOU ...
...LOOK JUST LIKE SAWAKO.
I KNEW YOU IN-STANTLY.
UH... YES, MA'AM.
UMMM.
は
GASP

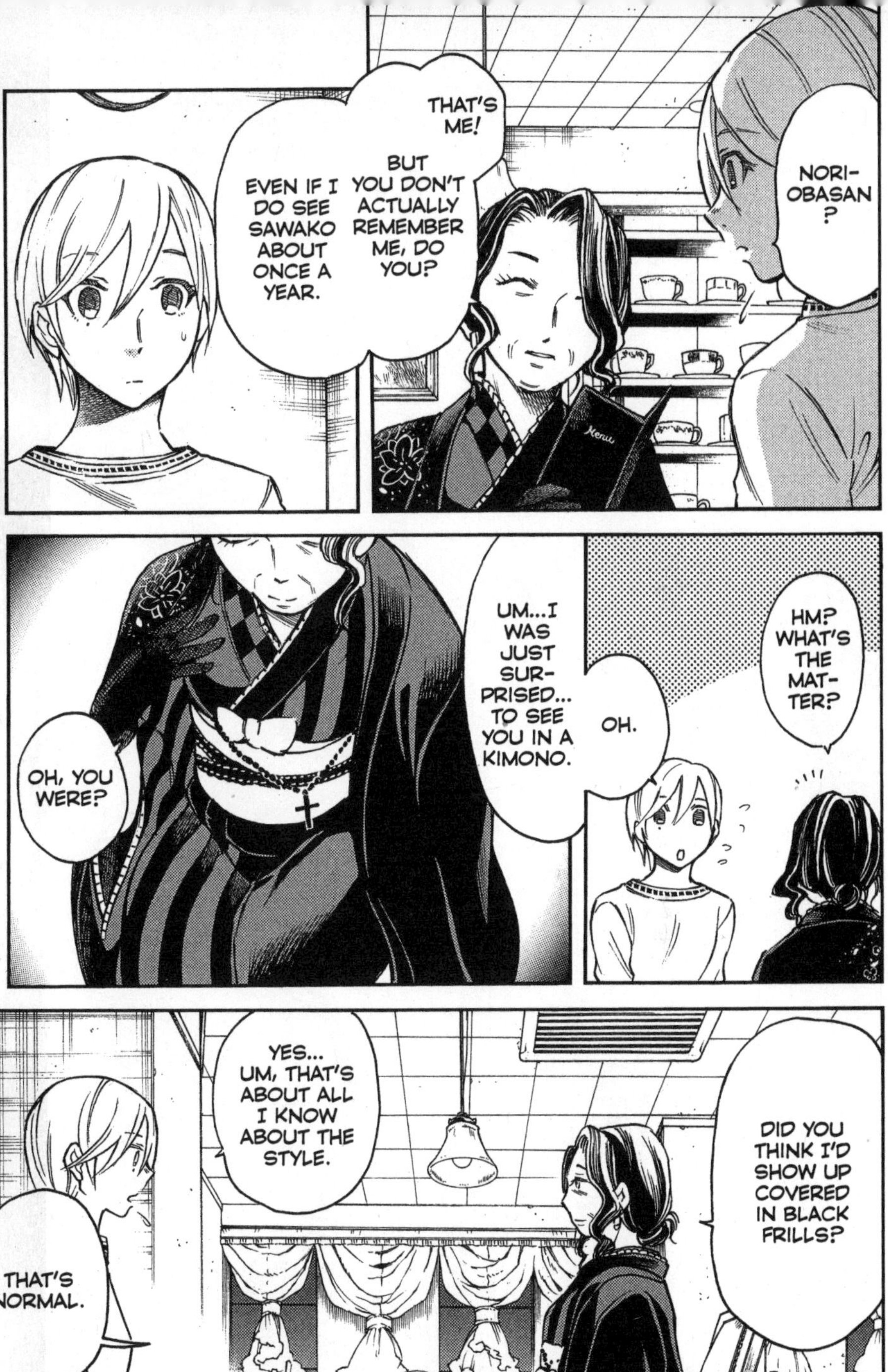
NORI-OBASAN?
THAT'S ME!
BUT YOU DON'T ACTUALLY REMEMBER ME, DO YOU?
EVEN IF I DO SEE SAWAKO ABOUT ONCE A YEAR.
HM? WHAT'S THE MATTER?
OH.
UM...I WAS JUST SURPRISED... TO SEE YOU IN A KIMONO.
OH, YOU WERE?
DID YOU THINK I'D SHOW UP COVERED IN BLACK FRILLS?
YES... UM, THAT'S ABOUT ALL I KNOW ABOUT THE STYLE.
THAT'S NORMAL.

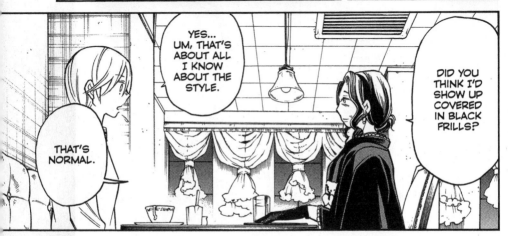

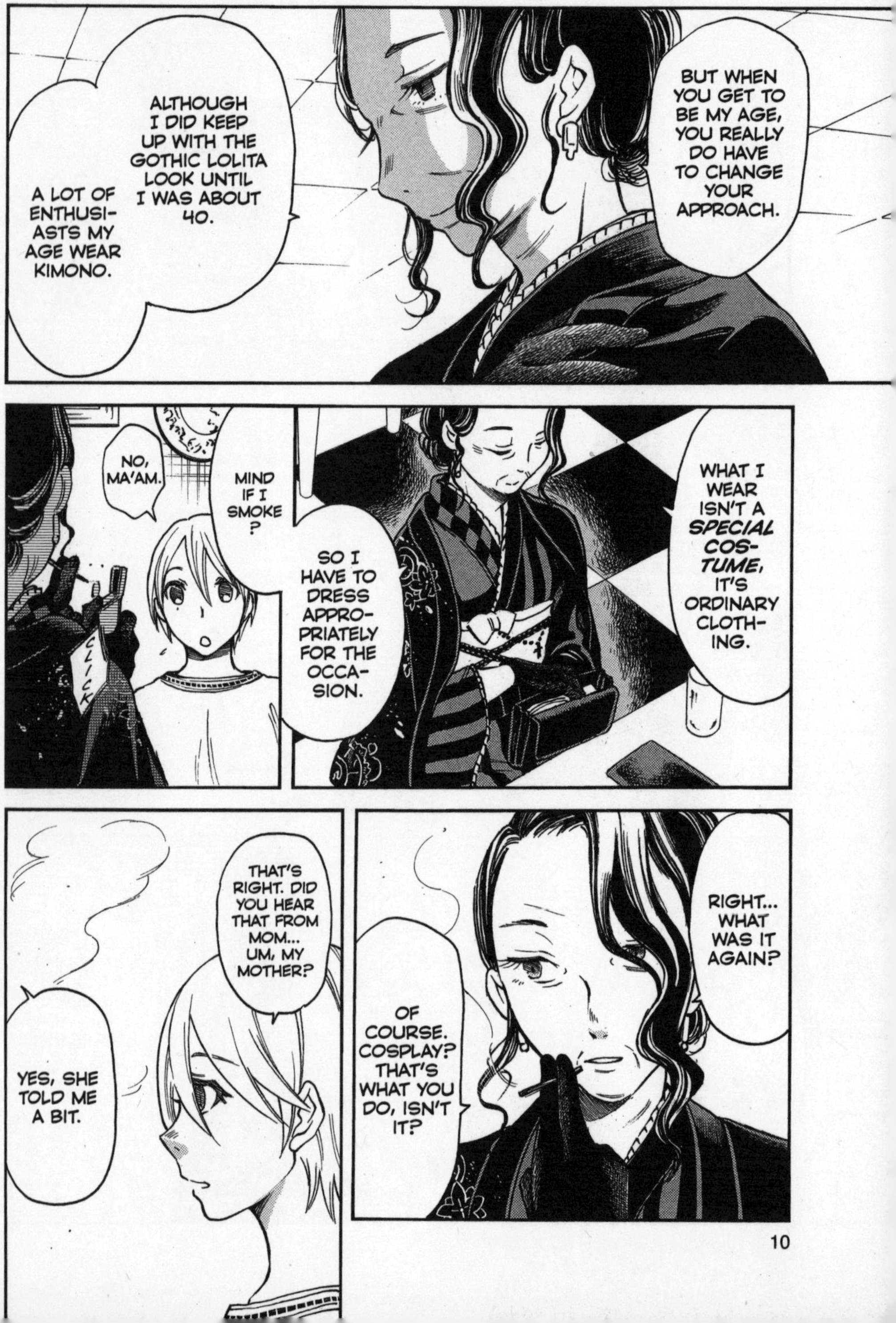
BUT WHEN YOU GET TO BE MY AGE, YOU REALLY DO HAVE TO CHANGE YOUR APPROACH.
ALTHOUGH I DID KEEP UP WITH THE GOTHIC LOLITA LOOK UNTIL I WAS ABOUT 40.
A LOT OF ENTHUSIASTS MY AGE WEAR KIMONO.
WHAT I WEAR ISN'T A *SPECIAL COSTUME*, IT'S ORDINARY CLOTHING.
SO I HAVE TO DRESS APPROPRIATELY FOR THE OCCASION.
MIND IF I SMOKE?
NO, MA'AM.
CLICK
RIGHT... WHAT WAS IT AGAIN?
OF COURSE. COSPLAY? THAT'S WHAT YOU DO, ISN'T IT?
THAT'S RIGHT. DID YOU HEAR THAT FROM MOM... UM, MY MOTHER?
YES, SHE TOLD ME A BIT.

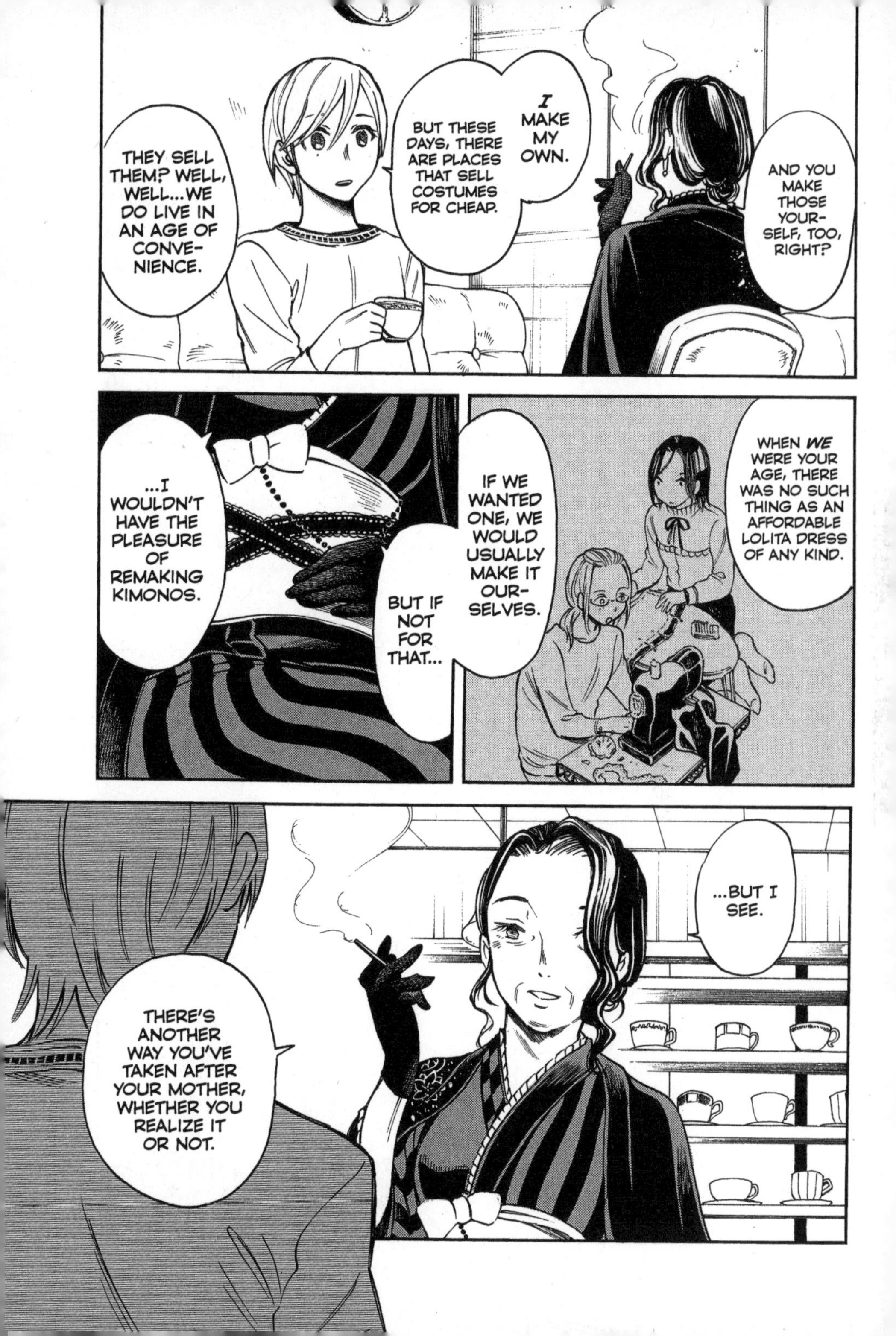
AND YOU MAKE THOSE YOUR-SELF, TOO, RIGHT?
I MAKE MY OWN.
BUT THESE DAYS, THERE ARE PLACES THAT SELL COSTUMES FOR CHEAP.
THEY SELL THEM? WELL, WELL...WE DO LIVE IN AN AGE OF CONVE-NIENCE.
WHEN *WE* WERE YOUR AGE, THERE WAS NO SUCH THING AS AN AFFORDABLE LOLITA DRESS OF ANY KIND.
IF WE WANTED ONE, WE WOULD USUALLY MAKE IT OUR-SELVES.
BUT IF NOT FOR THAT...
...I WOULDN'T HAVE THE PLEASURE OF REMAKING KIMONOS.
...BUT I SEE.
THERE'S ANOTHER WAY YOU'VE TAKEN AFTER YOUR MOTHER, WHETHER YOU REALIZE IT OR NOT.

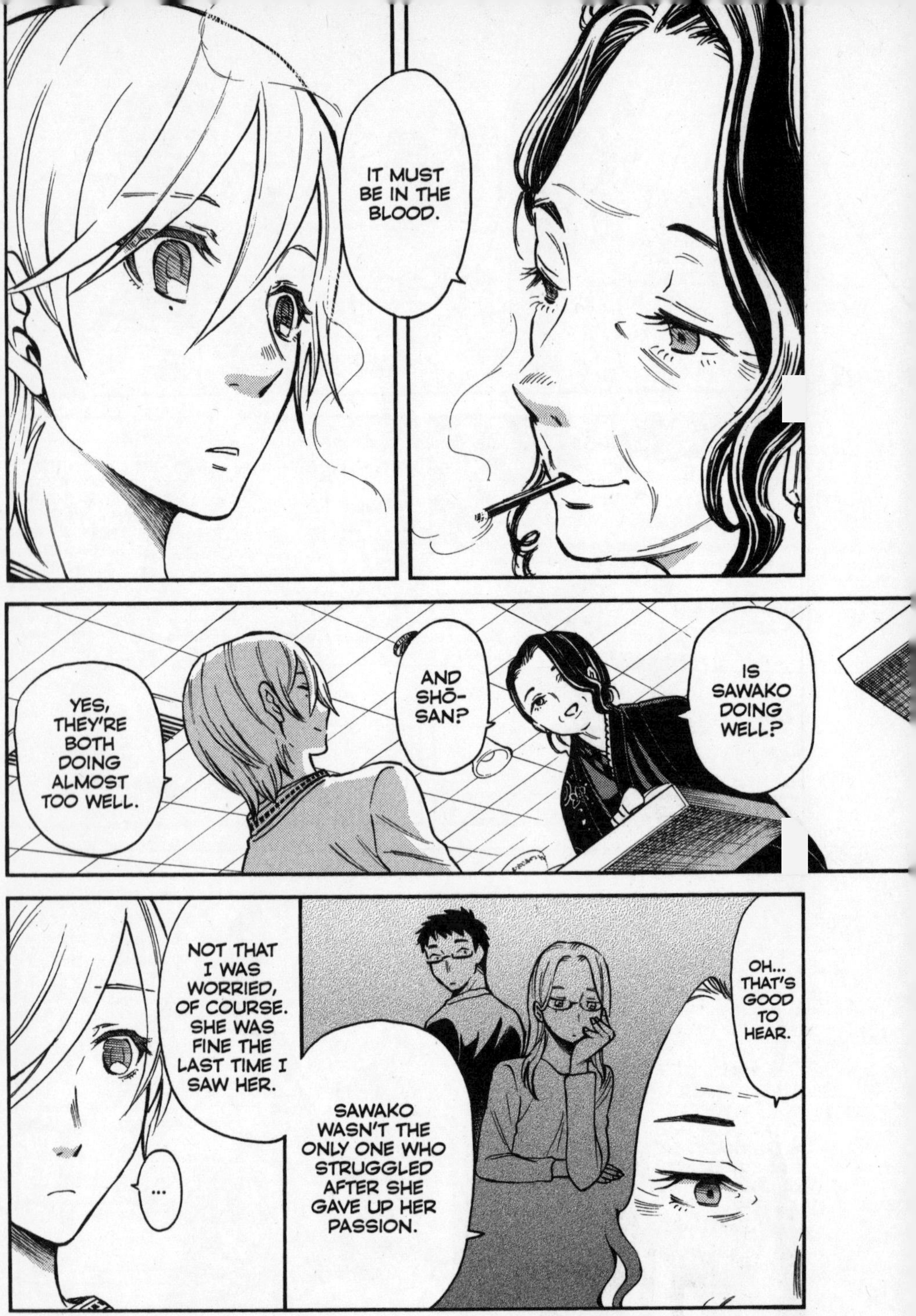
IT MUST BE IN THE BLOOD.
IS SAWAKO DOING WELL?
AND SHŌ-SAN?
YES, THEY'RE BOTH DOING ALMOST TOO WELL.
OH... THAT'S GOOD TO HEAR.
NOT THAT I WAS WORRIED, OF COURSE. SHE WAS FINE THE LAST TIME I SAW HER.
SAWAKO WASN'T THE ONLY ONE WHO STRUGGLED AFTER SHE GAVE UP HER PASSION.
...

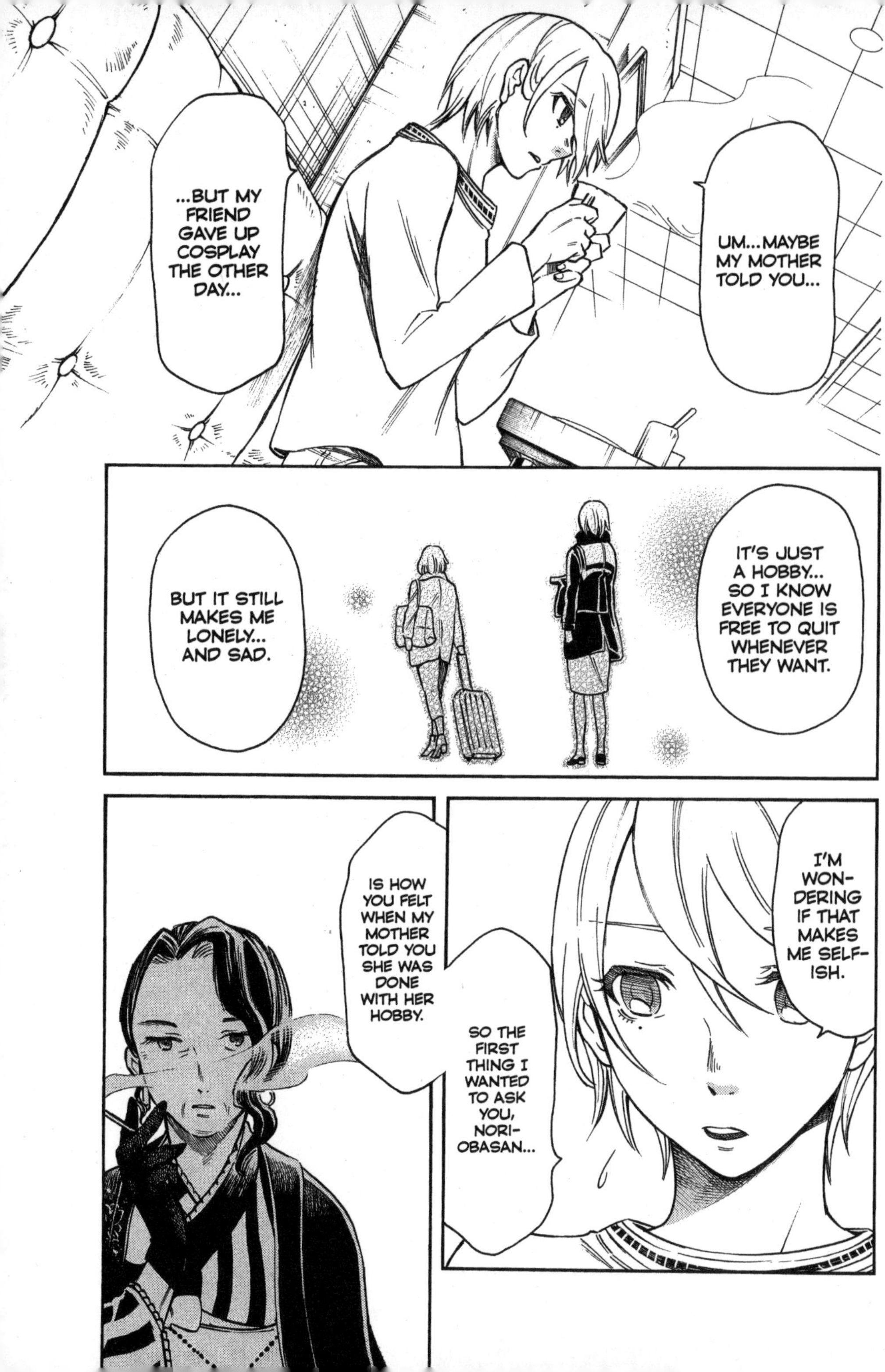
UM...MAYBE MY MOTHER TOLD YOU...
...BUT MY FRIEND GAVE UP COSPLAY THE OTHER DAY...
IT'S JUST A HOBBY... SO I KNOW EVERYONE IS FREE TO QUIT WHENEVER THEY WANT.
BUT IT STILL MAKES ME LONELY... AND SAD.
I'M WON-DERING IF THAT MAKES ME SELF-ISH.
SO THE FIRST THING I WANTED TO ASK YOU, NORI-OBASAN...
IS HOW YOU FELT WHEN MY MOTHER TOLD YOU SHE WAS DONE WITH HER HOBBY.

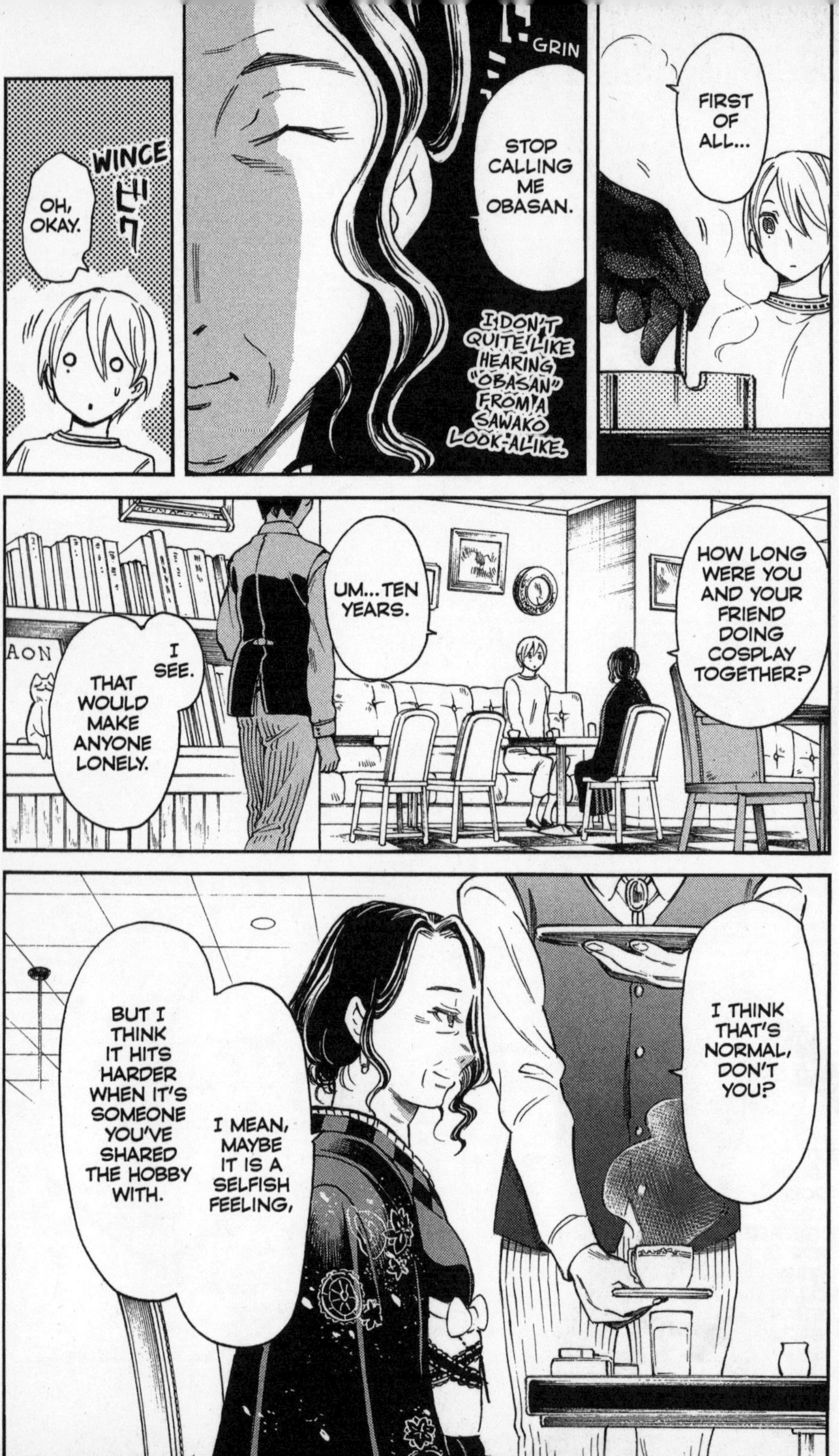
FIRST OF ALL...
GRIN
STOP CALLING ME OBASAN.
I DON'T QUITE LIKE HEARING "OBASAN" FROM A SAWAKO LOOK-ALIKE.
WINCE
ビク
OH, OKAY.
HOW LONG WERE YOU AND YOUR FRIEND DOING COSPLAY TOGETHER?
UM...TEN YEARS.
I SEE.
THAT WOULD MAKE ANYONE LONELY.
I THINK THAT'S NORMAL, DON'T YOU?
I MEAN, MAYBE IT IS A SELFISH FEELING,
BUT I THINK IT HITS HARDER WHEN IT'S SOMEONE YOU'VE SHARED THE HOBBY WITH.

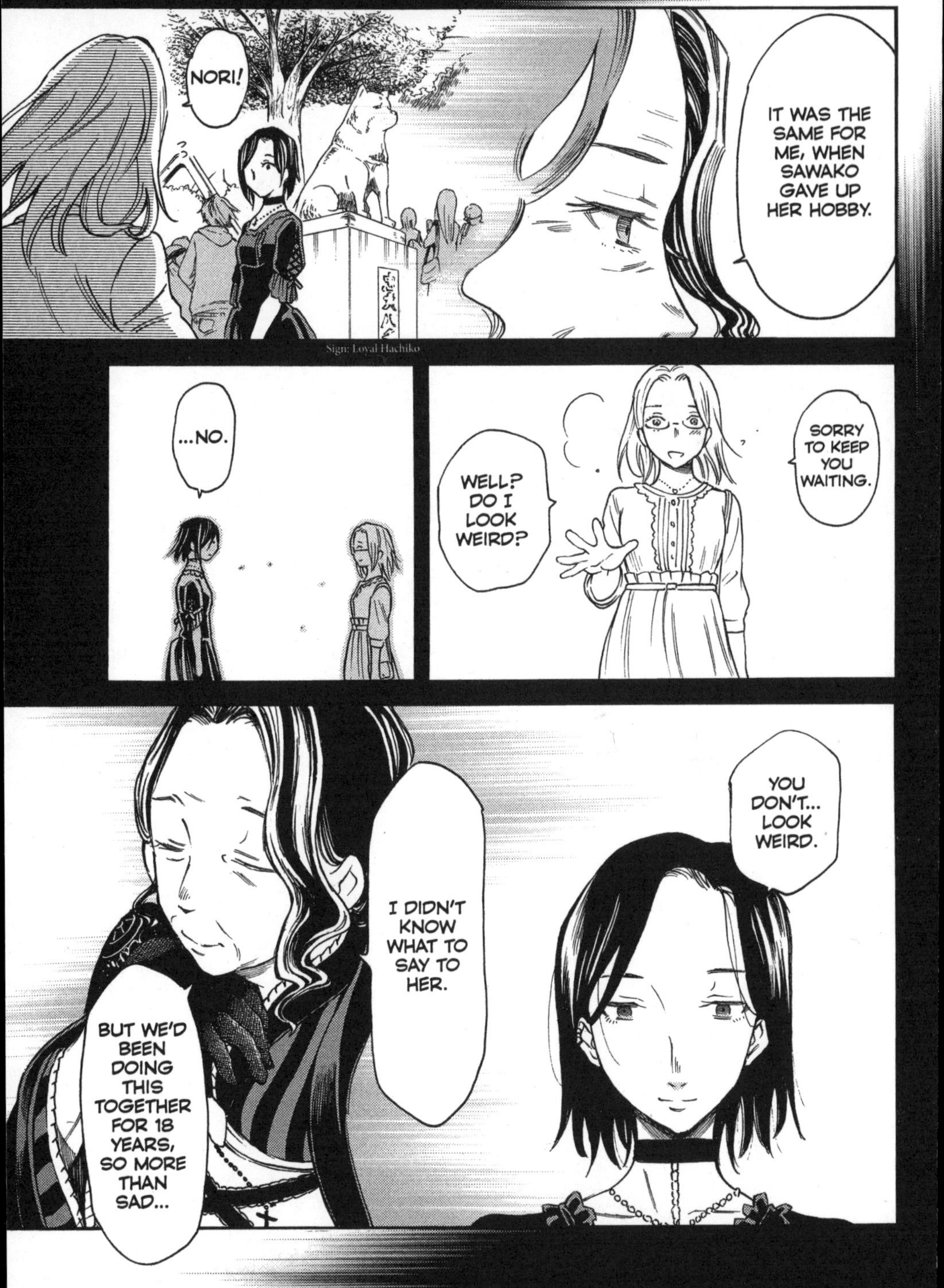
IT WAS THE SAME FOR ME, WHEN SAWAKO GAVE UP HER HOBBY.
NORI!
Sign: Loyal Hachiko
SORRY TO KEEP YOU WAITING.
WELL? DO I LOOK WEIRD?
...NO.
YOU DON'T... LOOK WEIRD.
I DIDN'T KNOW WHAT TO SAY TO HER.
BUT WE'D BEEN DOING THIS TOGETHER FOR 18 YEARS, SO MORE THAN SAD...

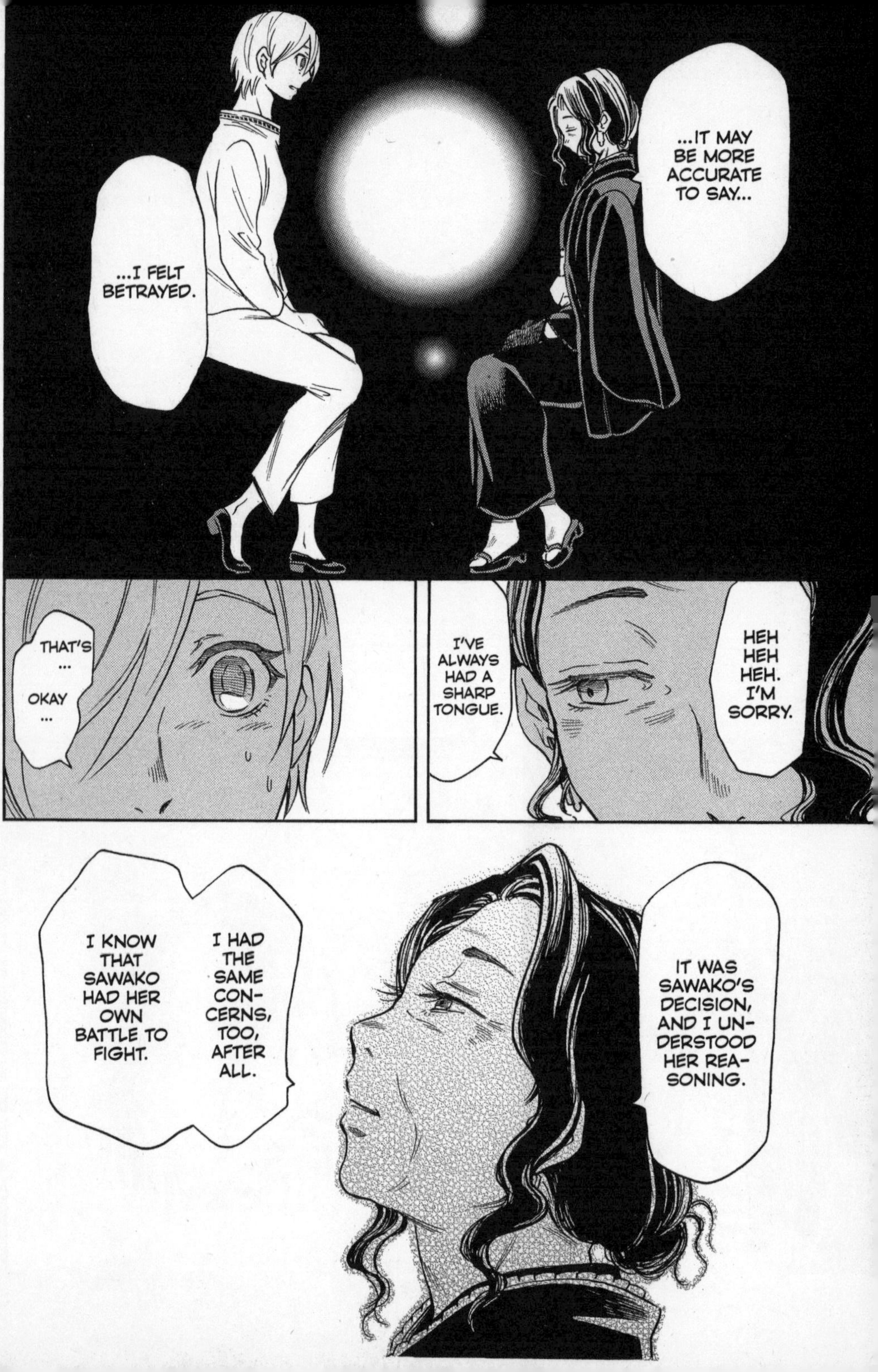
...IT MAY BE MORE ACCURATE TO SAY...
...I FELT BETRAYED.
HEH HEH HEH. I'M SORRY.
I'VE ALWAYS HAD A SHARP TONGUE.
THAT'S... OKAY...
IT WAS SAWAKO'S DECISION, AND I UNDERSTOOD HER REASONING.
I HAD THE SAME CONCERNS, TOO, AFTER ALL.
I KNOW THAT SAWAKO HAD HER OWN BATTLE TO FIGHT.

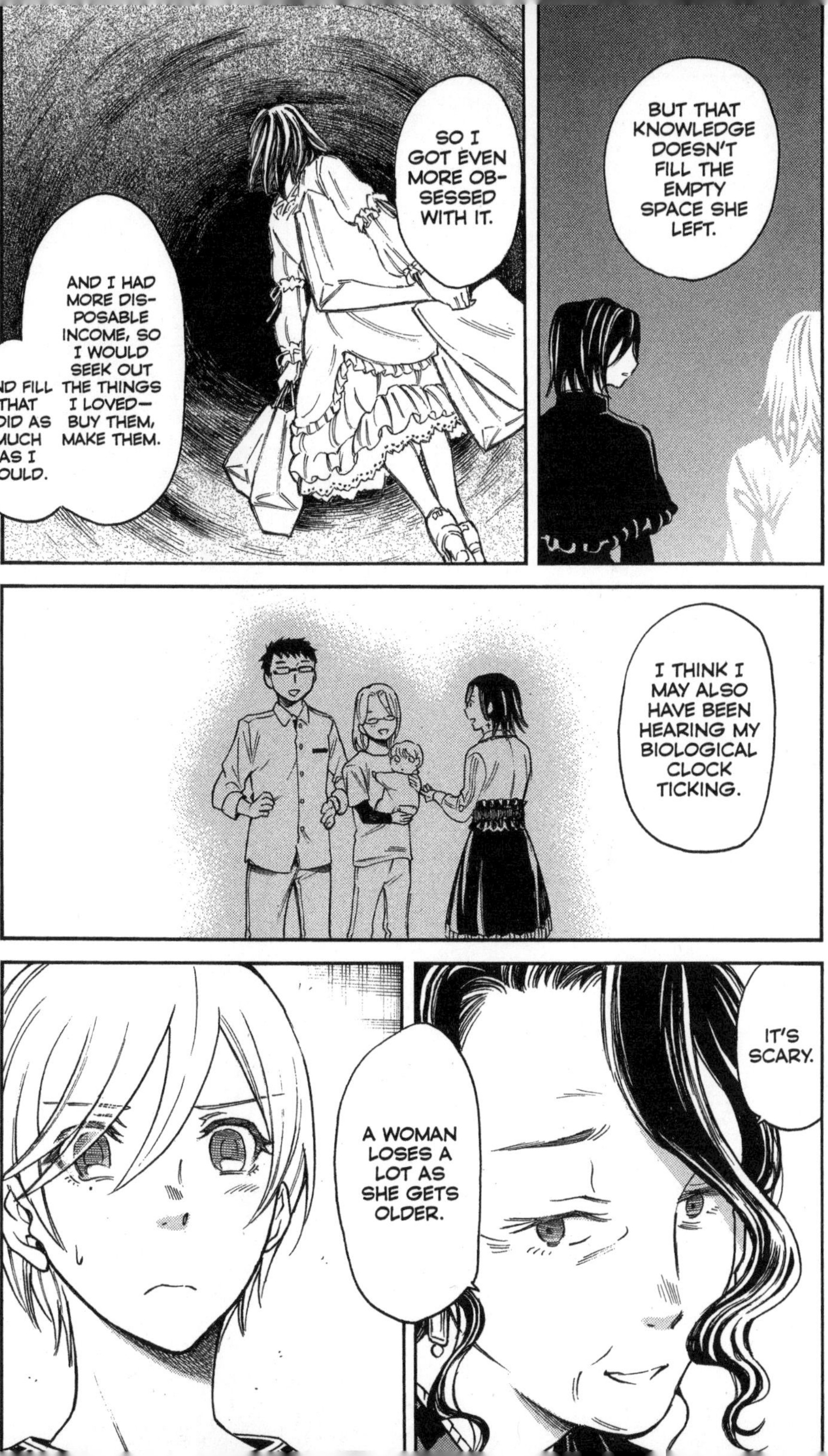

BUT THAT KNOWLEDGE DOESN'T FILL THE EMPTY SPACE SHE LEFT.
SO I GOT EVEN MORE OBSESSED WITH IT.
AND I HAD MORE DISPOSABLE INCOME, SO I WOULD SEEK OUT THE THINGS I LOVED—BUY THEM, MAKE THEM.
AND FILL THAT VOID AS MUCH AS I COULD.
I THINK I MAY ALSO HAVE BEEN HEARING MY BIOLOGICAL CLOCK TICKING.
IT'S SCARY.
A WOMAN LOSES A LOT AS SHE GETS OLDER.

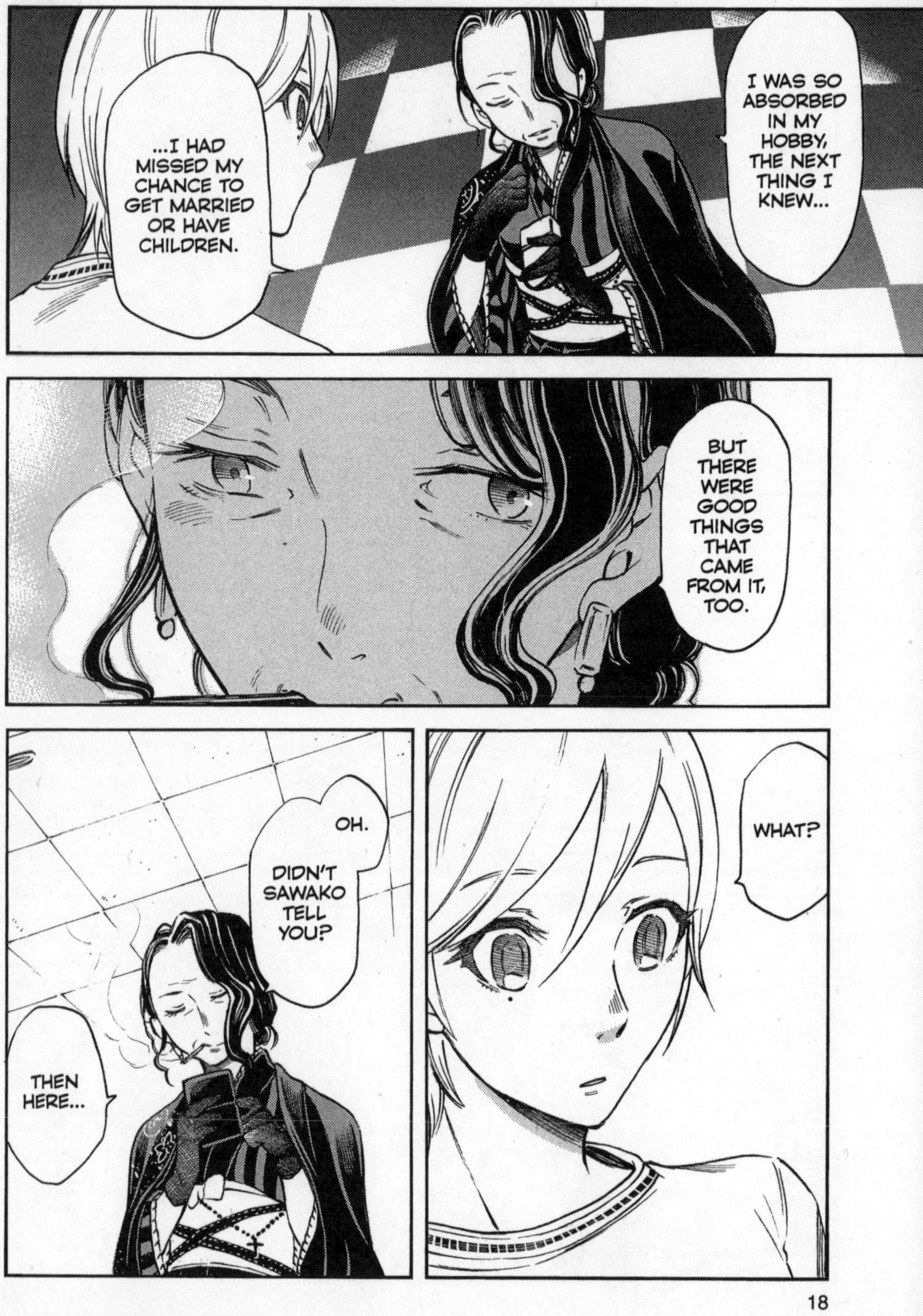
I WAS SO ABSORBED IN MY HOBBY, THE NEXT THING I KNEW...
...I HAD MISSED MY CHANCE TO GET MARRIED OR HAVE CHILDREN.
BUT THERE WERE GOOD THINGS THAT CAME FROM IT, TOO.
WHAT?
OH.
DIDN'T SAWAKO TELL YOU?
THEN HERE...

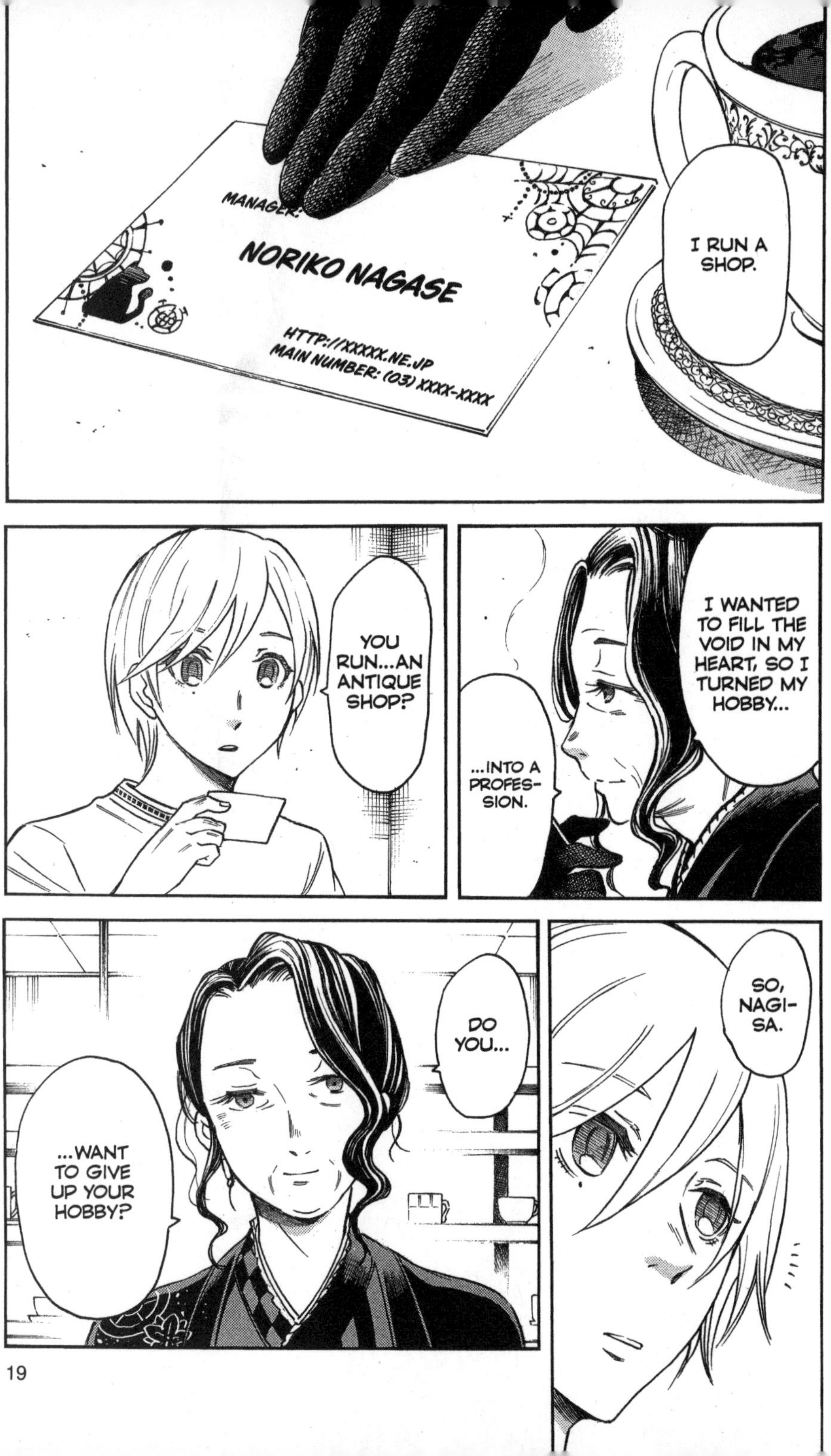
I RUN A SHOP.
MANAGER:
NORIKO NAGASE
HTTP://XXXXX.NE.JP
MAIN NUMBER: (03) XXXX-XXXX
I WANTED TO FILL THE VOID IN MY HEART, SO I TURNED MY HOBBY...
...INTO A PROFES-SION.
YOU RUN...AN ANTIQUE SHOP?
SO, NAGI-SA.
DO YOU...
...WANT TO GIVE UP YOUR HOBBY?

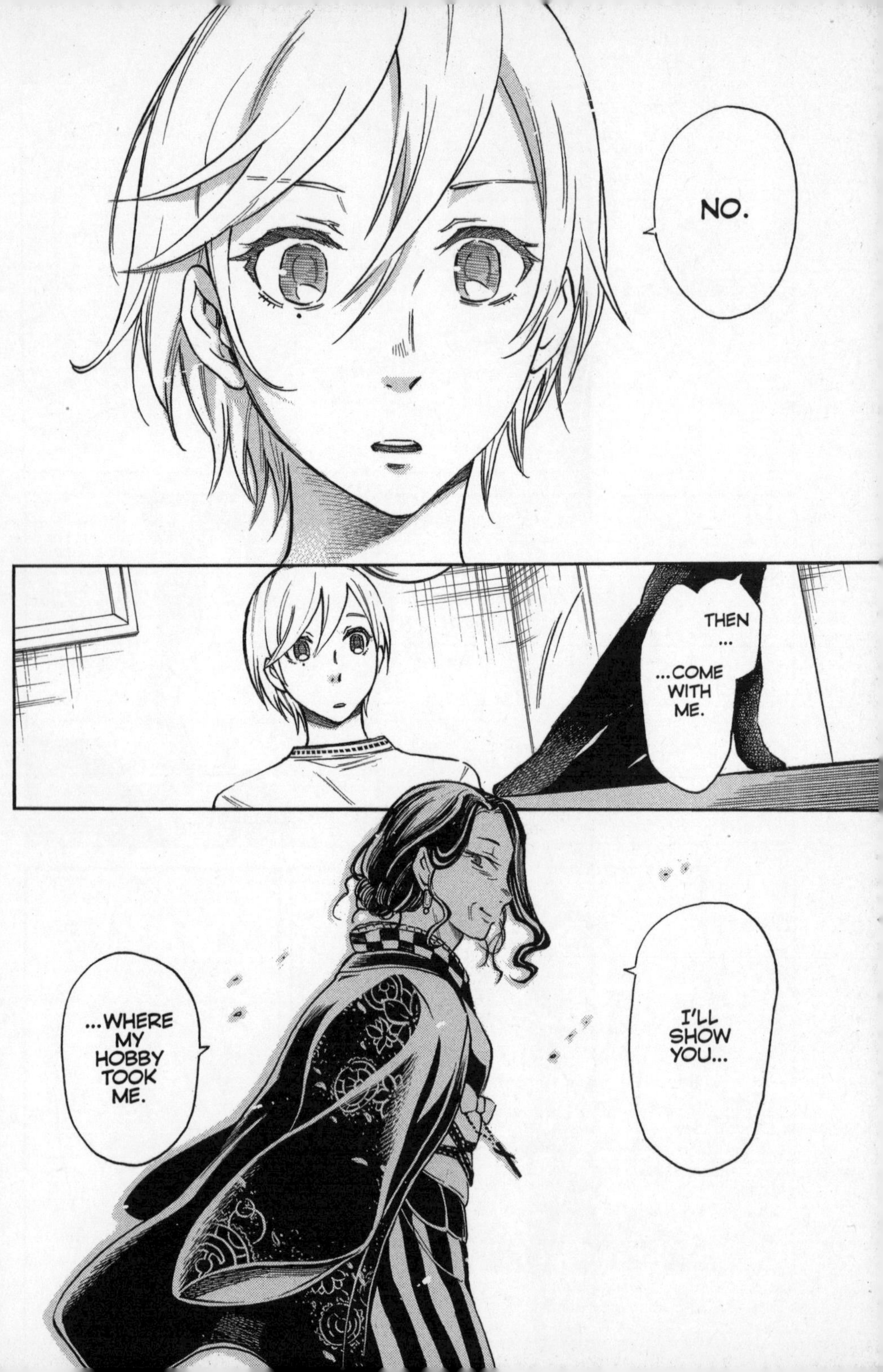
NO.
THEN ... ...COME WITH ME.
I'LL SHOW YOU...
...WHERE MY HOBBY TOOK ME.

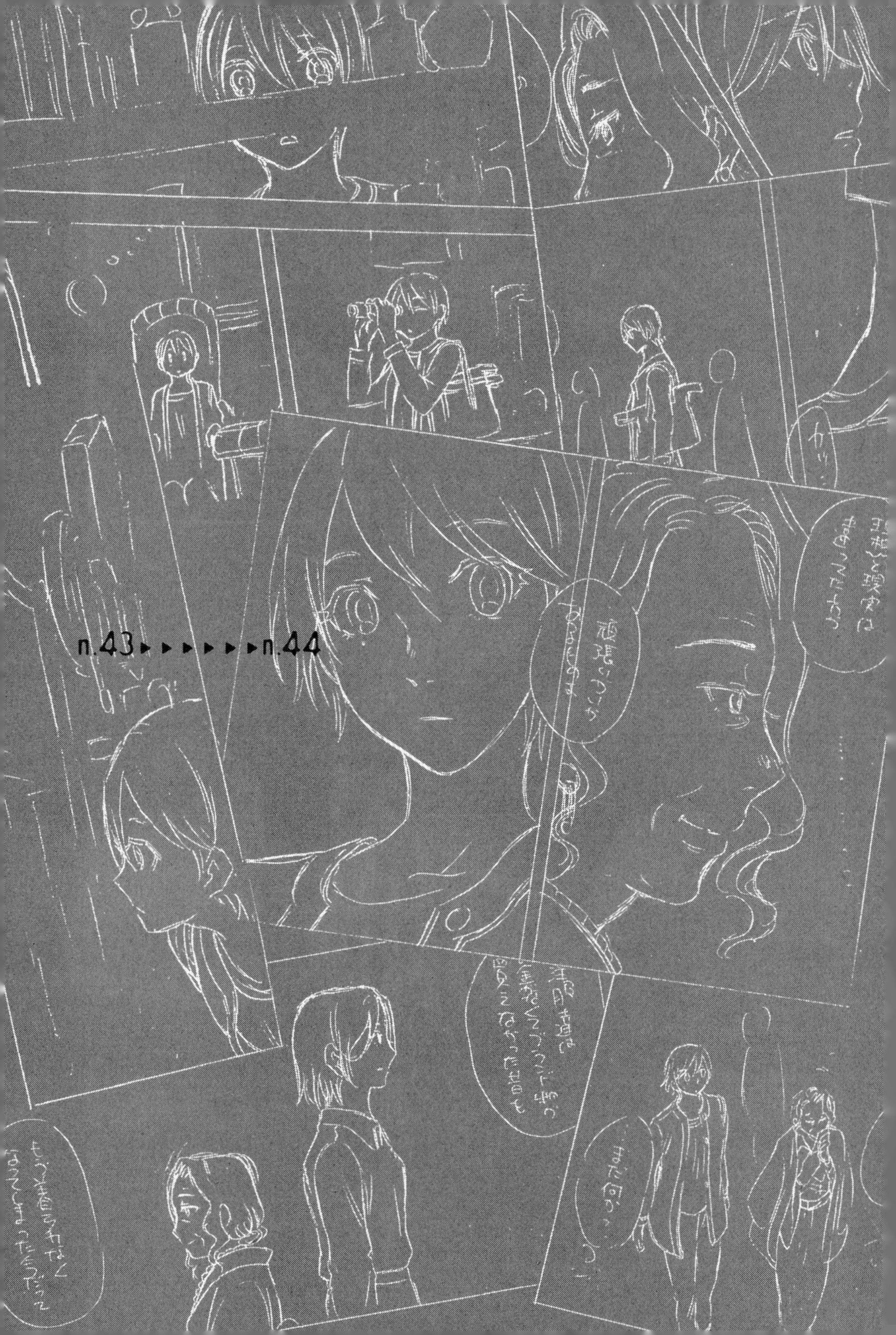

カッ…
変わったよ
頑張ってる
n.43▸▸▸▸▸▸▸n.44
毎日市場に
また何か…

THIS SERIES HAS REACHED ITS FINAL VOLUME. THANK YOU FOR STICKING WITH IT TO THE END.

NOW, FOR THIS VOLUME, I HOPE TO TALK ABOUT HOW THIS SERIES CAME TO BE, AND WHAT IT'S LIKE AT WORK.

MY FIRST WEEKLY SERIES ...

IT WAS THE MOST JAM-PACKED YEAR OF MY LIFE SO FAR.

I WANT MY LIFE TO KEEP BEING SO PACKED AND EXHAUSTING THAT IT MAKES ME WANT TO VOMIT.

佐久間結衣

YUI SAKUMA

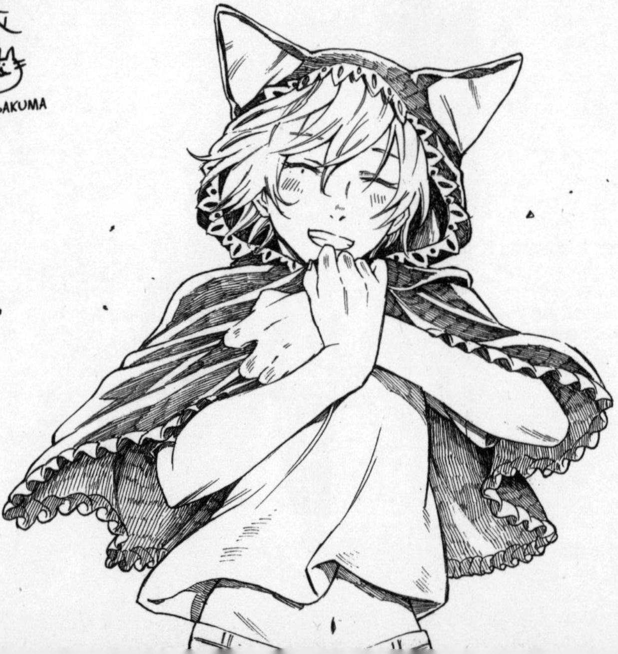

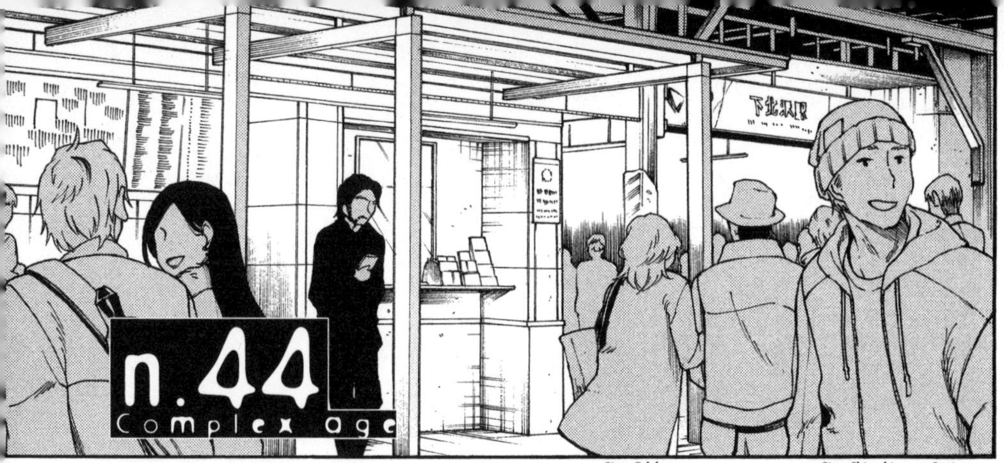
n.44
Complex age

Sign: Odakyu

Sign: Shimokitazawa Station

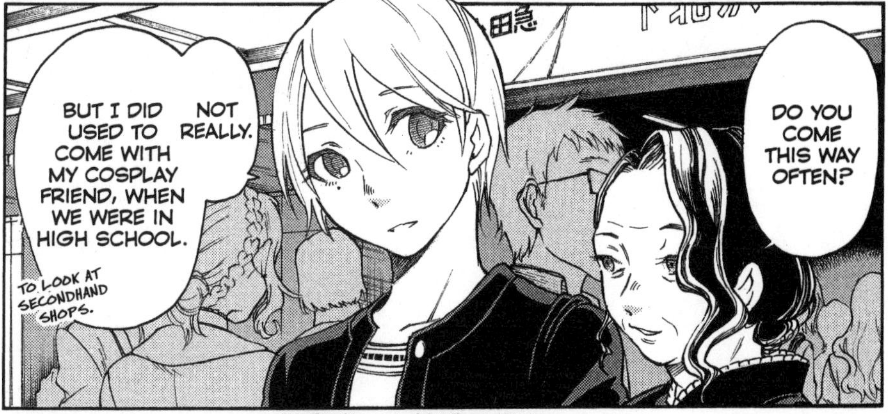
DO YOU COME THIS WAY OFTEN?
NOT REALLY.
BUT I DID USED TO COME WITH MY COSPLAY FRIEND, WHEN WE WERE IN HIGH SCHOOL.
TO LOOK AT SECONDHAND SHOPS.

Sign: Shimokitazawa South Exit Shopping District

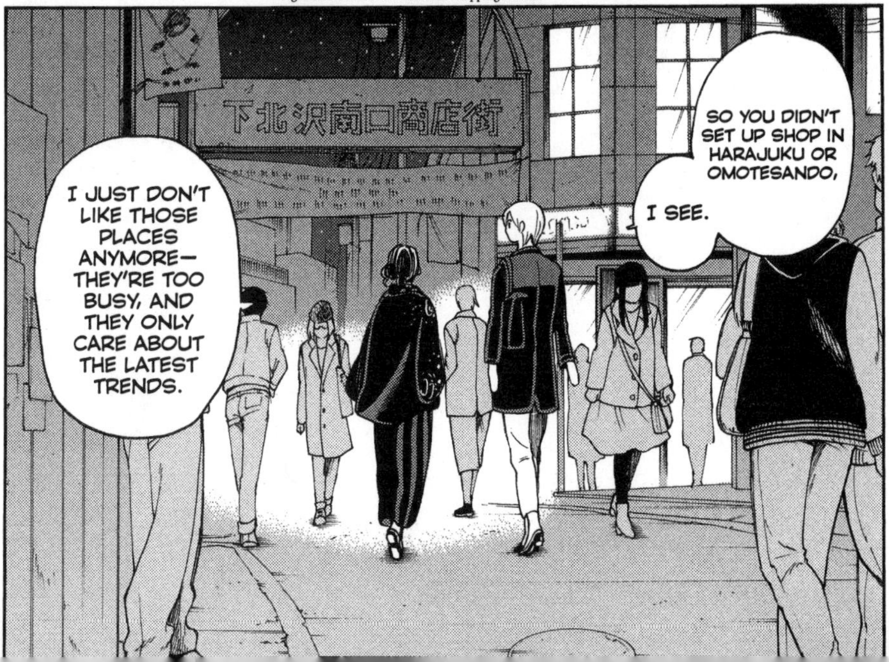
SO YOU DIDN'T SET UP SHOP IN HARAJUKU OR OMOTESANDO,
I SEE.
I JUST DON'T LIKE THOSE PLACES ANYMORE—THEY'RE TOO BUSY, AND THEY ONLY CARE ABOUT THE LATEST TRENDS.

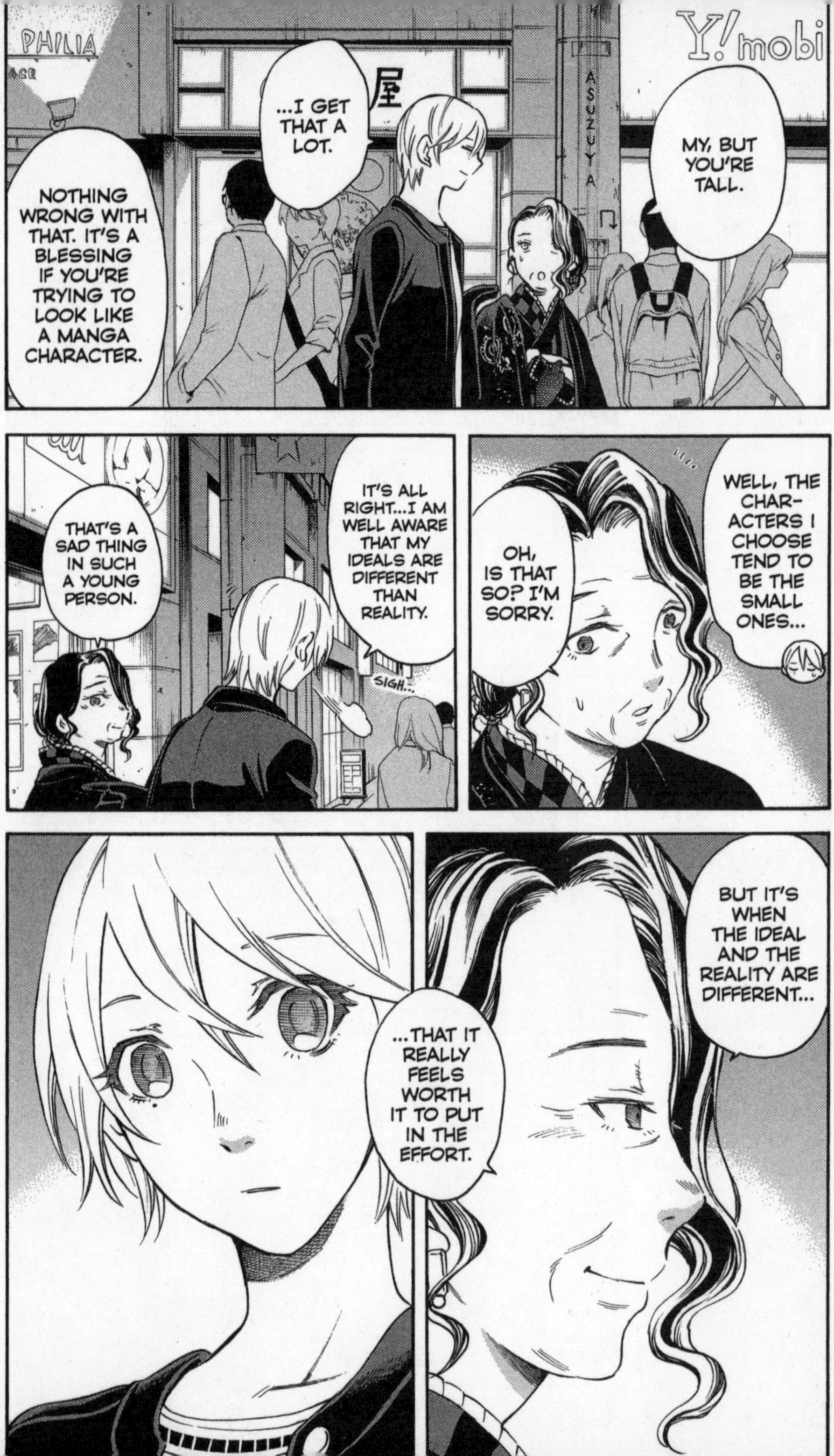
Y!mobi
ASUZUYA
屋
PHILIA
MY, BUT YOU'RE TALL.
...I GET THAT A LOT.
NOTHING WRONG WITH THAT. IT'S A BLESSING IF YOU'RE TRYING TO LOOK LIKE A MANGA CHARACTER.
WELL, THE CHAR-ACTERS I CHOOSE TEND TO BE THE SMALL ONES...
OH, IS THAT SO? I'M SORRY.
IT'S ALL RIGHT...I AM WELL AWARE THAT MY IDEALS ARE DIFFERENT THAN REALITY.
SIGH...
THAT'S A SAD THING IN SUCH A YOUNG PERSON.
BUT IT'S WHEN THE IDEAL AND THE REALITY ARE DIFFERENT...
...THAT IT REALLY FEELS WORTH IT TO PUT IN THE EFFORT.

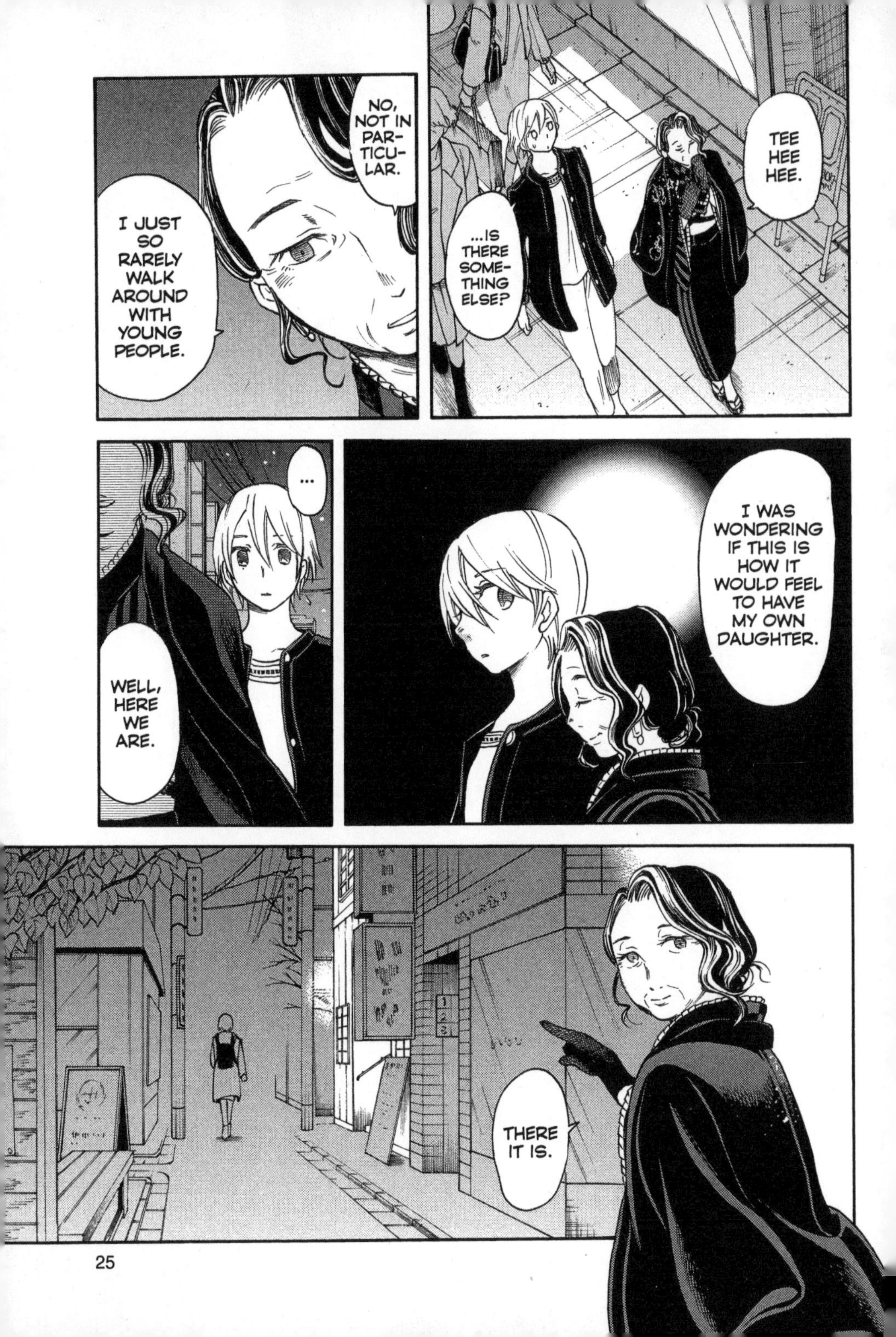
TEE HEE HEE.
...IS THERE SOME-THING ELSE?
NO, NOT IN PAR-TICU-LAR.
I JUST SO RARELY WALK AROUND WITH YOUNG PEOPLE.
I WAS WONDERING IF THIS IS HOW IT WOULD FEEL TO HAVE MY OWN DAUGHTER.
...
WELL, HERE WE ARE.
THERE IT IS.

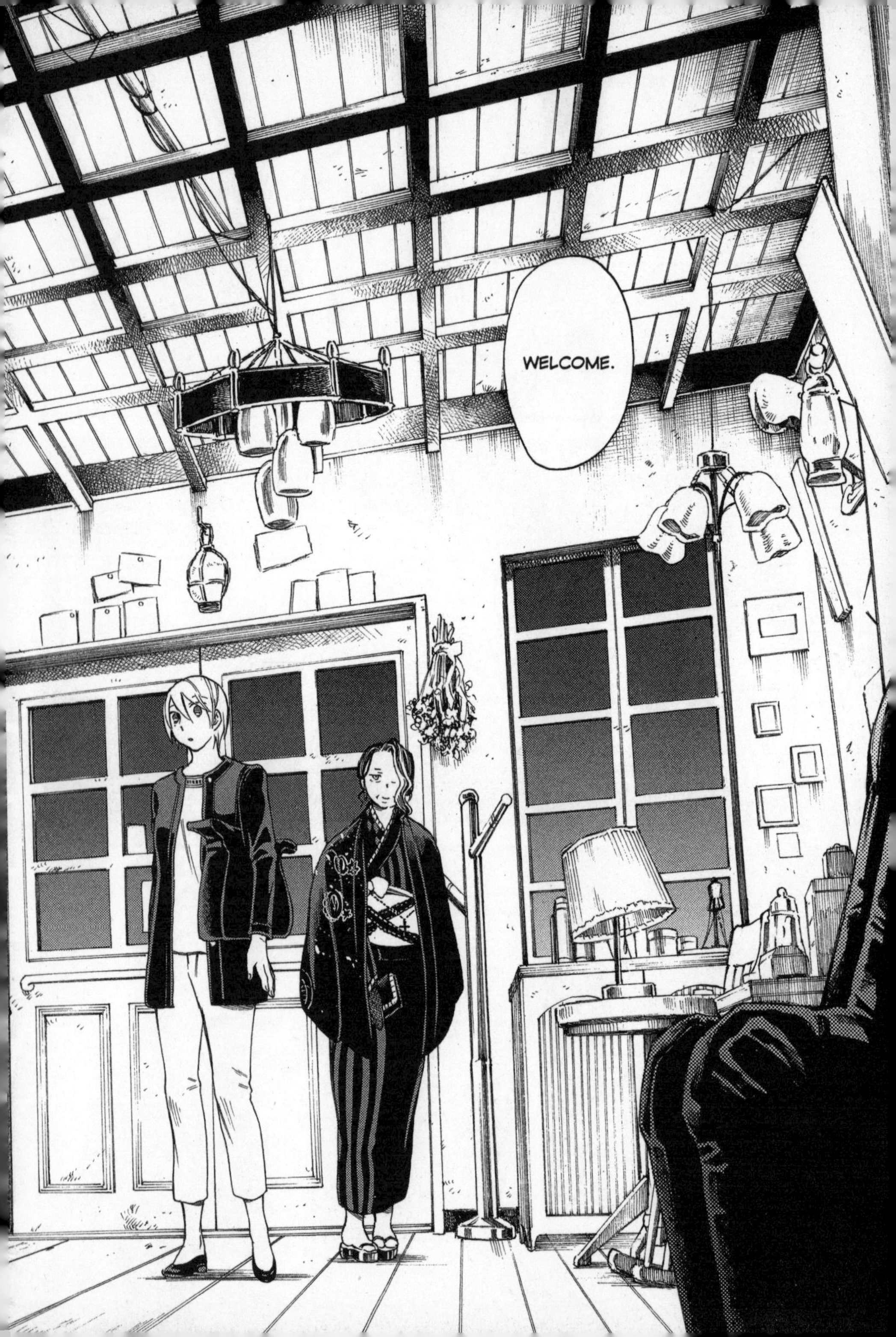
WELCOME.

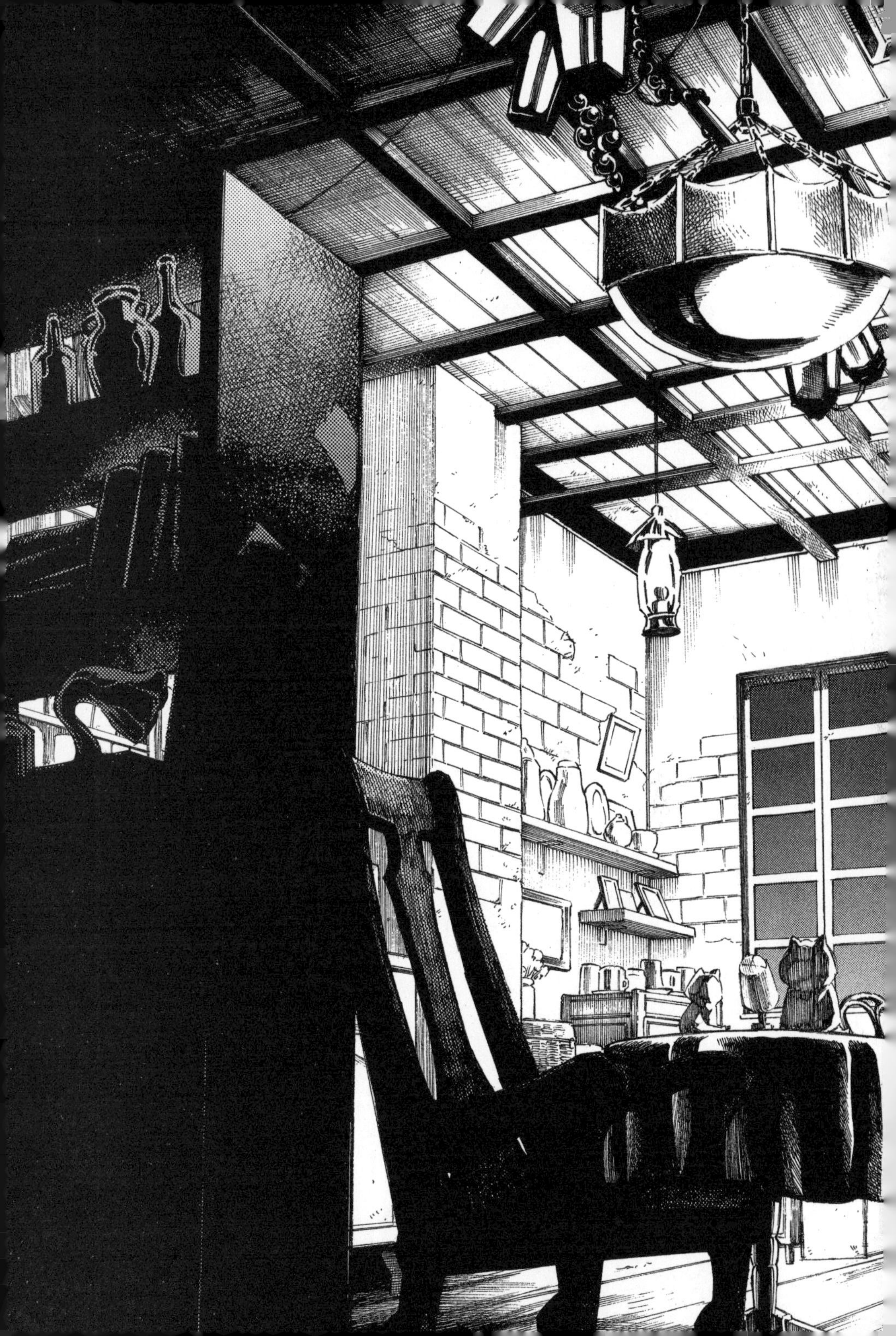

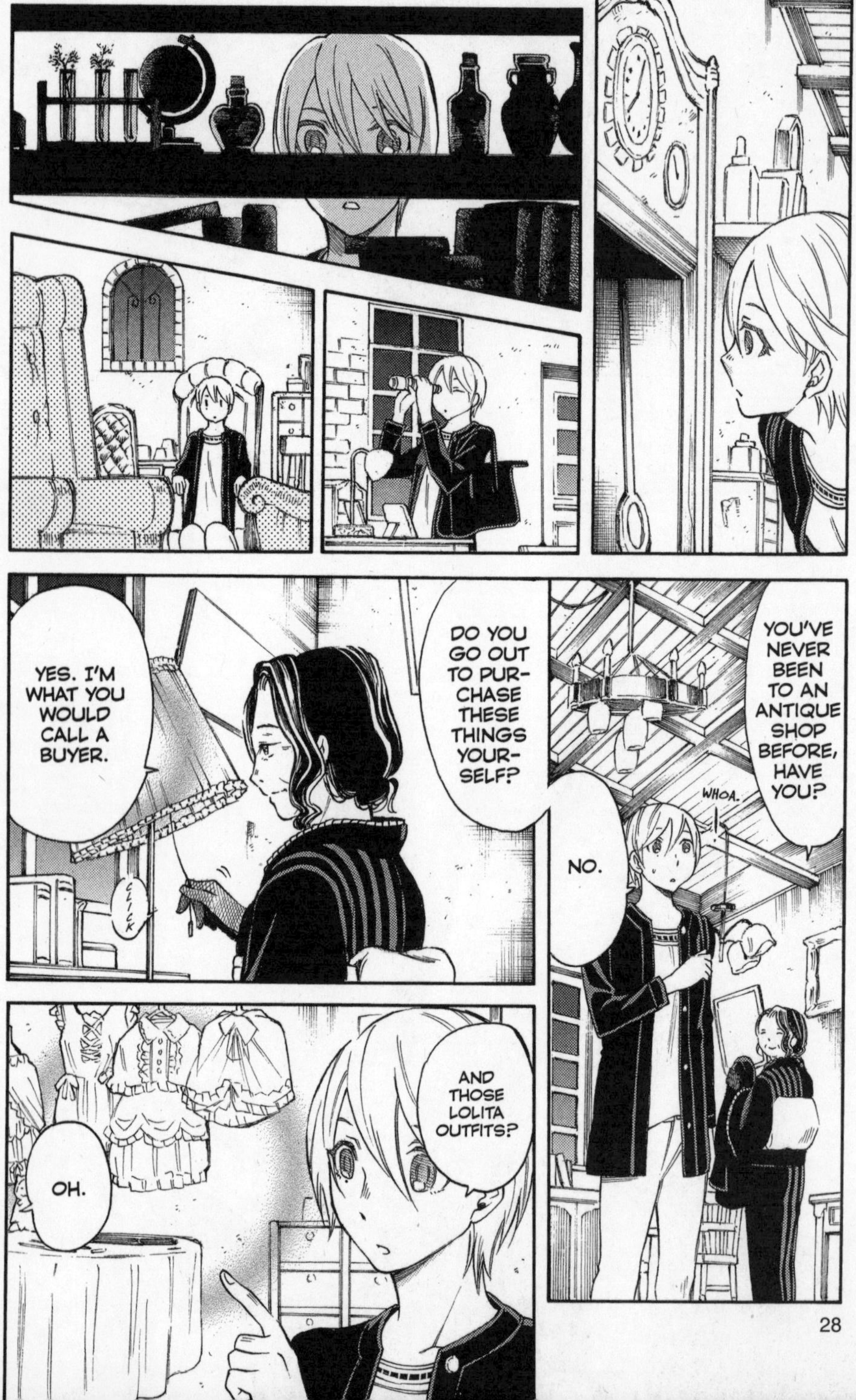
YOU'VE NEVER BEEN TO AN ANTIQUE SHOP BEFORE, HAVE YOU?
WHOA.
NO.
DO YOU GO OUT TO PUR-CHASE THESE THINGS YOUR-SELF?
YES. I'M WHAT YOU WOULD CALL A BUYER.
CLICK
AND THOSE LOLITA OUTFITS?
OH.

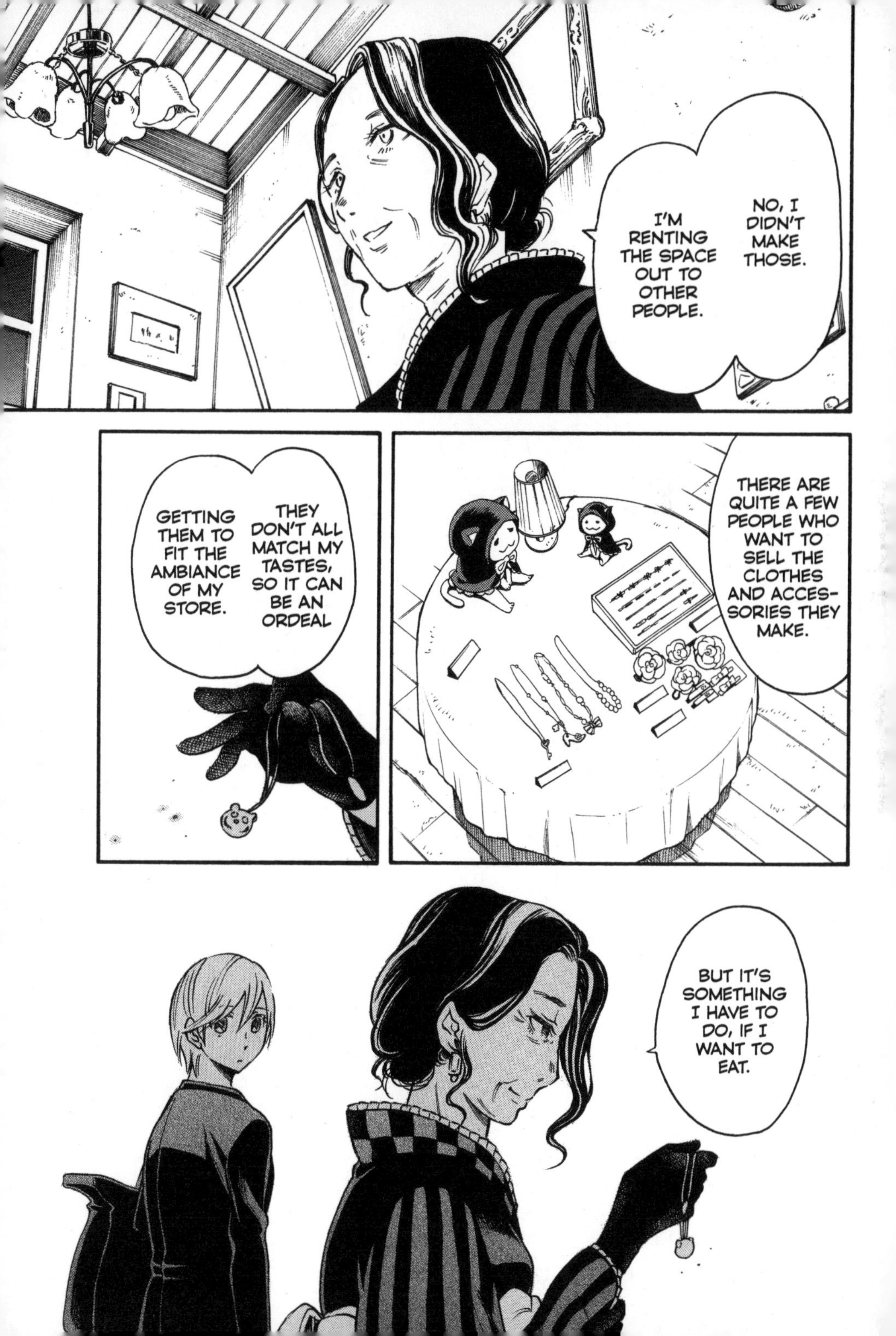
NO, I DIDN'T MAKE THOSE.
I'M RENTING THE SPACE OUT TO OTHER PEOPLE.
THERE ARE QUITE A FEW PEOPLE WHO WANT TO SELL THE CLOTHES AND ACCES-SORIES THEY MAKE.
THEY DON'T ALL MATCH MY TASTES, SO IT CAN BE AN ORDEAL
GETTING THEM TO FIT THE AMBIANCE OF MY STORE.
BUT IT'S SOMETHING I HAVE TO DO, IF I WANT TO EAT.

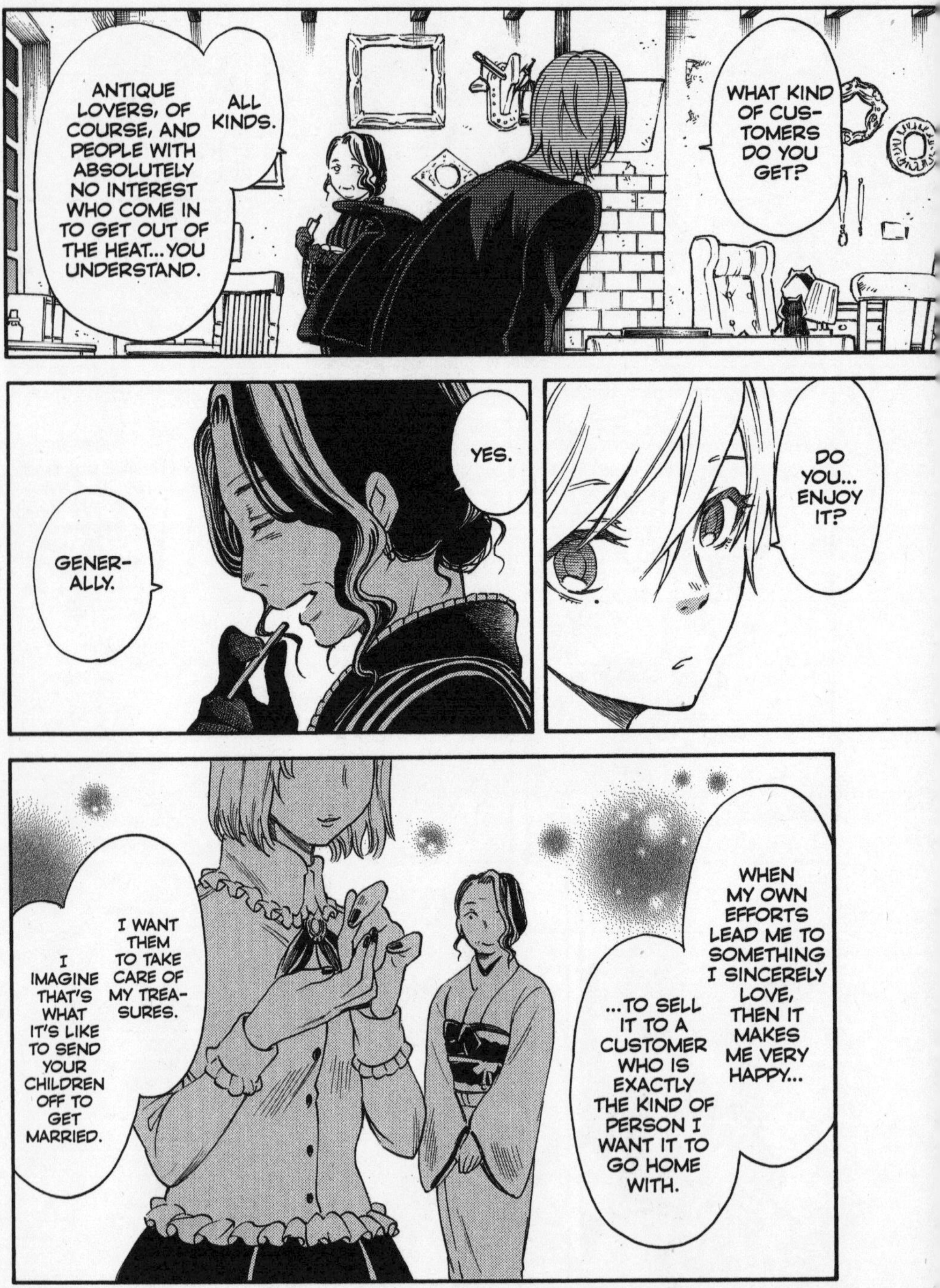
WHAT KIND OF CUS-TOMERS DO YOU GET?
ALL KINDS.
ANTIQUE LOVERS, OF COURSE, AND PEOPLE WITH ABSOLUTELY NO INTEREST WHO COME IN TO GET OUT OF THE HEAT...YOU UNDERSTAND.
DO YOU... ENJOY IT?
YES.
GENER-ALLY.
WHEN MY OWN EFFORTS LEAD ME TO SOMETHING I SINCERELY LOVE, THEN IT MAKES ME VERY HAPPY...
...TO SELL IT TO A CUSTOMER WHO IS EXACTLY THE KIND OF PERSON I WANT IT TO GO HOME WITH.
I WANT THEM TO TAKE CARE OF MY TREA-SURES.
I IMAGINE THAT'S WHAT IT'S LIKE TO SEND YOUR CHILDREN OFF TO GET MARRIED.

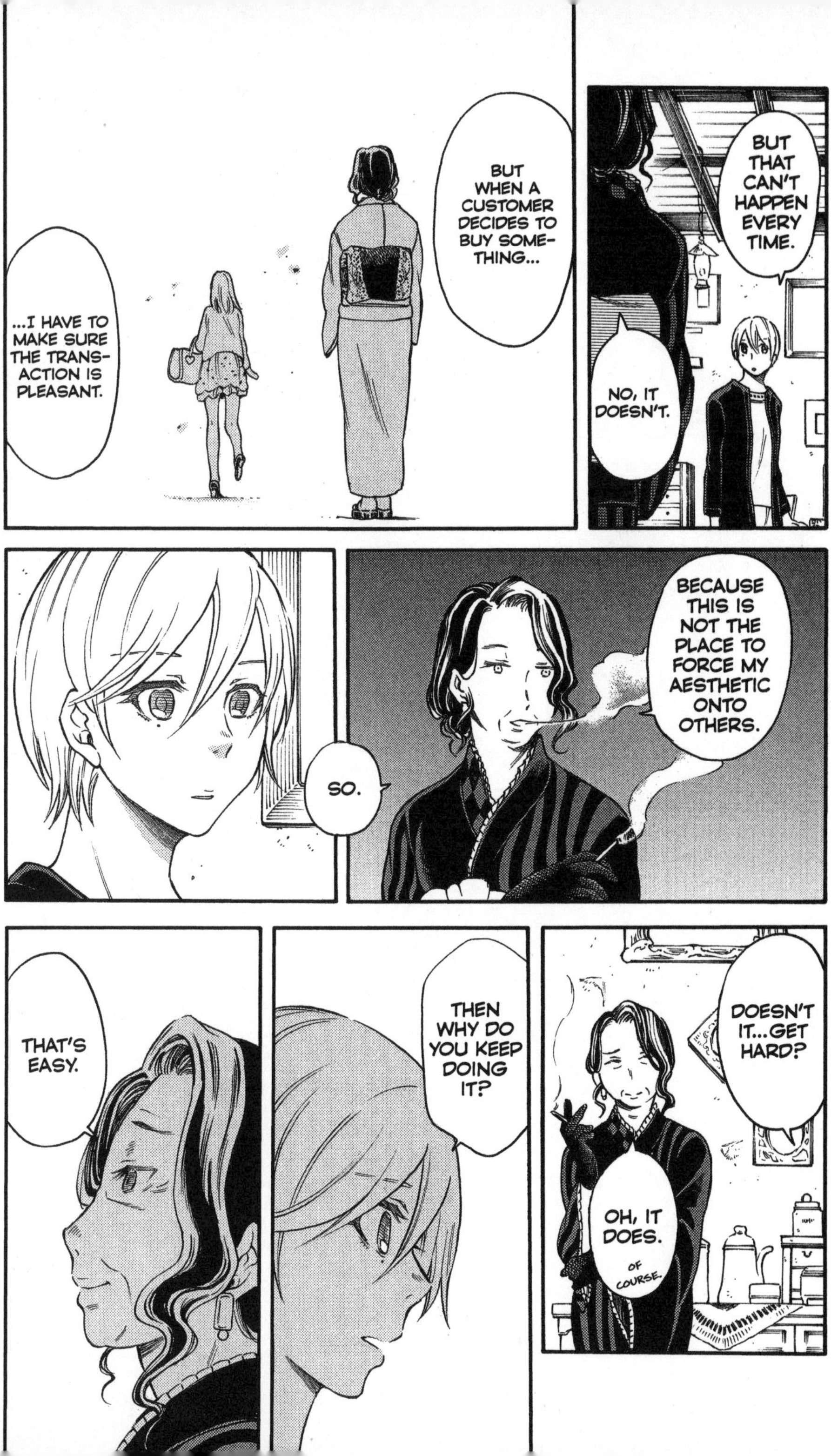
BUT THAT CAN'T HAPPEN EVERY TIME.
NO, IT DOESN'T.
BUT WHEN A CUSTOMER DECIDES TO BUY SOME-THING...
...I HAVE TO MAKE SURE THE TRANS-ACTION IS PLEASANT.
BECAUSE THIS IS NOT THE PLACE TO FORCE MY AESTHETIC ONTO OTHERS.
SO.
DOESN'T IT...GET HARD?
OH, IT DOES.
OF COURSE.
THEN WHY DO YOU KEEP DOING IT?
THAT'S EASY.

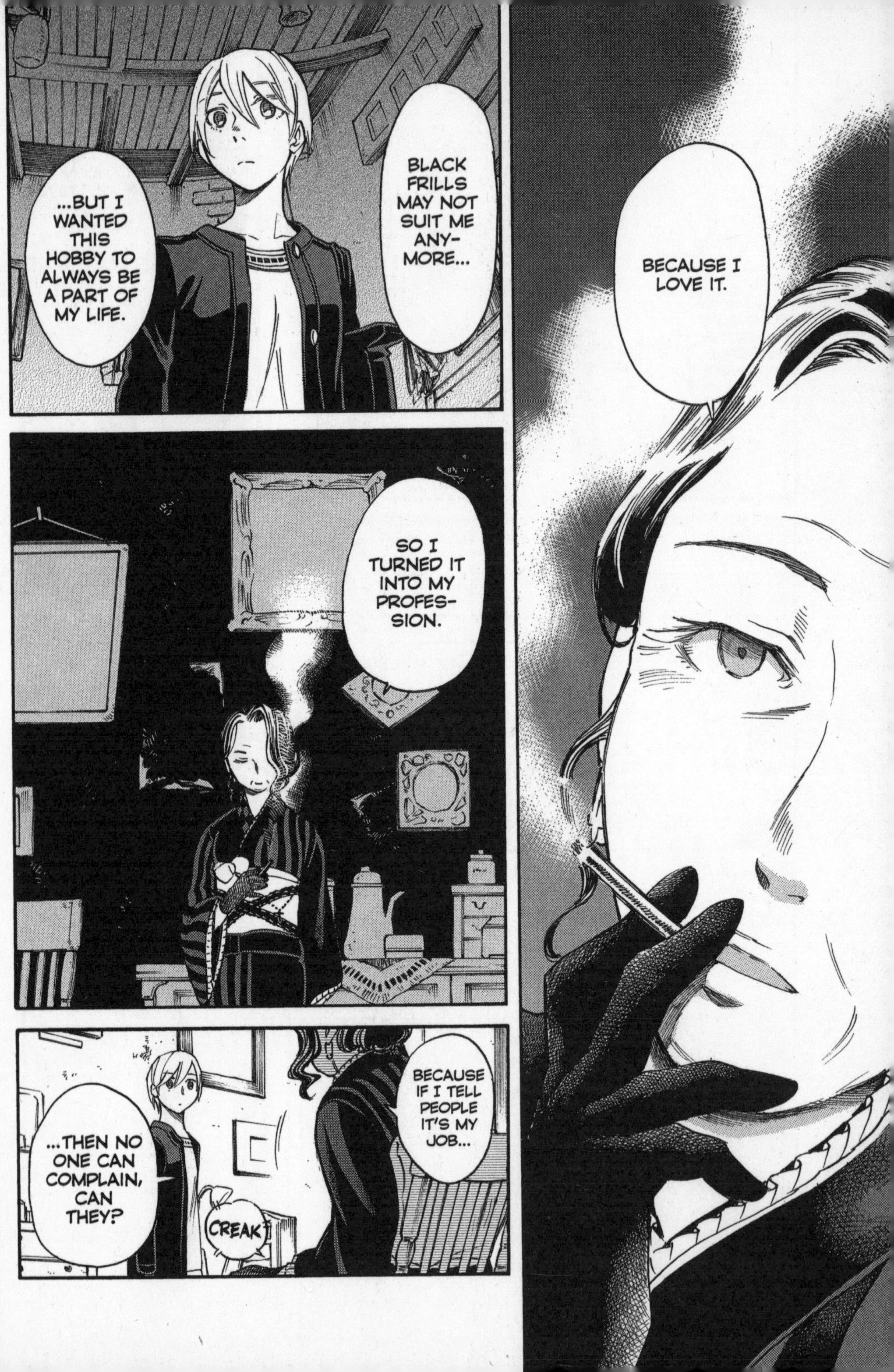
BECAUSE I LOVE IT.
BLACK FRILLS MAY NOT SUIT ME ANY-MORE...
...BUT I WANTED THIS HOBBY TO ALWAYS BE A PART OF MY LIFE.
SO I TURNED IT INTO MY PROFES-SION.
BECAUSE IF I TELL PEOPLE IT'S MY JOB...
...THEN NO ONE CAN COMPLAIN, CAN THEY?
CREAK

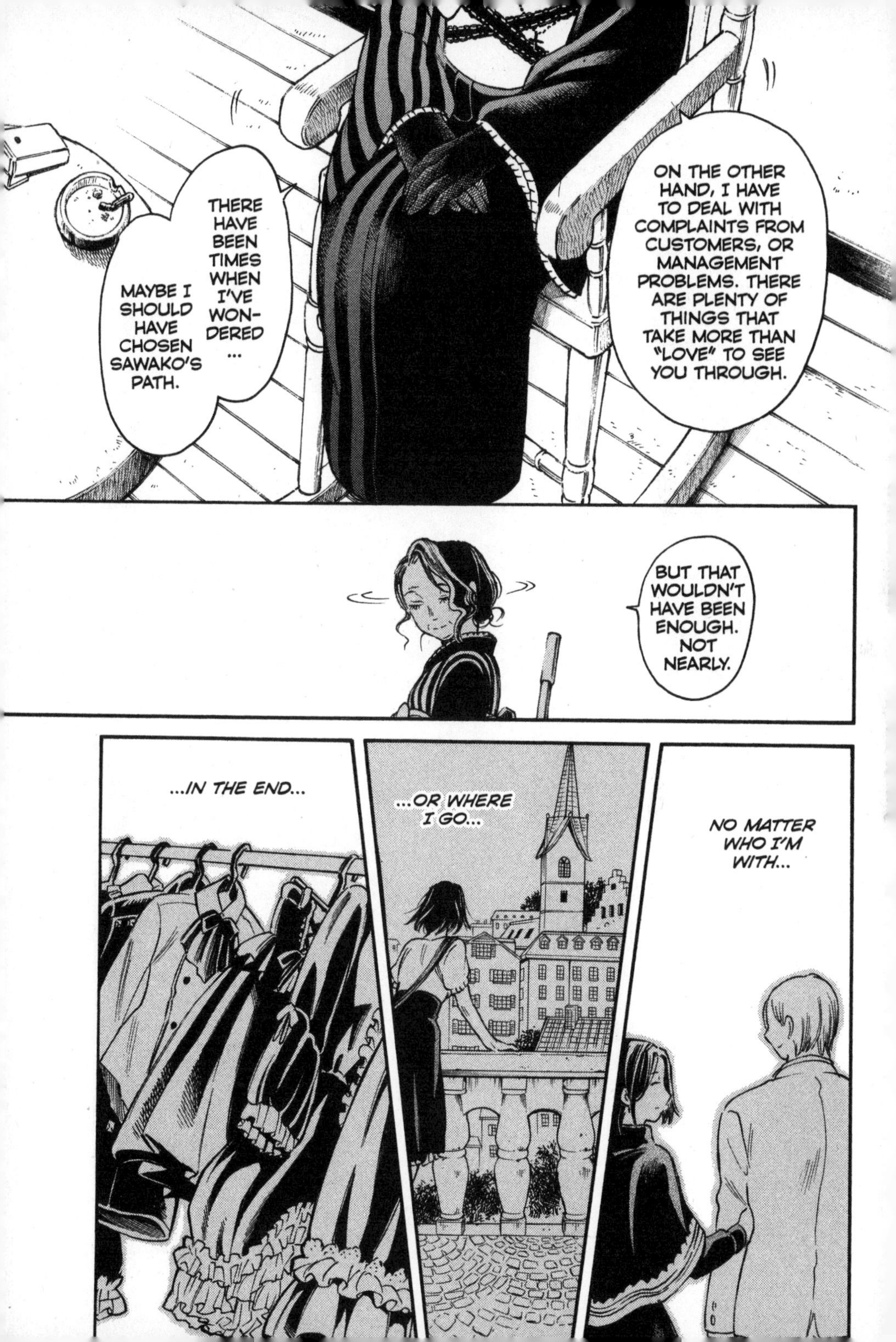
ON THE OTHER HAND, I HAVE TO DEAL WITH COMPLAINTS FROM CUSTOMERS, OR MANAGEMENT PROBLEMS. THERE ARE PLENTY OF THINGS THAT TAKE MORE THAN "LOVE" TO SEE YOU THROUGH.
THERE HAVE BEEN TIMES WHEN I'VE WONDERED ...
MAYBE I SHOULD HAVE CHOSEN SAWAKO'S PATH.
BUT THAT WOULDN'T HAVE BEEN ENOUGH. NOT NEARLY.
NO MATTER WHO I'M WITH...
...OR WHERE I GO...
...IN THE END...

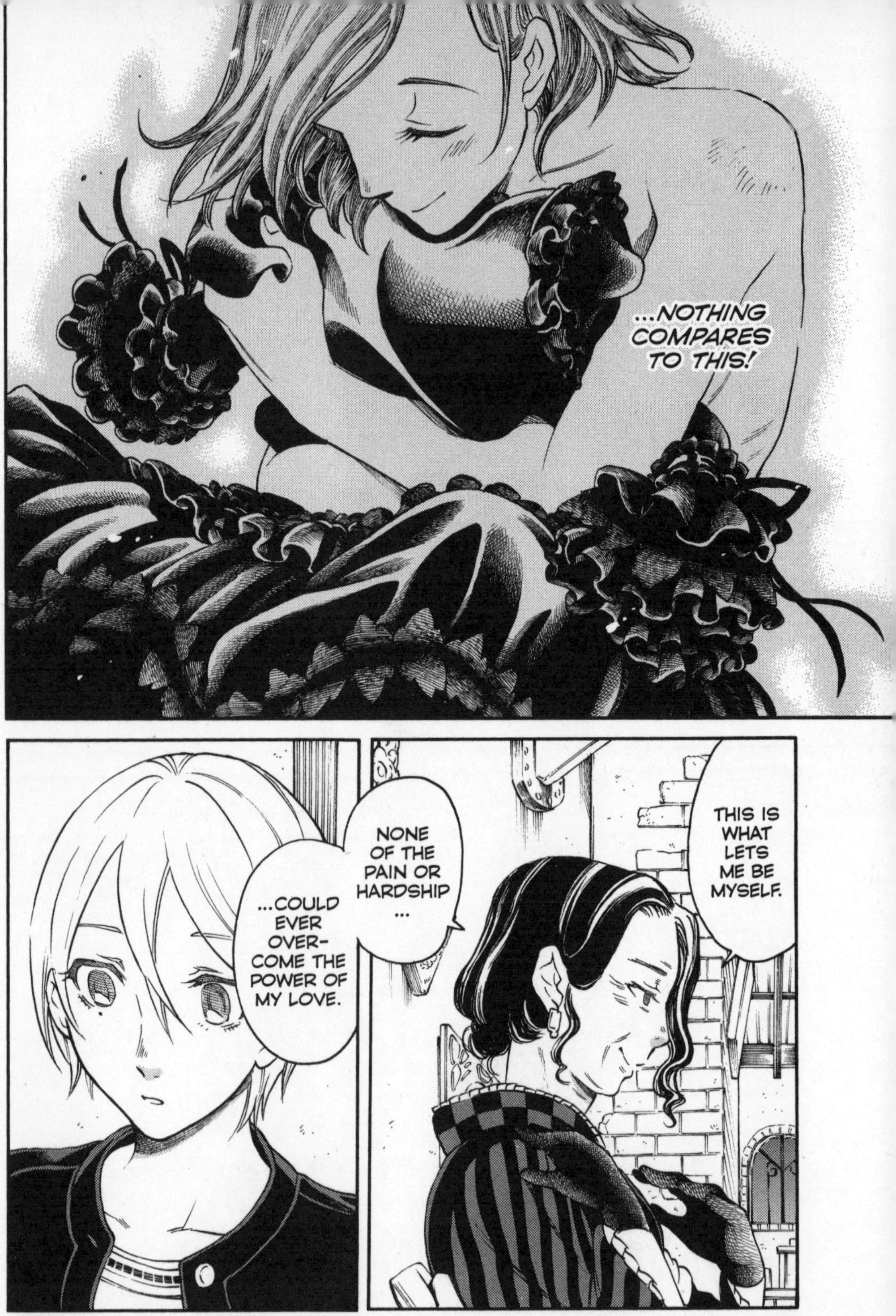
...NOTHING COMPARES TO THIS!
THIS IS WHAT LETS ME BE MYSELF.
NONE OF THE PAIN OR HARDSHIP ...
...COULD EVER OVER-COME THE POWER OF MY LOVE.

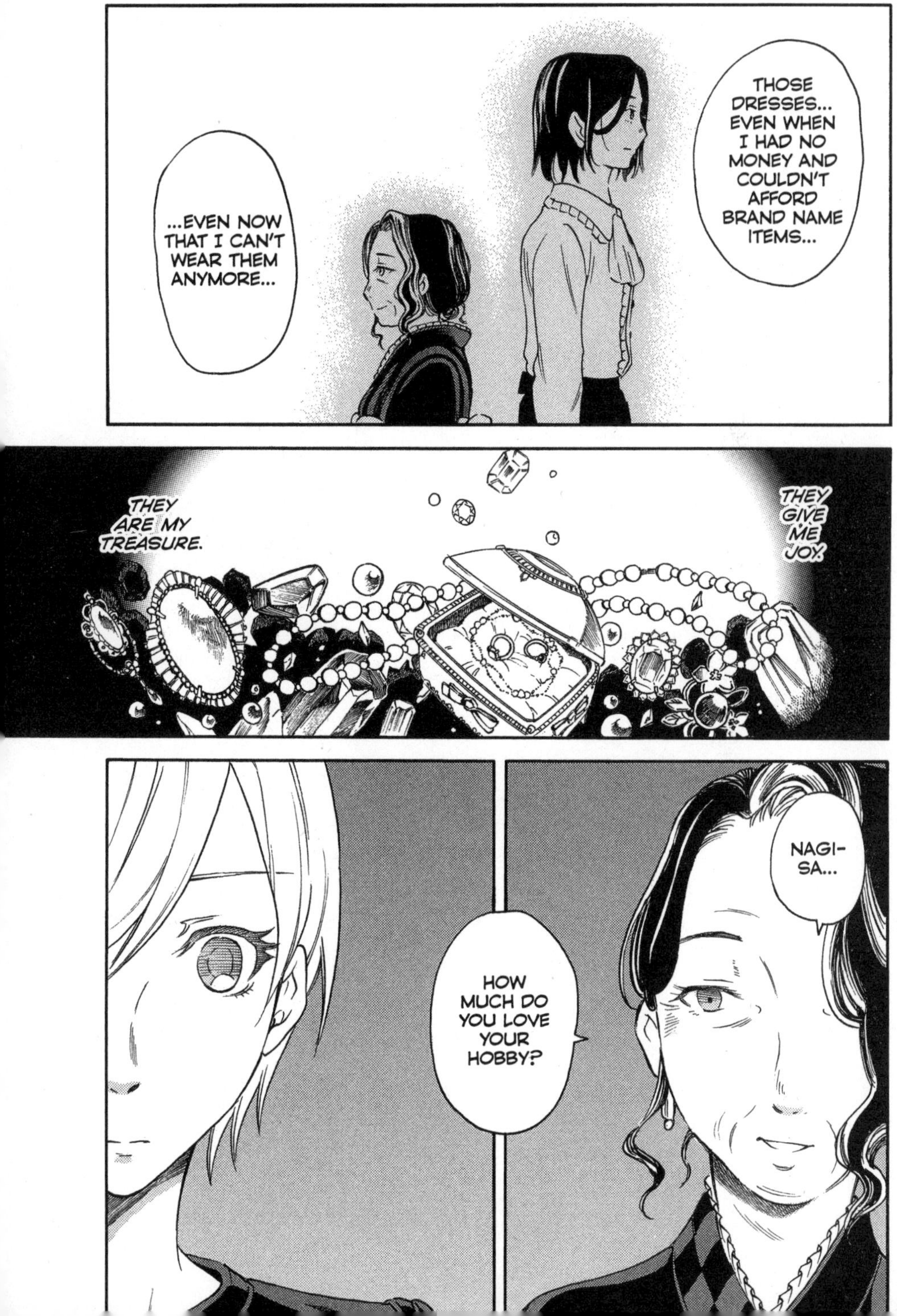
THOSE DRESSES... EVEN WHEN I HAD NO MONEY AND COULDN'T AFFORD BRAND NAME ITEMS...
...EVEN NOW THAT I CAN'T WEAR THEM ANYMORE...
THEY GIVE ME JOY.
THEY ARE MY TREASURE.
NAGI-SA...
HOW MUCH DO YOU LOVE YOUR HOBBY?

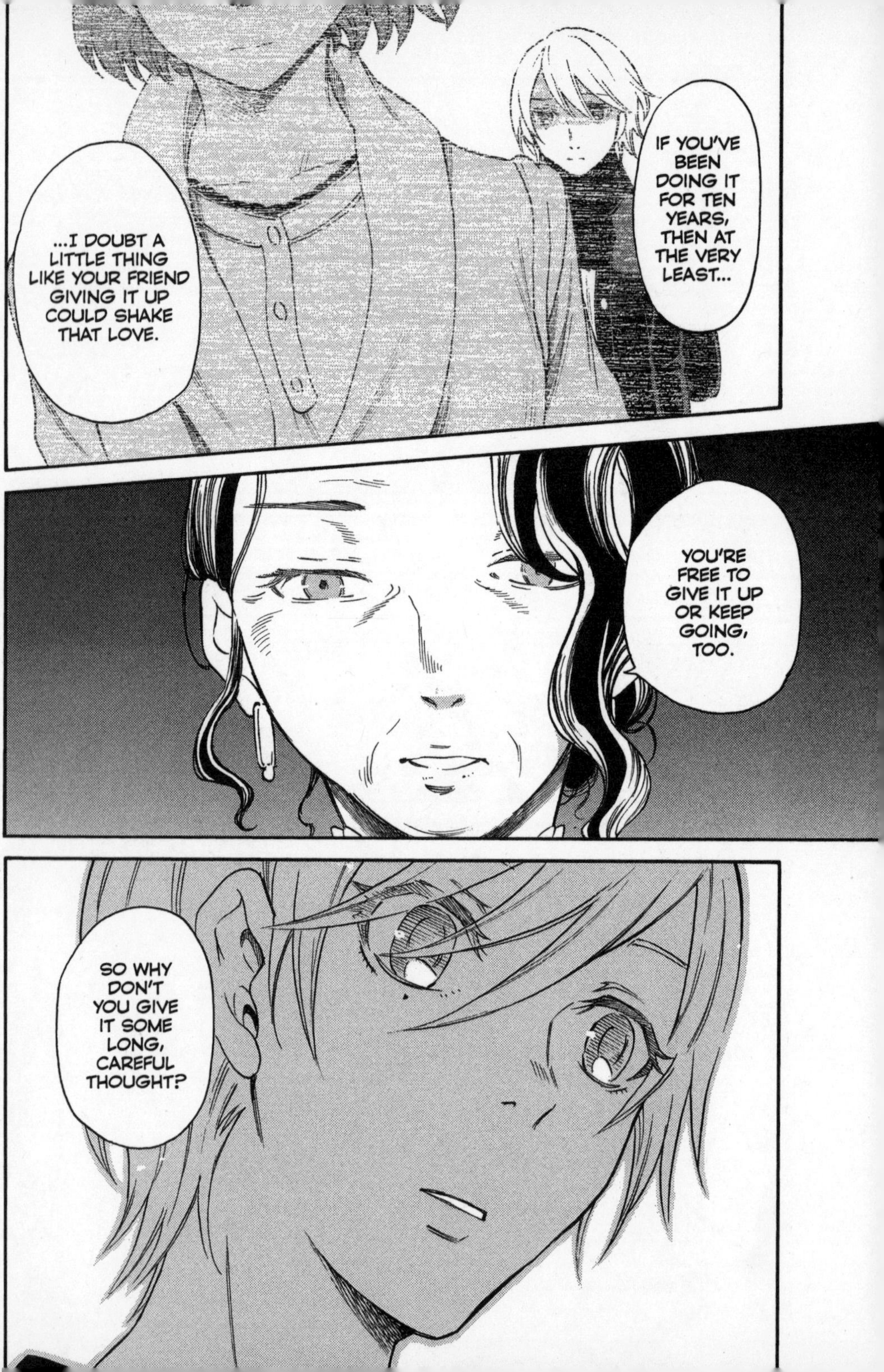
IF YOU'VE BEEN DOING IT FOR TEN YEARS, THEN AT THE VERY LEAST...
...I DOUBT A LITTLE THING LIKE YOUR FRIEND GIVING IT UP COULD SHAKE THAT LOVE.
YOU'RE FREE TO GIVE IT UP OR KEEP GOING, TOO.
SO WHY DON'T YOU GIVE IT SOME LONG, CAREFUL THOUGHT?

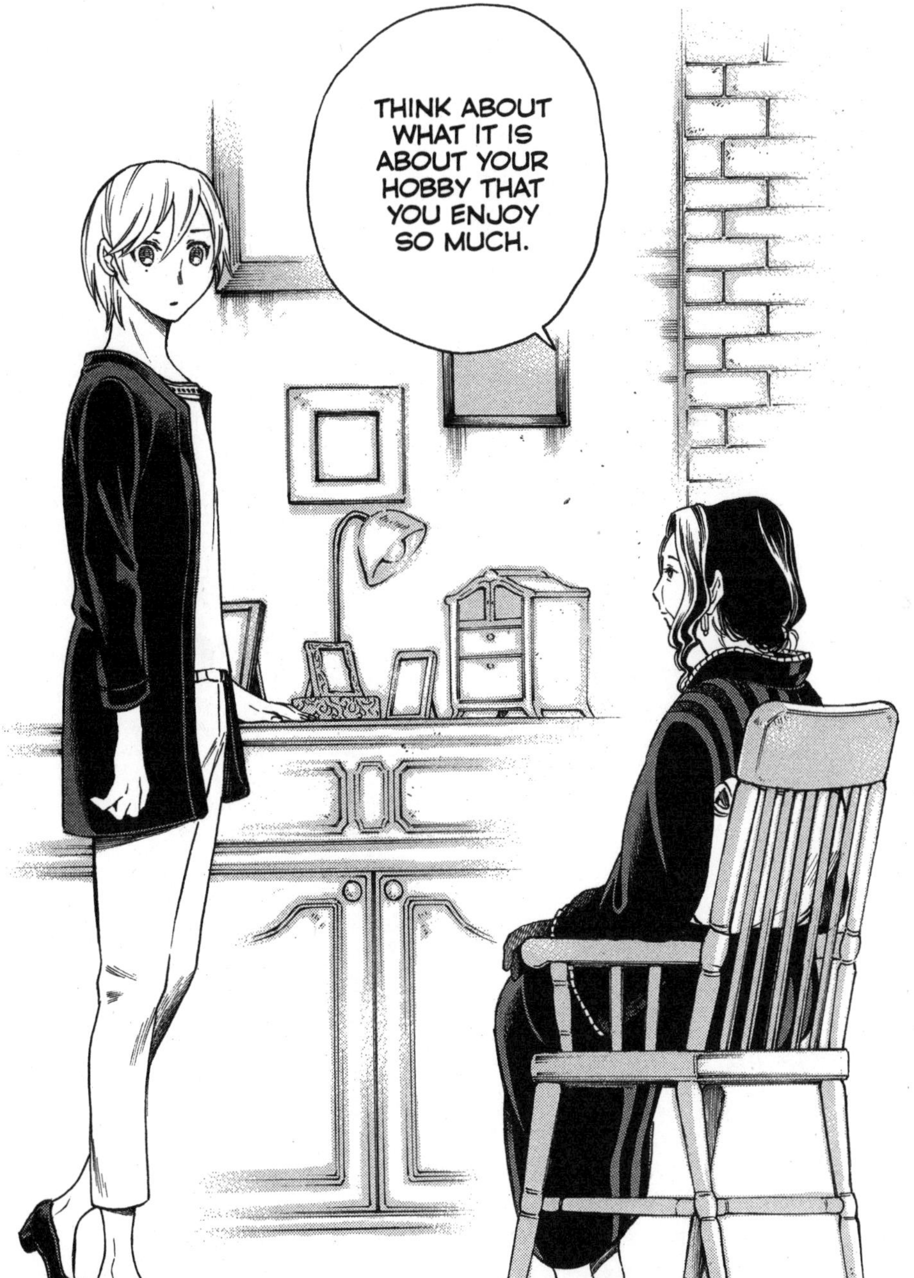
THINK ABOUT WHAT IT IS ABOUT YOUR HOBBY THAT YOU ENJOY SO MUCH.

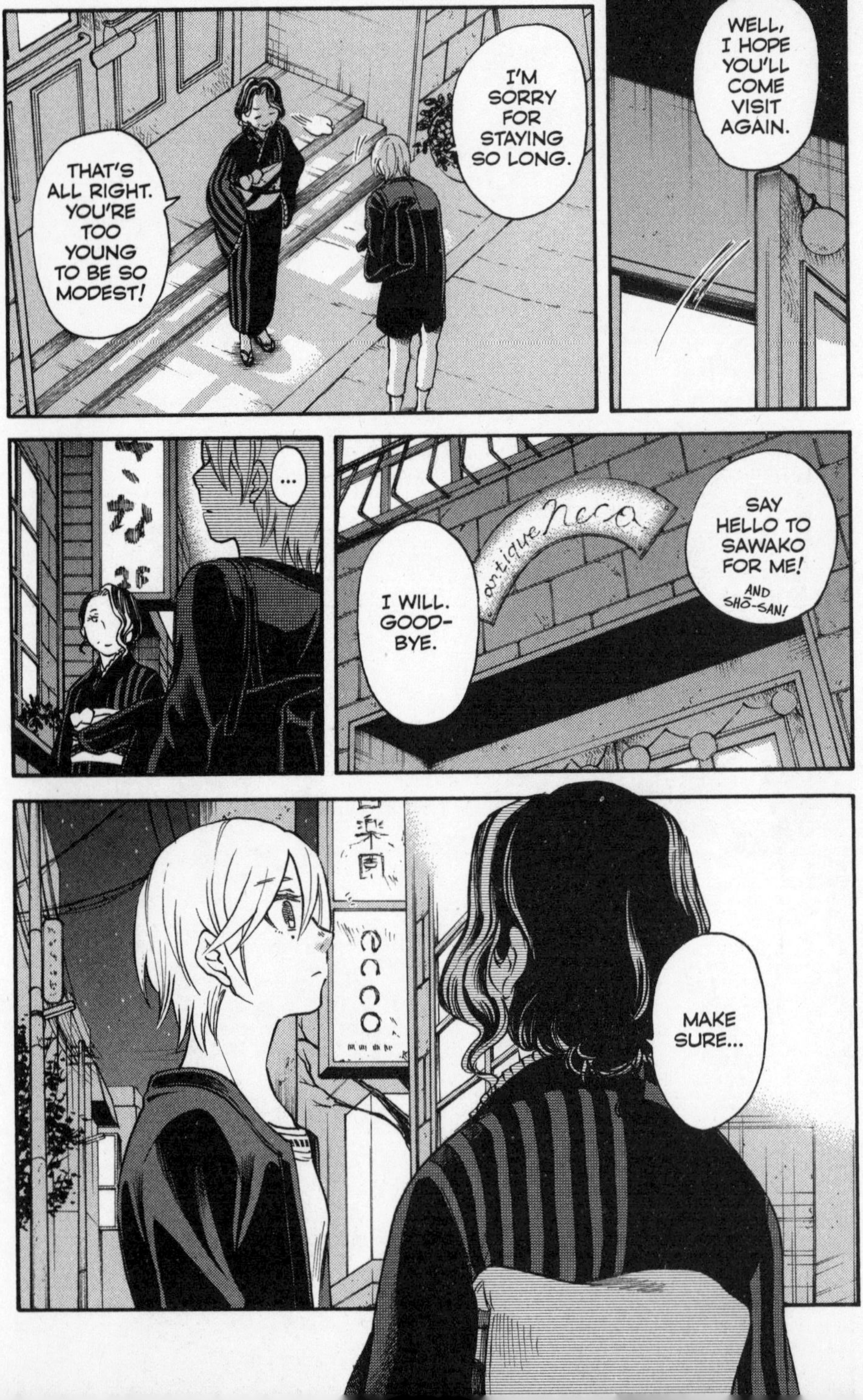
WELL, I HOPE YOU'LL COME VISIT AGAIN.
I'M SORRY FOR STAYING SO LONG.
THAT'S ALL RIGHT. YOU'RE TOO YOUNG TO BE SO MODEST!
SAY HELLO TO SAWAKO FOR ME!
AND SHŌ-SAN!
antique neco
I WILL. GOOD-BYE.
...
MAKE SURE...

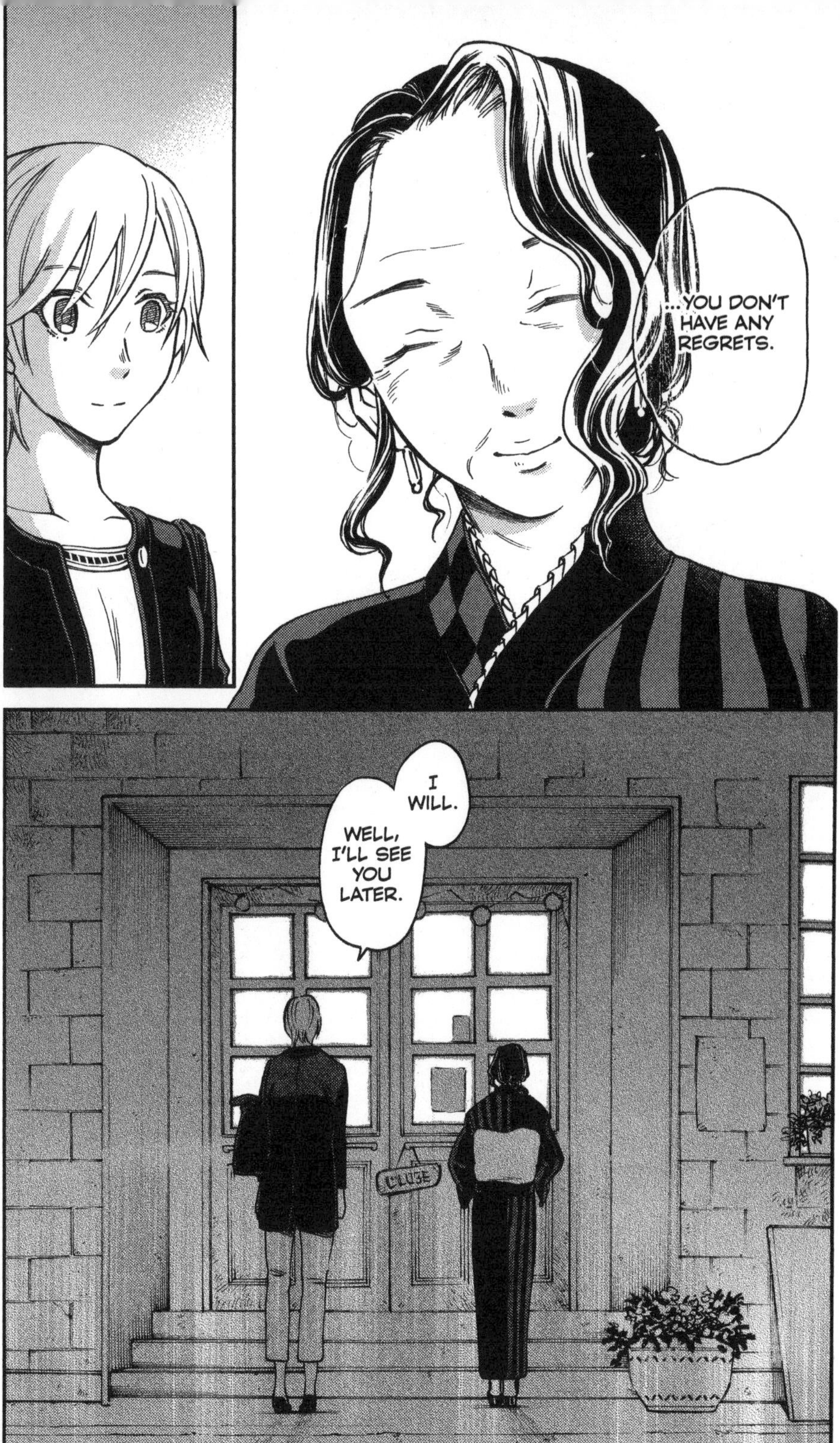
...YOU DON'T HAVE ANY REGRETS.
I WILL.
WELL, I'LL SEE YOU LATER.

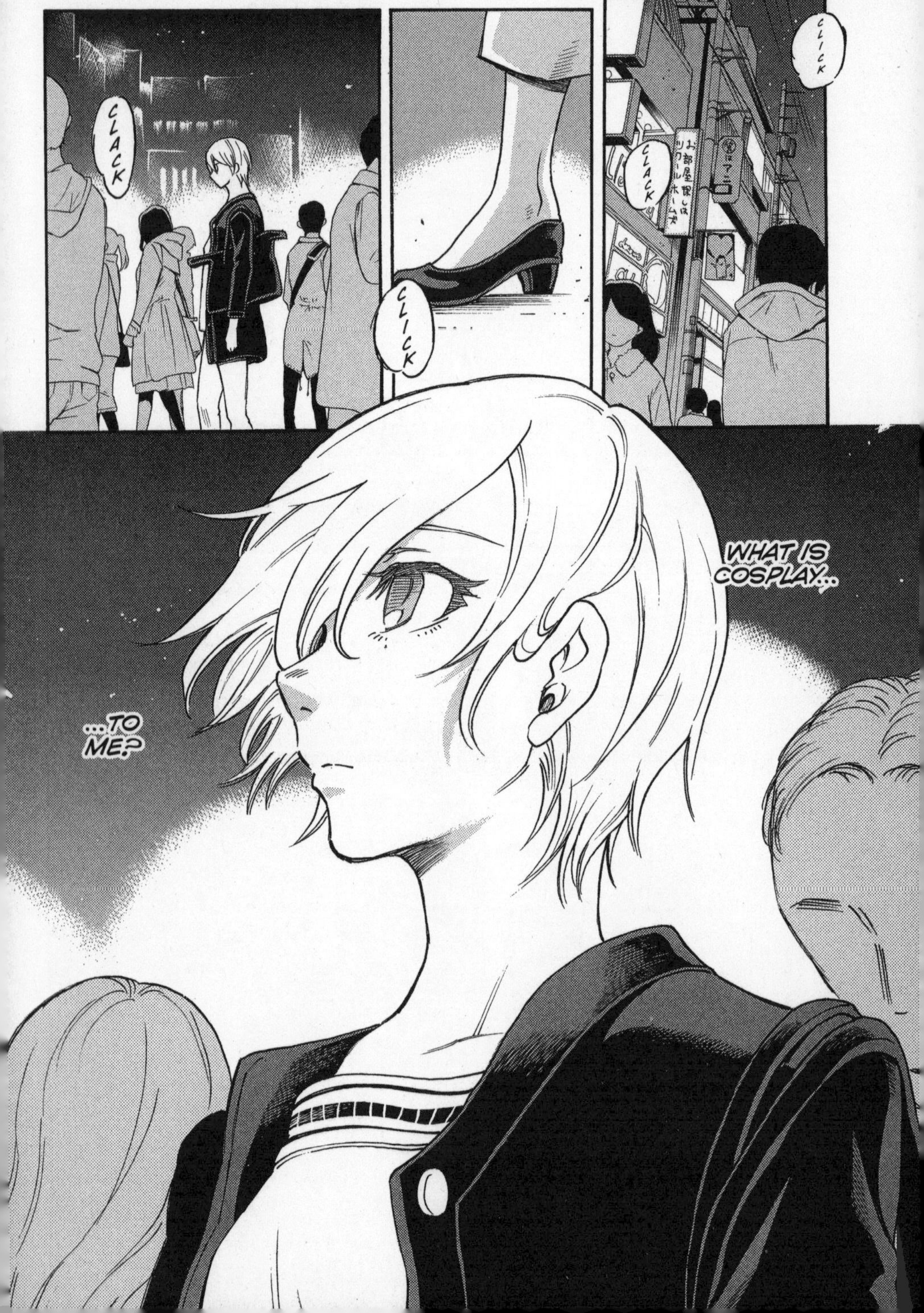
CLICK
CLACK
CLICK
CLACK
WHAT IS COSPLAY...
...TO ME?

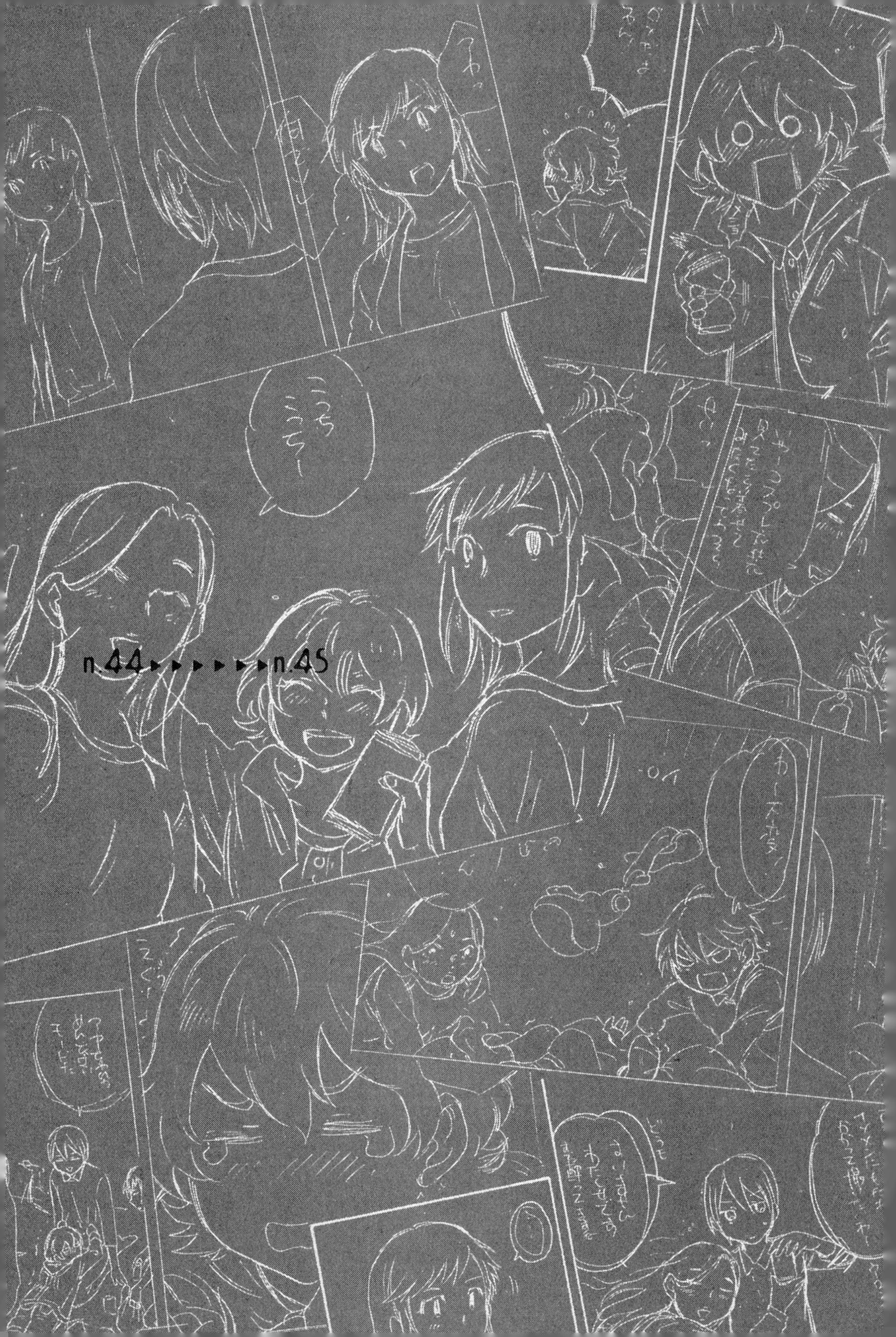
n.44▸▸▸▸▸▸▸▸n.45

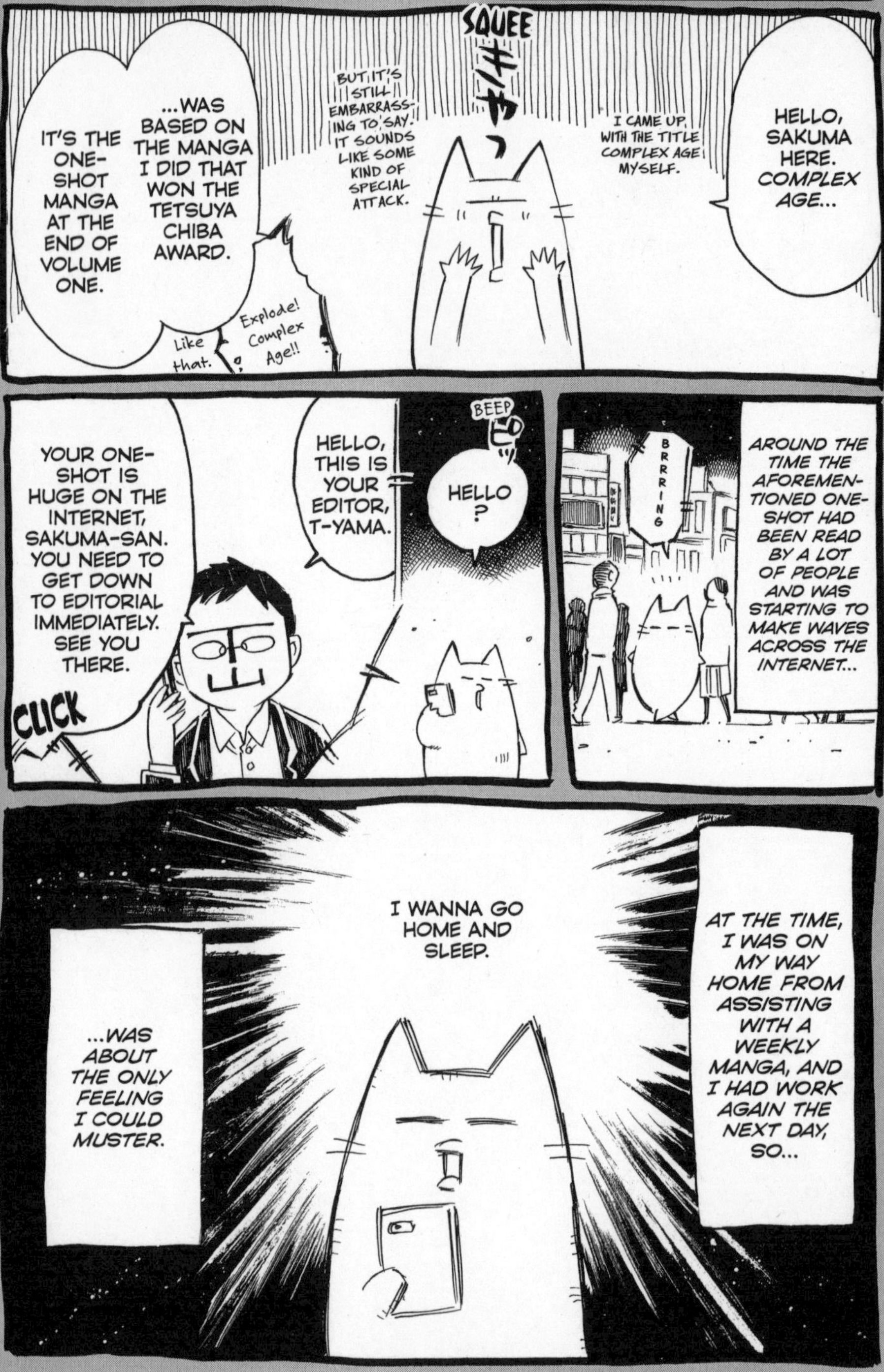
HELLO, SAKUMA HERE. COMPLEX AGE...
I CAME UP WITH THE TITLE COMPLEX AGE MYSELF.
SQUEE
BUT IT'S STILL EMBARRASSING TO SAY. IT SOUNDS LIKE SOME KIND OF SPECIAL ATTACK.
...WAS BASED ON THE MANGA I DID THAT WON THE TETSUYA CHIBA AWARD.
IT'S THE ONE-SHOT MANGA AT THE END OF VOLUME ONE.
Explode! Complex Age!!
Like that.
AROUND THE TIME THE AFOREMENTIONED ONE-SHOT HAD BEEN READ BY A LOT OF PEOPLE AND WAS STARTING TO MAKE WAVES ACROSS THE INTERNET...
BRRRING
BEEP
HELLO?
HELLO, THIS IS YOUR EDITOR, T-YAMA.
YOUR ONE-SHOT IS HUGE ON THE INTERNET, SAKUMA-SAN. YOU NEED TO GET DOWN TO EDITORIAL IMMEDIATELY. SEE YOU THERE.
CLICK
AT THE TIME, I WAS ON MY WAY HOME FROM ASSISTING WITH A WEEKLY MANGA, AND I HAD WORK AGAIN THE NEXT DAY, SO...
I WANNA GO HOME AND SLEEP.
...WAS ABOUT THE ONLY FEELING I COULD MUSTER.

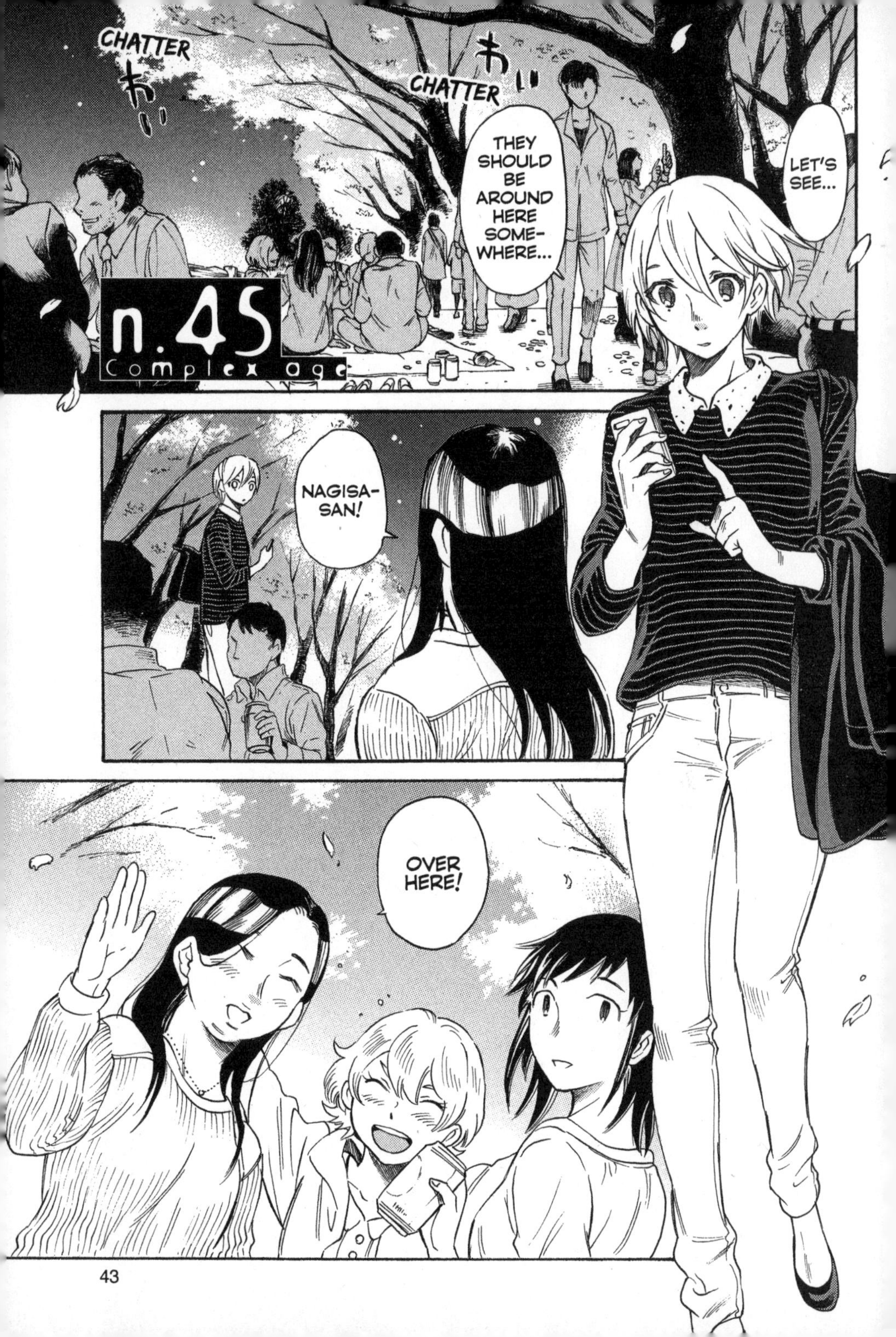

LET'S SEE...
CHATTER
わい
THEY SHOULD BE AROUND HERE SOMEWHERE...
CHATTER
わい
n.45
Complex age
NAGISA-SAN!
OVER HERE!

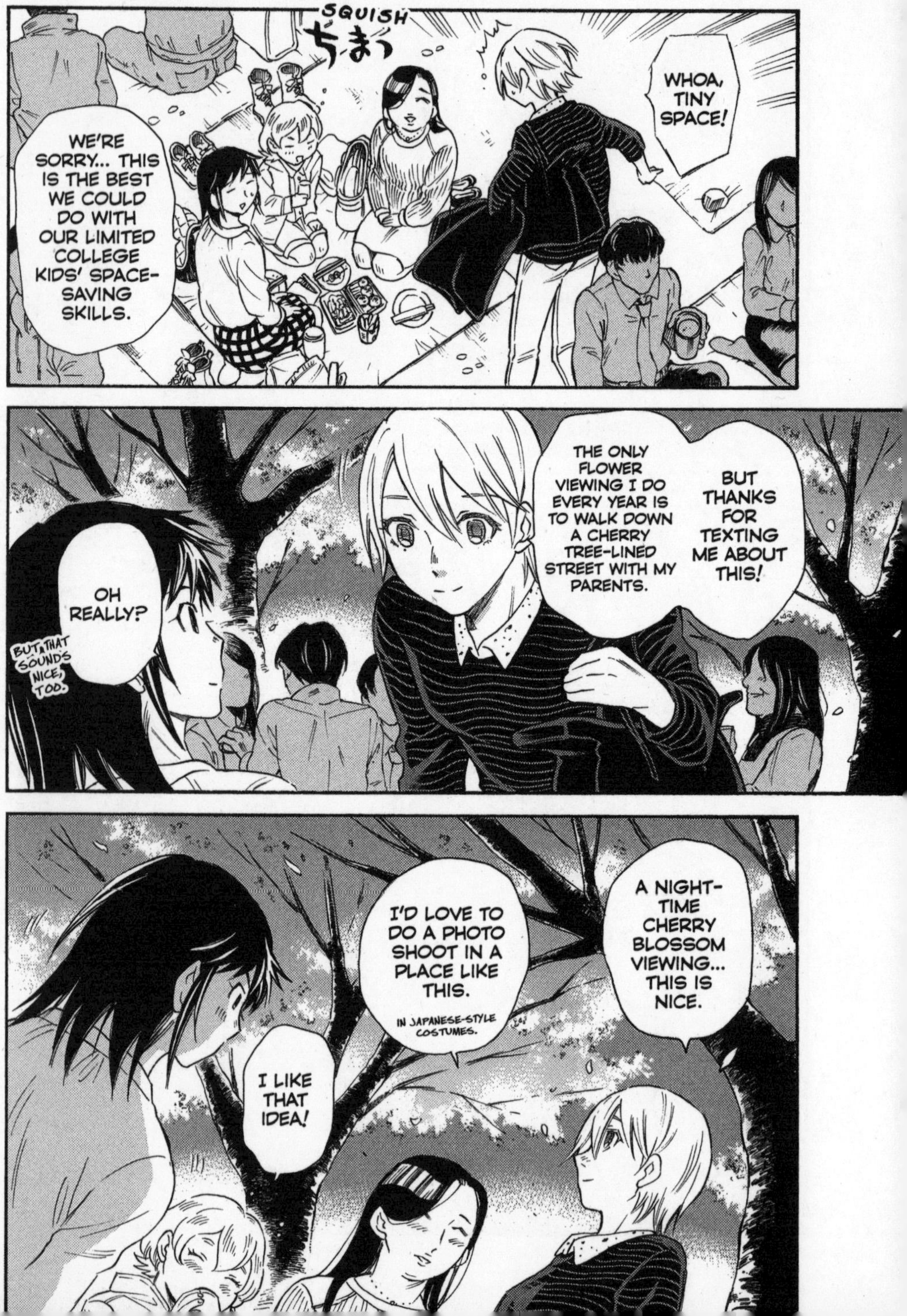
WHOA, TINY SPACE!
SQUISH
ちまっ
WE'RE SORRY... THIS IS THE BEST WE COULD DO WITH OUR LIMITED COLLEGE KIDS' SPACE-SAVING SKILLS.
THE ONLY FLOWER VIEWING I DO EVERY YEAR IS TO WALK DOWN A CHERRY TREE-LINED STREET WITH MY PARENTS.
BUT THANKS FOR TEXTING ME ABOUT THIS!
OH REALLY?
BUT THAT SOUNDS NICE, TOO.
A NIGHT-TIME CHERRY BLOSSOM VIEWING... THIS IS NICE.
I'D LOVE TO DO A PHOTO SHOOT IN A PLACE LIKE THIS.
IN JAPANESE-STYLE COSTUMES.
I LIKE THAT IDEA!

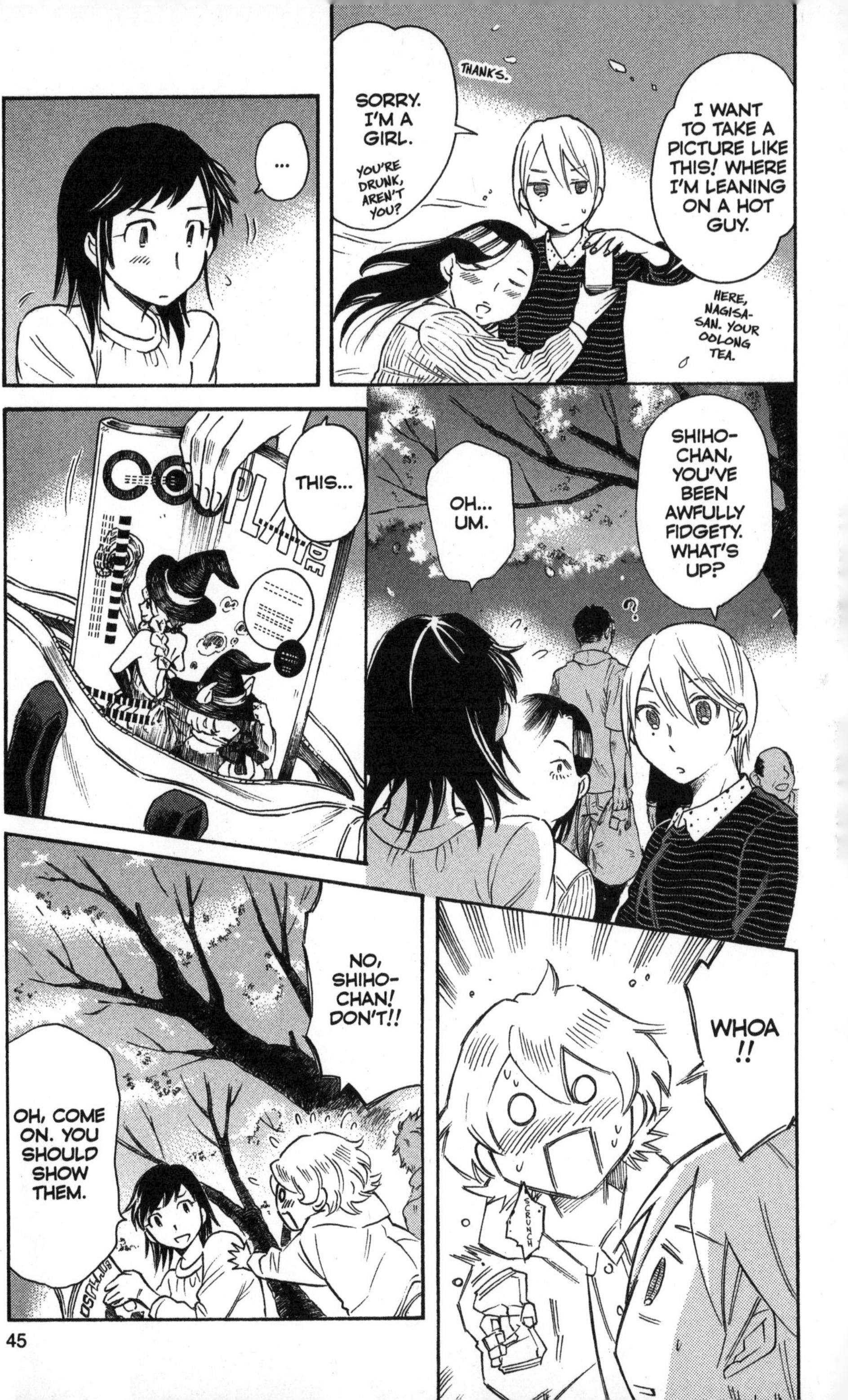
I WANT TO TAKE A PICTURE LIKE THIS! WHERE I'M LEANING ON A HOT GUY.
THANKS.
SORRY. I'M A GIRL.
HERE, NAGISA-SAN. YOUR OOLONG TEA.
YOU'RE DRUNK, AREN'T YOU?
...
SHIHO-CHAN, YOU'VE BEEN AWFULLY FIDGETY. WHAT'S UP?
OH... UM.
THIS...
WHOA!!
SCRUNCH
NO, SHIHO-CHAN! DON'T!!
OH, COME ON. YOU SHOULD SHOW THEM.

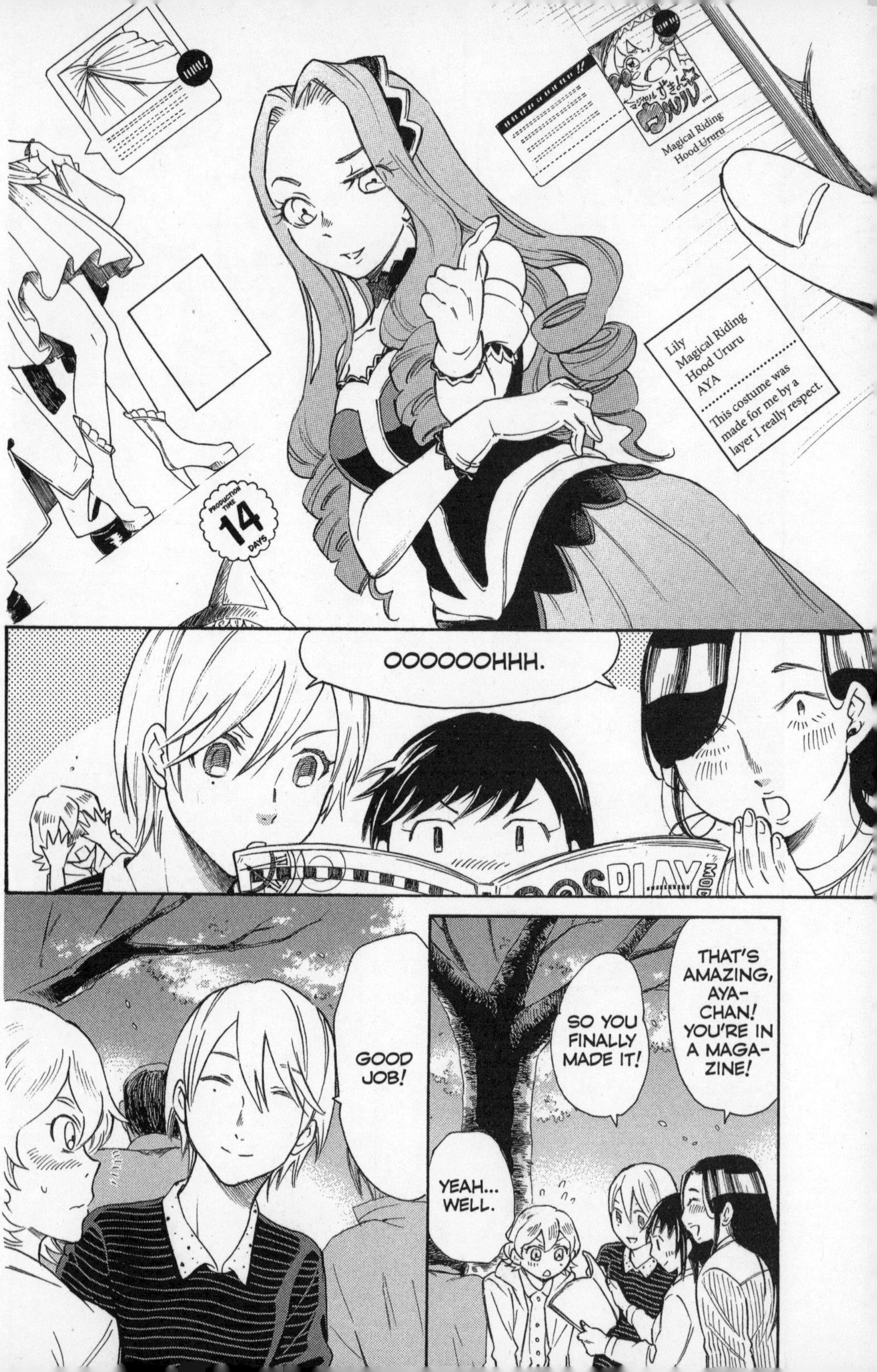
Magical Riding Hood Ururu
Lily
Magical Riding Hood Ururu
AYA
This costume was made for me by a layer I really respect.
PRODUCTION TIME 14 DAYS
OOOOOOHHH.
THAT'S AMAZING, AYA-CHAN! YOU'RE IN A MAGAZINE!
SO YOU FINALLY MADE IT!
YEAH... WELL.
GOOD JOB!

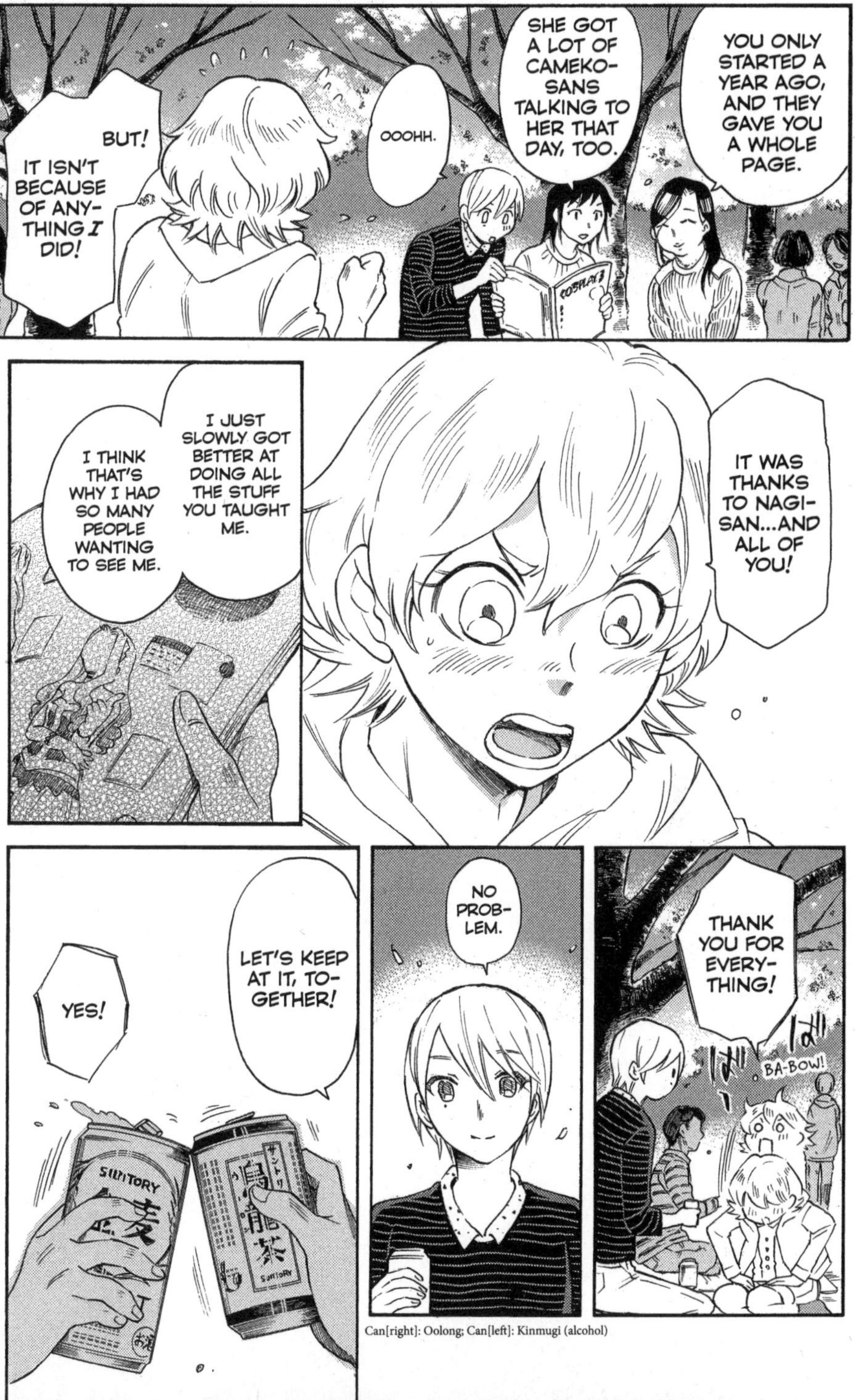
YOU ONLY STARTED A YEAR AGO, AND THEY GAVE YOU A WHOLE PAGE.
SHE GOT A LOT OF CAMEKO-SANS TALKING TO HER THAT DAY, TOO.
OOOHH.
BUT! IT ISN'T BECAUSE OF ANY-THING *I* DID!
IT WAS THANKS TO NAGI-SAN...AND ALL OF YOU!
I JUST SLOWLY GOT BETTER AT DOING ALL THE STUFF YOU TAUGHT ME.
I THINK THAT'S WHY I HAD SO MANY PEOPLE WANTING TO SEE ME.
THANK YOU FOR EVERY-THING!
BA-BOW!
NO PROB-LEM.
LET'S KEEP AT IT, TO-GETHER!
YES!

Can[right]: Oolong; Can[left]: Kinmugi (alcohol)

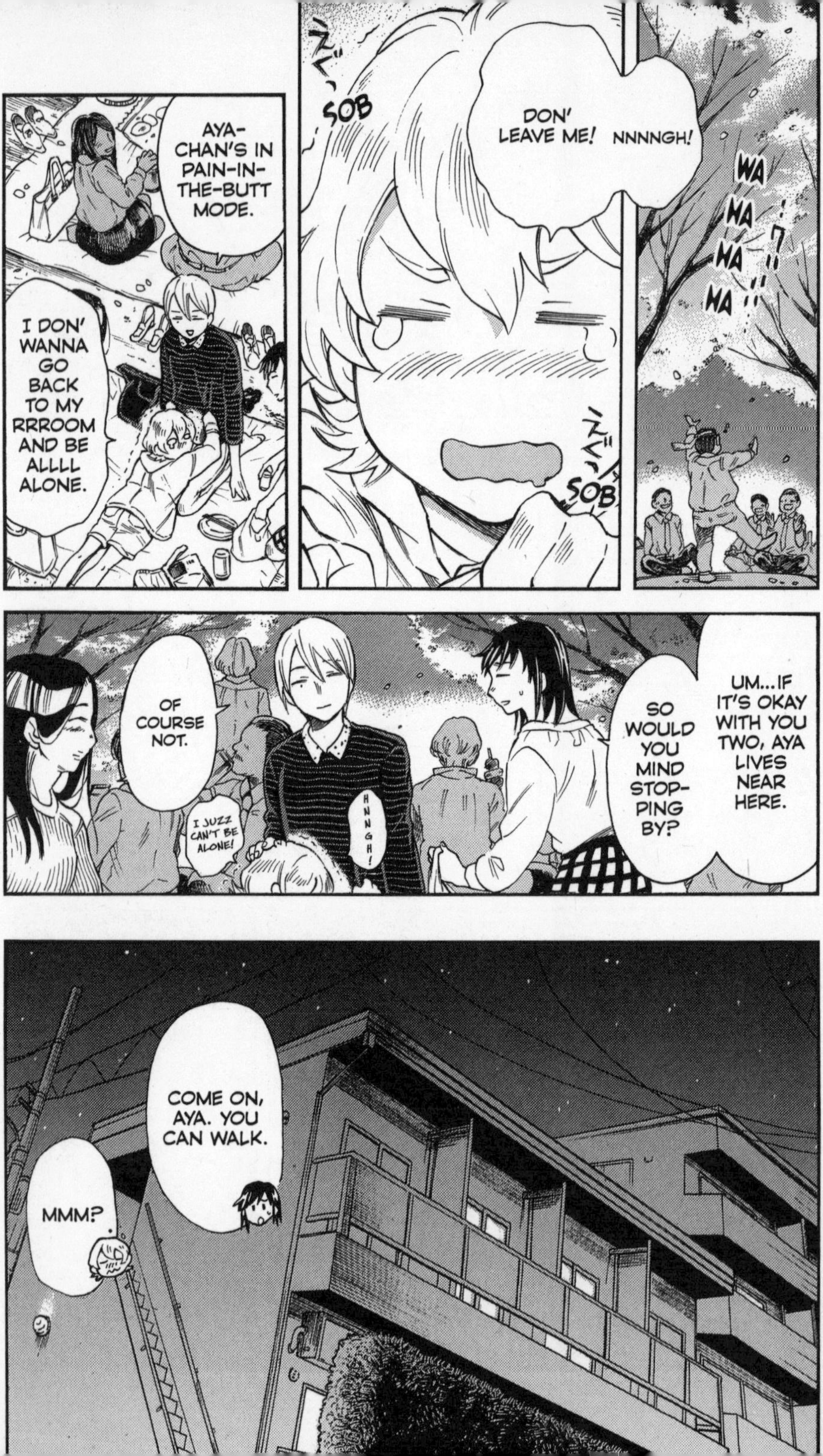
WA HA HA HA HA
DON' LEAVE ME!
NNNNGH!
SOB
SOB
AYA-CHAN'S IN PAIN-IN-THE-BUTT MODE.
I DON' WANNA GO BACK TO MY RRROOM AND BE ALLLL ALONE.
UM...IF IT'S OKAY WITH YOU TWO, AYA LIVES NEAR HERE.
SO WOULD YOU MIND STOPPING BY?
OF COURSE NOT.
HNNGH!
I JUZZ CAN'T BE ALONE!
COME ON, AYA. YOU CAN WALK.
MMM?

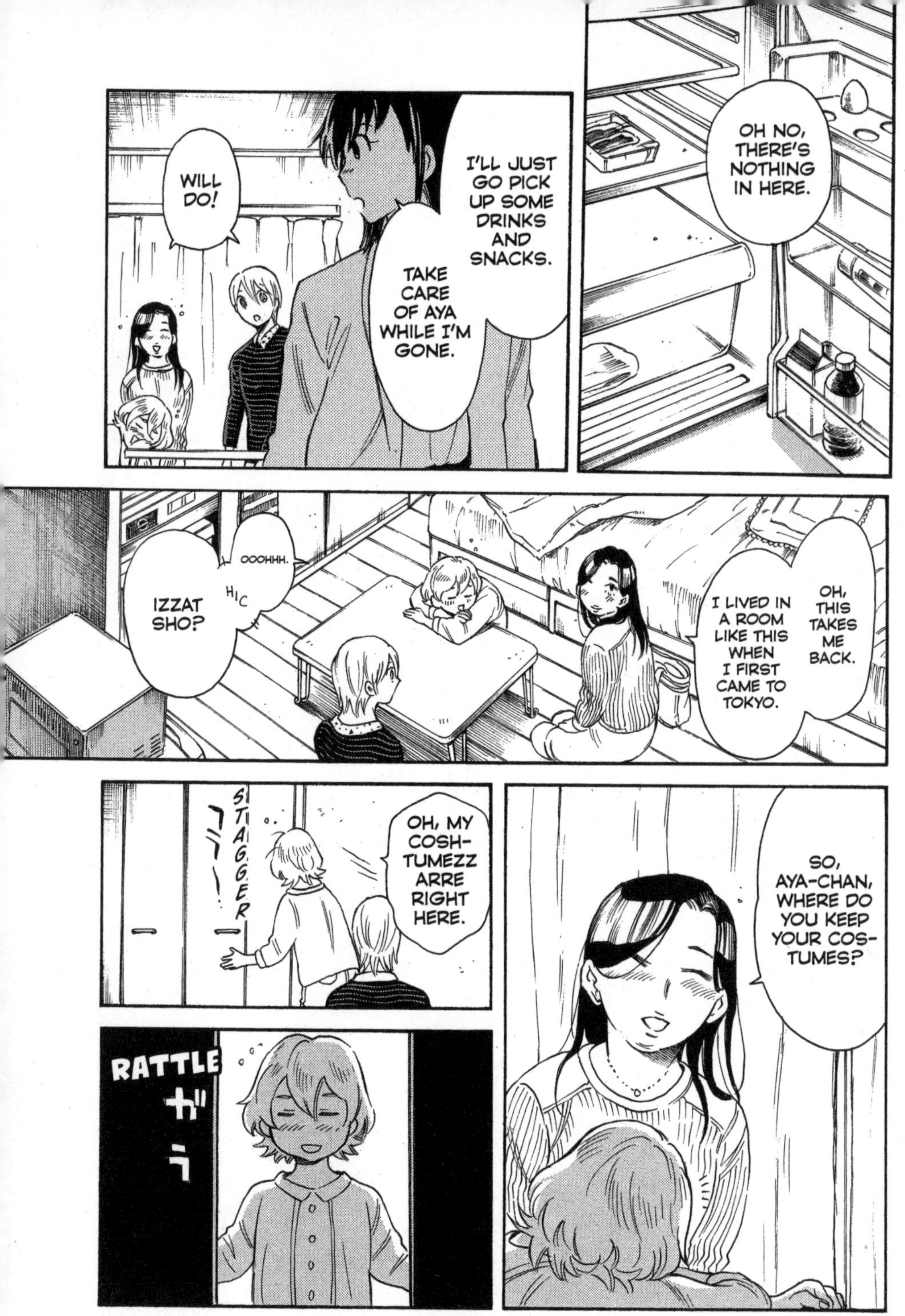
OH NO, THERE'S NOTHING IN HERE.
I'LL JUST GO PICK UP SOME DRINKS AND SNACKS.
TAKE CARE OF AYA WHILE I'M GONE.
WILL DO!
OH, THIS TAKES ME BACK.
I LIVED IN A ROOM LIKE THIS WHEN I FIRST CAME TO TOKYO.
OOOHHH.
HIC
IZZAT SHO?
SO, AYA-CHAN, WHERE DO YOU KEEP YOUR COS-TUMES?
OH, MY COSH-TUMEZZ ARRE RIGHT HERE.
STAGGER
RATTLE
ガラ

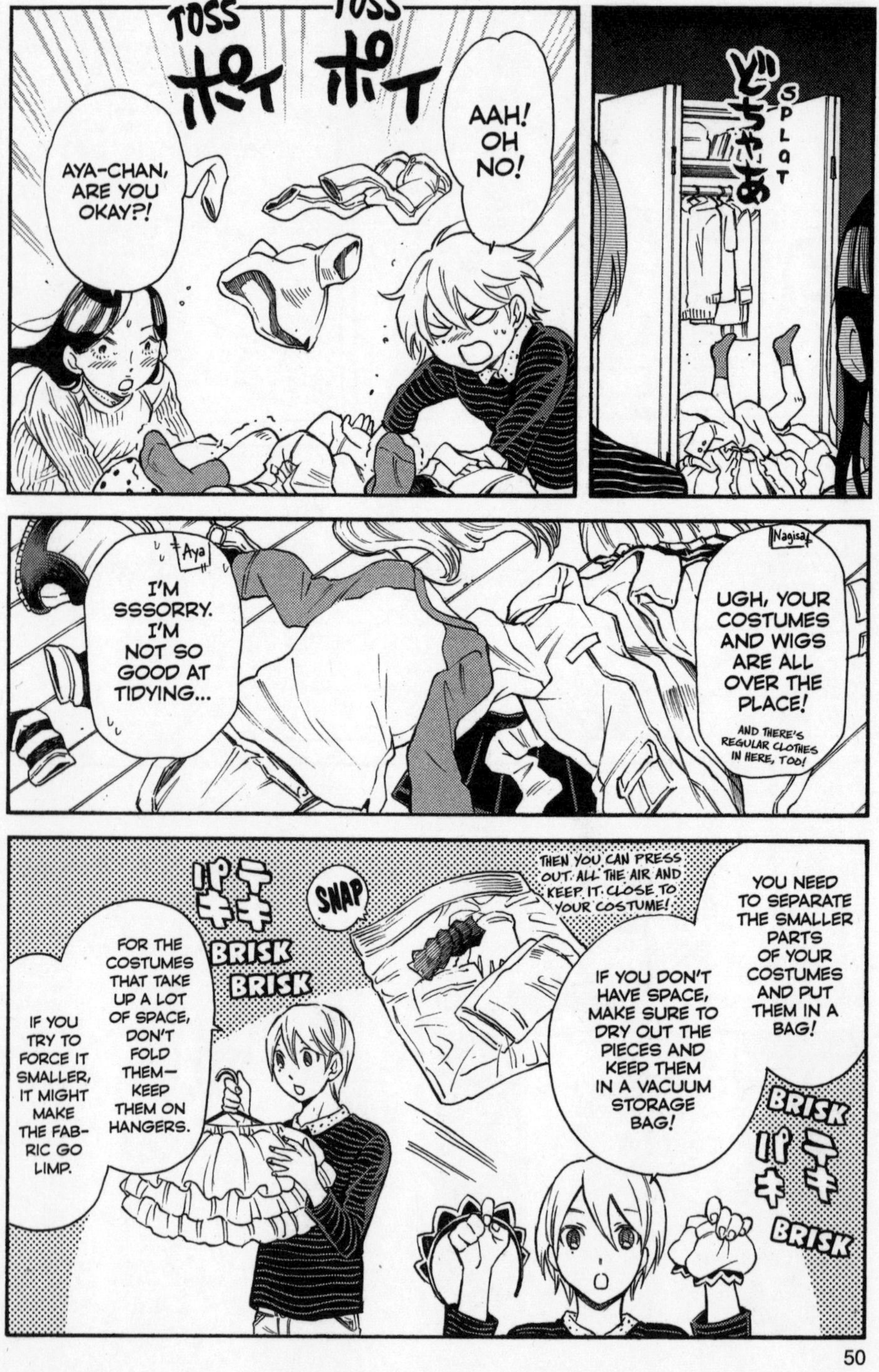
どちゃあ
SPLAT
TOSS TOSS
ポイポイ
AAH! OH NO!
AYA-CHAN, ARE YOU OKAY?!
Nagisa
UGH, YOUR COSTUMES AND WIGS ARE ALL OVER THE PLACE!
AND THERE'S REGULAR CLOTHES IN HERE, TOO!
Aya
I'M SSSORRY. I'M NOT SO GOOD AT TIDYING...
YOU NEED TO SEPARATE THE SMALLER PARTS OF YOUR COSTUMES AND PUT THEM IN A BAG!
THEN YOU CAN PRESS OUT ALL THE AIR AND KEEP IT CLOSE TO YOUR COSTUME!
SNAP
IF YOU DON'T HAVE SPACE, MAKE SURE TO DRY OUT THE PIECES AND KEEP THEM IN A VACUUM STORAGE BAG!
BRISK
テキパキ
BRISK
テキパキ
BRISK BRISK
FOR THE COSTUMES THAT TAKE UP A LOT OF SPACE, DON'T FOLD THEM—KEEP THEM ON HANGERS.
IF YOU TRY TO FORCE IT SMALLER, IT MIGHT MAKE THE FAB-RIC GO LIMP.

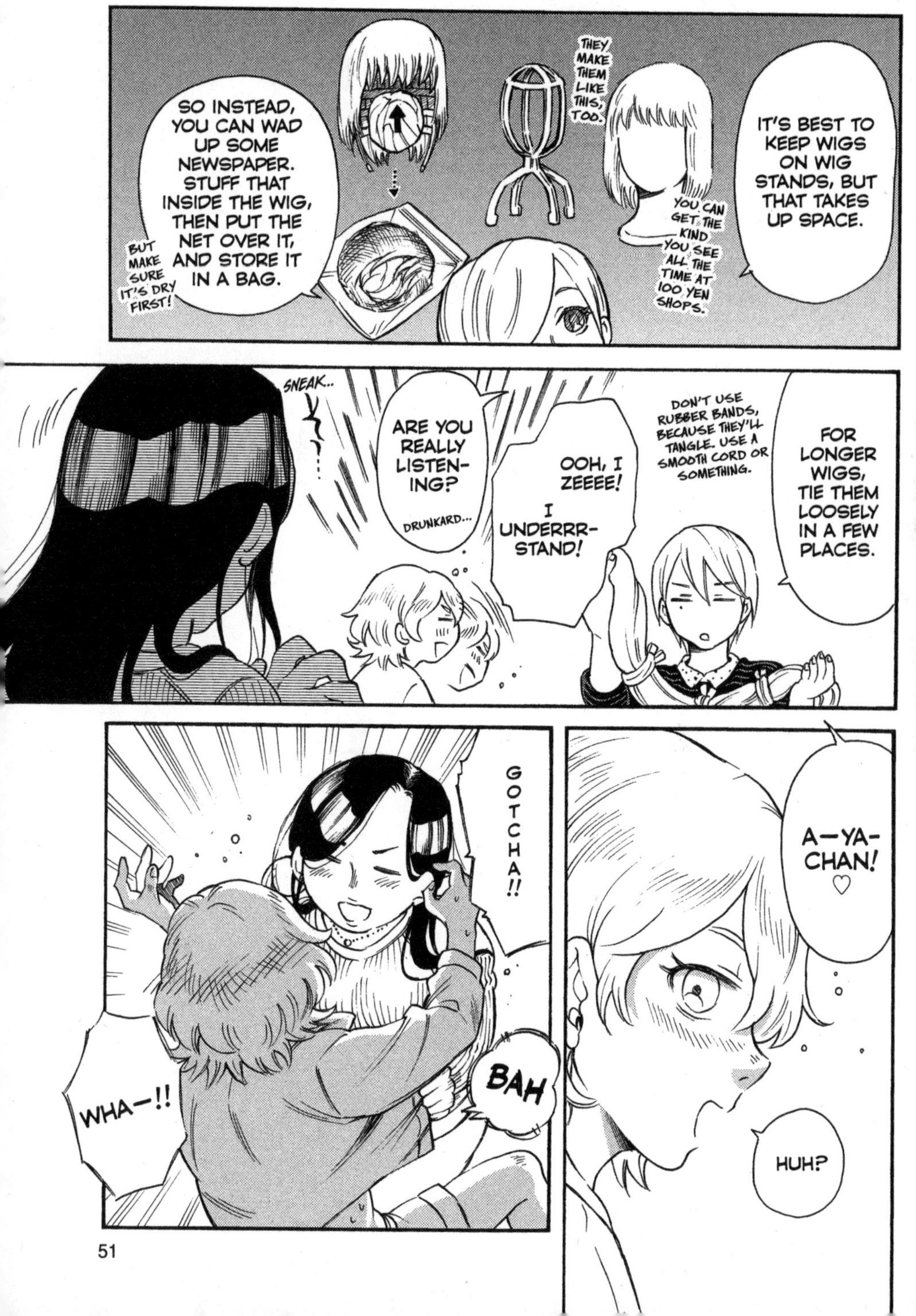

IT'S BEST TO KEEP WIGS ON WIG STANDS, BUT THAT TAKES UP SPACE.
YOU CAN GET THE KIND YOU SEE ALL THE TIME AT 100 YEN SHOPS.
THEY MAKE THEM LIKE THIS, TOO.
SO INSTEAD, YOU CAN WAD UP SOME NEWSPAPER. STUFF THAT INSIDE THE WIG, THEN PUT THE NET OVER IT, AND STORE IT IN A BAG.
BUT MAKE SURE IT'S DRY FIRST!
FOR LONGER WIGS, TIE THEM LOOSELY IN A FEW PLACES.
DON'T USE RUBBER BANDS, BECAUSE THEY'LL TANGLE. USE A SMOOTH CORD OR SOMETHING.
OOH, I ZEEEE!
I UNDERRR-STAND!
ARE YOU REALLY LISTEN-ING?
DRUNKARD...
SNEAK...
A—YA-CHAN! ♡
HUH?
GOTCHA!!
BAH
WHA—!!

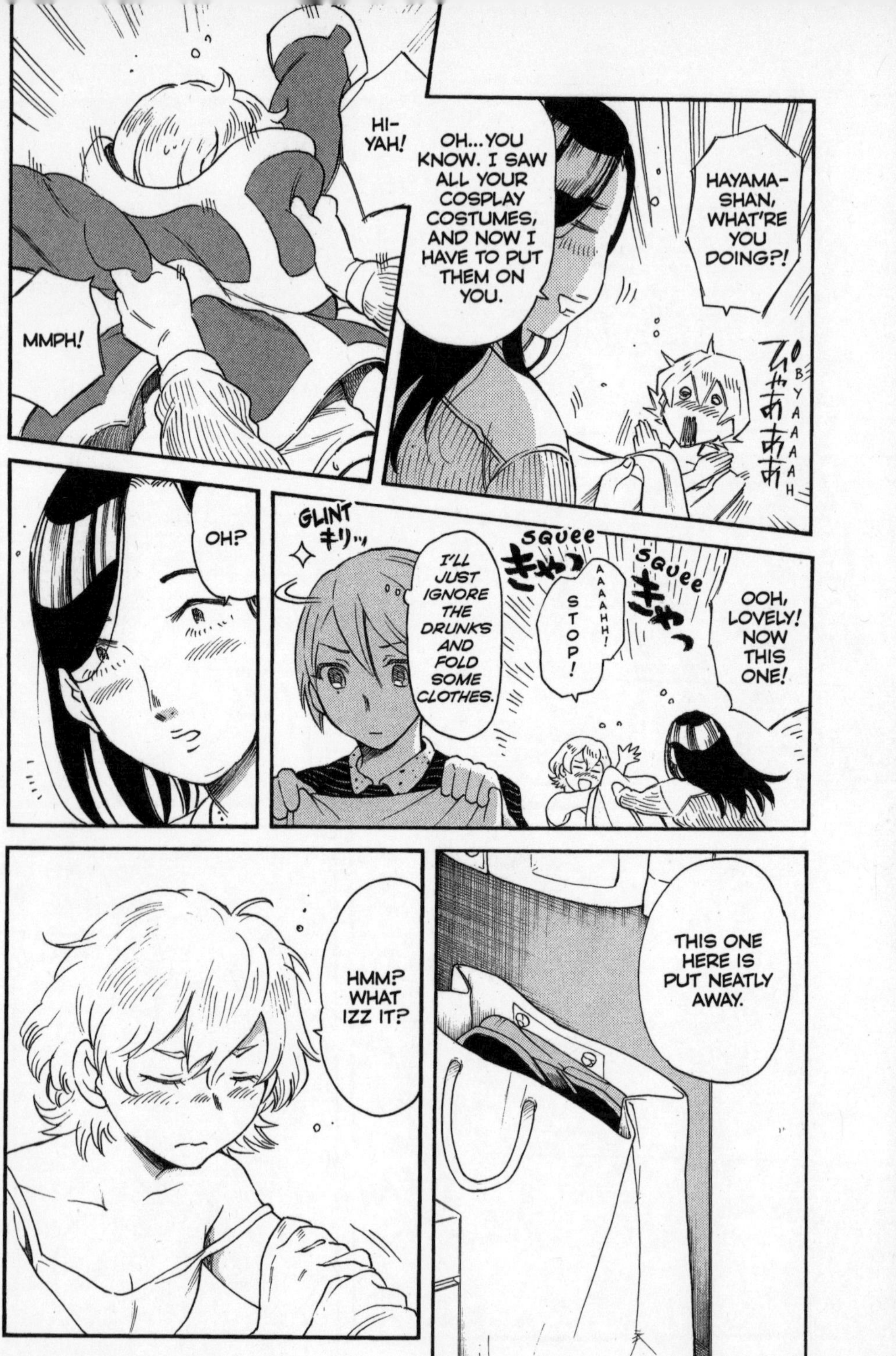
HAYAMA-SHAN, WHAT'RE YOU DOING?!
ぴゃあああ
BYAAAAH
OH...YOU KNOW. I SAW ALL YOUR COSPLAY COSTUMES, AND NOW I HAVE TO PUT THEM ON YOU.
HI-YAH!
MMPH!
OOH, LOVELY! NOW THIS ONE!
SQUEE
きゃっ
AAAAHH!
STOP!
SQUEE
きゃっ
I'LL JUST IGNORE THE DRUNKS AND FOLD SOME CLOTHES.
GLINT
キリッ
OH?
THIS ONE HERE IS PUT NEATLY AWAY.
HMM? WHAT IZZ IT?

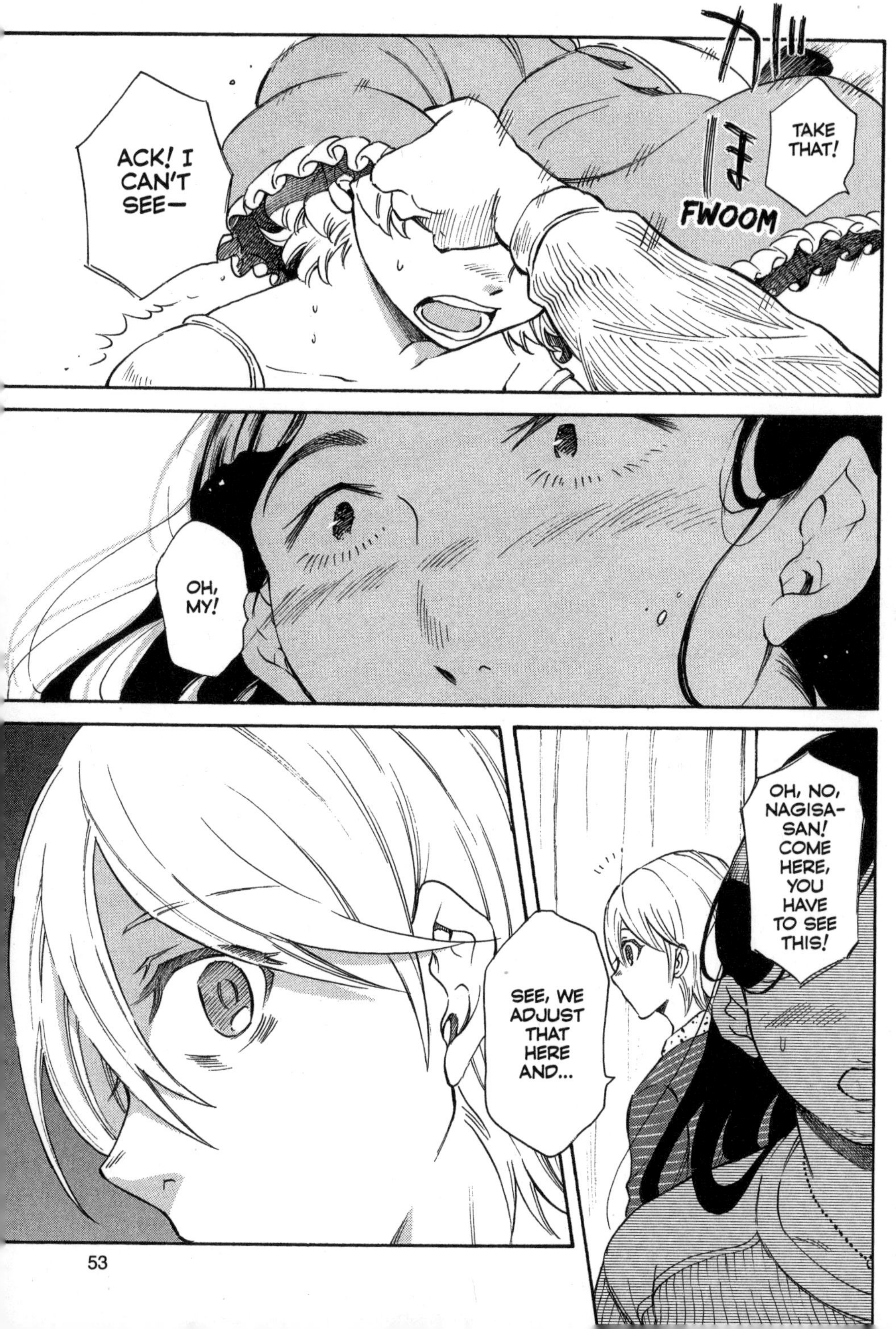
TAKE THAT!
FWOOM
ACK! I CAN'T SEE—
OH, MY!
OH, NO, NAGISA-SAN! COME HERE, YOU HAVE TO SEE THIS!
SEE, WE ADJUST THAT HERE AND...

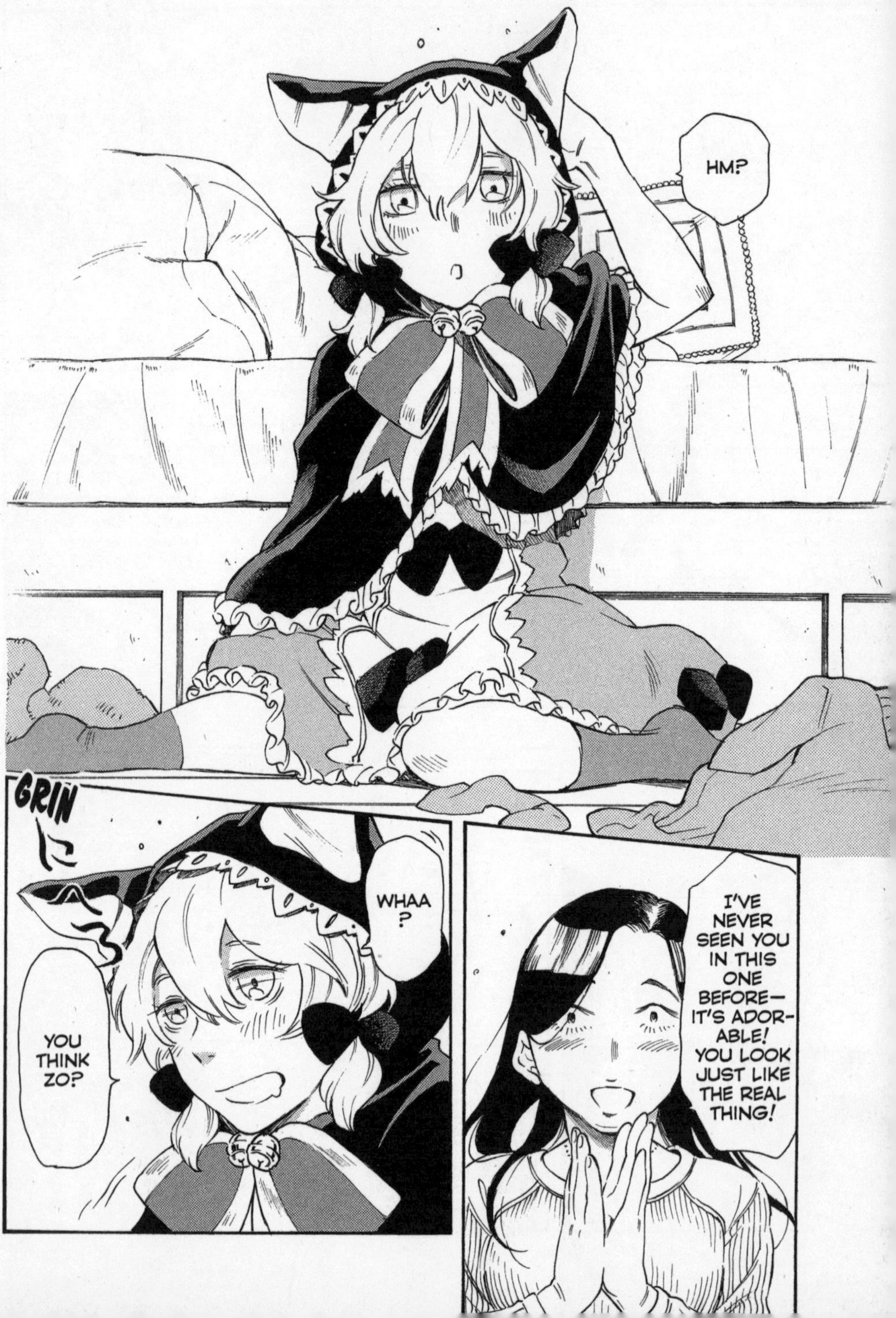
HM?
I'VE NEVER SEEN YOU IN THIS ONE BEFORE—IT'S ADORABLE! YOU LOOK JUST LIKE THE REAL THING!
GRIN
WHAA?
YOU THINK ZO?

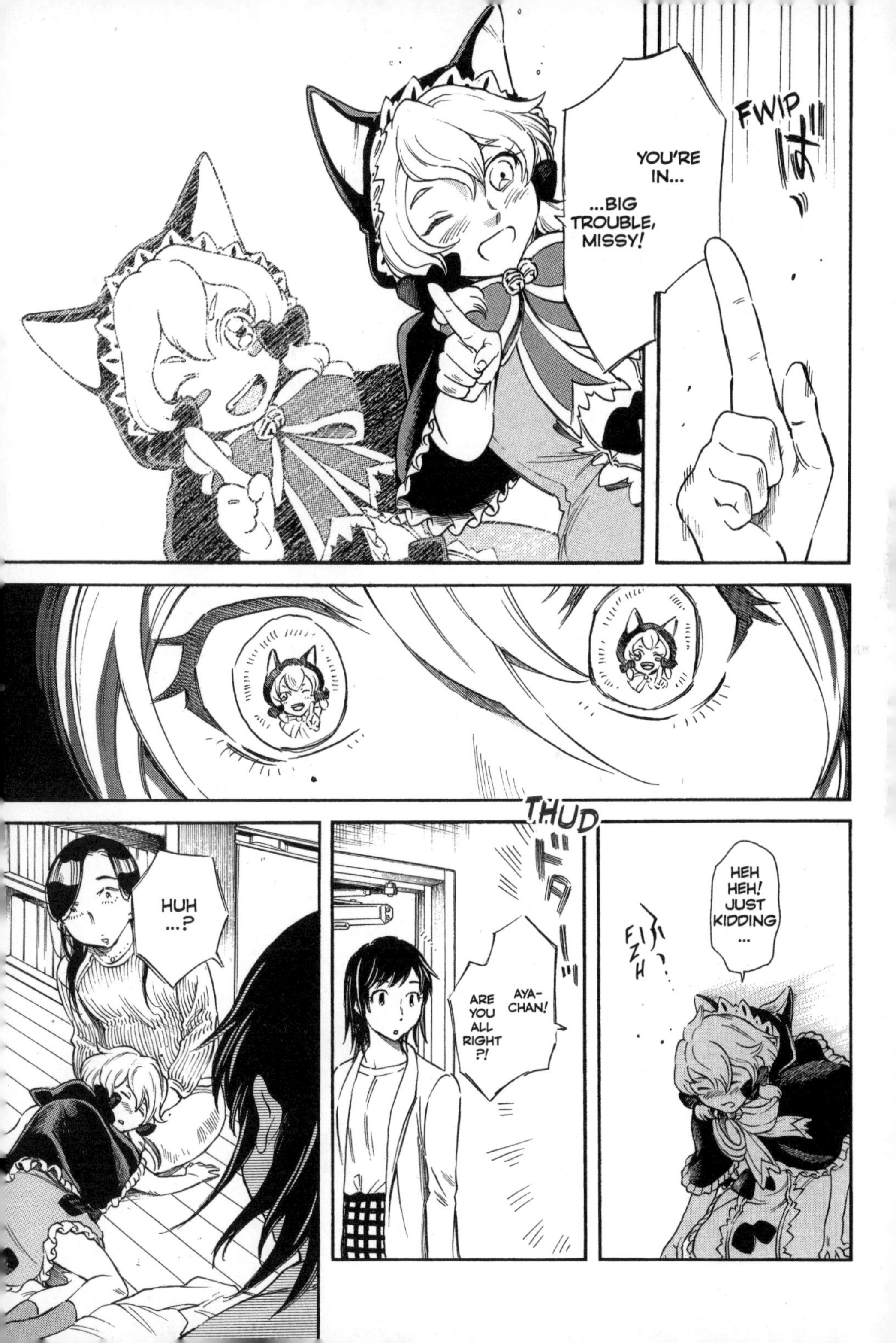
FWIP
YOU'RE IN...
...BIG TROUBLE, MISSY!
HEH HEH! JUST KIDDING ...
FIZH
THUD
AYA-CHAN!
ARE YOU ALL RIGHT ?!
HUH ...?

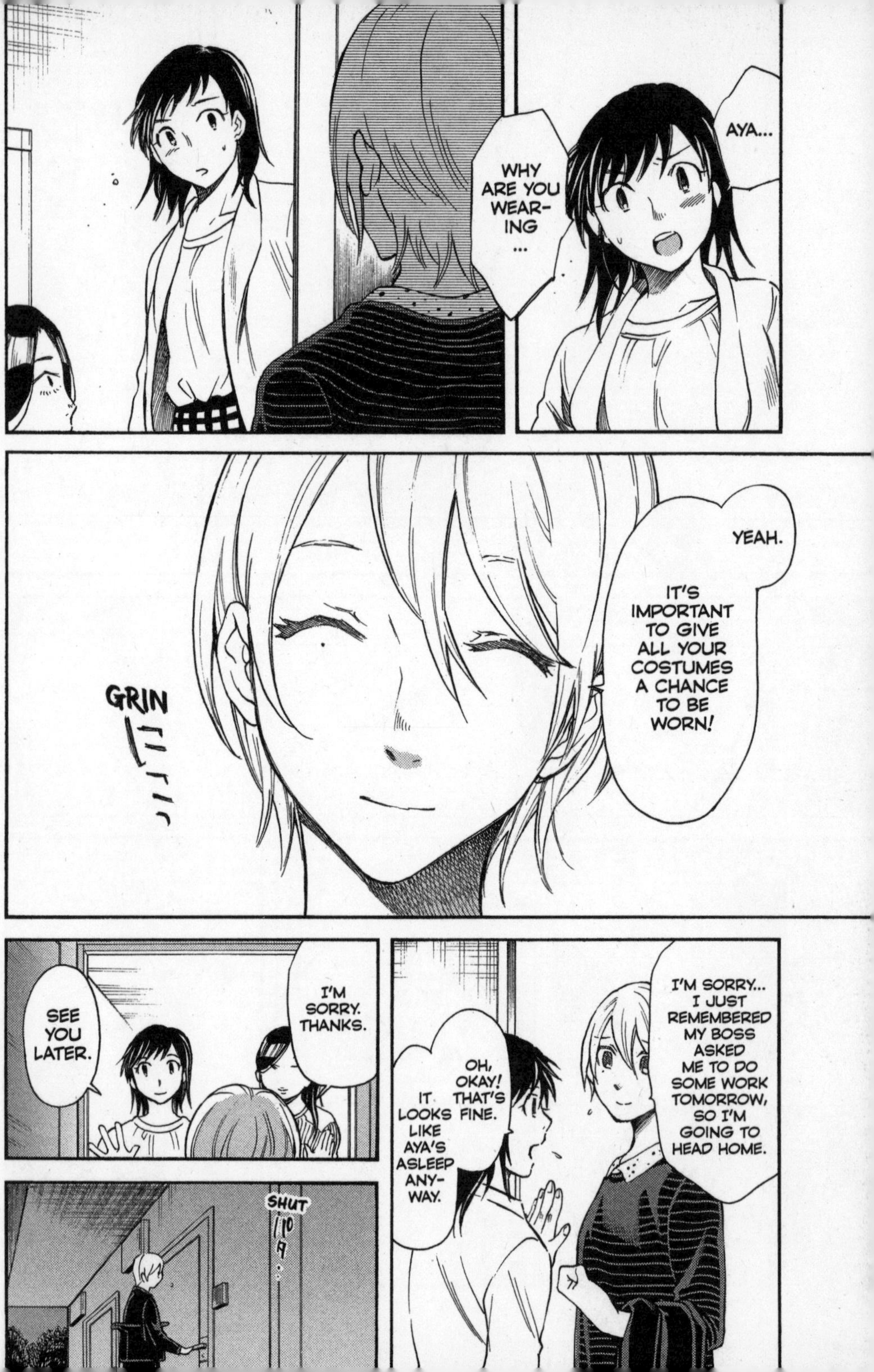
AYA...
WHY ARE YOU WEARING...
YEAH.
IT'S IMPORTANT TO GIVE ALL YOUR COSTUMES A CHANCE TO BE WORN!
GRIN
I'M SORRY... I JUST REMEMBERED MY BOSS ASKED ME TO DO SOME WORK TOMORROW, SO I'M GOING TO HEAD HOME.
OH, OKAY! THAT'S FINE.
IT LOOKS LIKE AYA'S ASLEEP ANYWAY.
I'M SORRY. THANKS.
SEE YOU LATER.
SHUT

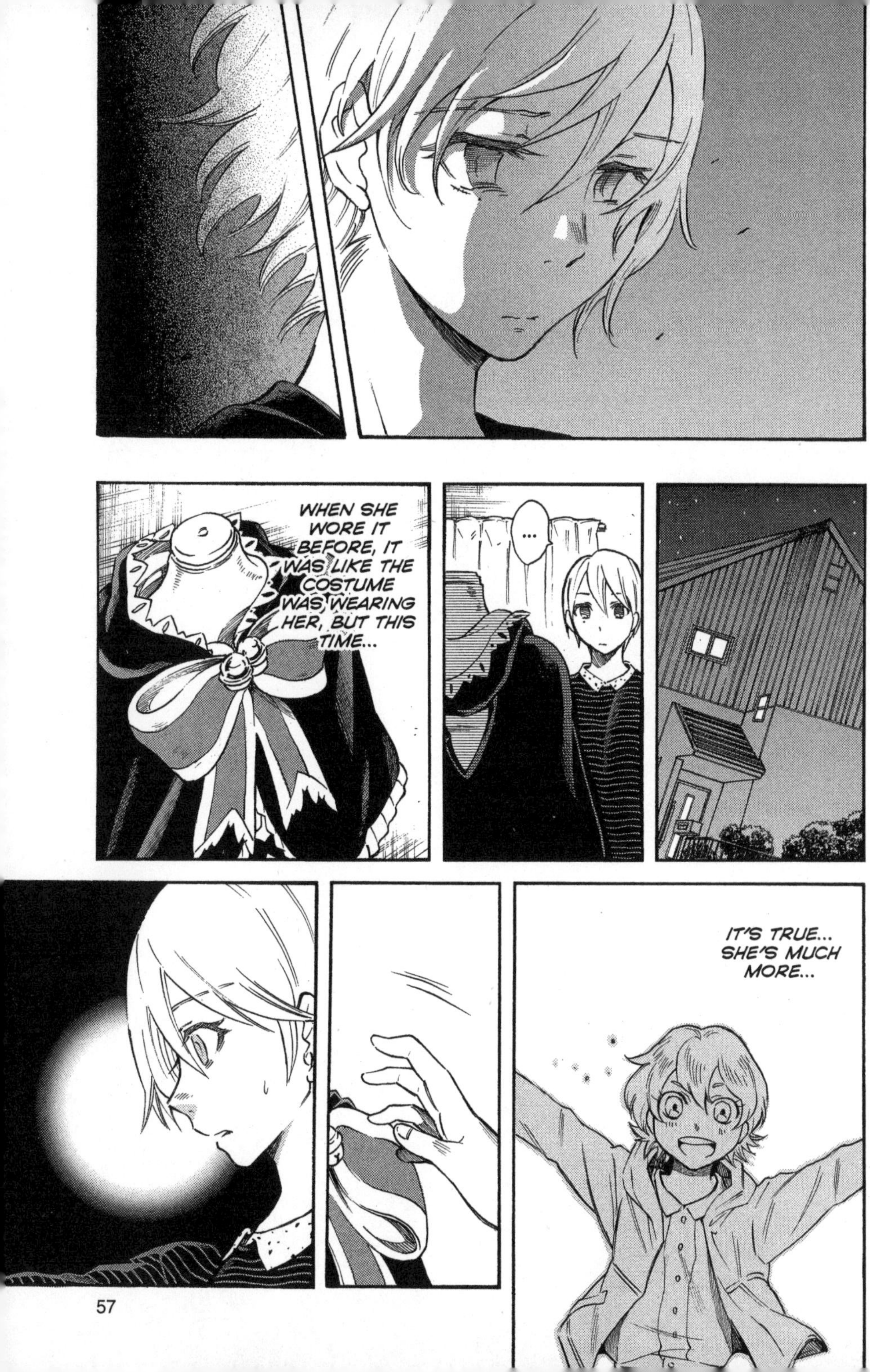
...
WHEN SHE WORE IT BEFORE, IT WAS LIKE THE COSTUME WAS WEARING HER, BUT THIS TIME...
IT'S TRUE... SHE'S MUCH MORE...

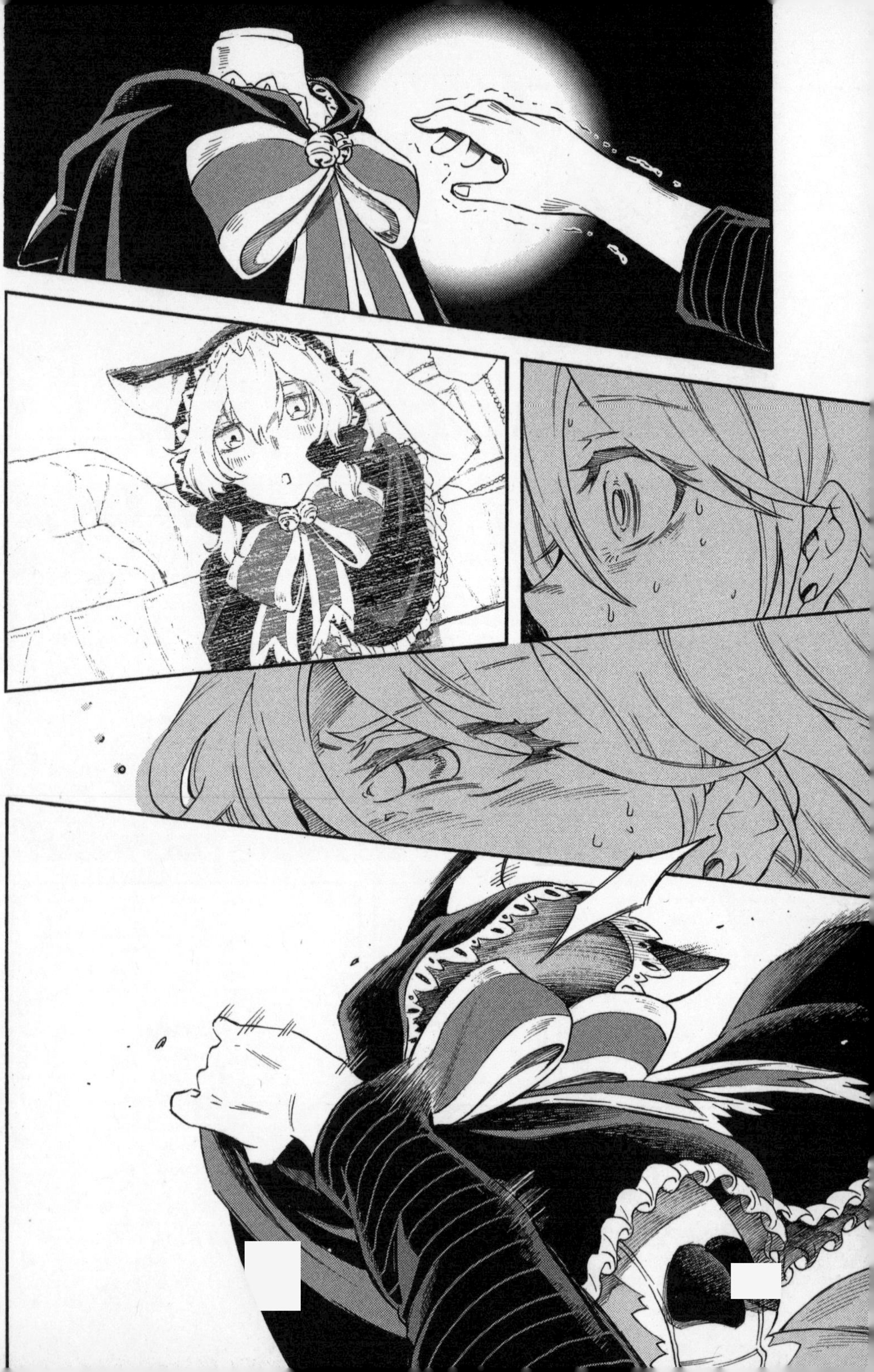

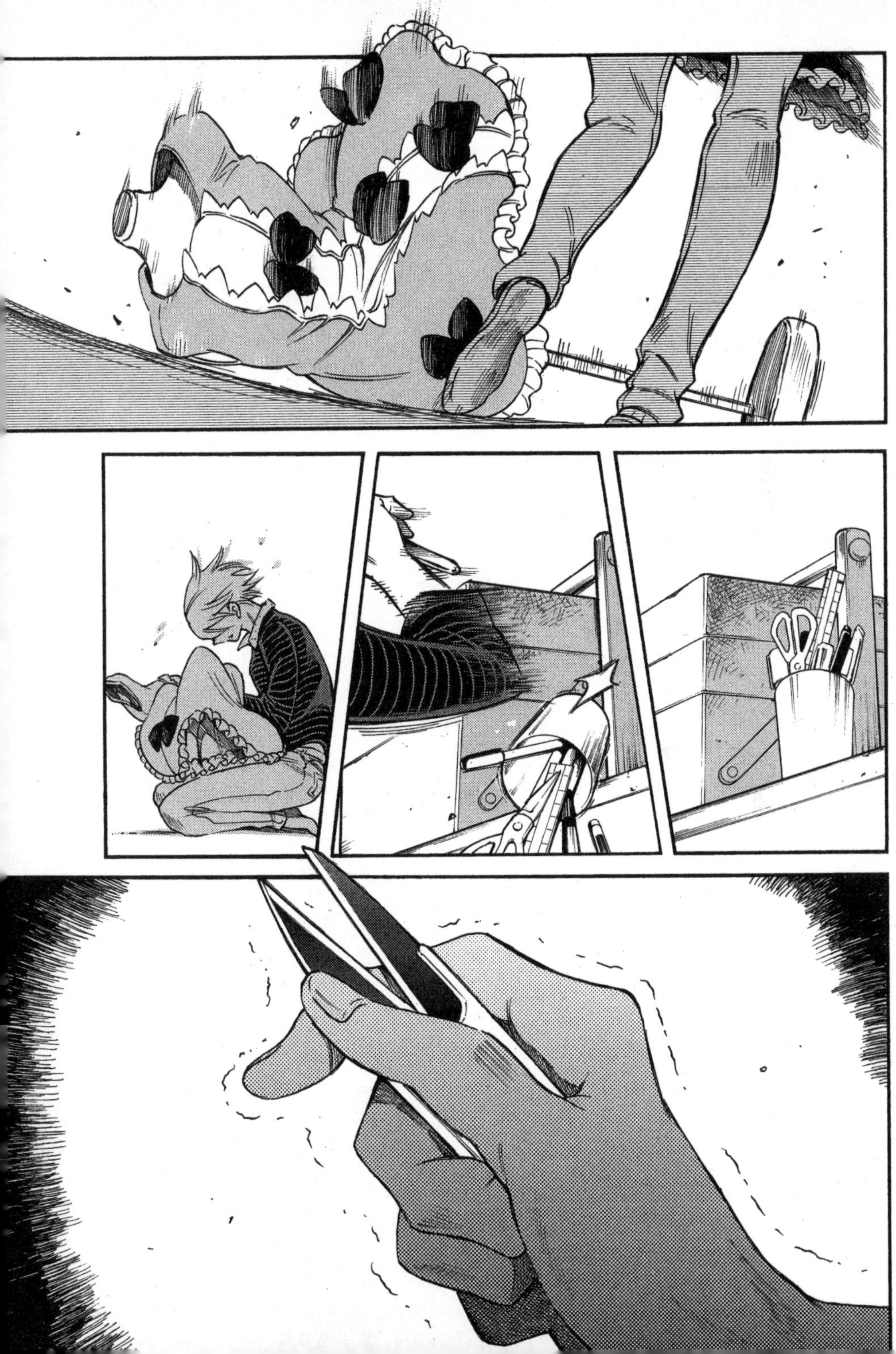

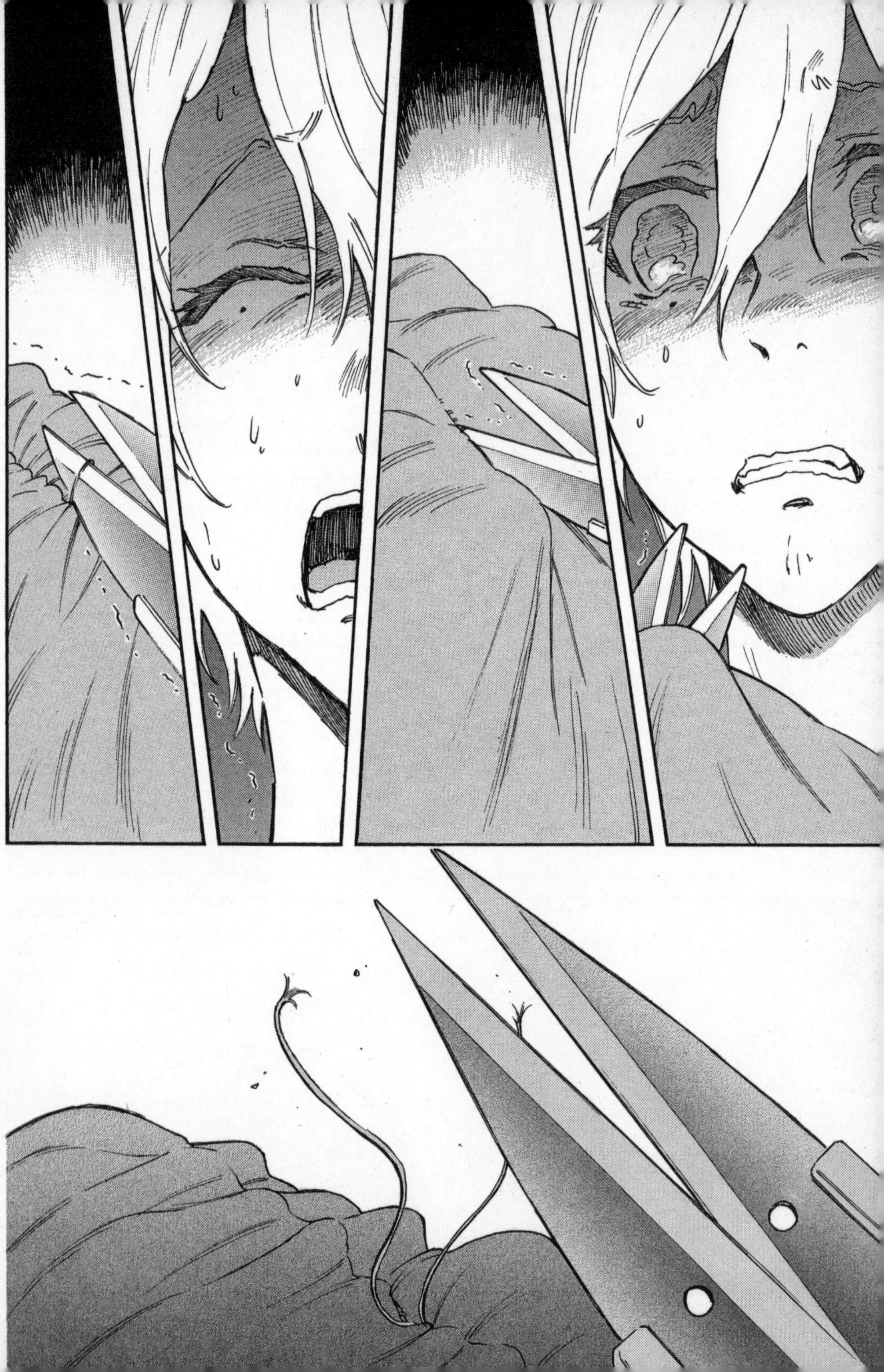

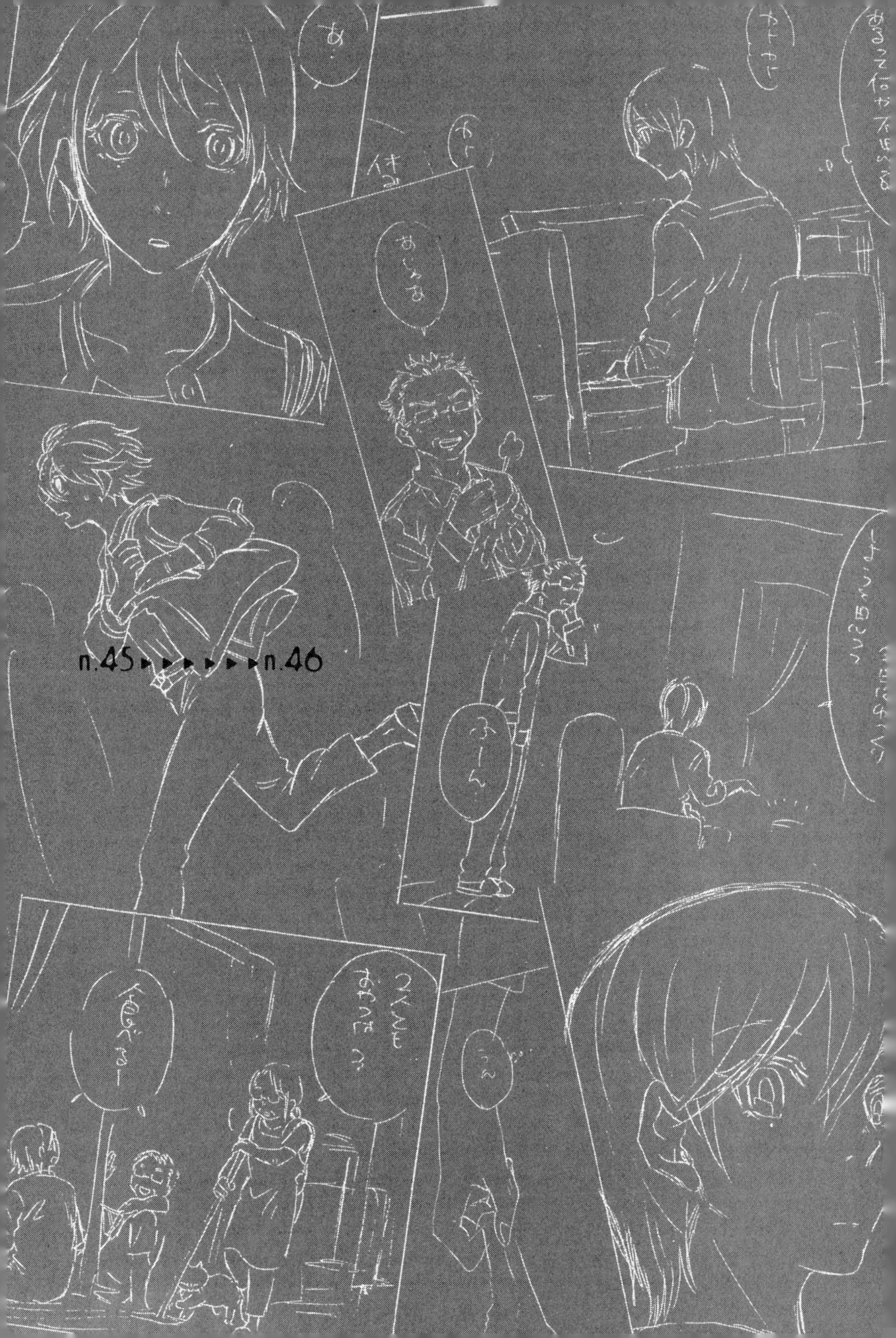
n.45▶▶▶▶▶▶▶n.46

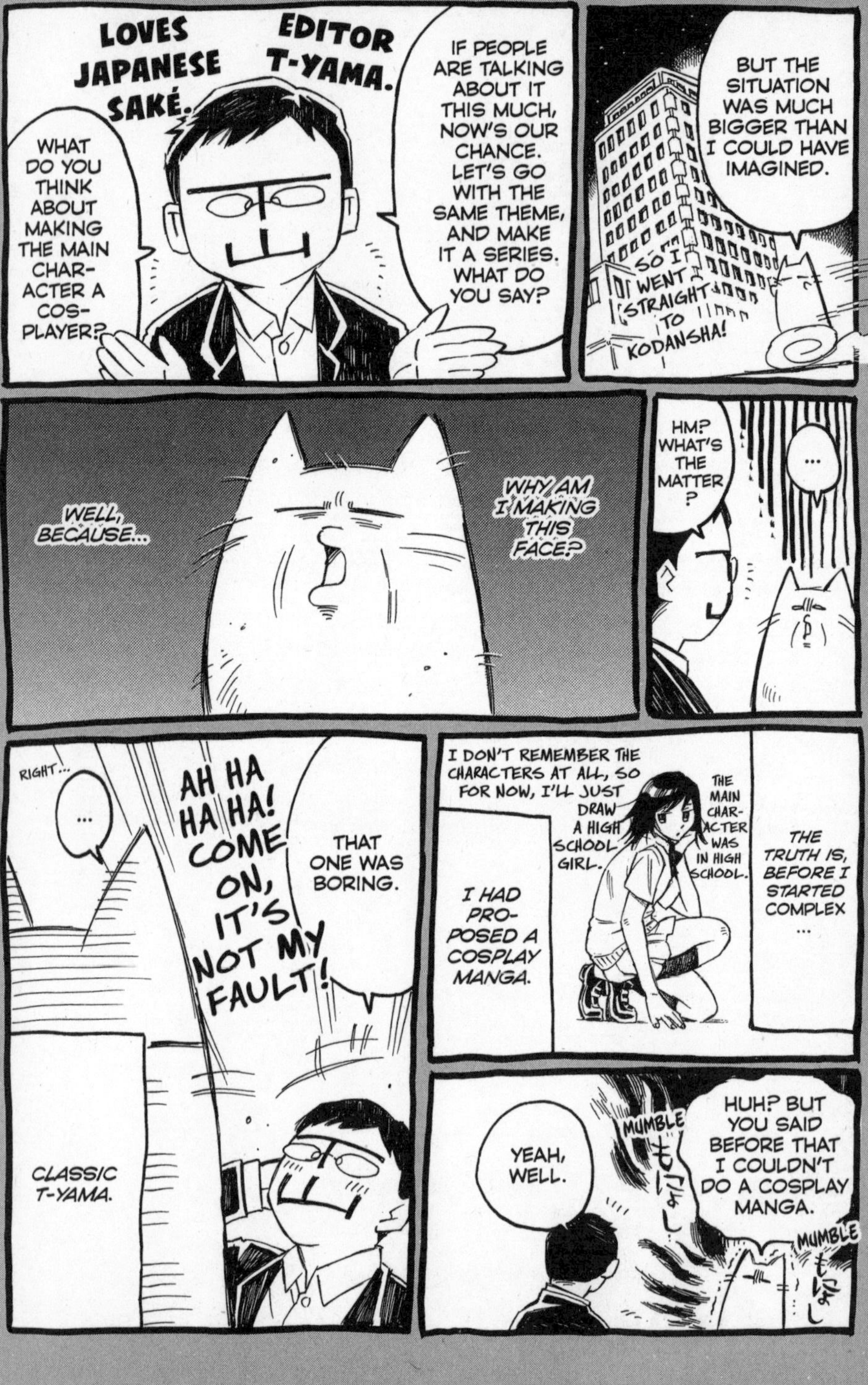
BUT THE SITUATION WAS MUCH BIGGER THAN I COULD HAVE IMAGINED.
SO I WENT STRAIGHT TO KODANSHA!
IF PEOPLE ARE TALKING ABOUT IT THIS MUCH, NOW'S OUR CHANCE. LET'S GO WITH THE SAME THEME, AND MAKE IT A SERIES. WHAT DO YOU SAY?
EDITOR T-YAMA.
LOVES JAPANESE SAKÉ.
WHAT DO YOU THINK ABOUT MAKING THE MAIN CHAR-ACTER A COS-PLAYER?
HM? WHAT'S THE MATTER?
...
WHY AM I MAKING THIS FACE?
WELL, BECAUSE...
THE TRUTH IS, BEFORE I STARTED COMPLEX...
THE MAIN CHAR-ACTER WAS IN HIGH SCHOOL.
I DON'T REMEMBER THE CHARACTERS AT ALL, SO FOR NOW, I'LL JUST DRAW A HIGH SCHOOL GIRL.
I HAD PRO-POSED A COSPLAY MANGA.
HUH? BUT YOU SAID BEFORE THAT I COULDN'T DO A COSPLAY MANGA.
MUMBLE
YEAH, WELL.
MUMBLE
THAT ONE WAS BORING.
AH HA HA HA! COME ON, IT'S NOT MY FAULT!
RIGHT...
...
CLASSIC T-YAMA.

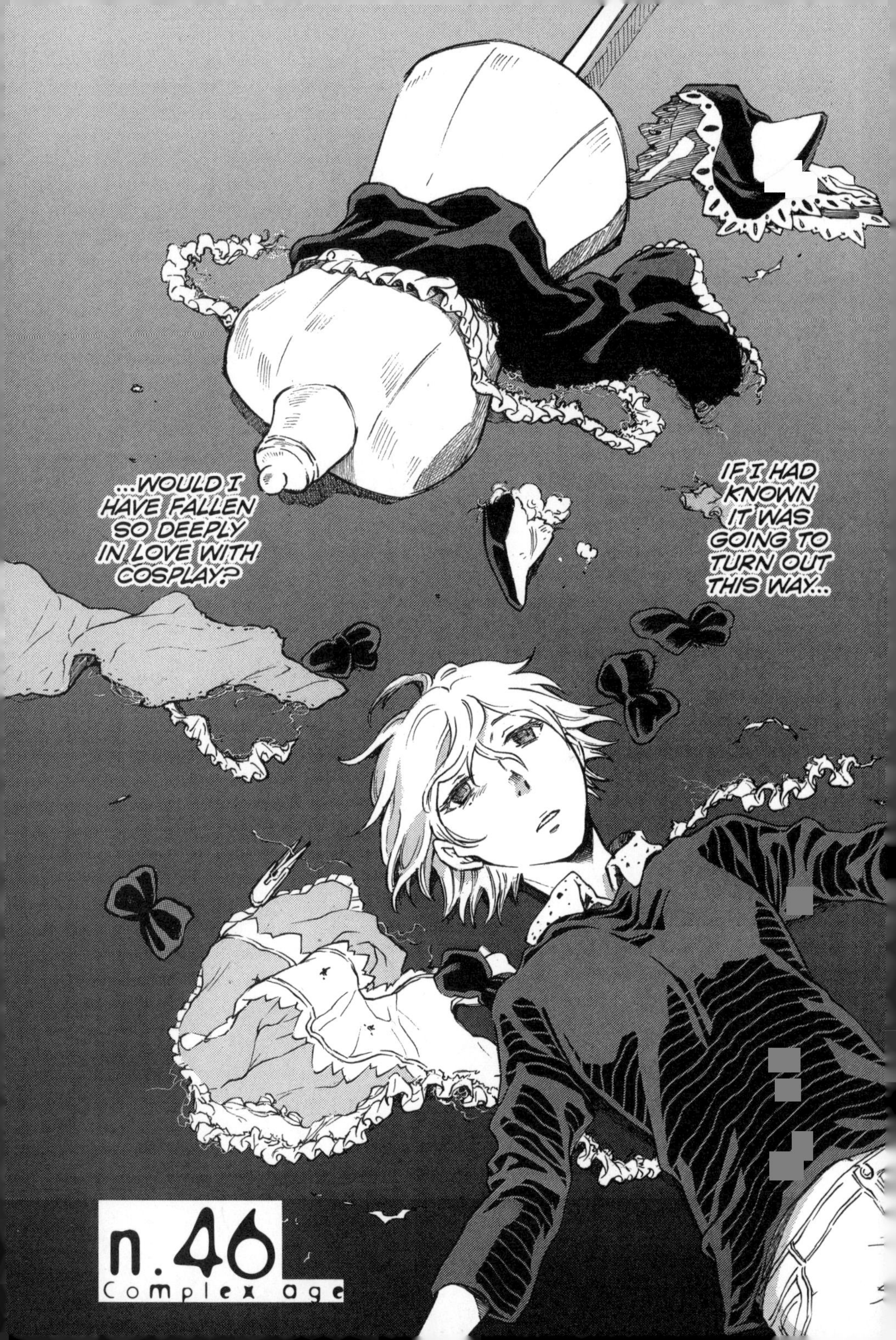
IF I HAD KNOWN IT WAS GOING TO TURN OUT THIS WAY...
...WOULD I HAVE FALLEN SO DEEPLY IN LOVE WITH COSPLAY?
n.46
Complex age

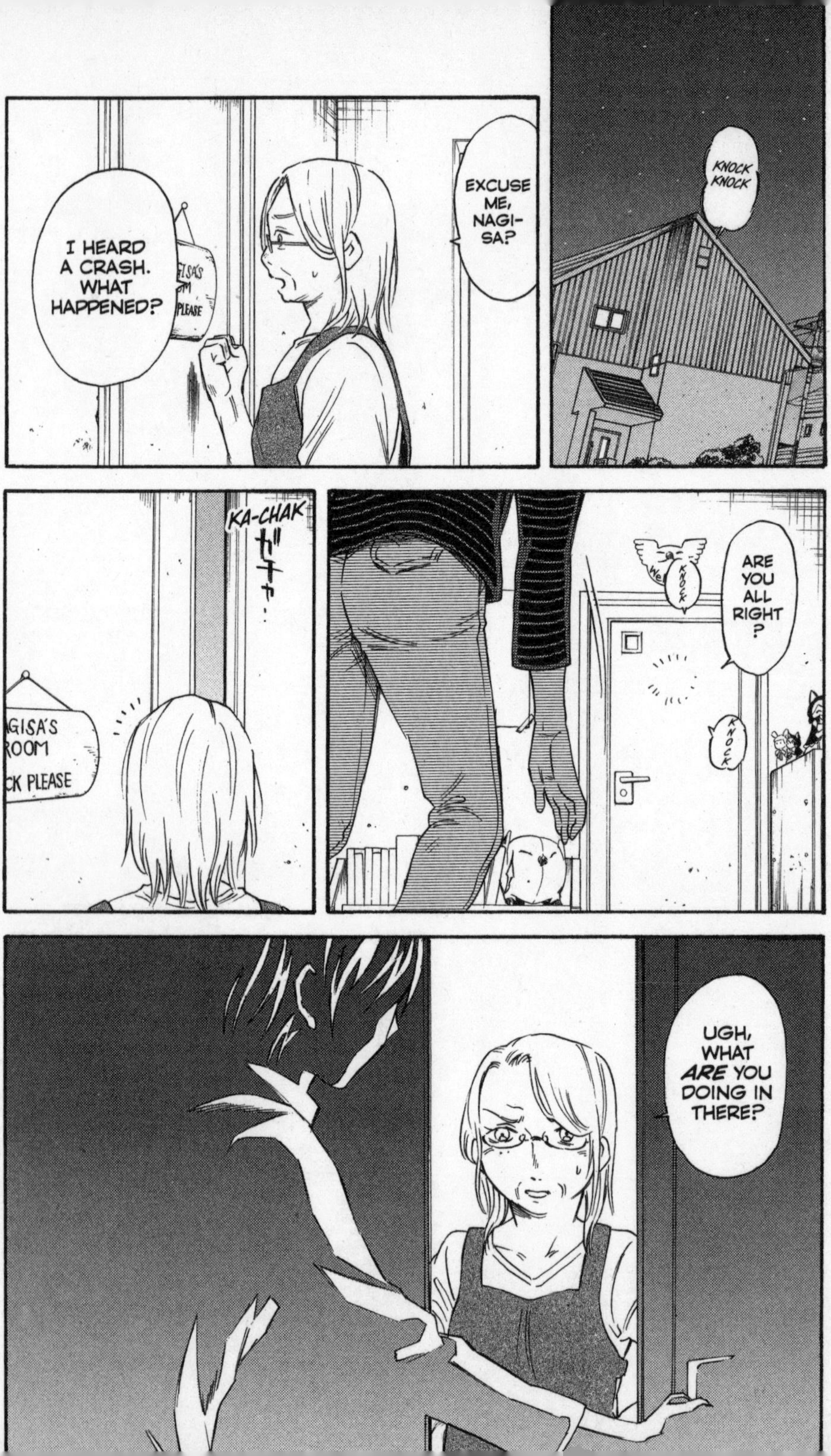
KNOCK KNOCK
EXCUSE ME, NAGISA?
I HEARD A CRASH. WHAT HAPPENED?
KNOCK
ARE YOU ALL RIGHT?
KNOCK
KA-CHAK
ガチャ
UGH, WHAT *ARE* YOU DOING IN THERE?

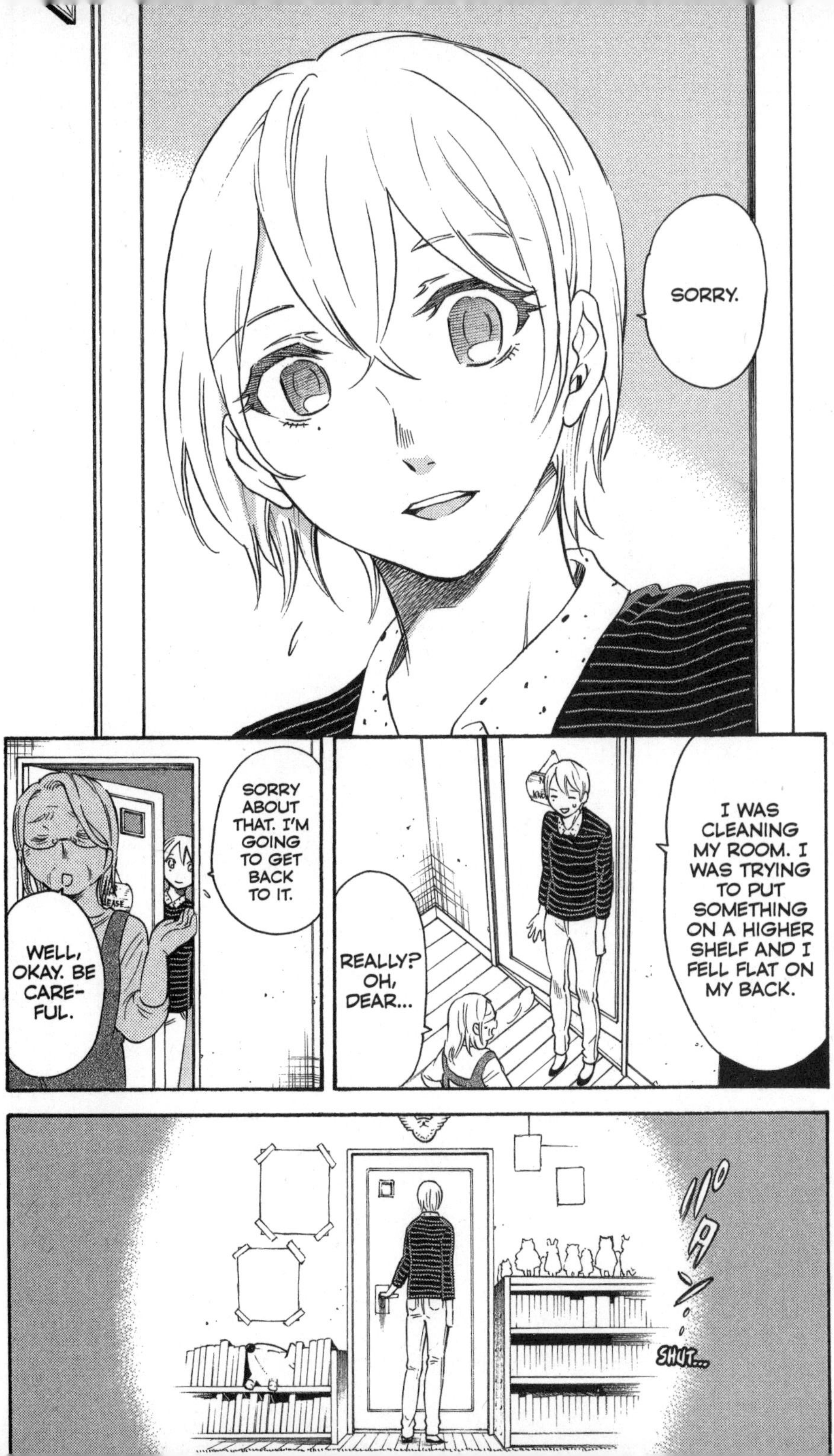
SORRY.
I WAS CLEANING MY ROOM. I WAS TRYING TO PUT SOMETHING ON A HIGHER SHELF AND I FELL FLAT ON MY BACK.
REALLY? OH, DEAR...
SORRY ABOUT THAT. I'M GOING TO GET BACK TO IT.
WELL, OKAY. BE CARE-FUL.
パタン
SHUT...

YEAH
...

IT'S NOT AS BIG A DEAL AS I THOUGHT IT WOULD BE.

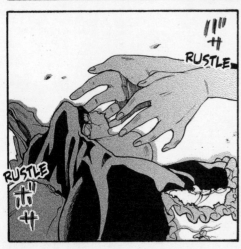

RUSTLE

RUSTLE

CLATTER

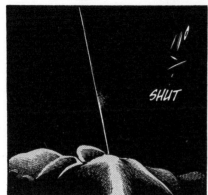

SHUT

SO THIS IS WHAT IT'S LIKE TO WAKE UP FROM THE DREAM.

Home Tutoring Service
MORE

New Hiring Tutors!

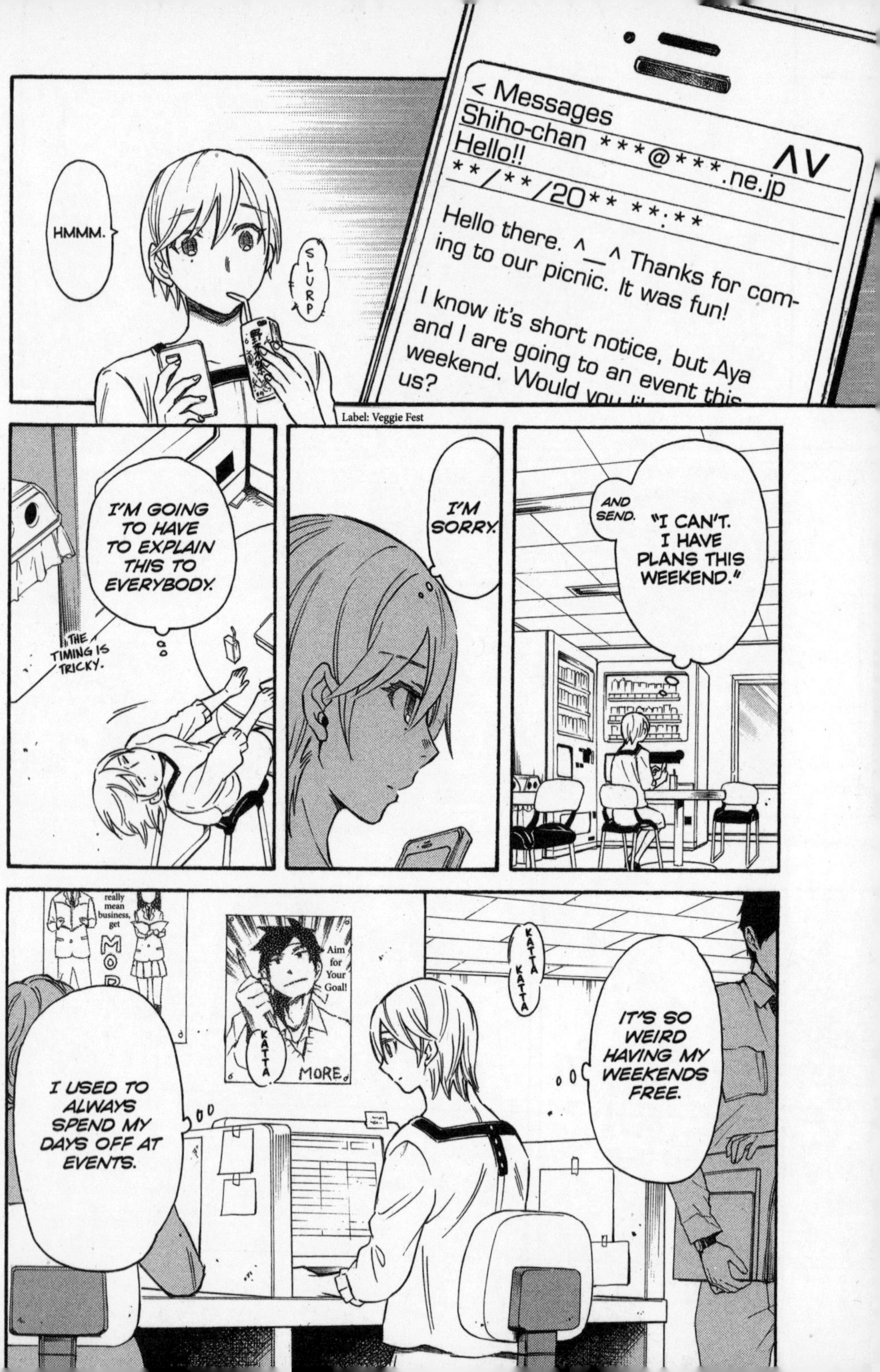
< Messages
Shiho-chan ***@***.ne.jp
Hello!!
//20** **:**
Hello there. ^__^ Thanks for coming to our picnic. It was fun!
I know it's short notice, but Aya and I are going to an event this weekend. Would you li
us?
HMMM.
SLURP
Label: Veggie Fest
AND SEND.
"I CAN'T. I HAVE PLANS THIS WEEKEND."
I'M SORRY.
I'M GOING TO HAVE TO EXPLAIN THIS TO EVERYBODY.
THE TIMING IS TRICKY.
KATTA KATTA
IT'S SO WEIRD HAVING MY WEEKENDS FREE.
Aim for Your Goal!
KATTA
MORE
really mean business, get
MOR
I USED TO ALWAYS SPEND MY DAYS OFF AT EVENTS.

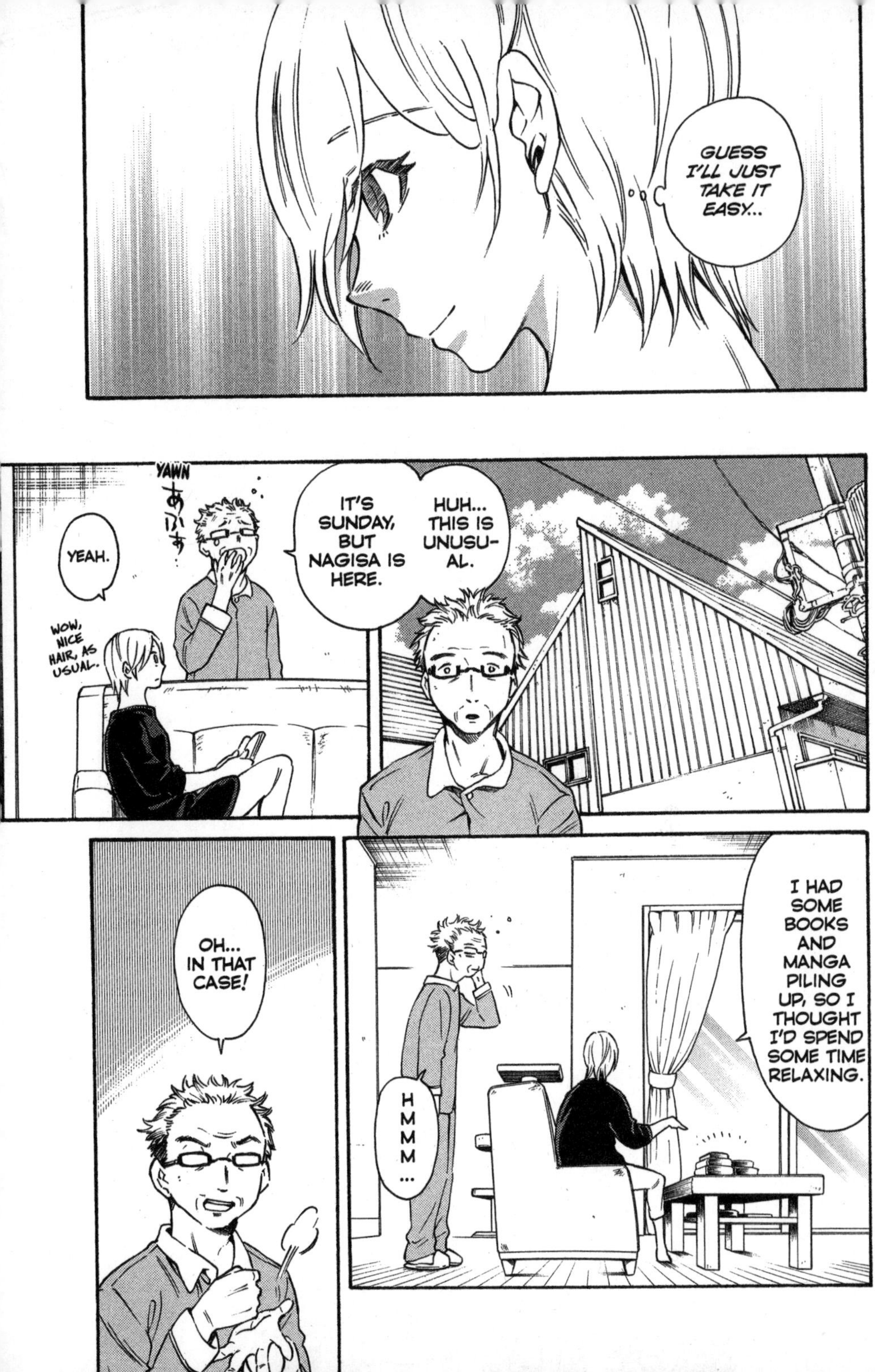
GUESS I'LL JUST TAKE IT EASY...
HUH... THIS IS UNUSU-AL.
IT'S SUNDAY, BUT NAGISA IS HERE.
YAWN
あふぁ
YEAH.
WOW, NICE HAIR, AS USUAL.
I HAD SOME BOOKS AND MANGA PILING UP, SO I THOUGHT I'D SPEND SOME TIME RELAXING.
HMMM...
OH... IN THAT CASE!

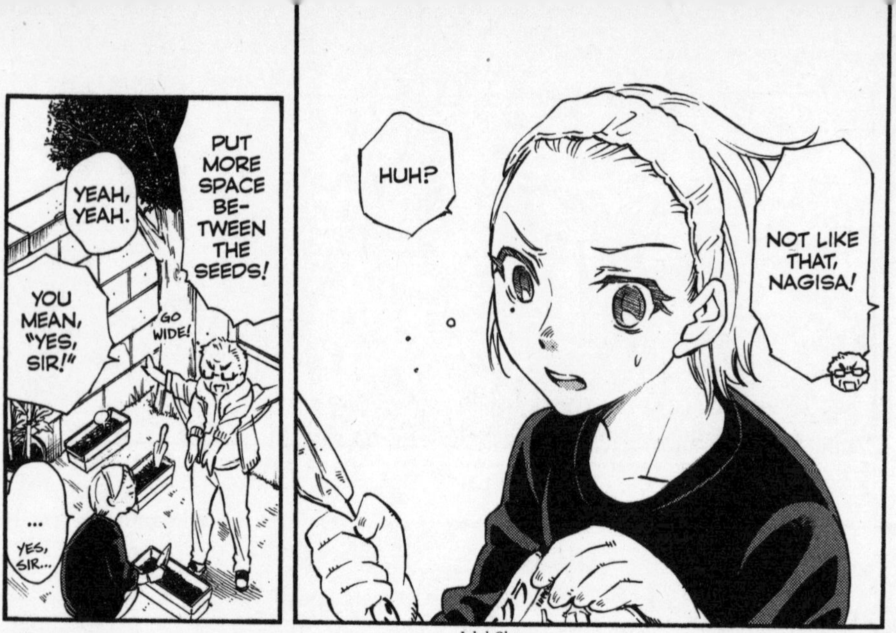
NOT LIKE THAT, NAGISA!
HUH?
PUT MORE SPACE BE-TWEEN THE SEEDS!
GO WIDE!
YEAH, YEAH.
YOU MEAN, "YES, SIR!"
... YES, SIR...

Label: Okra

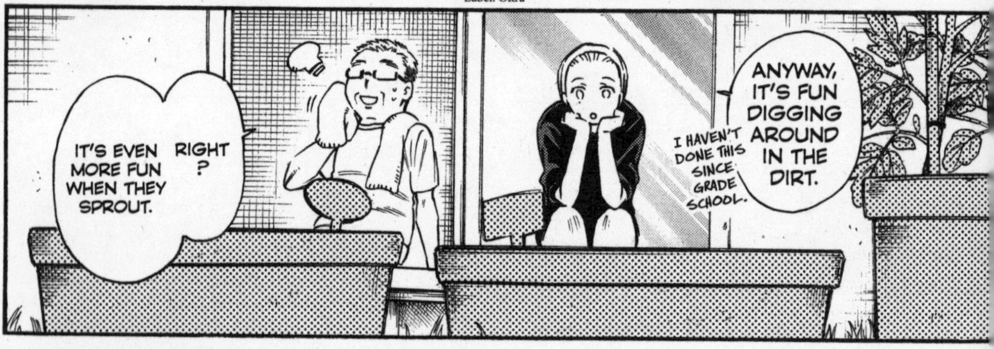
ANYWAY, IT'S FUN DIGGING AROUND IN THE DIRT.
I HAVEN'T DONE THIS SINCE GRADE SCHOOL.
RIGHT?
IT'S EVEN MORE FUN WHEN THEY SPROUT.

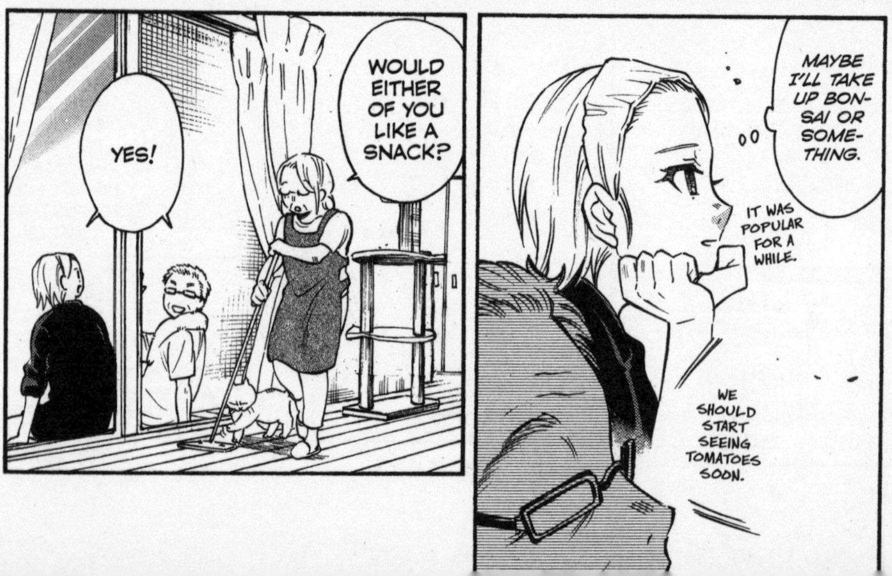
MAYBE I'LL TAKE UP BON-SAI OR SOME-THING.
IT WAS POPULAR FOR A WHILE.
WE SHOULD START SEEING TOMATOES SOON.
WOULD EITHER OF YOU LIKE A SNACK?
YES!

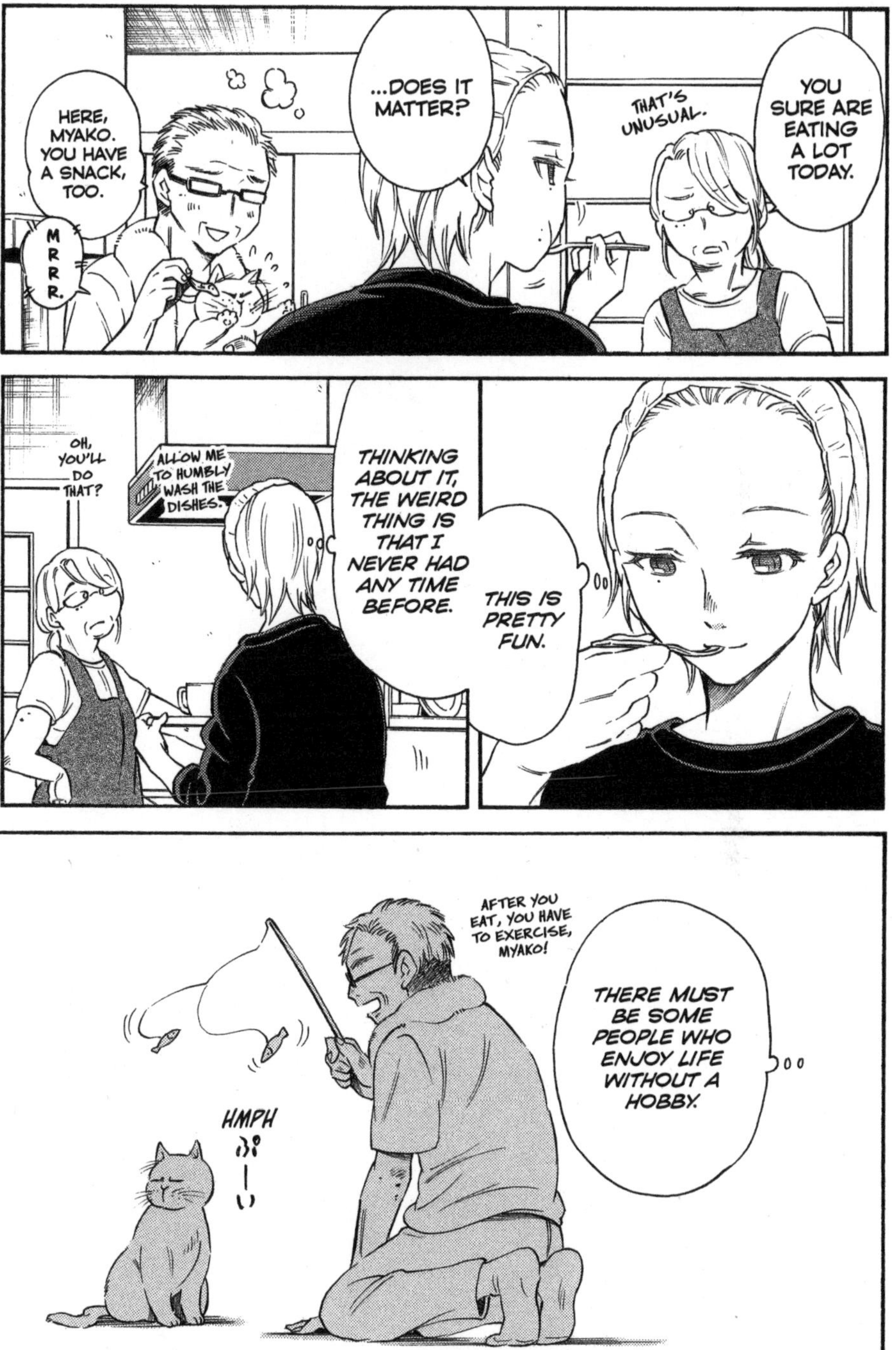
YOU SURE ARE EATING A LOT TODAY.
THAT'S UNUSUAL.
...DOES IT MATTER?
HERE, MYAKO. YOU HAVE A SNACK, TOO.
MRRR.
THIS IS PRETTY FUN.
THINKING ABOUT IT, THE WEIRD THING IS THAT I NEVER HAD ANY TIME BEFORE.
ALLOW ME TO HUMBLY WASH THE DISHES.
OH, YOU'LL DO THAT?
THERE MUST BE SOME PEOPLE WHO ENJOY LIFE WITHOUT A HOBBY.
AFTER YOU EAT, YOU HAVE TO EXERCISE, MYAKO!
HMPH
ぷーい

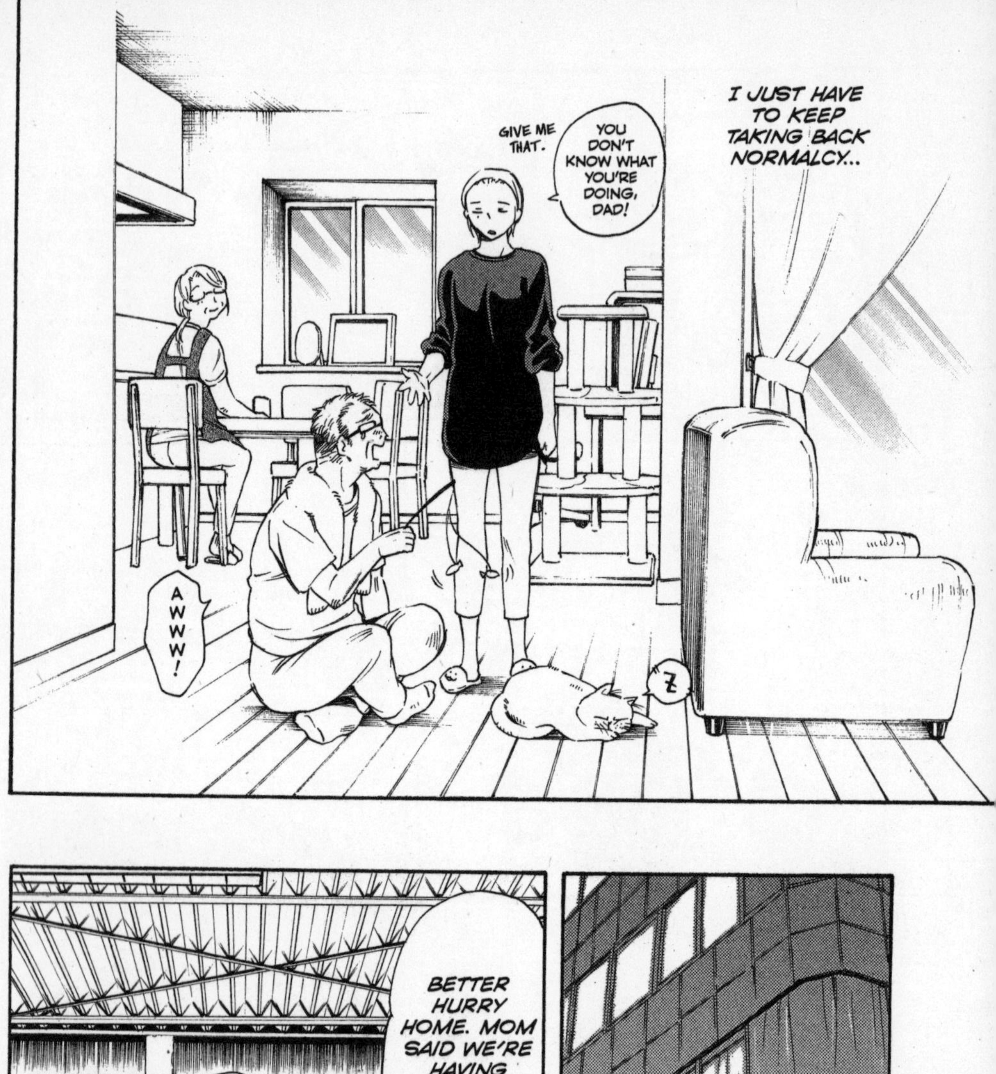
I JUST HAVE TO KEEP TAKING BACK NORMALCY...
YOU DON'T KNOW WHAT YOU'RE DOING, DAD!
GIVE ME THAT.
AWWW!
Z

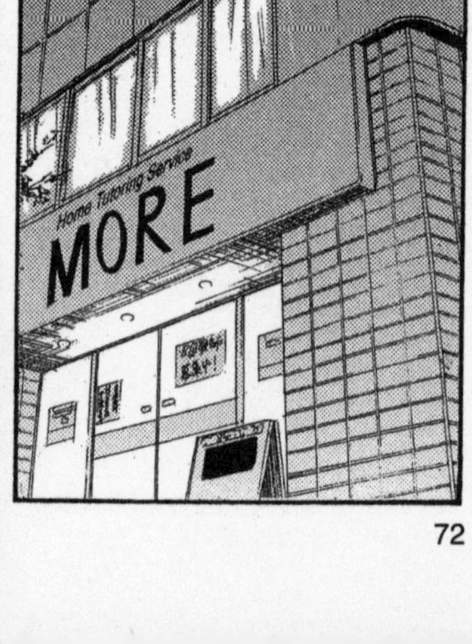
Home Tutoring Service
MORE

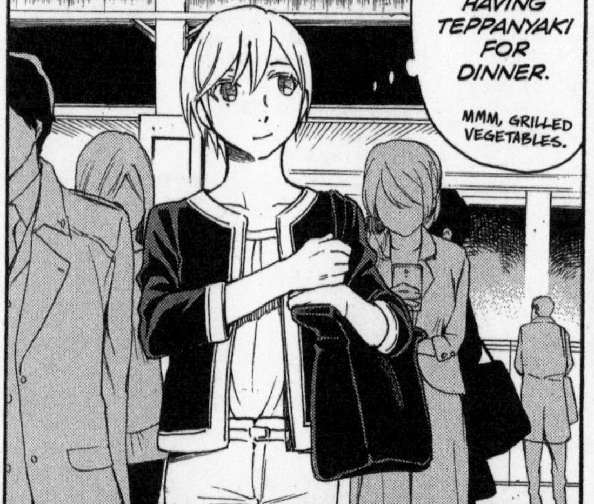
BETTER HURRY HOME. MOM SAID WE'RE HAVING TEPPANYAKI FOR DINNER.
MMM, GRILLED VEGETABLES.

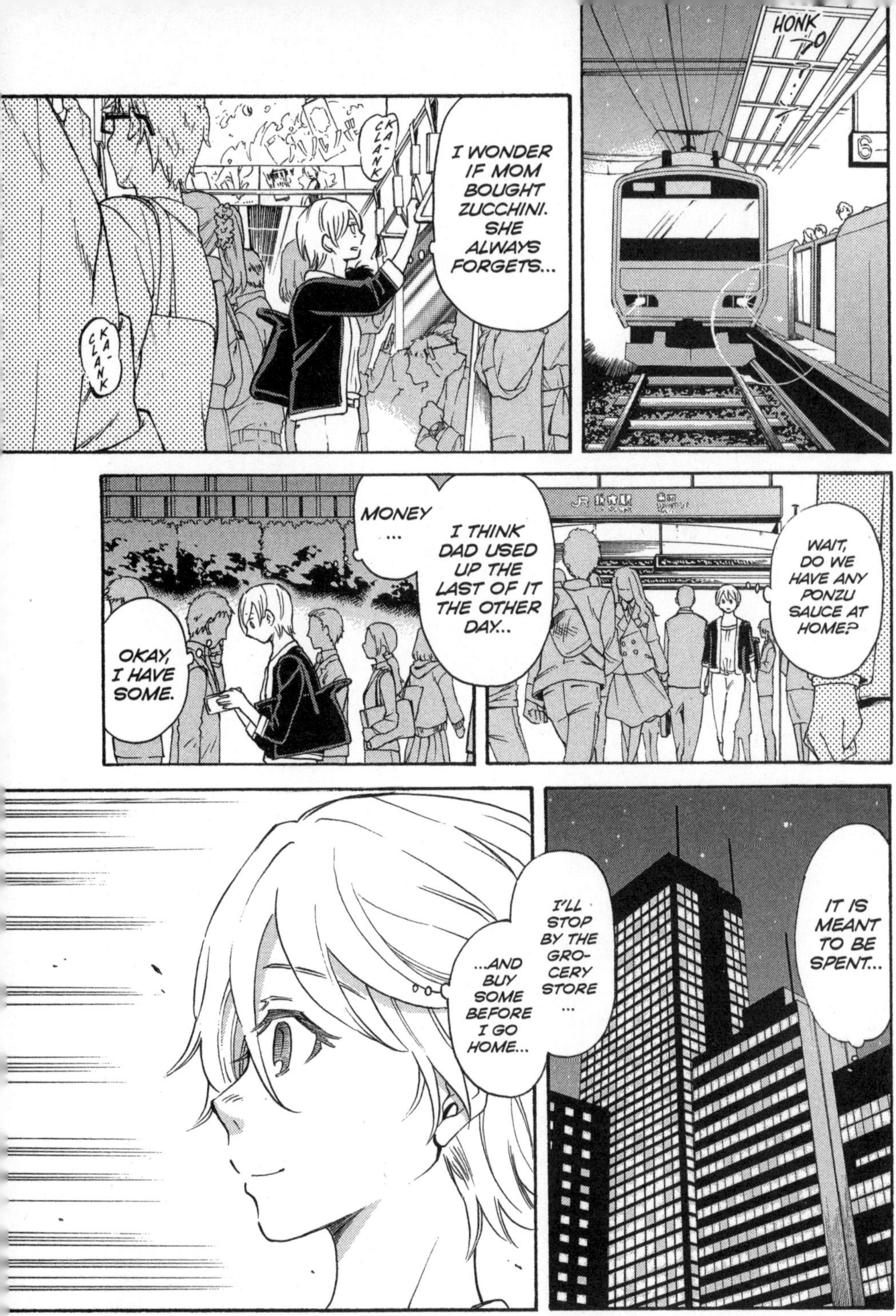
HONK
I WONDER IF MOM BOUGHT ZUCCHINI. SHE ALWAYS FORGETS...
KLA-ANK
KLA-ANK
WAIT, DO WE HAVE ANY PONZU SAUCE AT HOME?
I THINK DAD USED UP THE LAST OF IT THE OTHER DAY...
MONEY ...
OKAY, I HAVE SOME.
IT IS MEANT TO BE SPENT...
I'LL STOP BY THE GRO-CERY STORE ...
...AND BUY SOME BEFORE I GO HOME...

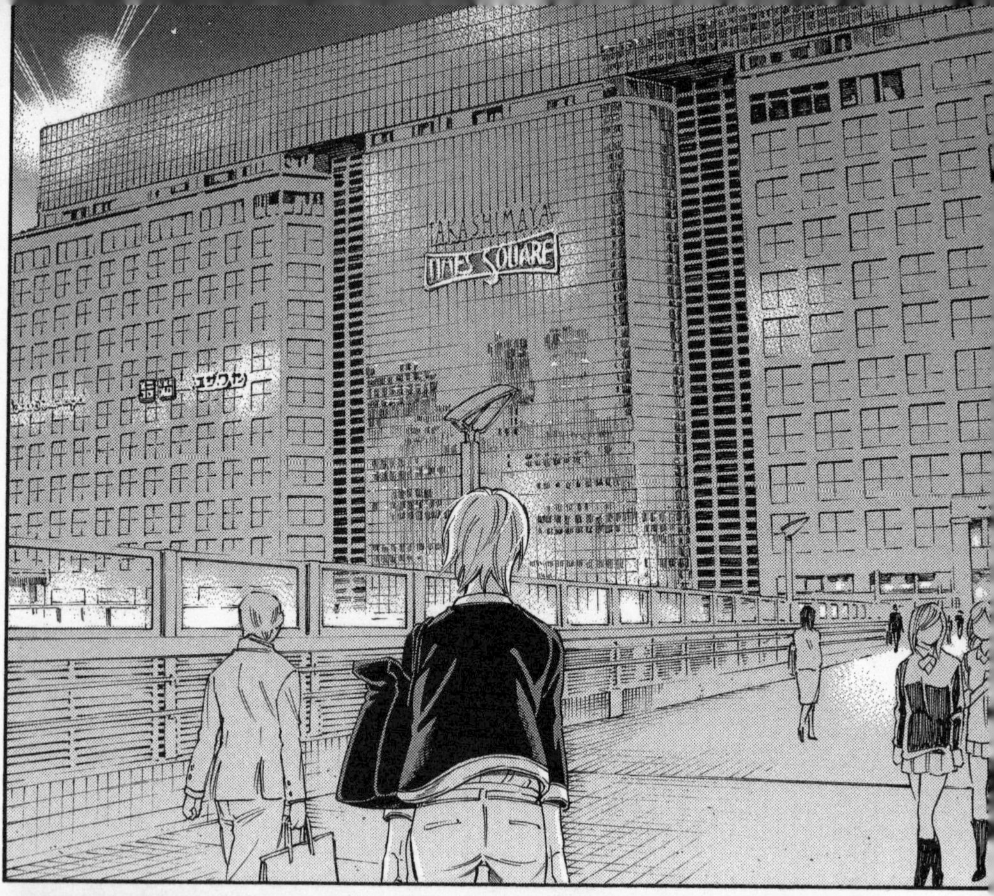
TAKASHIMAYA
TIMES SQUARE

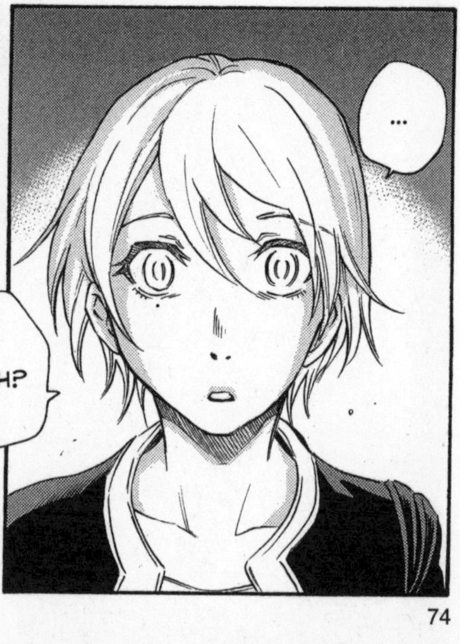
...
HUH?

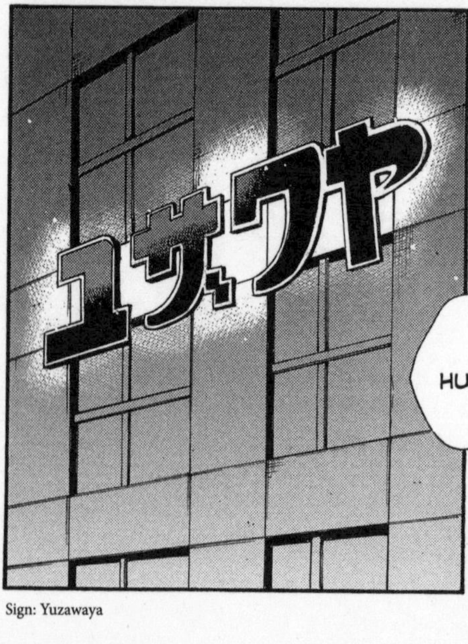
ユザワヤ

Sign: Yuzawaya

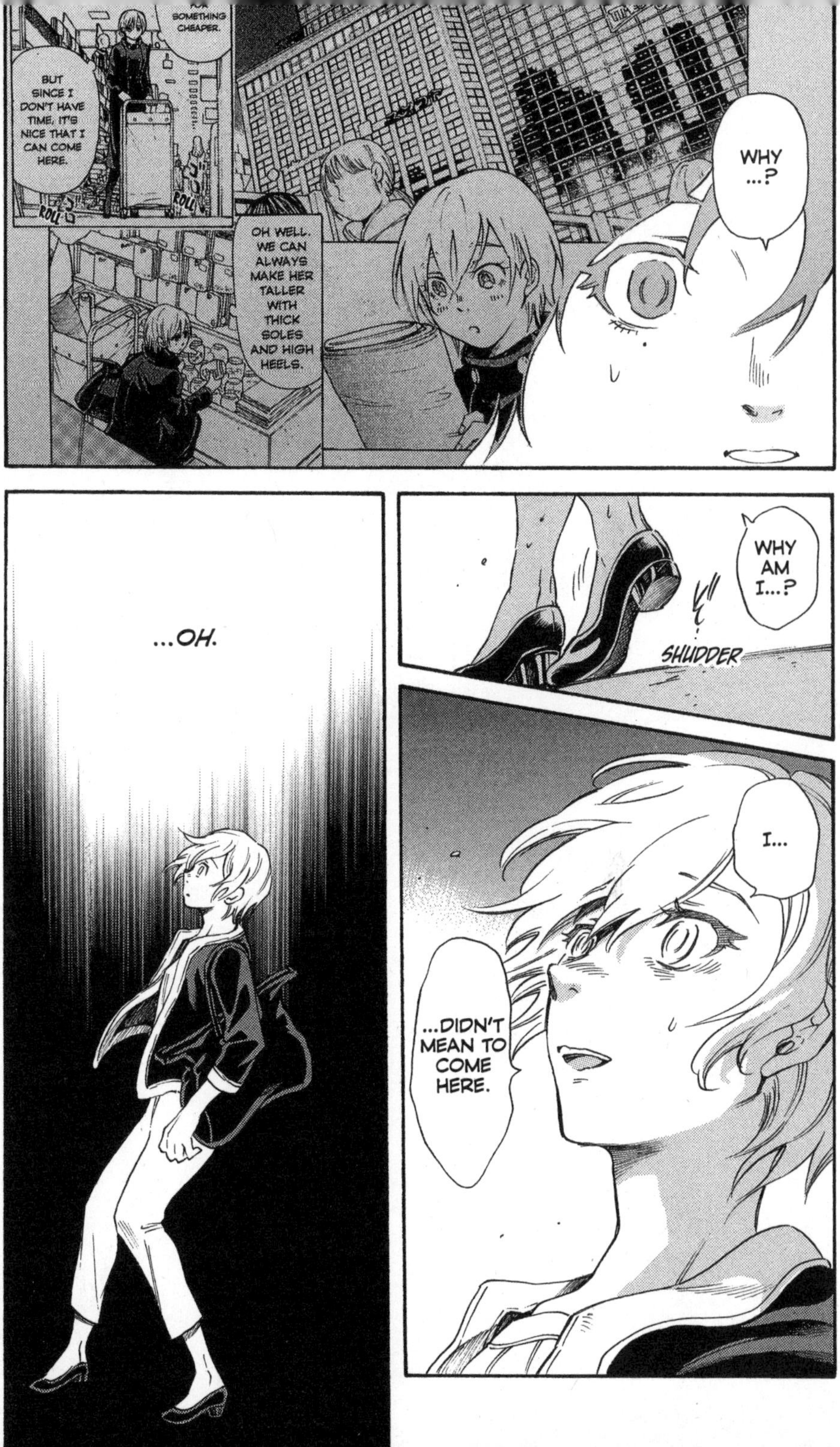
WHY ...?
SOMETHING CHEAPER.
BUT SINCE I DON'T HAVE TIME, IT'S NICE THAT I CAN COME HERE.
ROLL
ROLL
OH WELL. WE CAN ALWAYS MAKE HER TALLER WITH THICK SOLES AND HIGH HEELS.
WHY AM I...?
SHUDDER
I...
...DIDN'T MEAN TO COME HERE.
...OH.

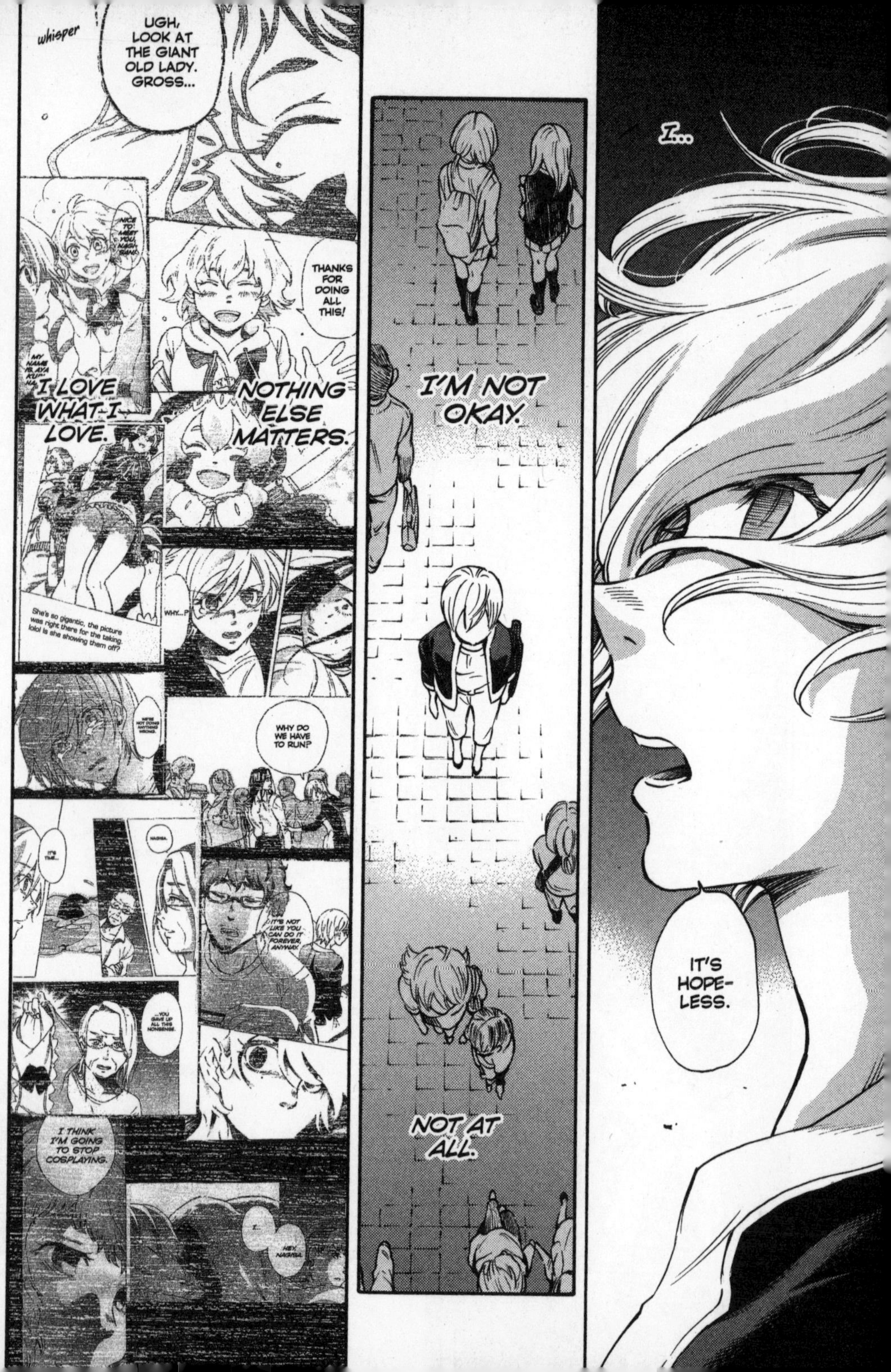
I...
IT'S HOPELESS.
I'M NOT OKAY.
NOT AT ALL.
whisper
UGH, LOOK AT THE GIANT OLD LADY. GROSS...
THANKS FOR DOING ALL THIS!
NICE TO MEET YOU, NAGI-SAN!
NOTHING ELSE MATTERS.
I LOVE WHAT I LOVE.
WHY...?
She's so gigantic, the picture was right there for the taking. lolol Is she showing them off?
WHY DO WE HAVE TO RUN?
WE'RE NOT DOING ANYTHING WRONG.
IT'S NOT LIKE YOU CAN DO IT FOREVER, ANYWAY.
NAGISA.
IT'S TIME...
...YOU GAVE UP ALL THIS NONSENSE.
HEY, NAGISA.
I...
I THINK I'M GOING TO STOP COSPLAYING.

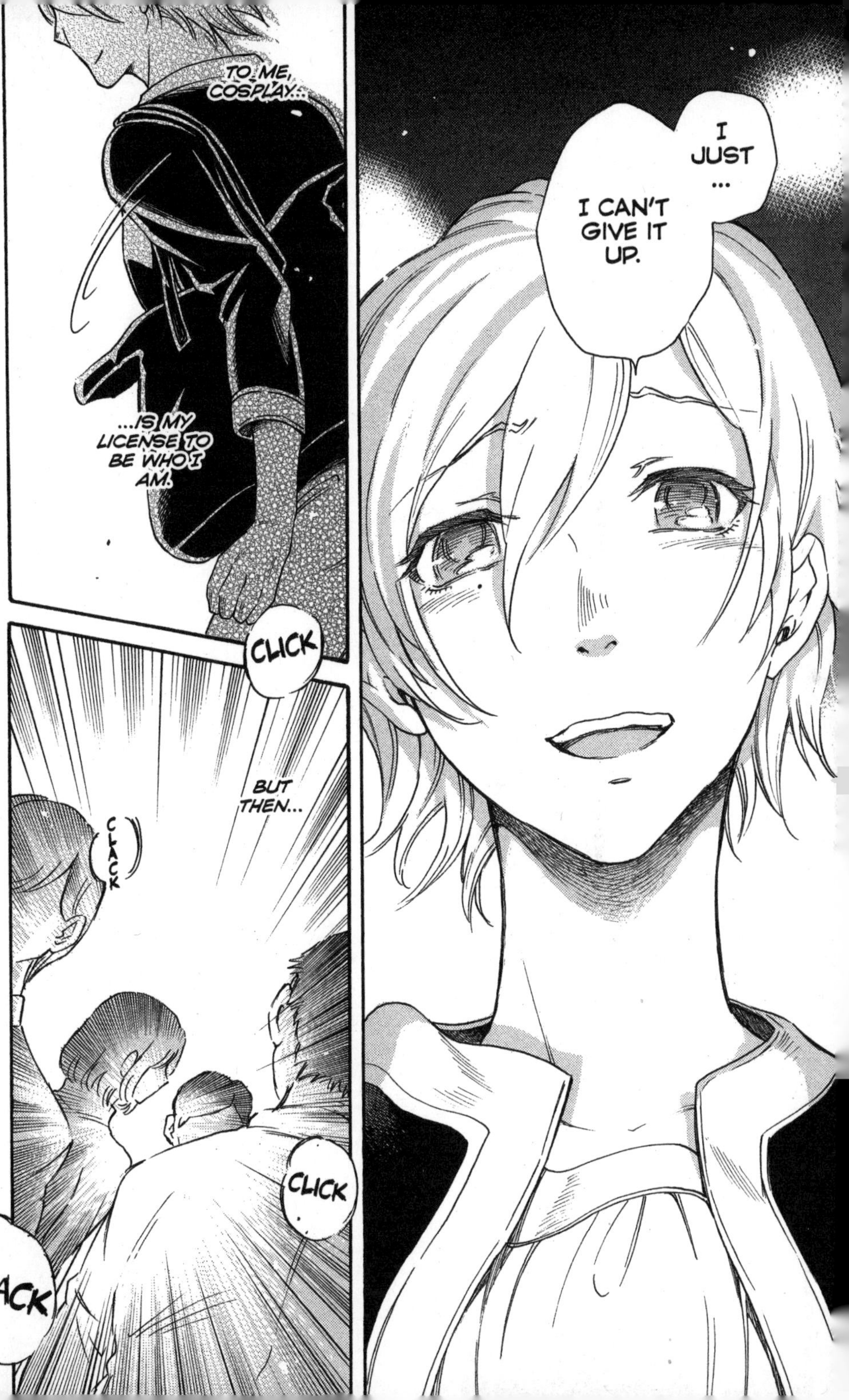
I JUST...
I CAN'T GIVE IT UP.
TO ME, COSPLAY...
...IS MY LICENSE TO BE WHO I AM.
CLICK
BUT THEN...
CLACK
CLICK
CLACK

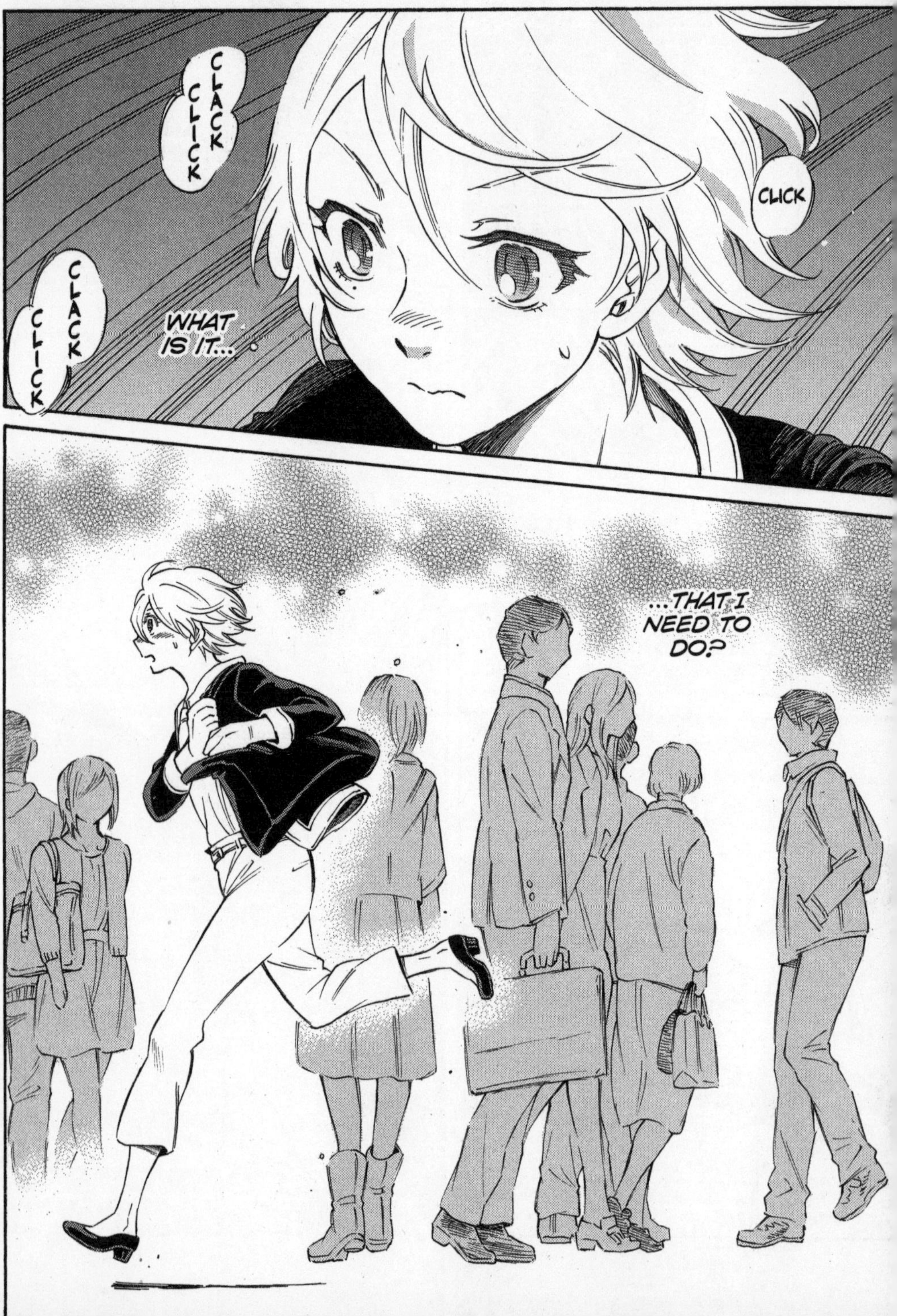
CLICK
CLACK CLICK
CLACK CLICK
WHAT IS IT...
...THAT I NEED TO DO?

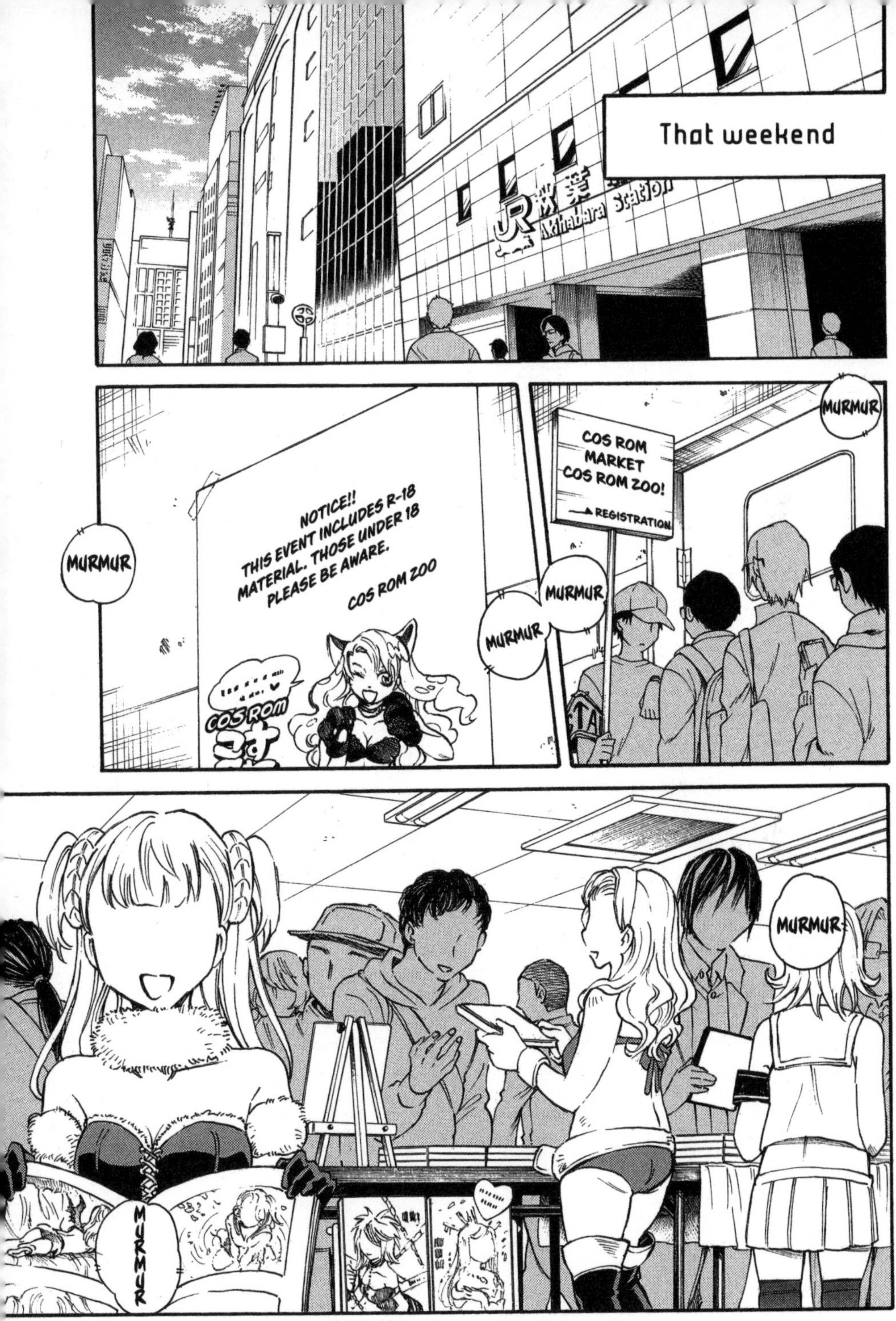
That weekend
Akihabara Station
MURMUR
COS ROM MARKET COS ROM ZOO!
REGISTRATION
MURMUR
MURMUR
NOTICE!! THIS EVENT INCLUDES R-18 MATERIAL. THOSE UNDER 18 PLEASE BE AWARE.
COS ROM ZOO
COS ROM
MURMUR
MURMUR
MURMUR

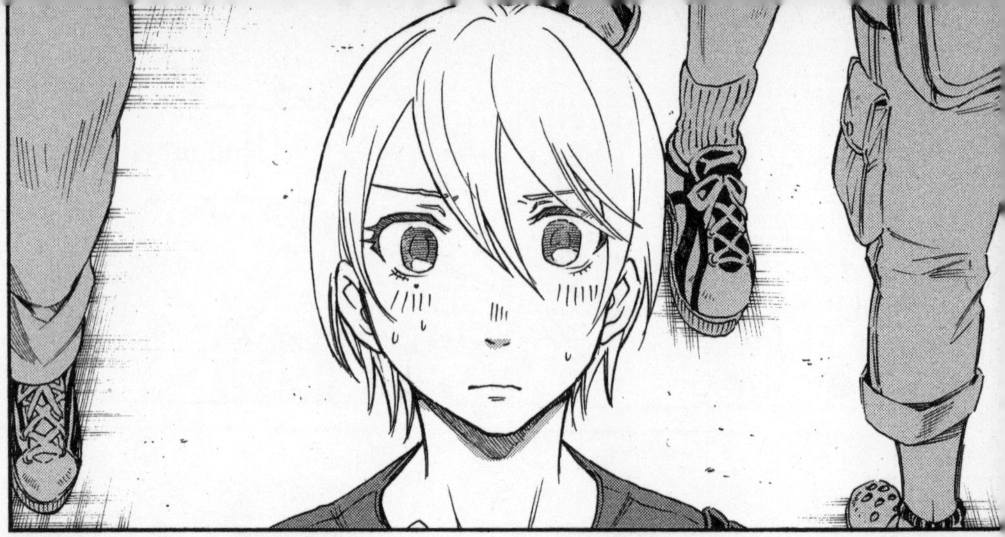

Flier: Cos Rom Market, Cos Rom Zoo

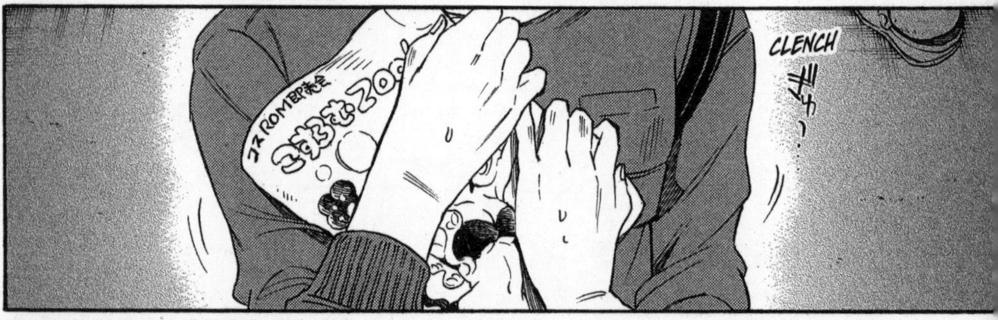
CLENCH

Poster: Cos Rom Market, Cos Rom

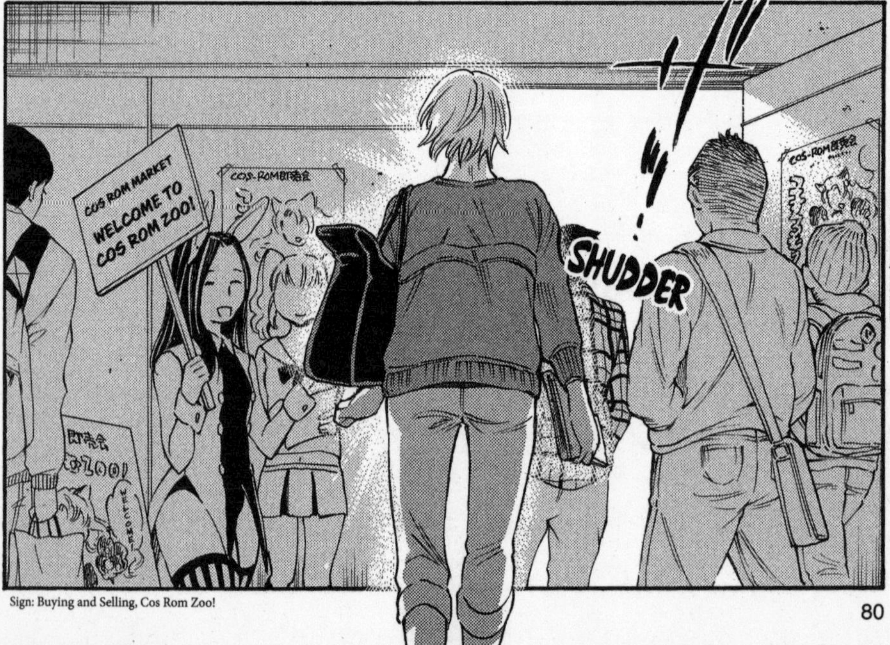
COS ROM MARKET
WELCOME TO COS ROM ZOO!
SHUDDER

Poster: Cos Rom Market, Cos Rom

Sign: Buying and Selling, Cos Rom Zoo!

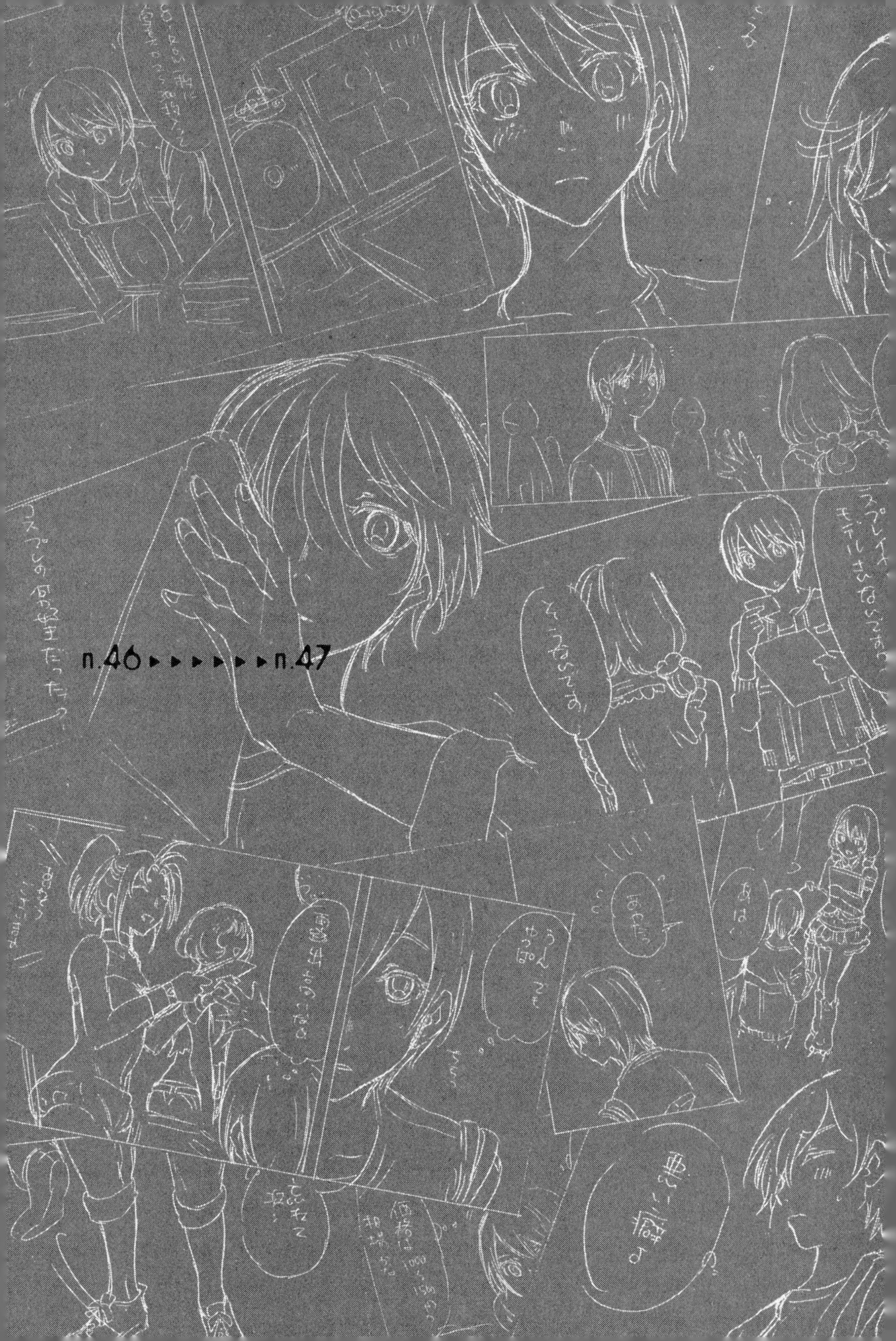
n.46▸▸▸▸▸▸▸▸n.47

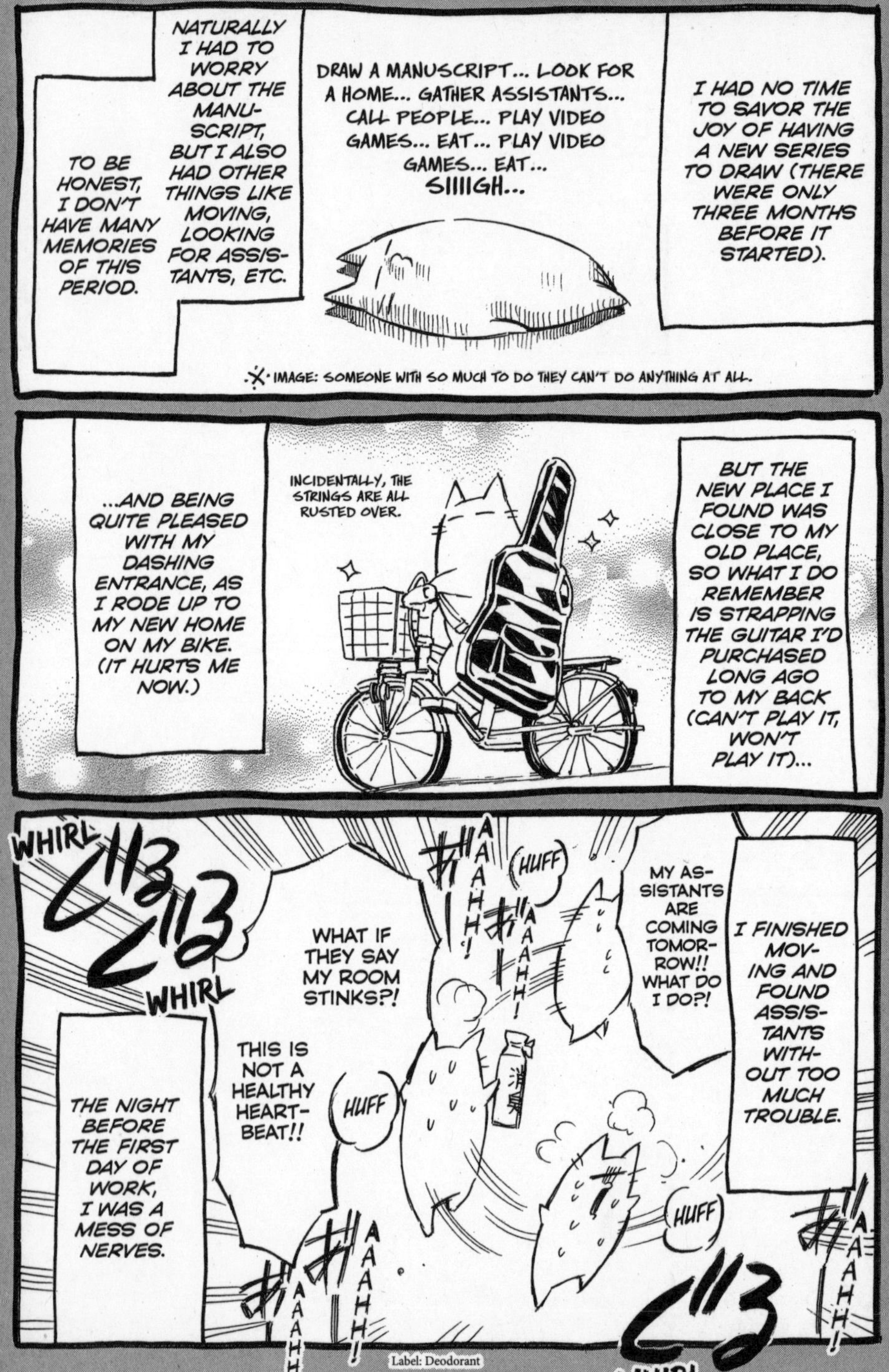
I HAD NO TIME TO SAVOR THE JOY OF HAVING A NEW SERIES TO DRAW (THERE WERE ONLY THREE MONTHS BEFORE IT STARTED).
DRAW A MANUSCRIPT... LOOK FOR A HOME... GATHER ASSISTANTS... CALL PEOPLE... PLAY VIDEO GAMES... EAT... PLAY VIDEO GAMES... EAT... SIIIIGH...
NATURALLY I HAD TO WORRY ABOUT THE MANU-SCRIPT, BUT I ALSO HAD OTHER THINGS LIKE MOVING, LOOKING FOR ASSIS-TANTS, ETC.
TO BE HONEST, I DON'T HAVE MANY MEMORIES OF THIS PERIOD.
※ IMAGE: SOMEONE WITH SO MUCH TO DO THEY CAN'T DO ANYTHING AT ALL.
BUT THE NEW PLACE I FOUND WAS CLOSE TO MY OLD PLACE, SO WHAT I DO REMEMBER IS STRAPPING THE GUITAR I'D PURCHASED LONG AGO TO MY BACK (CAN'T PLAY IT, WON'T PLAY IT)...
INCIDENTALLY, THE STRINGS ARE ALL RUSTED OVER.
...AND BEING QUITE PLEASED WITH MY DASHING ENTRANCE, AS I RODE UP TO MY NEW HOME ON MY BIKE. (IT HURTS ME NOW.)
I FINISHED MOV-ING AND FOUND ASSIS-TANTS WITH-OUT TOO MUCH TROUBLE.
MY AS-SISTANTS ARE COMING TOMOR-ROW!! WHAT DO I DO?!
HUFF
AAAHH!
AAAHH!
WHAT IF THEY SAY MY ROOM STINKS?!
WHIRL
WHIRL
HUFF
THIS IS NOT A HEALTHY HEART-BEAT!!
THE NIGHT BEFORE THE FIRST DAY OF WORK, I WAS A MESS OF NERVES.
HUFF
AAAHH!
AAAHH!
AAAHH!
Label: Deodorant
WHIRL

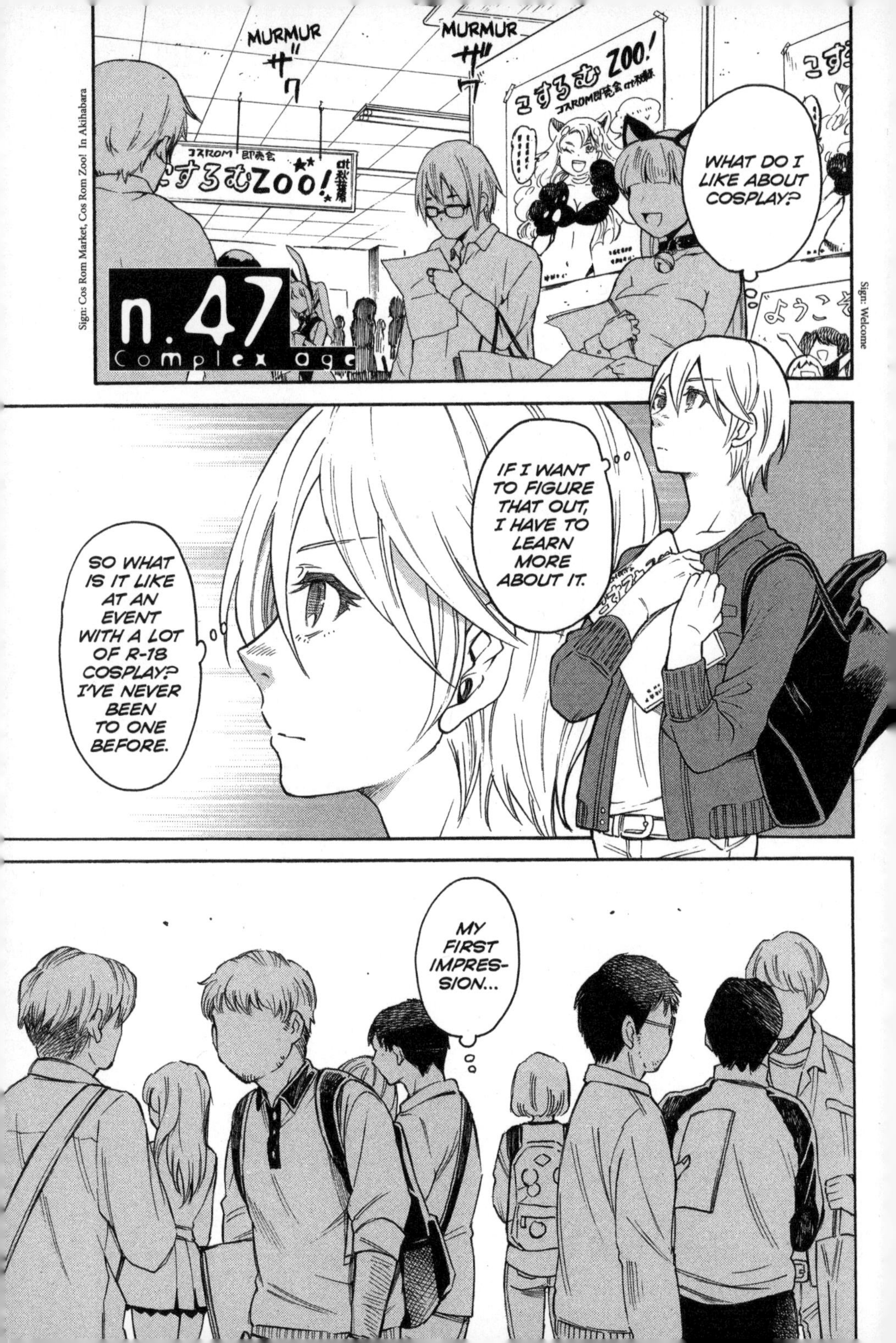
Sign: Welcome
WHAT DO I LIKE ABOUT COSPLAY?
こすろむ ZOO!
MURMUR
ザワ
MURMUR
ザワ
こすろむZoo!
Sign: Cos Rom Market, Cos Rom Zoo! In Akihabara
n.47
Complex age
IF I WANT TO FIGURE THAT OUT, I HAVE TO LEARN MORE ABOUT IT.
SO WHAT IS IT LIKE AT AN EVENT WITH A LOT OF R-18 COSPLAY? I'VE NEVER BEEN TO ONE BEFORE.
MY FIRST IMPRESSION...

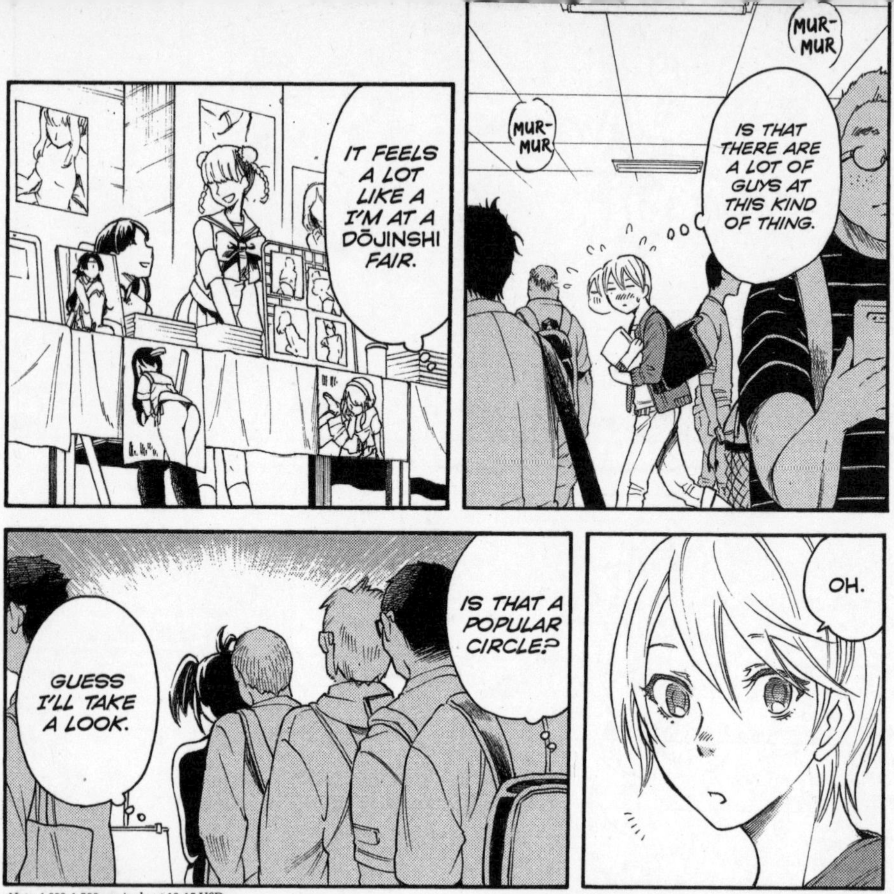
MUR-MUR
MUR-MUR
IS THAT THERE ARE A LOT OF GUYS AT THIS KIND OF THING.
IT FEELS A LOT LIKE A I'M AT A DŌJINSHI FAIR.
OH.
IS THAT A POPULAR CIRCLE?
GUESS I'LL TAKE A LOOK.

Note: 1,000-1,500 yen is about 10-15 USD.

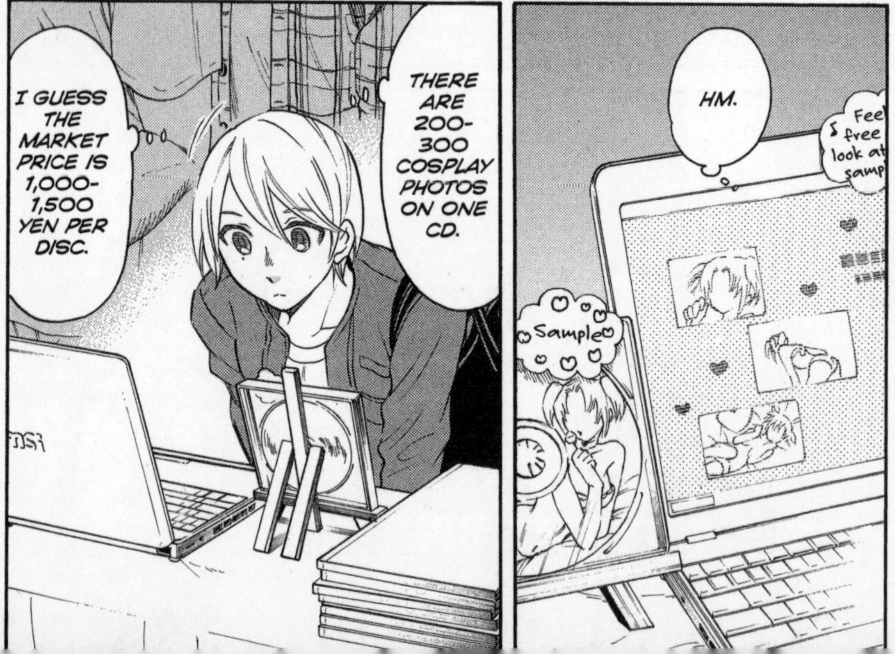
HM.
Feel free look at samp
Sample
THERE ARE 200-300 COSPLAY PHOTOS ON ONE CD.
I GUESS THE MARKET PRICE IS 1,000-1,500 YEN PER DISC.

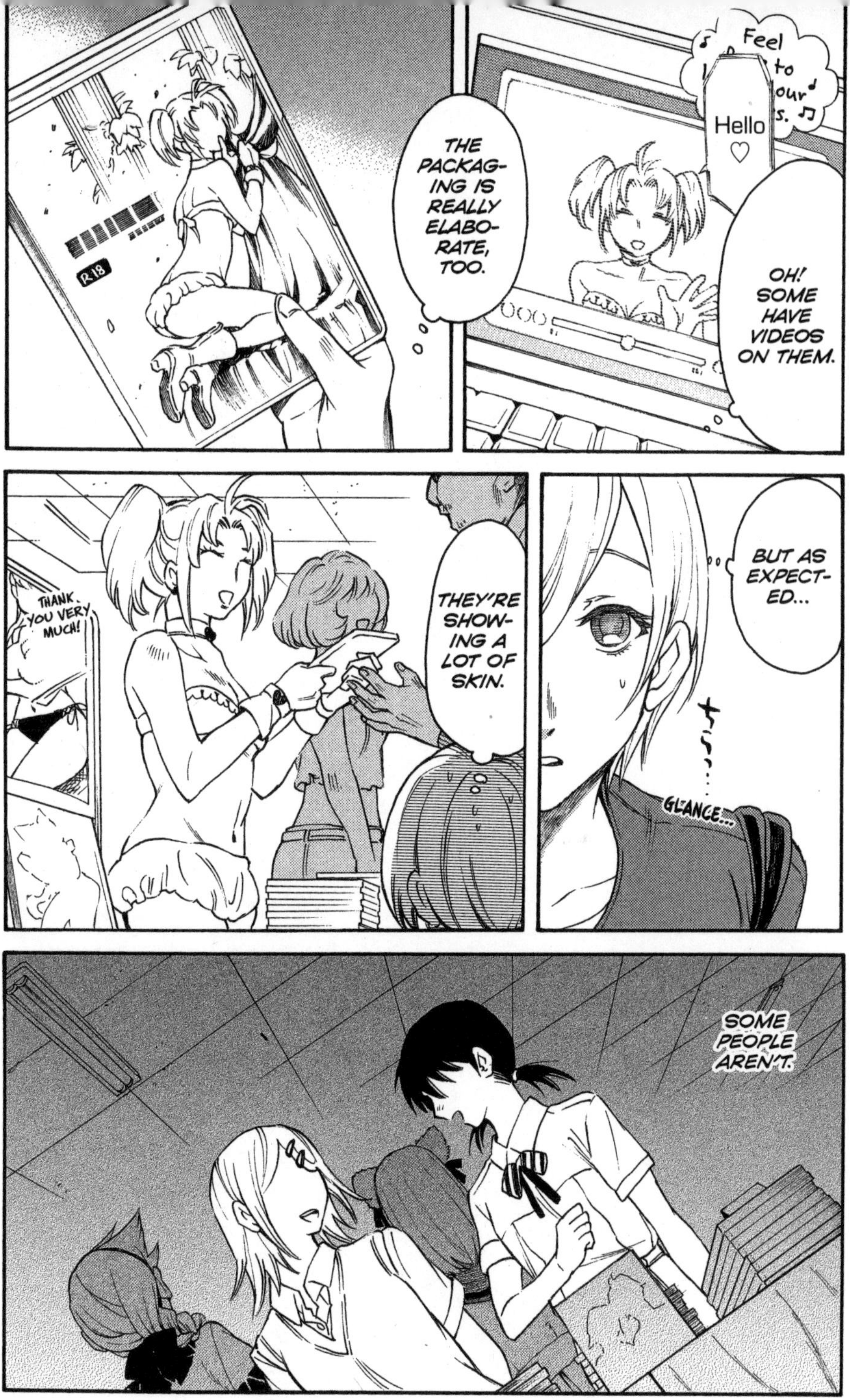
Hello ♡
OH! SOME HAVE VIDEOS ON THEM.
THE PACKAGING IS REALLY ELABORATE, TOO.
BUT AS EXPECTED...
GLANCE...
THEY'RE SHOWING A LOT OF SKIN.
THANK YOU VERY MUCH!
SOME PEOPLE AREN'T.

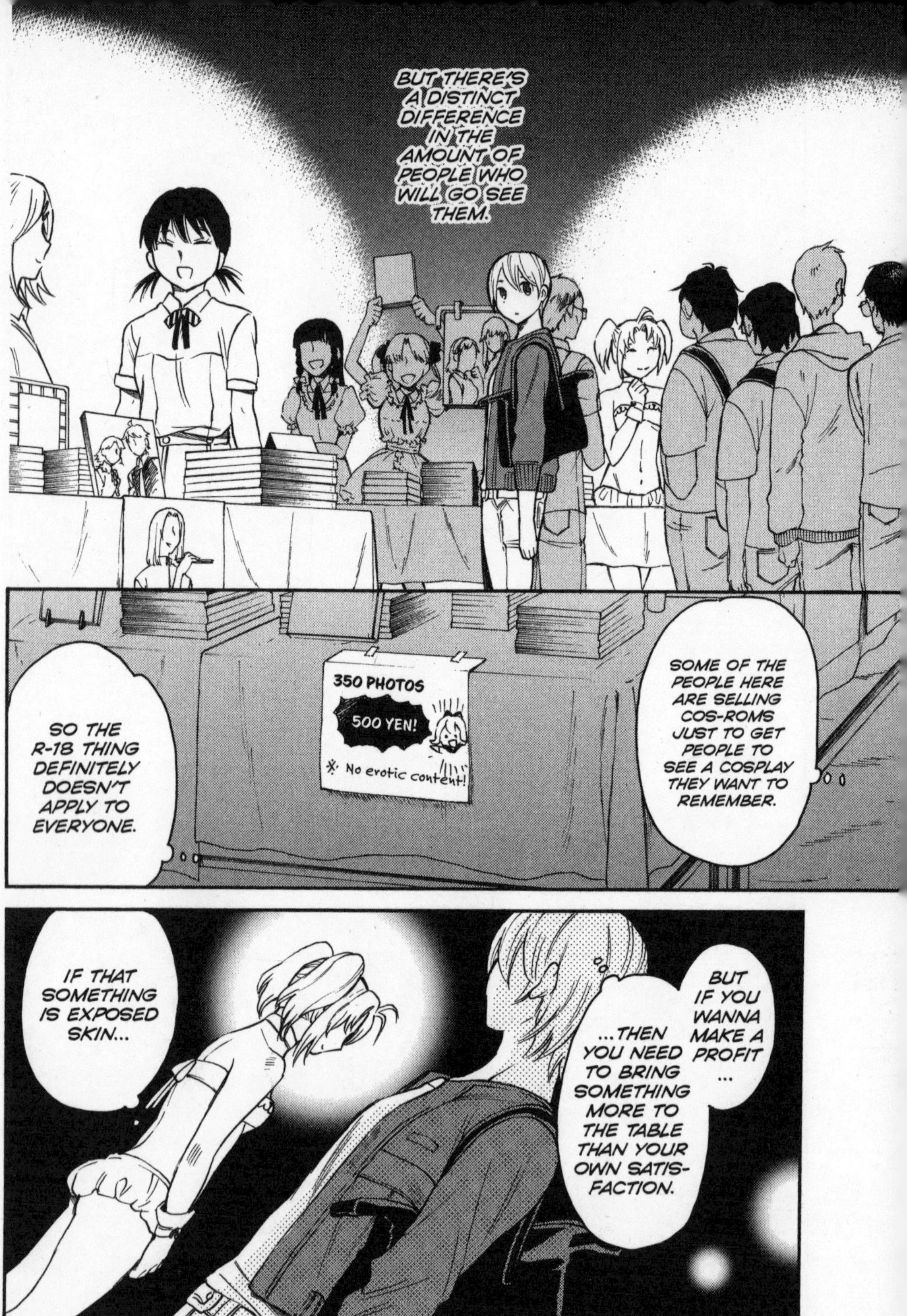
BUT THERE'S A DISTINCT DIFFERENCE IN THE AMOUNT OF PEOPLE WHO WILL GO SEE THEM.
SOME OF THE PEOPLE HERE ARE SELLING COS-ROMS JUST TO GET PEOPLE TO SEE A COSPLAY THEY WANT TO REMEMBER.
350 PHOTOS
500 YEN!
※ No erotic content!
SO THE R-18 THING DEFINITELY DOESN'T APPLY TO EVERYONE.
BUT IF YOU WANNA MAKE A PROFIT ...
...THEN YOU NEED TO BRING SOMETHING MORE TO THE TABLE THAN YOUR OWN SATIS-FACTION.
IF THAT SOMETHING IS EXPOSED SKIN...

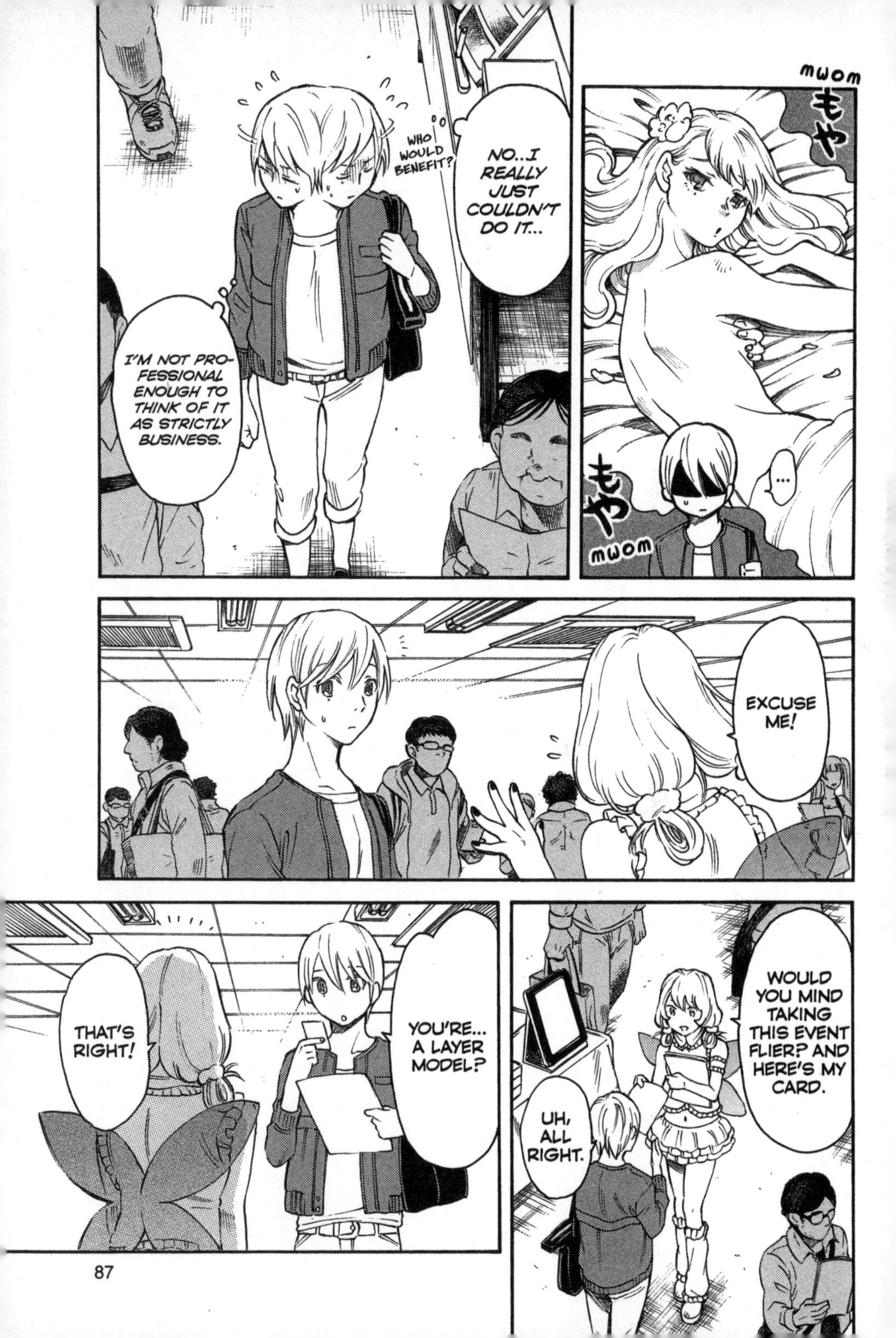
mwom
もや
...
もや
mwom
NO...I REALLY JUST COULDN'T DO IT...
WHO WOULD BENEFIT?
I'M NOT PRO-FESSIONAL ENOUGH TO THINK OF IT AS STRICTLY BUSINESS.
EXCUSE ME!
WOULD YOU MIND TAKING THIS EVENT FLIER? AND HERE'S MY CARD.
UH, ALL RIGHT.
YOU'RE... A LAYER MODEL?
THAT'S RIGHT!

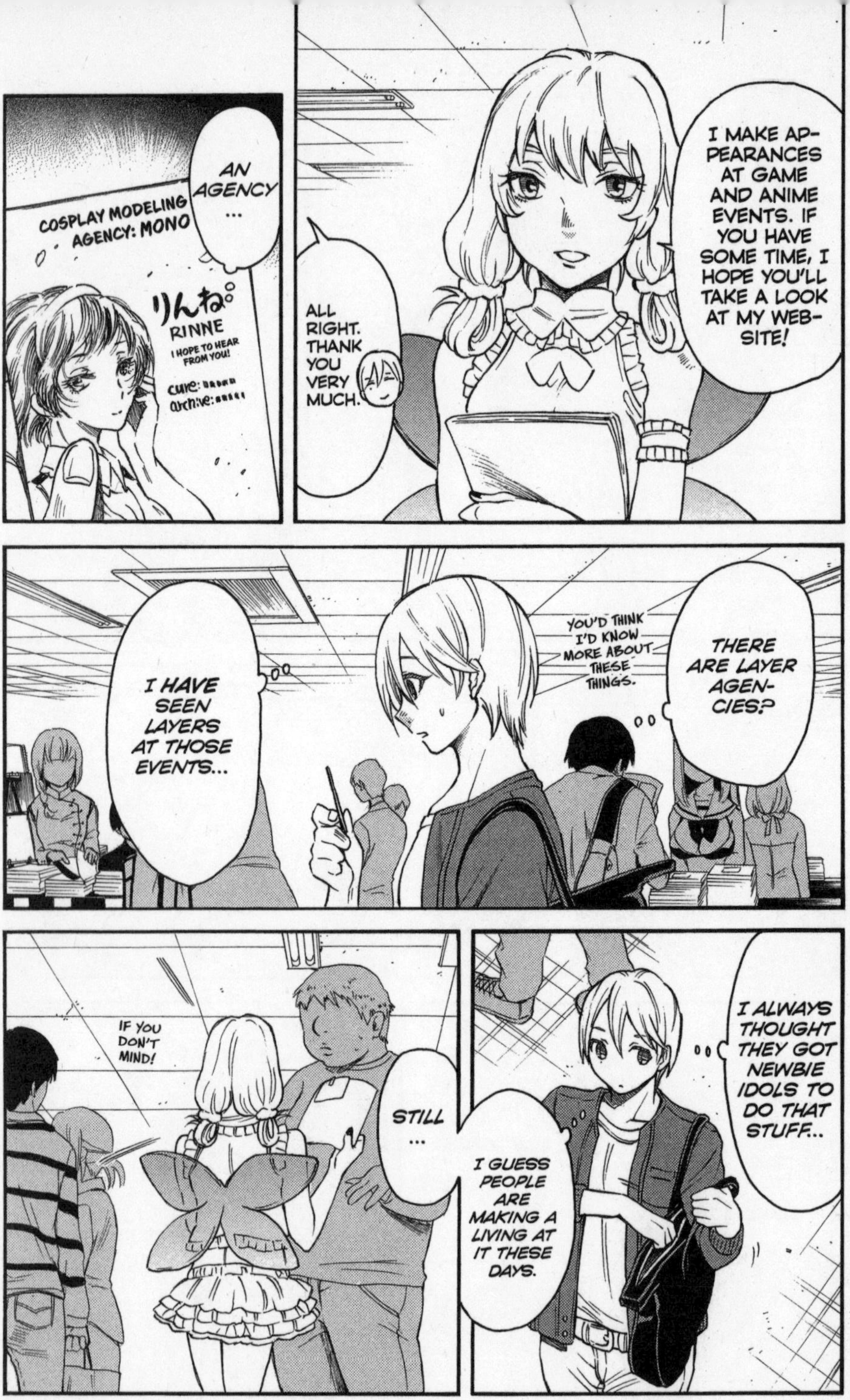
I MAKE APPEARANCES AT GAME AND ANIME EVENTS. IF YOU HAVE SOME TIME, I HOPE YOU'LL TAKE A LOOK AT MY WEBSITE!
ALL RIGHT. THANK YOU VERY MUCH.
AN AGENCY ...
COSPLAY MODELING AGENCY: MONO
りんね RINNE
I HOPE TO HEAR FROM YOU!
THERE ARE LAYER AGENCIES?
YOU'D THINK I'D KNOW MORE ABOUT THESE THINGS.
I HAVE SEEN LAYERS AT THOSE EVENTS...
I ALWAYS THOUGHT THEY GOT NEWBIE IDOLS TO DO THAT STUFF...
STILL ...
I GUESS PEOPLE ARE MAKING A LIVING AT IT THESE DAYS.
IF YOU DON'T MIND!

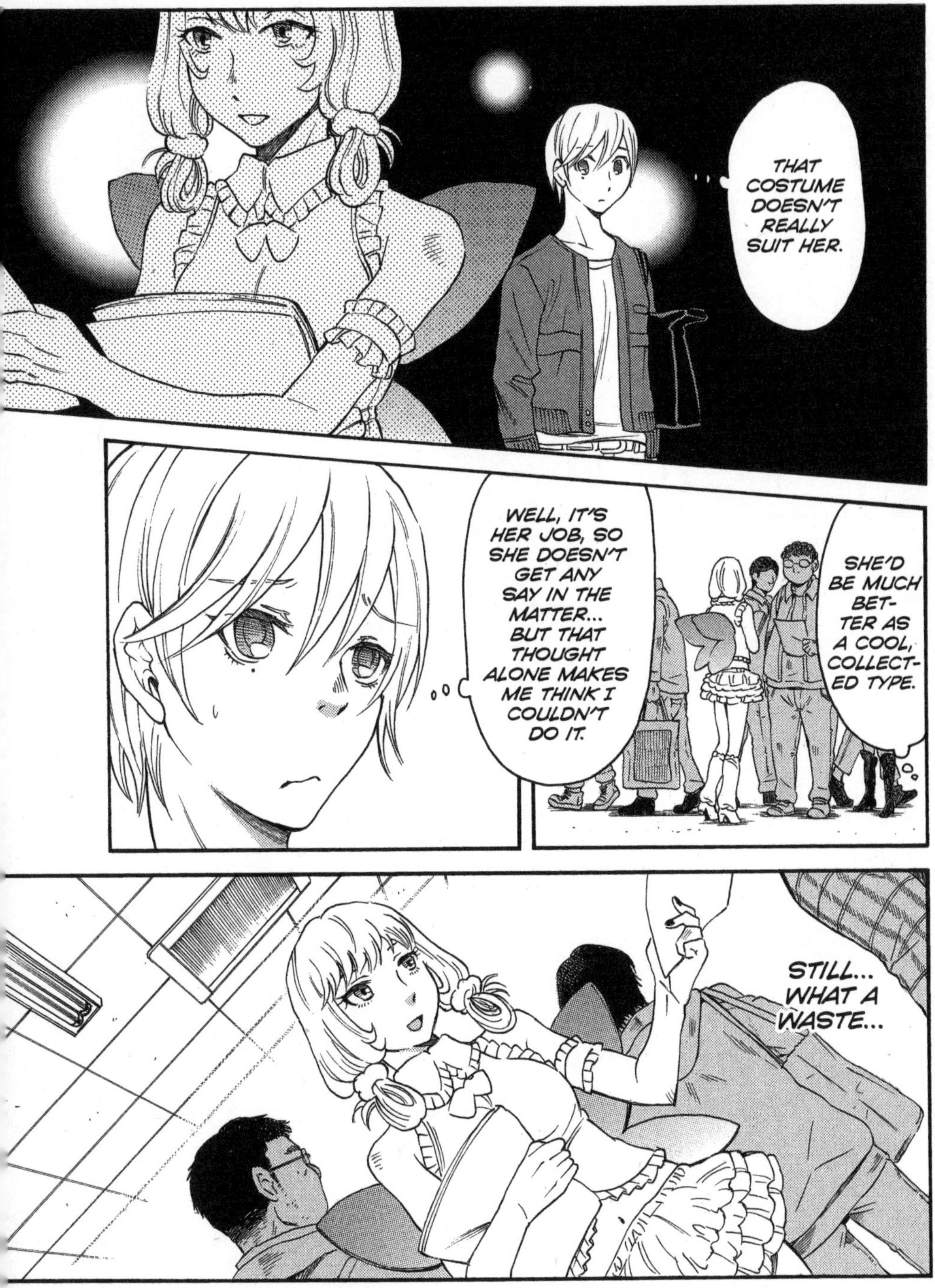
THAT COSTUME DOESN'T REALLY SUIT HER.
SHE'D BE MUCH BET-TER AS A COOL, COLLECT-ED TYPE.
WELL, IT'S HER JOB, SO SHE DOESN'T GET ANY SAY IN THE MATTER... BUT THAT THOUGHT ALONE MAKES ME THINK I COULDN'T DO IT.
STILL... WHAT A WASTE...

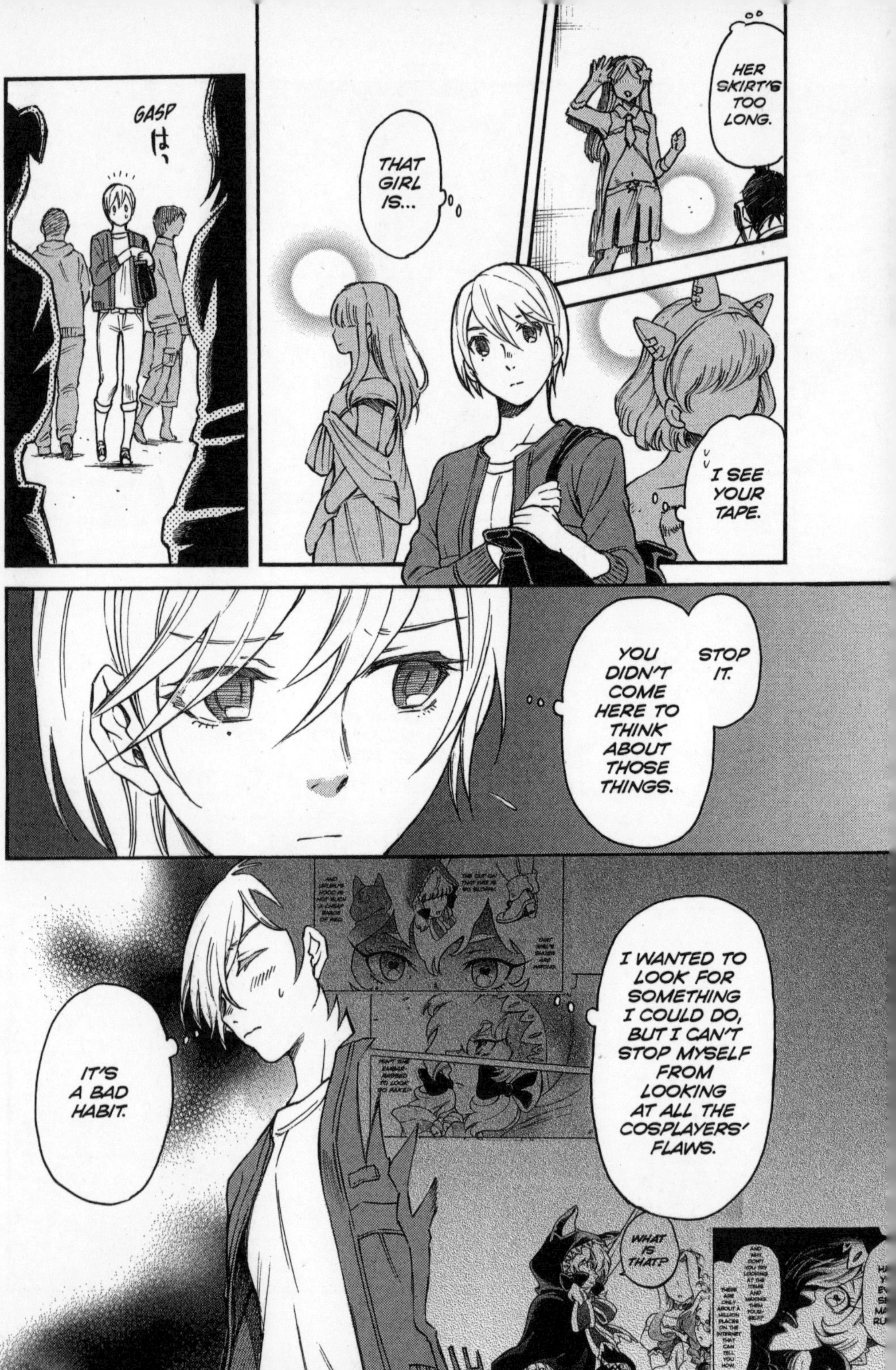
HER SKIRT'S TOO LONG.
THAT GIRL IS...
I SEE YOUR TAPE.
GASP
は、
STOP IT.
YOU DIDN'T COME HERE TO THINK ABOUT THOSE THINGS.
I WANTED TO LOOK FOR SOMETHING I COULD DO, BUT I CAN'T STOP MYSELF FROM LOOKING AT ALL THE COSPLAYERS' FLAWS.
IT'S A BAD HABIT.
WHAT IS THAT?

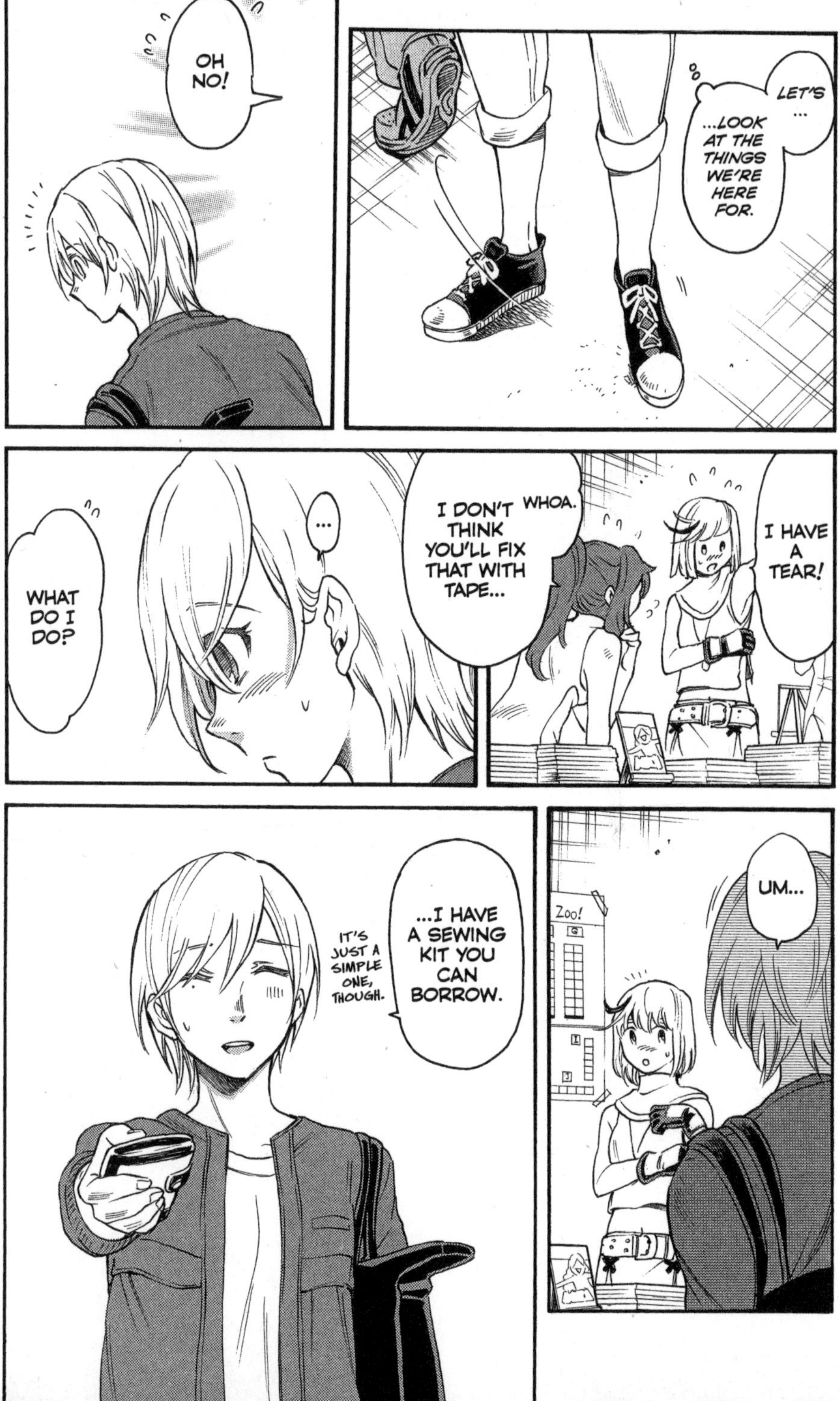
LET'S... ...LOOK AT THE THINGS WE'RE HERE FOR.
OH NO!
I HAVE A TEAR!
WHOA.
I DON'T THINK YOU'LL FIX THAT WITH TAPE...
...
WHAT DO I DO?
UM...
Zoo!
...I HAVE A SEWING KIT YOU CAN BORROW.
IT'S JUST A SIMPLE ONE, THOUGH.

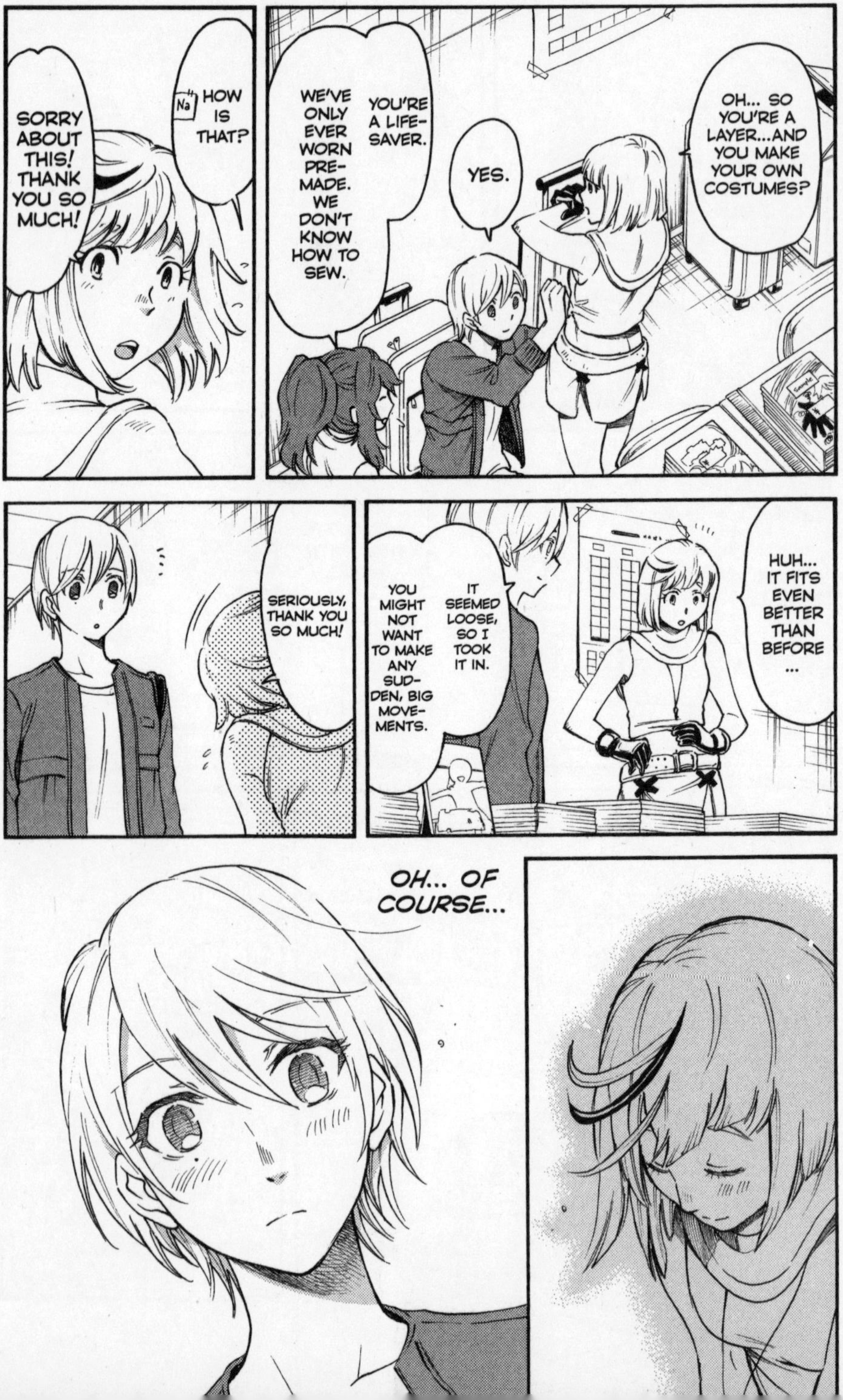
OH... SO YOU'RE A LAYER...AND YOU MAKE YOUR OWN COSTUMES?
YES.
YOU'RE A LIFE-SAVER.
WE'VE ONLY EVER WORN PRE-MADE. WE DON'T KNOW HOW TO SEW.
HOW IS THAT?
SORRY ABOUT THIS! THANK YOU SO MUCH!
HUH... IT FITS EVEN BETTER THAN BEFORE ...
IT SEEMED LOOSE, SO I TOOK IT IN.
YOU MIGHT NOT WANT TO MAKE ANY SUD-DEN, BIG MOVE-MENTS.
SERIOUSLY, THANK YOU SO MUCH!
OH... OF COURSE...

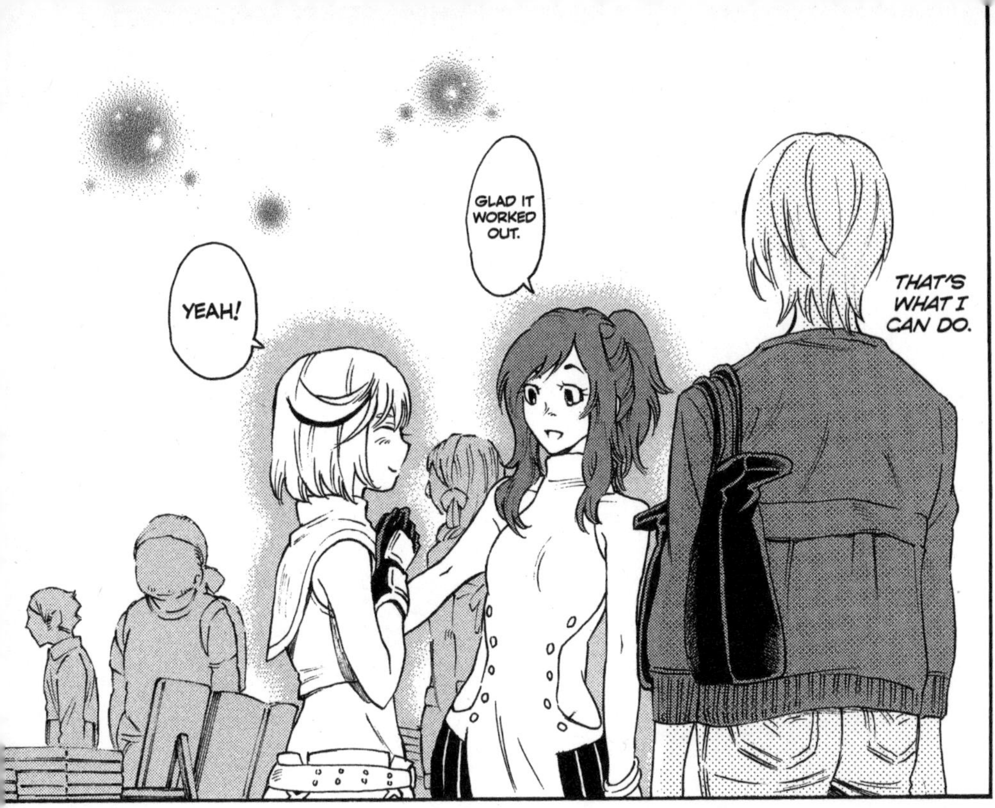
THAT'S WHAT I CAN DO.
GLAD IT WORKED OUT.
YEAH!
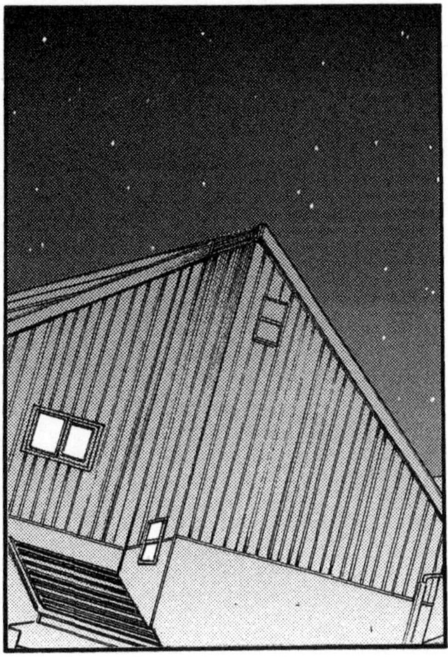
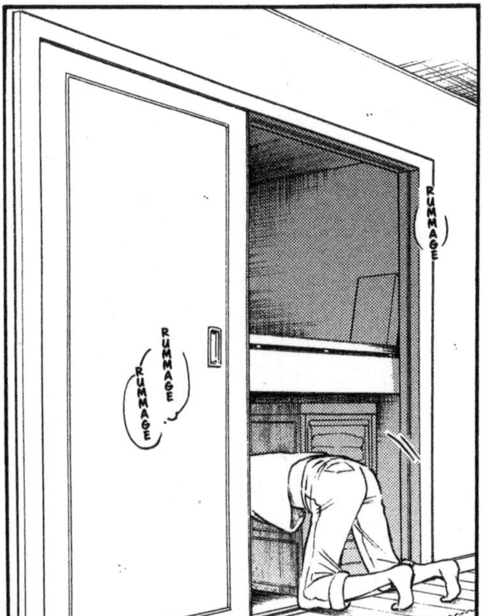
RUMMAGE
RUMMAGE
RUMMAGE

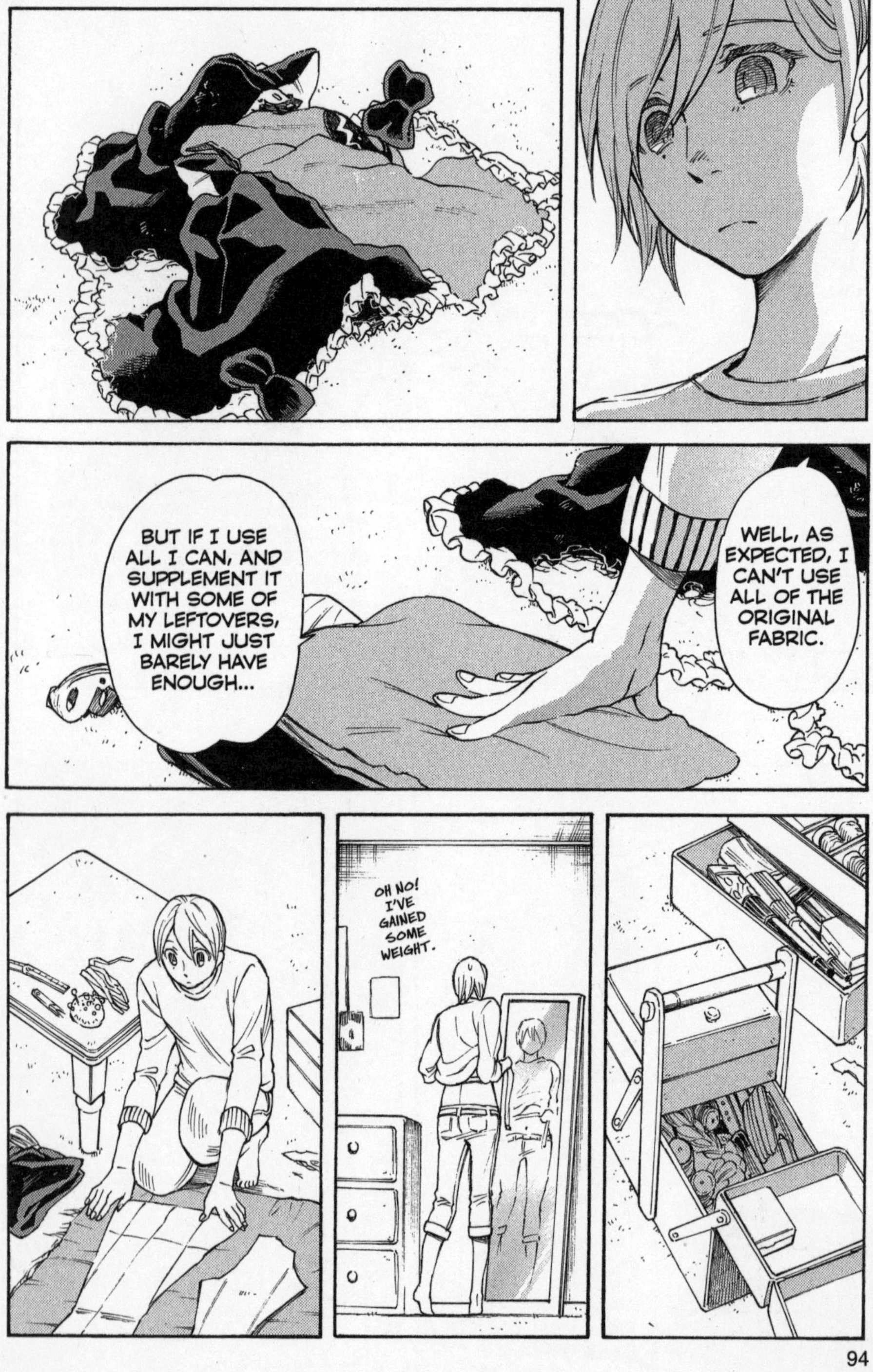
WELL, AS EXPECTED, I CAN'T USE ALL OF THE ORIGINAL FABRIC.
BUT IF I USE ALL I CAN, AND SUPPLEMENT IT WITH SOME OF MY LEFTOVERS, I MIGHT JUST BARELY HAVE ENOUGH...
OH NO! I'VE GAINED SOME WEIGHT.

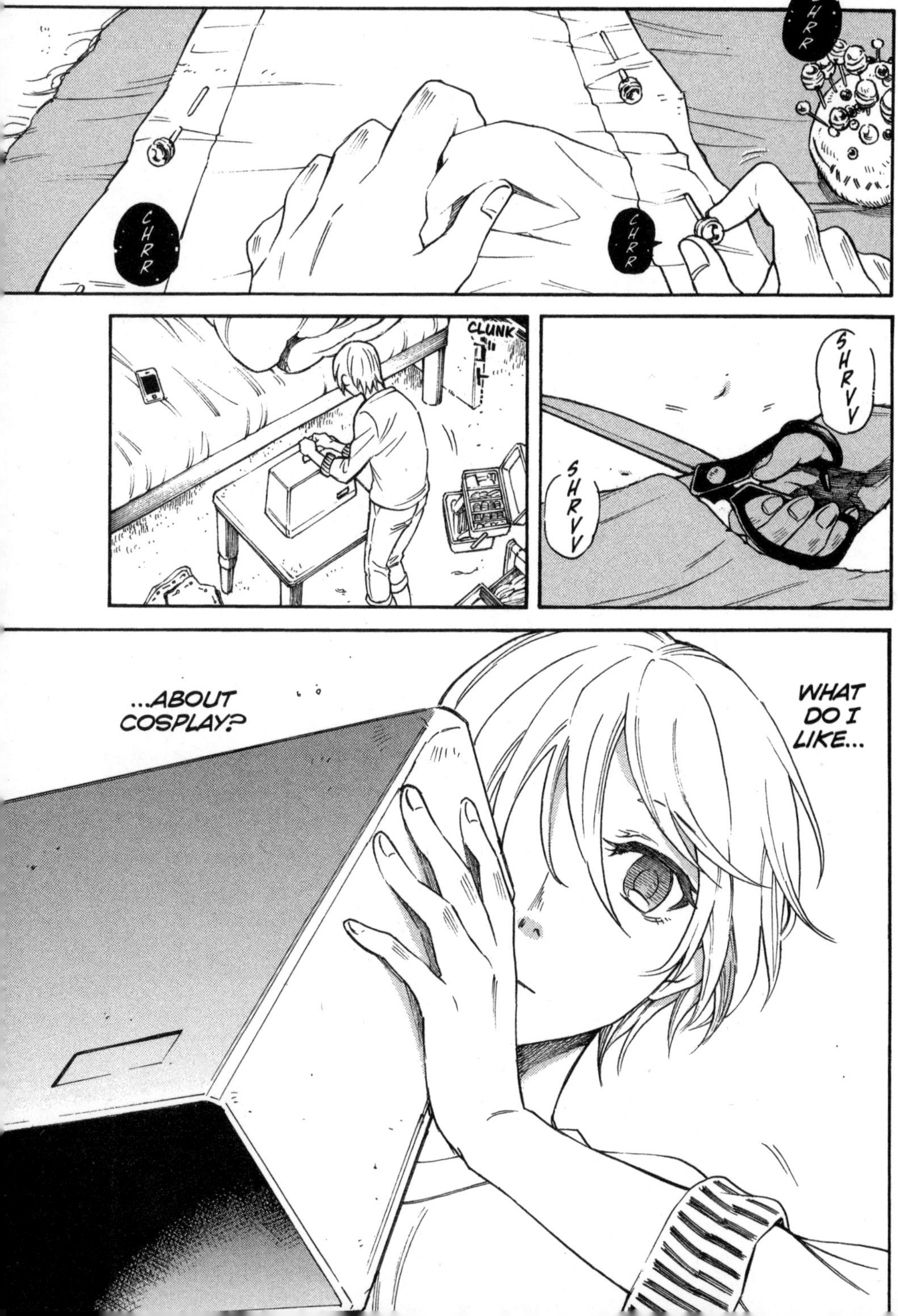
CHRR
CHRR
CHRR
SHRVV
SHRVV
CLUNK
WHAT DO I LIKE...
...ABOUT COSPLAY?

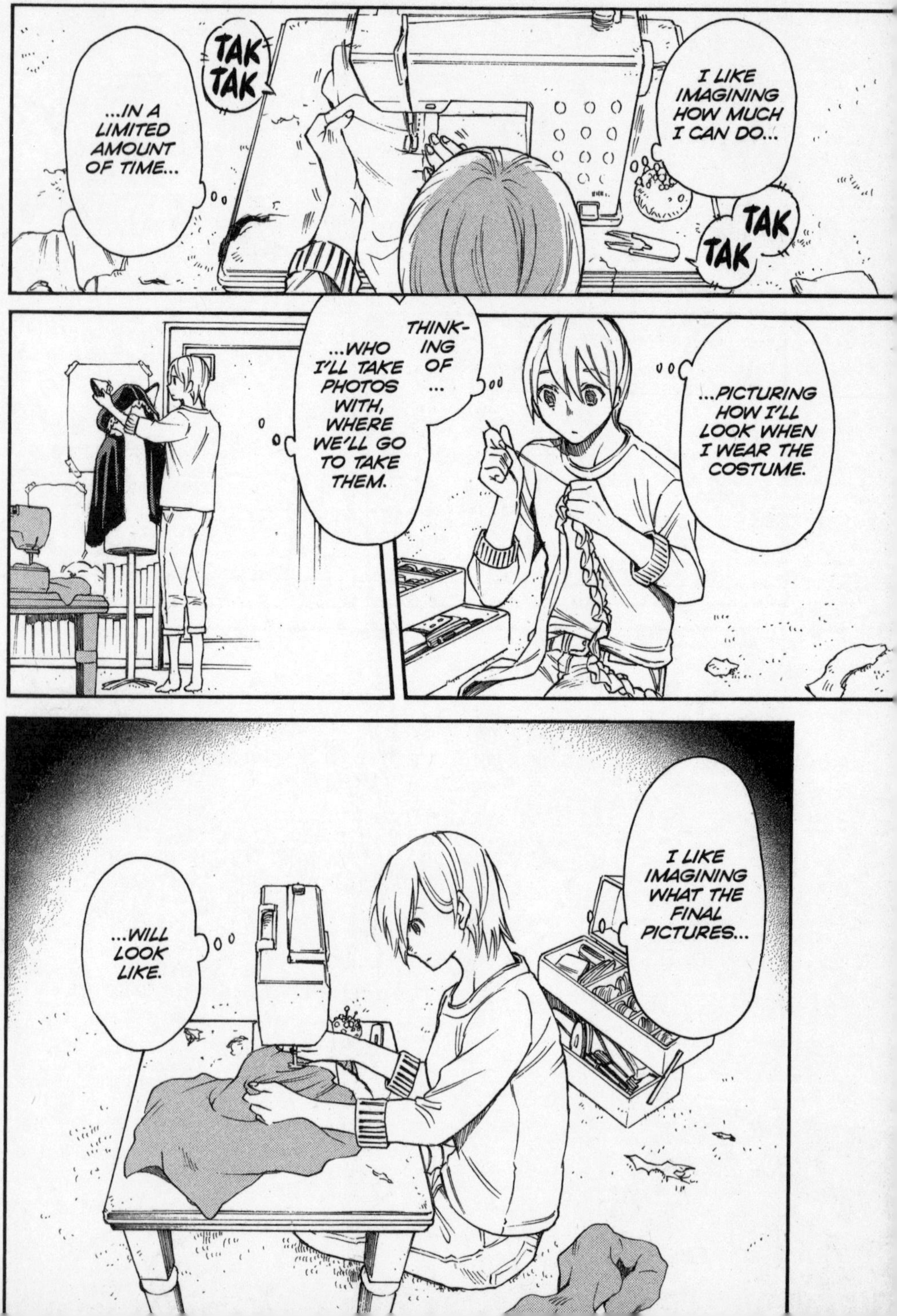
I LIKE IMAGINING HOW MUCH I CAN DO...
TAK TAK
TAK TAK
...IN A LIMITED AMOUNT OF TIME...
...PICTURING HOW I'LL LOOK WHEN I WEAR THE COSTUME.
THINKING OF ...
...WHO I'LL TAKE PHOTOS WITH, WHERE WE'LL GO TO TAKE THEM.
I LIKE IMAGINING WHAT THE FINAL PICTURES...
...WILL LOOK LIKE.

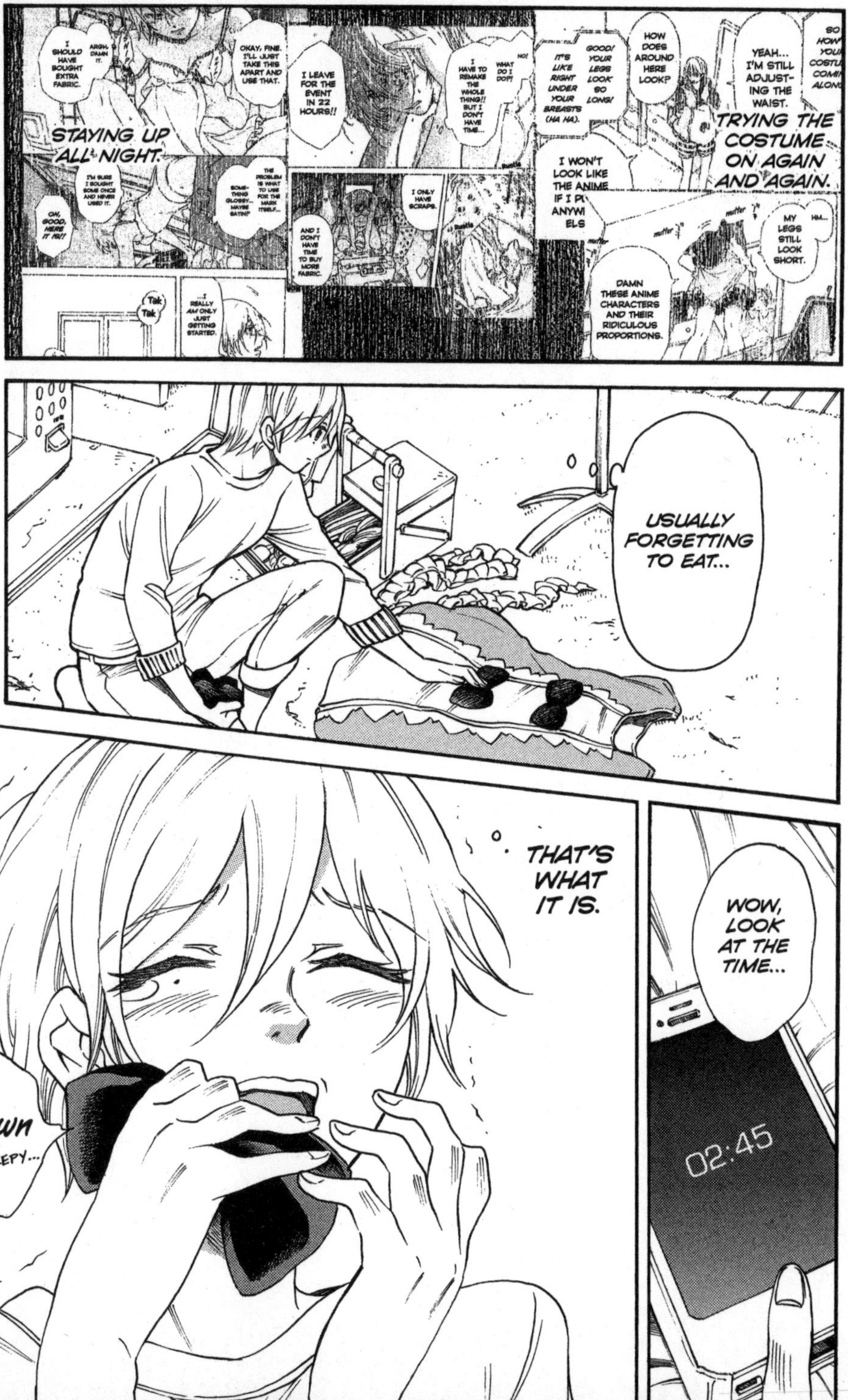
SO HOW YOU COSTU COMI ALONG
YEAH... I'M STILL ADJUSTING THE WAIST.
HOW DOES AROUND HERE LOOK?
GOOD! YOUR LEGS LOOK SO LONG!
IT'S LIKE RIGHT UNDER YOUR BREASTS (HA HA).
TRYING THE COSTUME ON AGAIN AND AGAIN.
HM...
MY LEGS STILL LOOK SHORT.
mutter
mutter
mutter
I WON'T LOOK LIKE THE ANIME IF I PU ANYWI ELS
DAMN THESE ANIME CHARACTERS AND THEIR RIDICULOUS PROPORTIONS.
NO!
WHAT DO I DO?!
I HAVE TO REMAKE THE WHOLE THING!! BUT I DON'T HAVE TIME...
I LEAVE FOR THE EVENT IN 22 HOURS!!
Rustle
I ONLY HAVE SCRAPS.
Rustle
AND I DON'T HAVE TIME TO BUY MORE FABRIC.
OKAY, FINE. I'LL JUST TAKE THIS APART AND USE THAT.
ARGH, DAMN IT.
I SHOULD HAVE BOUGHT EXTRA FABRIC.
STAYING UP ALL NIGHT.
THE PROBLEM IS WHAT TO USE FOR THE MARK ITSELF...
SOMETHING GLOSSY... MAYBE SATIN?
I'M SURE I BOUGHT SOME ONCE AND NEVER USED IT.
OH, GOOD, HERE IT IS!!
...I REALLY AM ONLY JUST GETTING STARTED.
Tak
Tak
USUALLY FORGETTING TO EAT...
WOW, LOOK AT THE TIME...
02:45
THAT'S WHAT IT IS.
Yawn
SLEEPY...

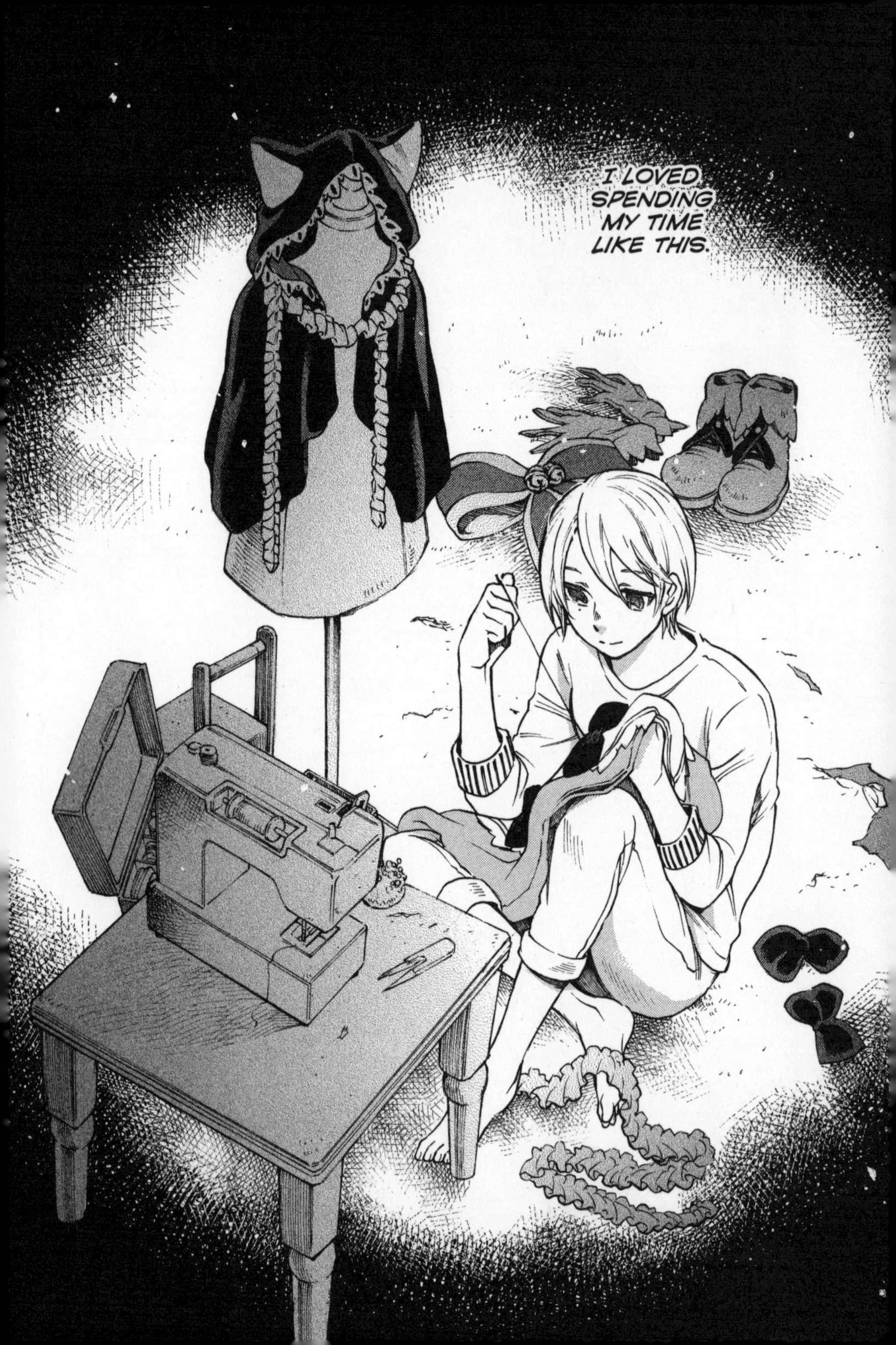
I LOVED SPENDING MY TIME LIKE THIS.

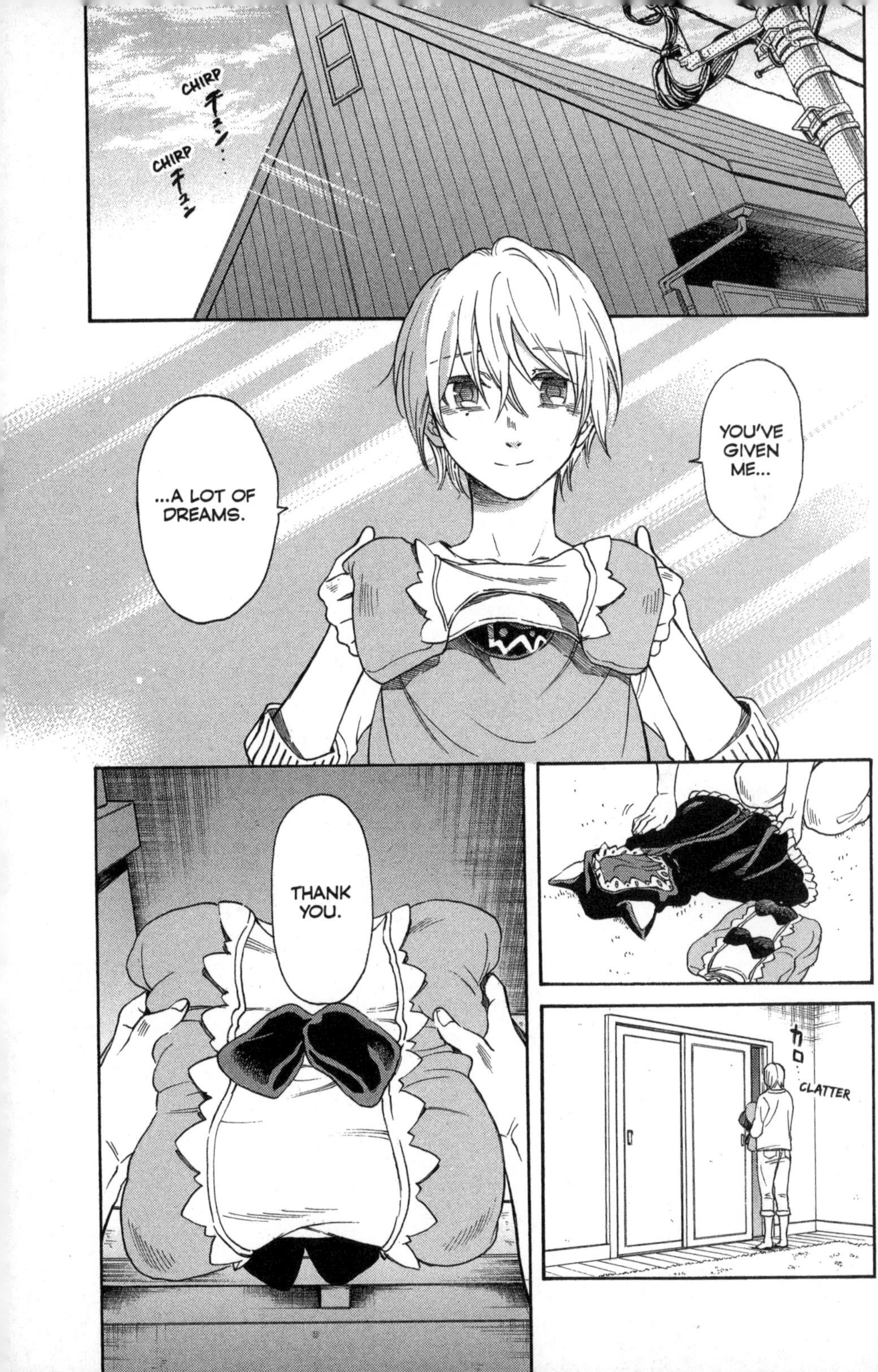
CHIRP
チュン…
CHIRP
チュン
YOU'VE GIVEN ME...
...A LOT OF DREAMS.
カロ…
CLATTER
THANK YOU.

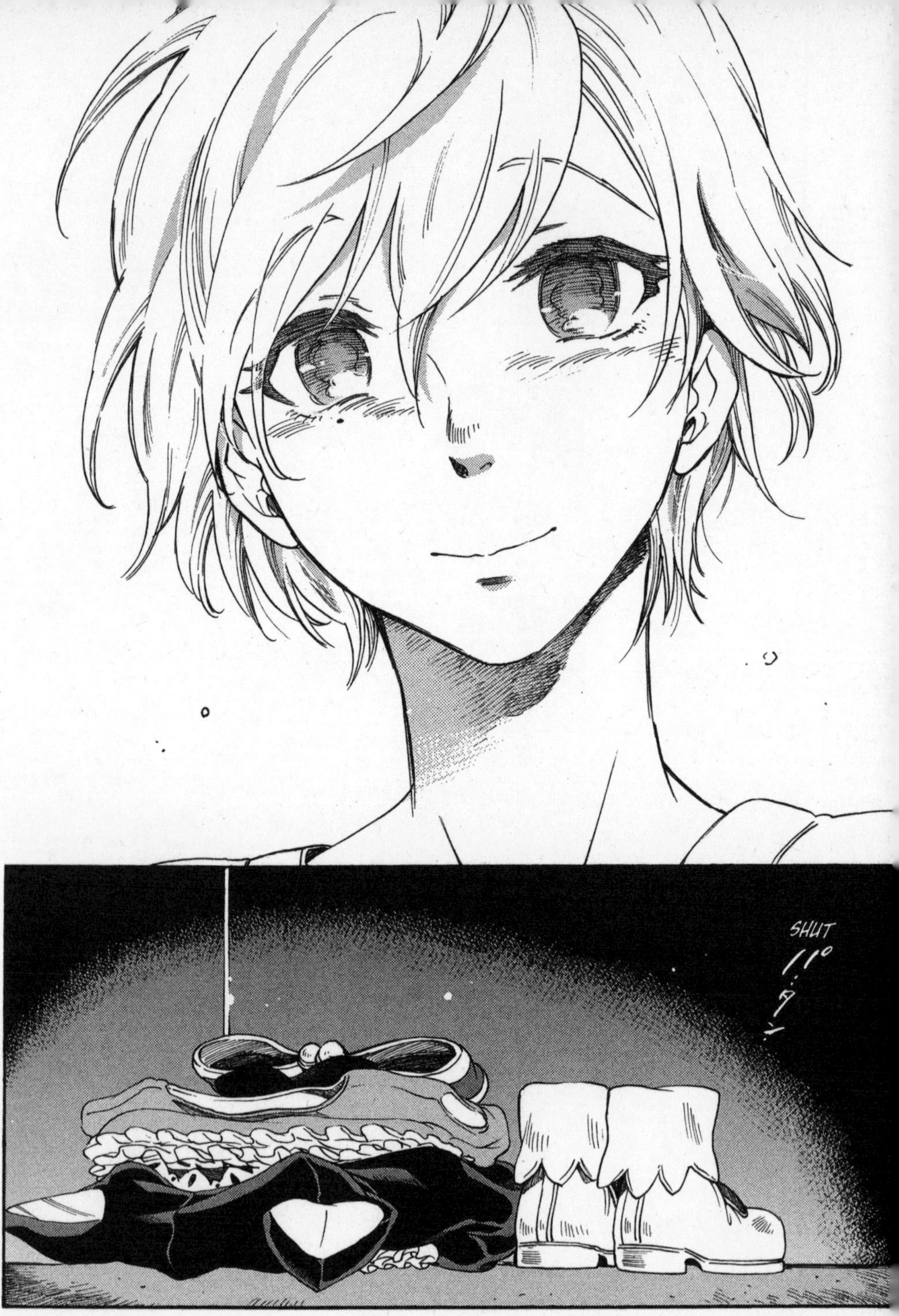
SHUT

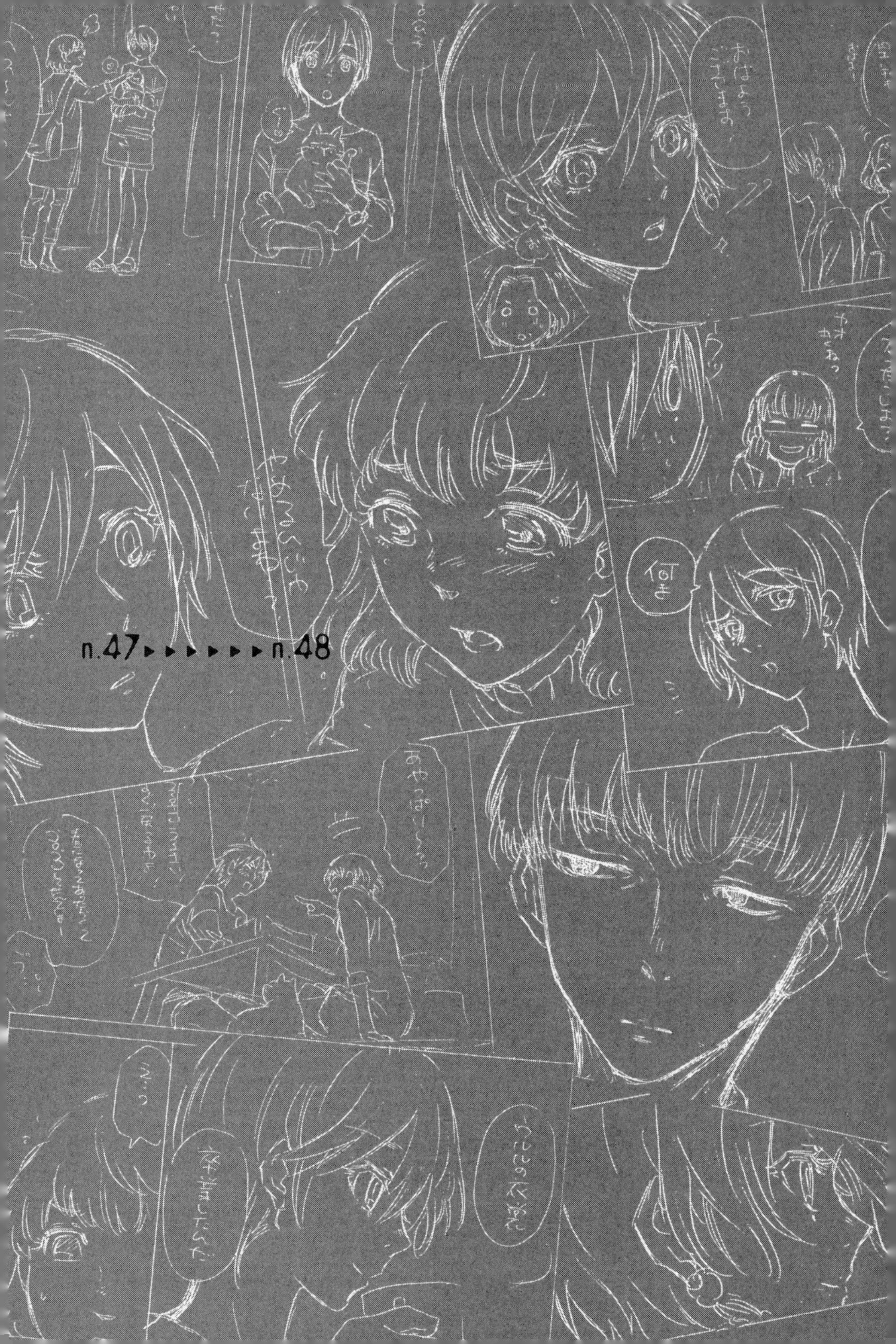
おはようございます
何

n.47▸▸▸▸▸▸▸▸n.48

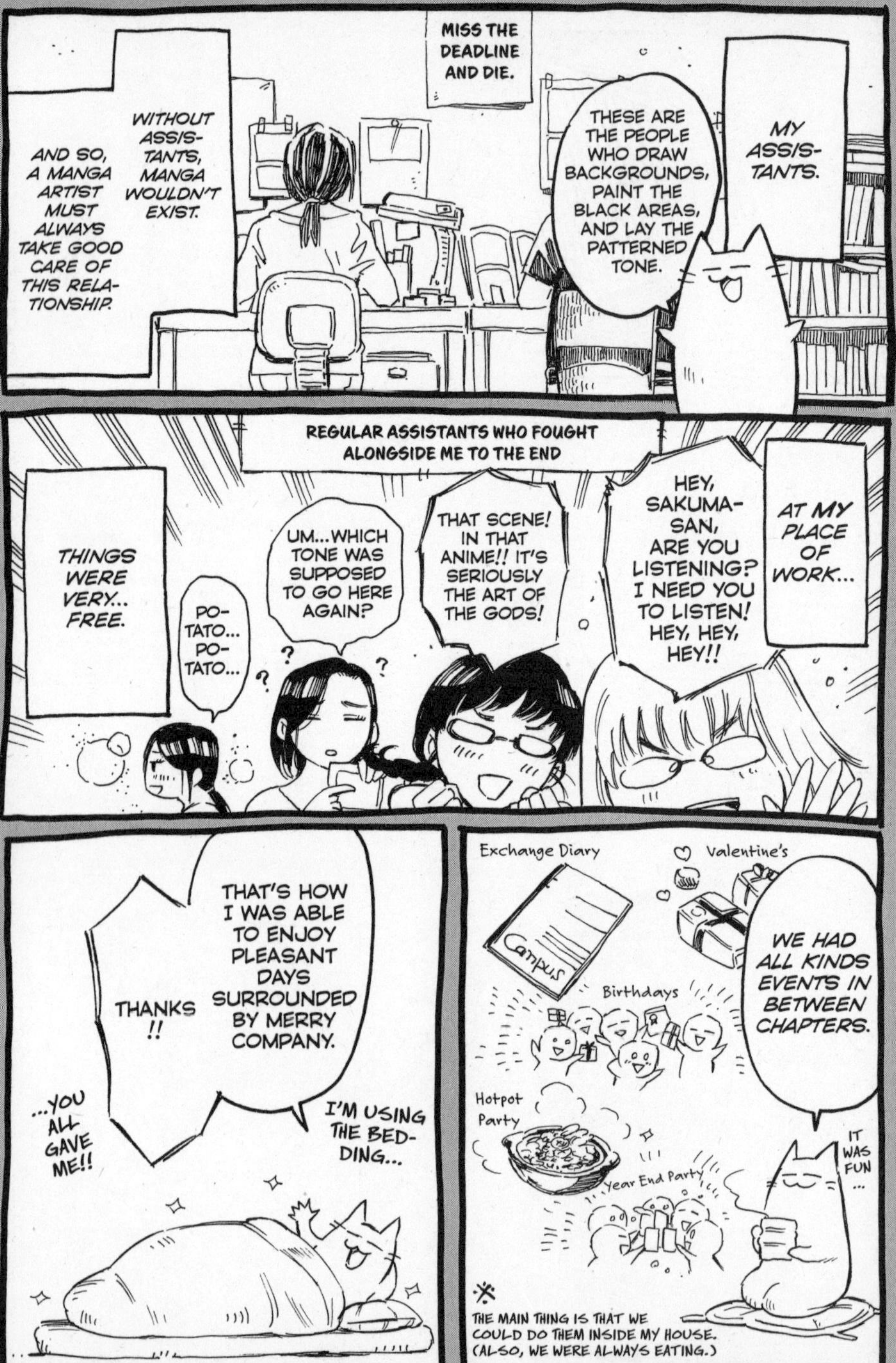
MY ASSIS-TANTS.
THESE ARE THE PEOPLE WHO DRAW BACKGROUNDS, PAINT THE BLACK AREAS, AND LAY THE PATTERNED TONE.
MISS THE DEADLINE AND DIE.
WITHOUT ASSIS-TANTS, MANGA WOULDN'T EXIST.
AND SO, A MANGA ARTIST MUST ALWAYS TAKE GOOD CARE OF THIS RELA-TIONSHIP.
AT MY PLACE OF WORK...
REGULAR ASSISTANTS WHO FOUGHT ALONGSIDE ME TO THE END
HEY, SAKUMA-SAN, ARE YOU LISTENING? I NEED YOU TO LISTEN! HEY, HEY, HEY!!
THAT SCENE! IN THAT ANIME!! IT'S SERIOUSLY THE ART OF THE GODS!
UM...WHICH TONE WAS SUPPOSED TO GO HERE AGAIN?
PO-TATO... PO-TATO...
THINGS WERE VERY... FREE.
WE HAD ALL KINDS EVENTS IN BETWEEN CHAPTERS.
Valentine's
Exchange Diary
Campus
Birthdays
Hotpot Party
Year End Party
IT WAS FUN ...
THE MAIN THING IS THAT WE COULD DO THEM INSIDE MY HOUSE. (ALSO, WE WERE ALWAYS EATING.)
THAT'S HOW I WAS ABLE TO ENJOY PLEASANT DAYS SURROUNDED BY MERRY COMPANY.
THANKS !!
I'M USING THE BED-DING...
...YOU ALL GAVE ME!!

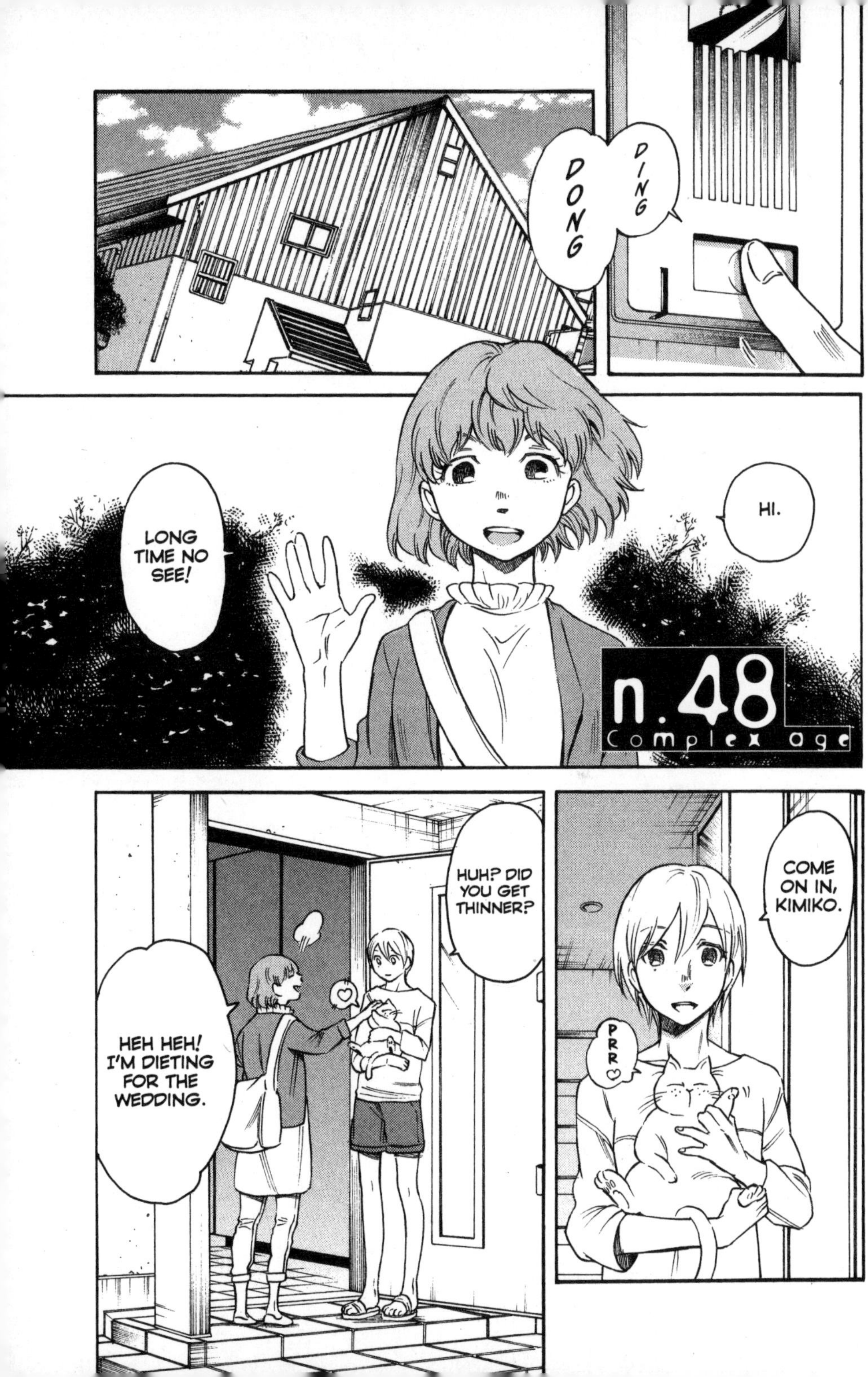
DING DONG
HI.
LONG TIME NO SEE!
n.48
Complex age
COME ON IN, KIMIKO.
PRR♡
HUH? DID YOU GET THINNER?
HEH HEH! I'M DIETING FOR THE WEDDING.

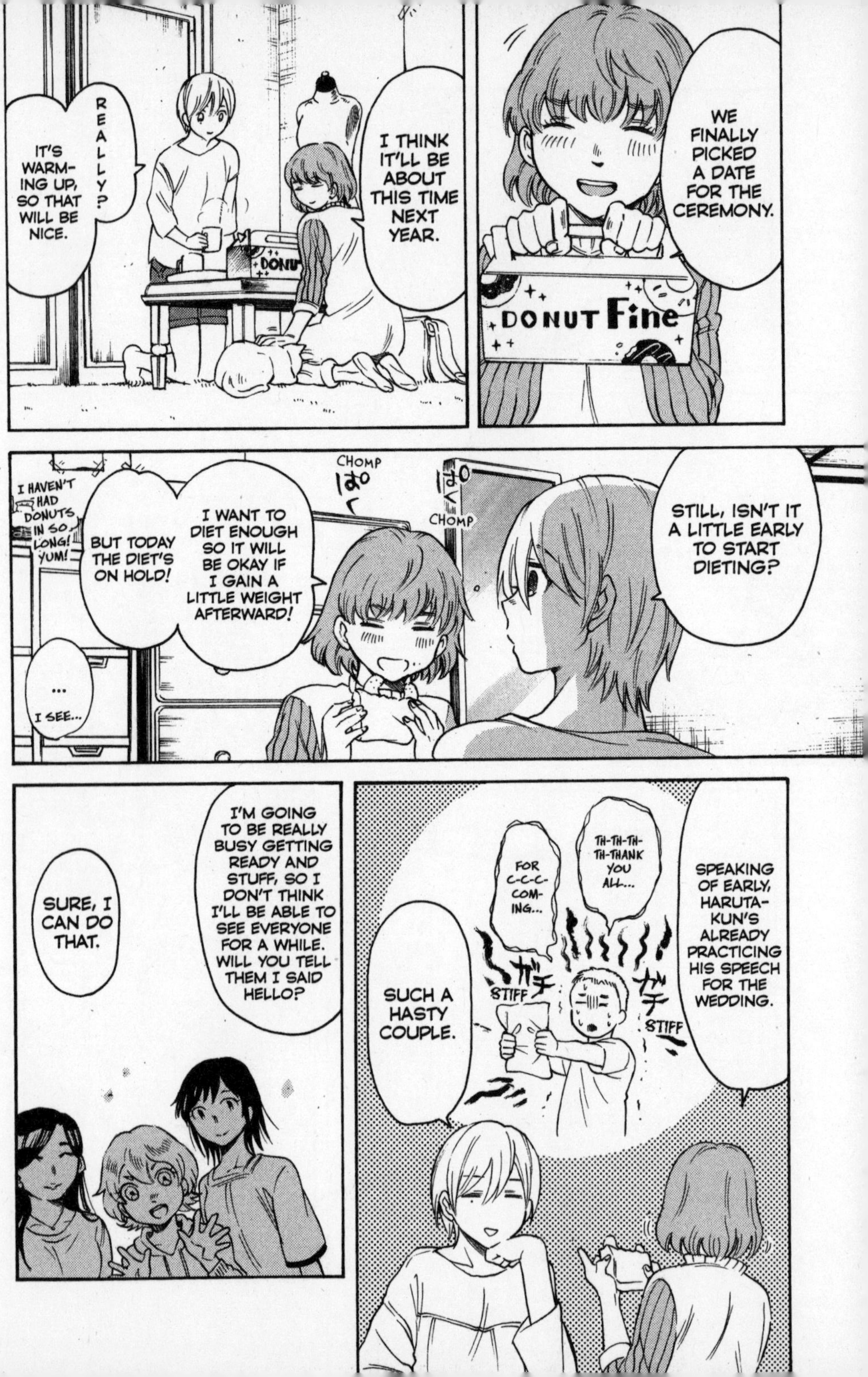
WE FINALLY PICKED A DATE FOR THE CEREMONY.
DONUT Fine
DONUT
I THINK IT'LL BE ABOUT THIS TIME NEXT YEAR.
REALLY?
IT'S WARMING UP, SO THAT WILL BE NICE.
STILL, ISN'T IT A LITTLE EARLY TO START DIETING?
CHOMP
CHOMP
I WANT TO DIET ENOUGH SO IT WILL BE OKAY IF I GAIN A LITTLE WEIGHT AFTERWARD!
BUT TODAY THE DIET'S ON HOLD!
I HAVEN'T HAD DONUTS IN SO LONG! YUM!
... I SEE...
SPEAKING OF EARLY, HARUTA-KUN'S ALREADY PRACTICING HIS SPEECH FOR THE WEDDING.
TH-TH-TH-TH-THANK YOU ALL...
FOR C-C-C-COMING...
STIFF
STIFF
SUCH A HASTY COUPLE.
I'M GOING TO BE REALLY BUSY GETTING READY AND STUFF, SO I DON'T THINK I'LL BE ABLE TO SEE EVERYONE FOR A WHILE. WILL YOU TELL THEM I SAID HELLO?
SURE, I CAN DO THAT.

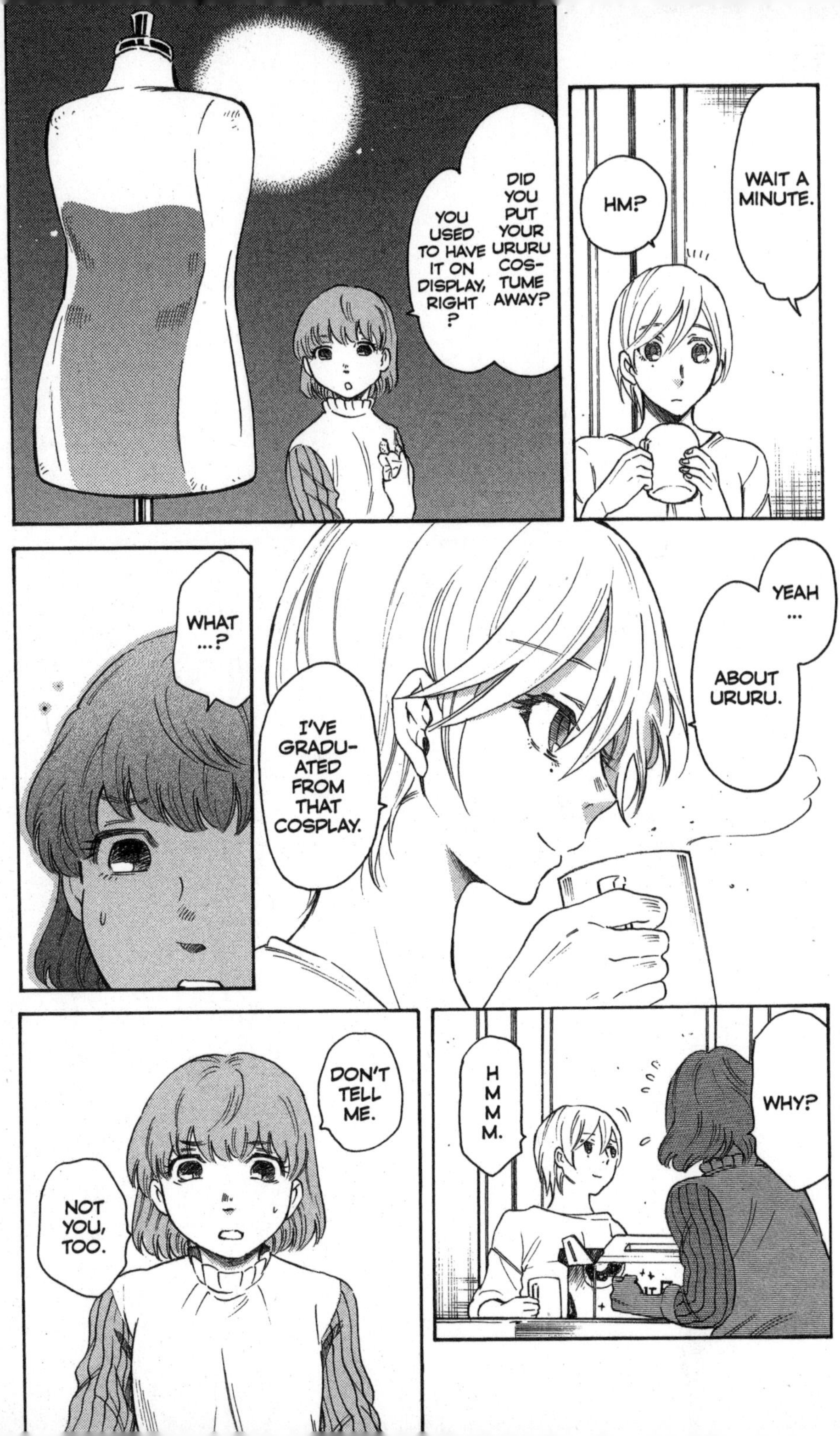
WAIT A MINUTE.
HM?
DID YOU PUT YOUR URURU COSTUME AWAY?
YOU USED TO HAVE IT ON DISPLAY, RIGHT?
YEAH... ABOUT URURU.
I'VE GRADUATED FROM THAT COSPLAY.
WHAT...?
WHY?
HMMM.
DON'T TELL ME.
NOT YOU, TOO.

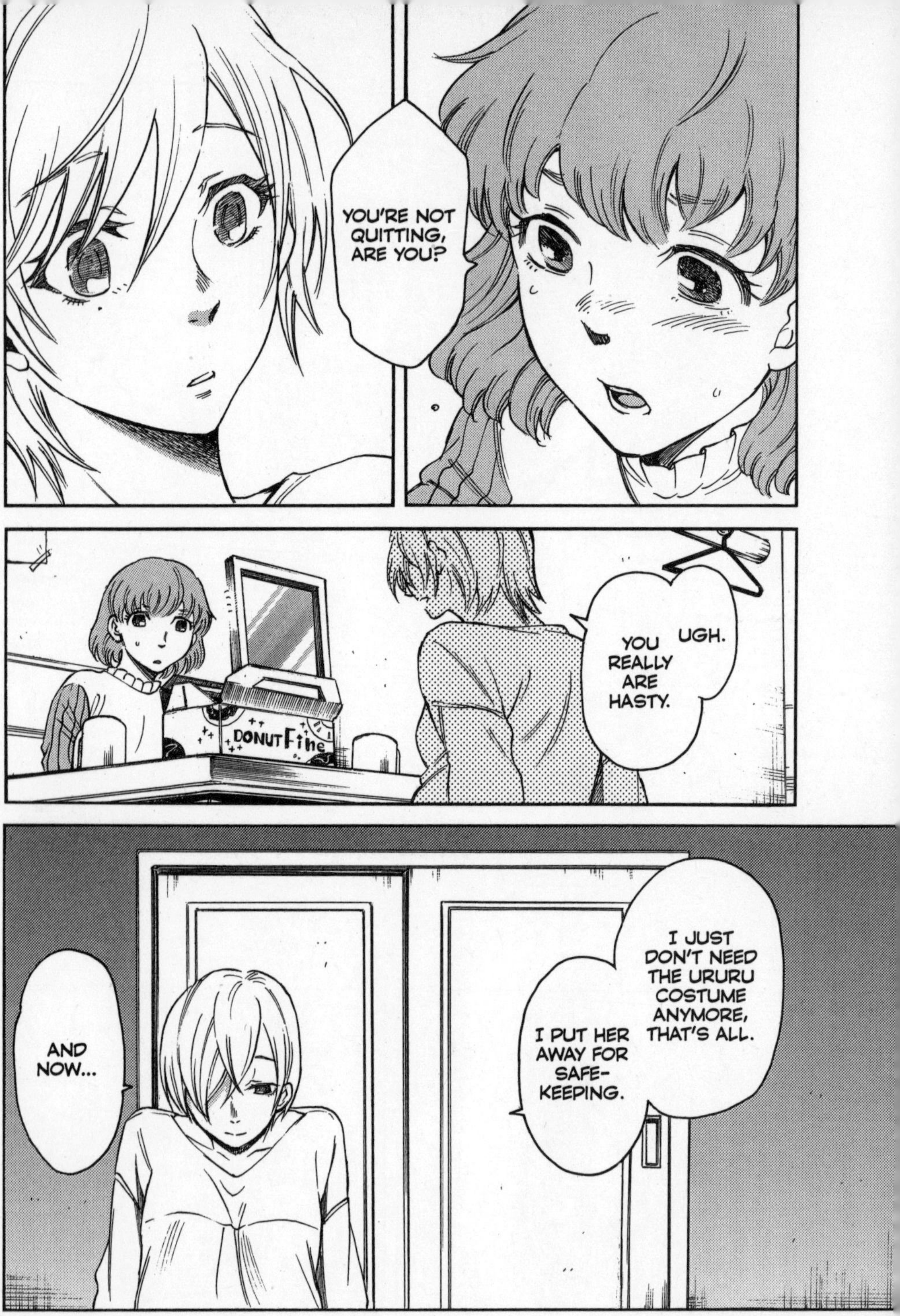
YOU'RE NOT QUITTING, ARE YOU?
UGH.
YOU REALLY ARE HASTY.
I JUST DON'T NEED THE URURU COSTUME ANYMORE, THAT'S ALL.
I PUT HER AWAY FOR SAFE-KEEPING.
AND NOW...

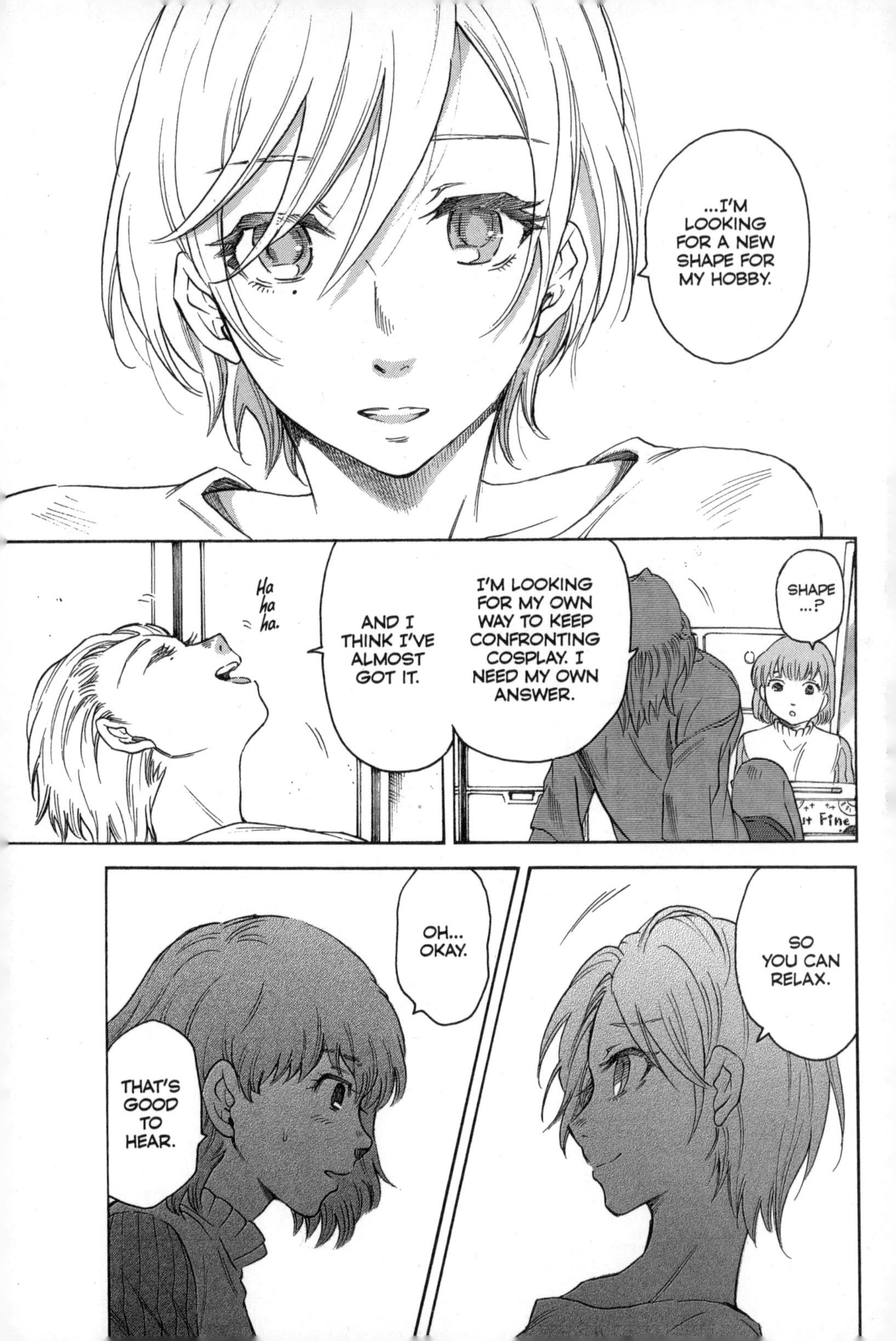
...I'M LOOKING FOR A NEW SHAPE FOR MY HOBBY.
SHAPE ...?
I'M LOOKING FOR MY OWN WAY TO KEEP CONFRONTING COSPLAY. I NEED MY OWN ANSWER.
AND I THINK I'VE ALMOST GOT IT.
Ha ha ha.
SO YOU CAN RELAX.
OH... OKAY.
THAT'S GOOD TO HEAR.

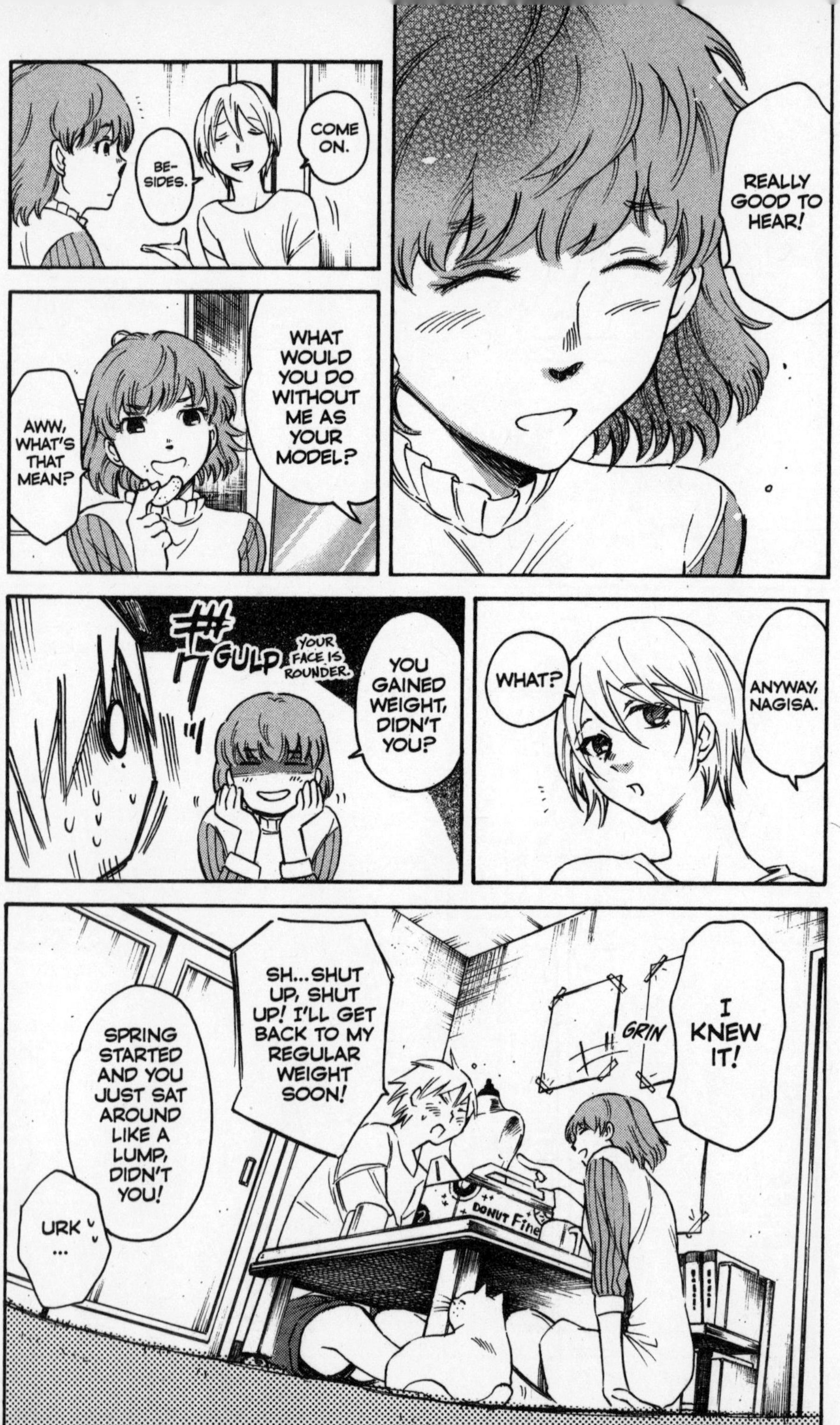
REALLY GOOD TO HEAR!
COME ON.
BE-SIDES.
WHAT WOULD YOU DO WITHOUT ME AS YOUR MODEL?
AWW, WHAT'S THAT MEAN?
ANYWAY, NAGISA.
WHAT?
YOU GAINED WEIGHT, DIDN'T YOU?
YOUR FACE IS ROUNDER.
GULP
I KNEW IT!
GRIN
SH...SHUT UP, SHUT UP! I'LL GET BACK TO MY REGULAR WEIGHT SOON!
SPRING STARTED AND YOU JUST SAT AROUND LIKE A LUMP, DIDN'T YOU!
URK ...
DONUT Fine

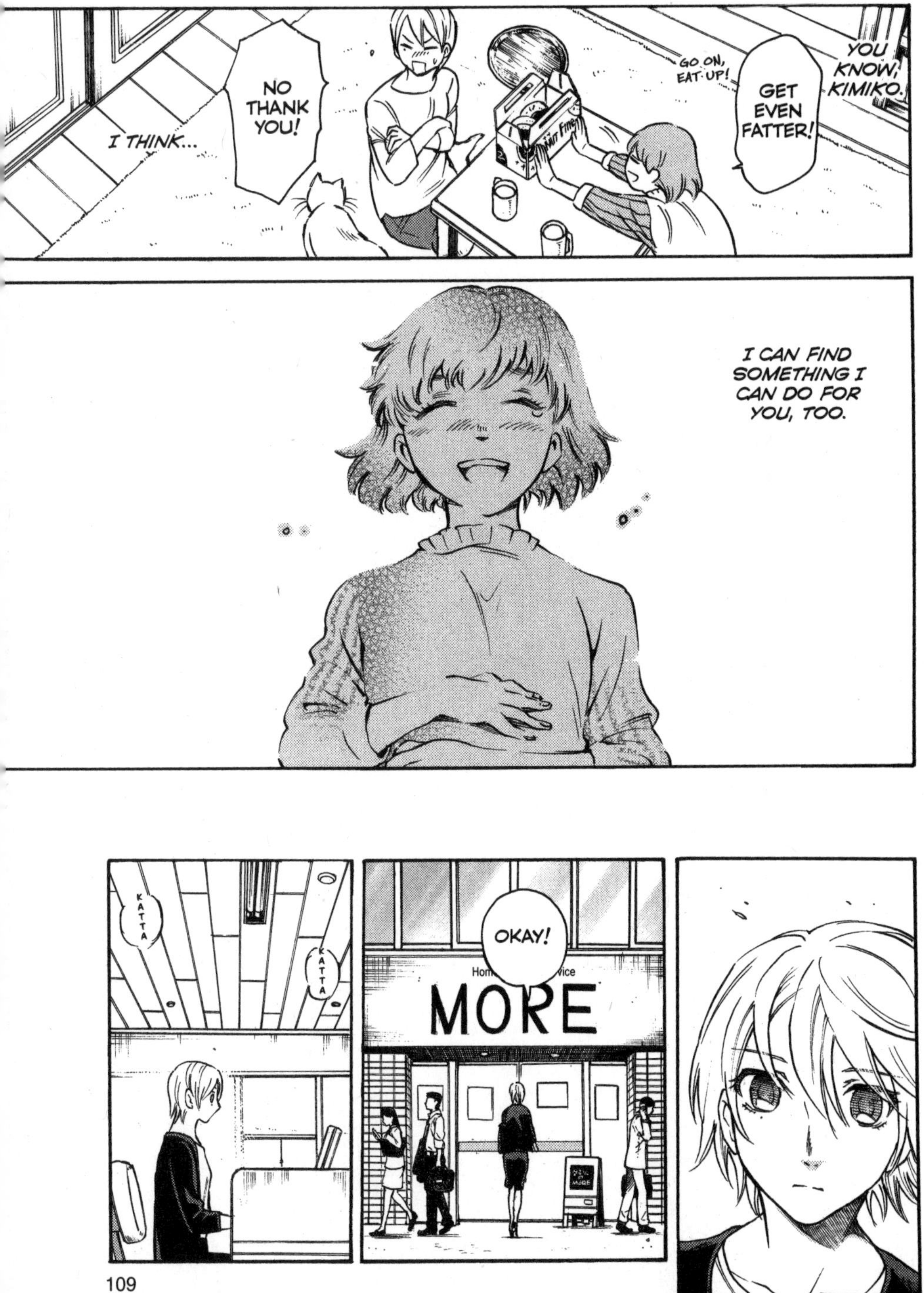
YOU KNOW, KIMIKO.
GET EVEN FATTER!
GO ON, EAT UP!
NO THANK YOU!
I THINK...
I CAN FIND SOMETHING I CAN DO FOR YOU, TOO.
OKAY!
MORE
KATTA
KATTA

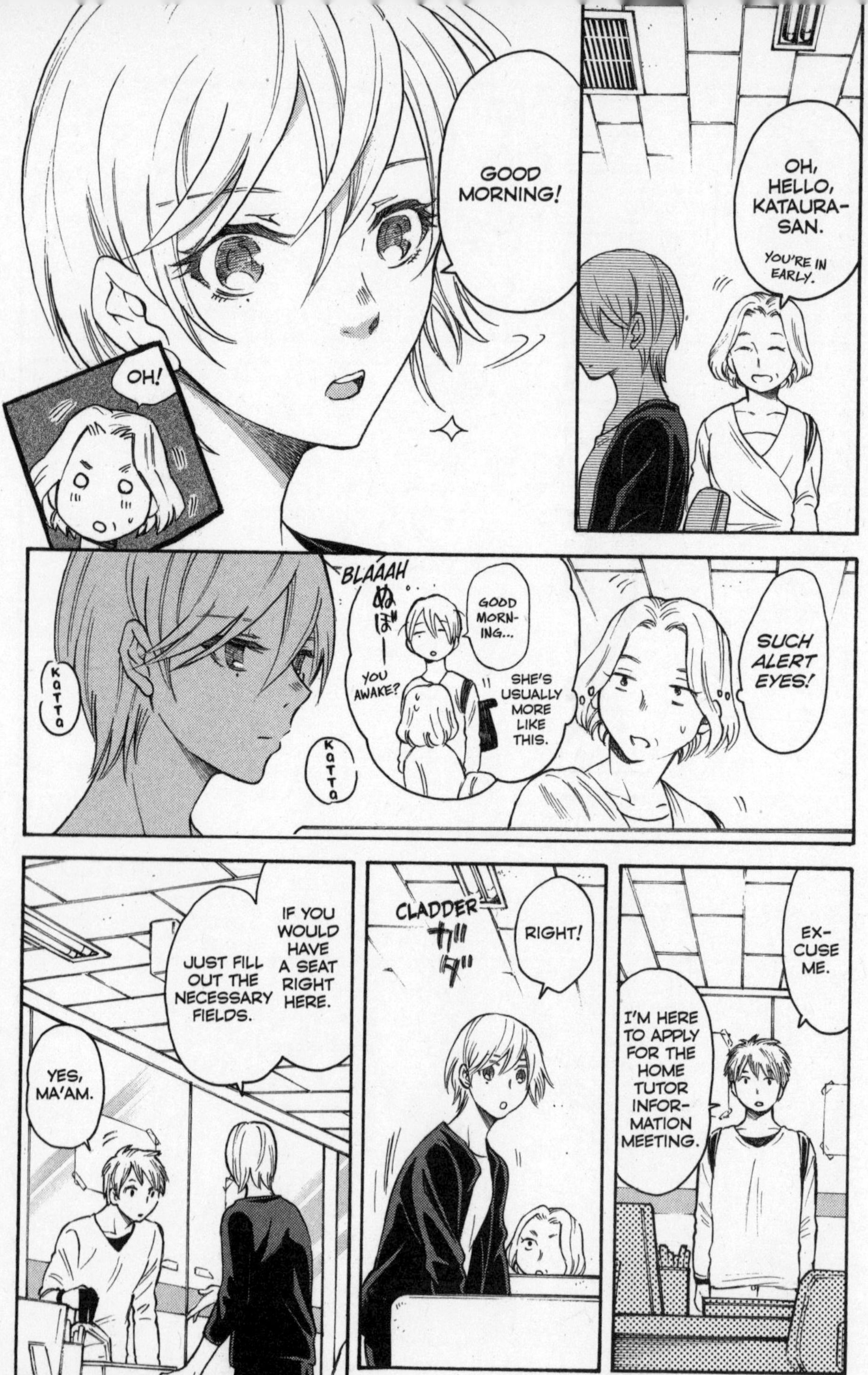
OH, HELLO, KATAURA-SAN.
YOU'RE IN EARLY.
GOOD MORNING!
OH!
SUCH ALERT EYES!
BLAAAH ぬぼー
GOOD MORNING...
YOU AWAKE?
SHE'S USUALLY MORE LIKE THIS.
Katta
Katta
EX-CUSE ME.
I'M HERE TO APPLY FOR THE HOME TUTOR INFOR-MATION MEETING.
RIGHT!
CLADDER ガダ
IF YOU WOULD HAVE A SEAT RIGHT HERE.
JUST FILL OUT THE NECESSARY FIELDS.
YES, MA'AM.

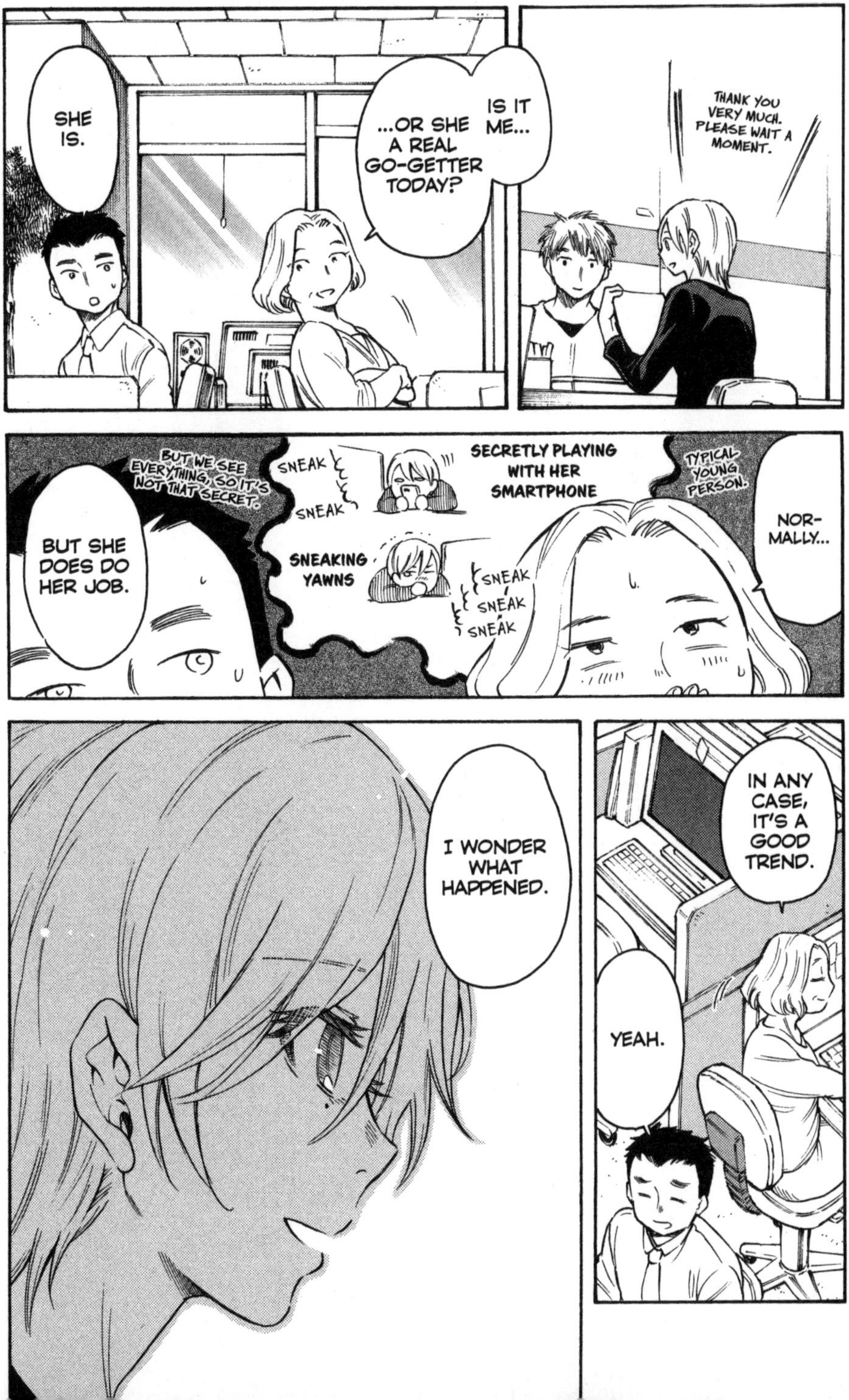
THANK YOU VERY MUCH. PLEASE WAIT A MOMENT.
IS IT ME...
...OR SHE A REAL GO-GETTER TODAY?
SHE IS.
NOR-MALLY...
TYPICAL YOUNG PERSON.
SECRETLY PLAYING WITH HER SMARTPHONE
SNEAK
SNEAK
SNEAKING YAWNS
SNEAK
SNEAK
SNEAK
BUT WE SEE EVERYTHING, SO IT'S NOT THAT SECRET.
BUT SHE DOES DO HER JOB.
IN ANY CASE, IT'S A GOOD TREND.
YEAH.
I WONDER WHAT HAPPENED.

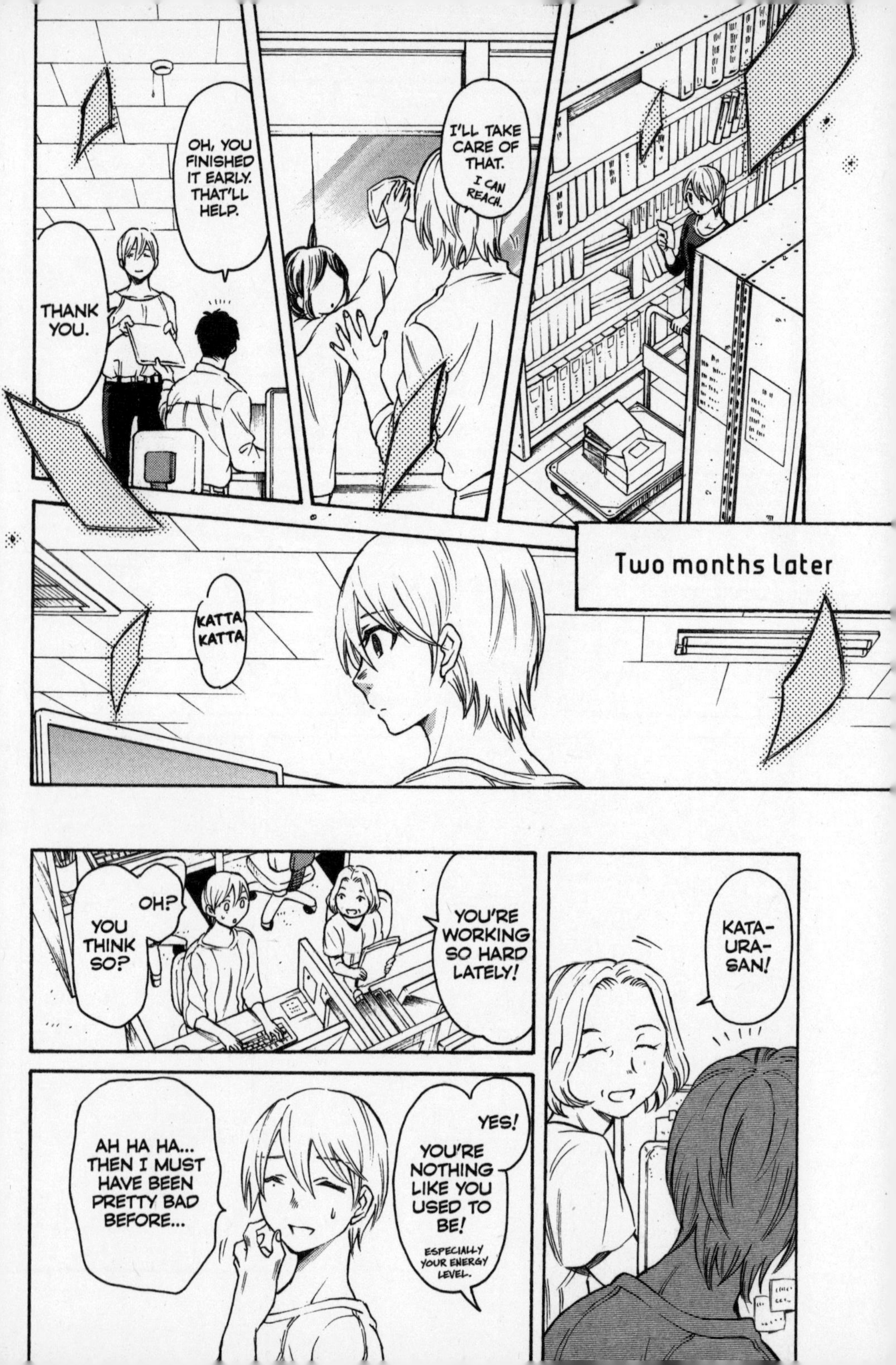
I'LL TAKE CARE OF THAT.
I CAN REACH.
OH, YOU FINISHED IT EARLY. THAT'LL HELP.
THANK YOU.
Two months later
KATTA KATTA
KATA-URA-SAN!
YOU'RE WORKING SO HARD LATELY!
OH? YOU THINK SO?
YES!
YOU'RE NOTHING LIKE YOU USED TO BE!
ESPECIALLY YOUR ENERGY LEVEL.
AH HA HA... THEN I MUST HAVE BEEN PRETTY BAD BEFORE...

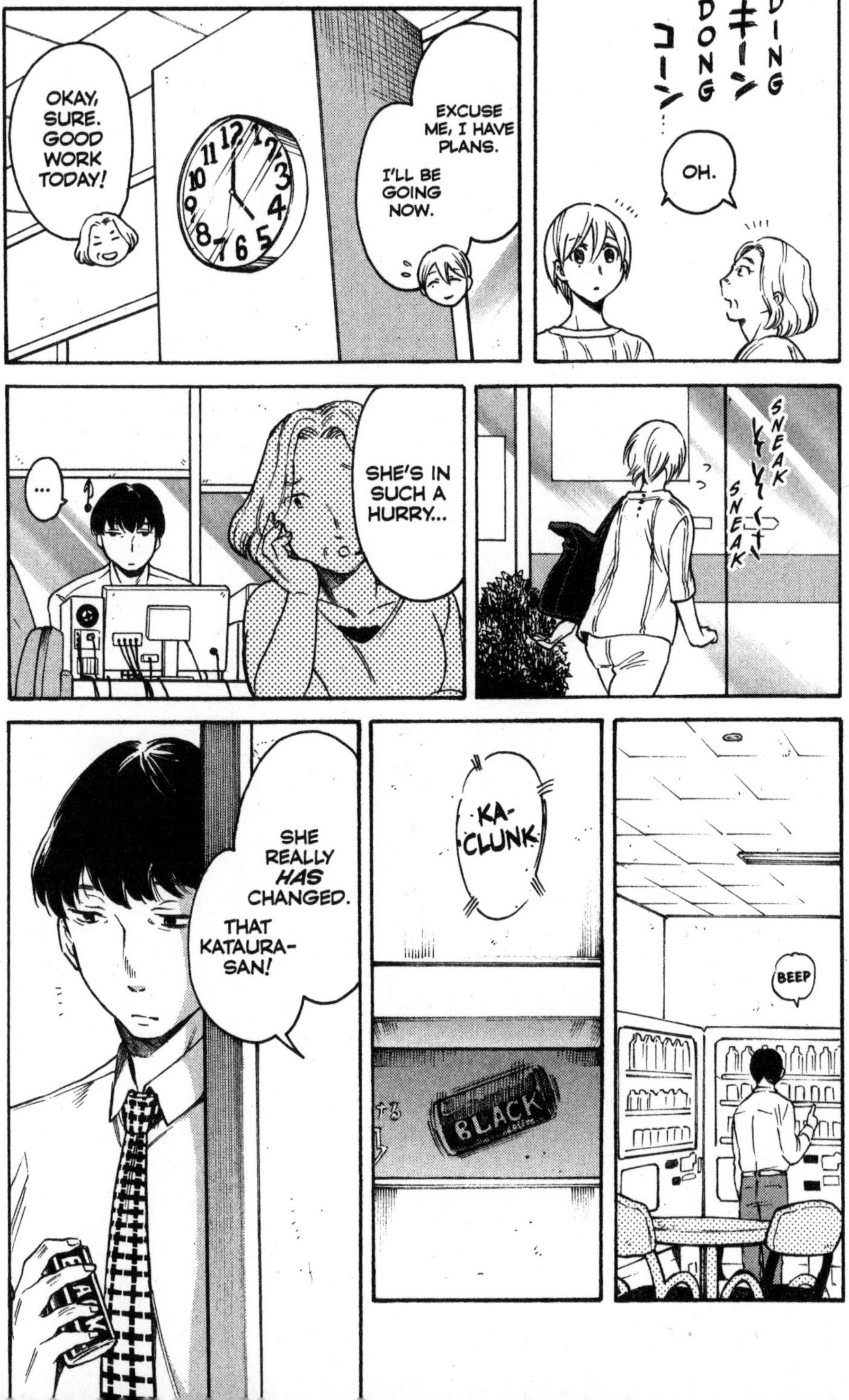
DING DONG
キーンコーン…
OH.
EXCUSE ME, I HAVE PLANS.
I'LL BE GOING NOW.
OKAY, SURE. GOOD WORK TODAY!
SNEAK SNEAK
SHE'S IN SUCH A HURRY...
...
BEEP
KA-CLUNK
BLACK
SHE REALLY *HAS* CHANGED.
THAT KATAURA-SAN!

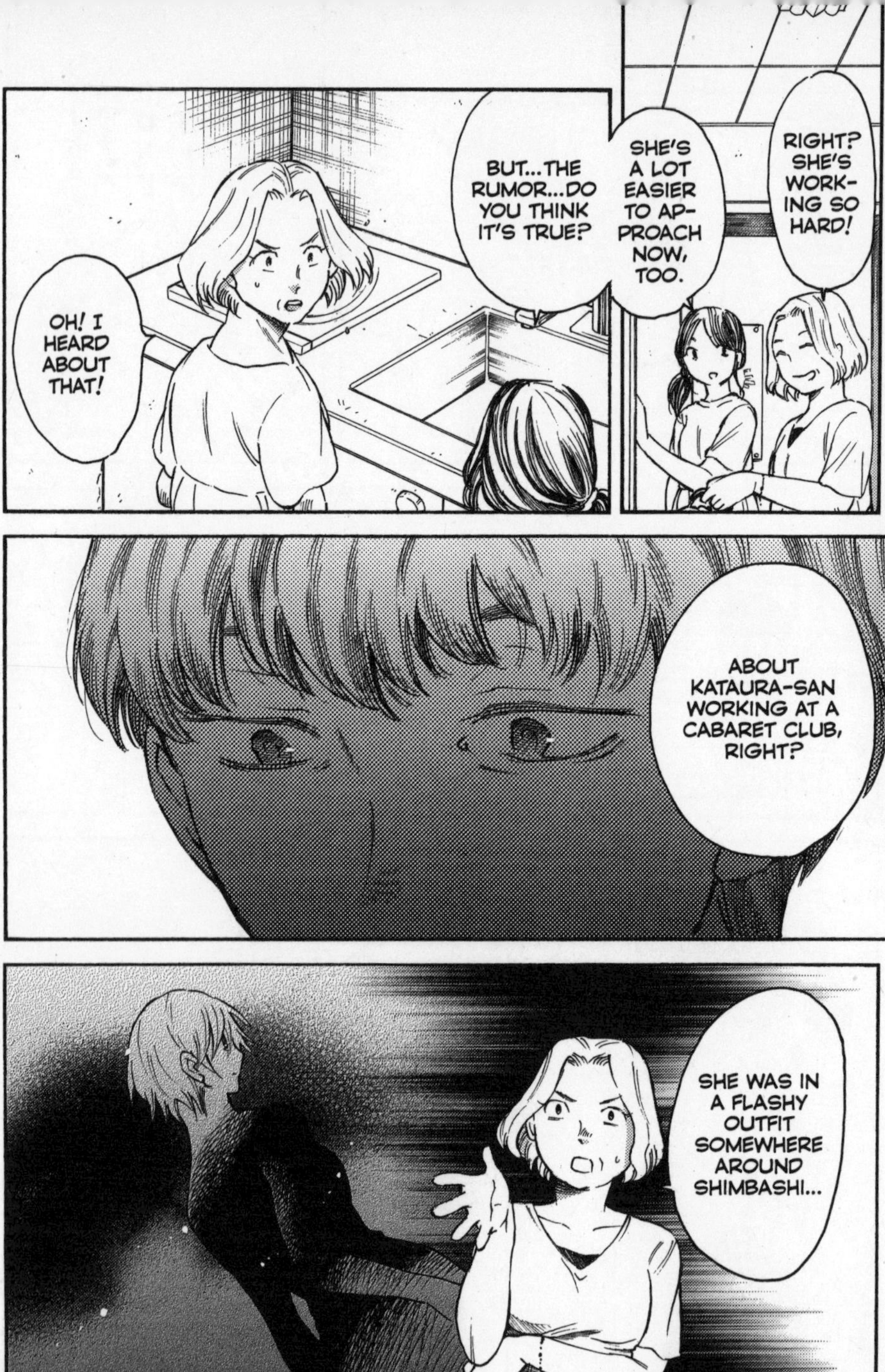
RIGHT? SHE'S WORKING SO HARD!
SHE'S A LOT EASIER TO APPROACH NOW, TOO.
BUT...THE RUMOR...DO YOU THINK IT'S TRUE?
OH! I HEARD ABOUT THAT!
ABOUT KATAURA-SAN WORKING AT A CABARET CLUB, RIGHT?
SHE WAS IN A FLASHY OUTFIT SOMEWHERE AROUND SHIMBASHI...

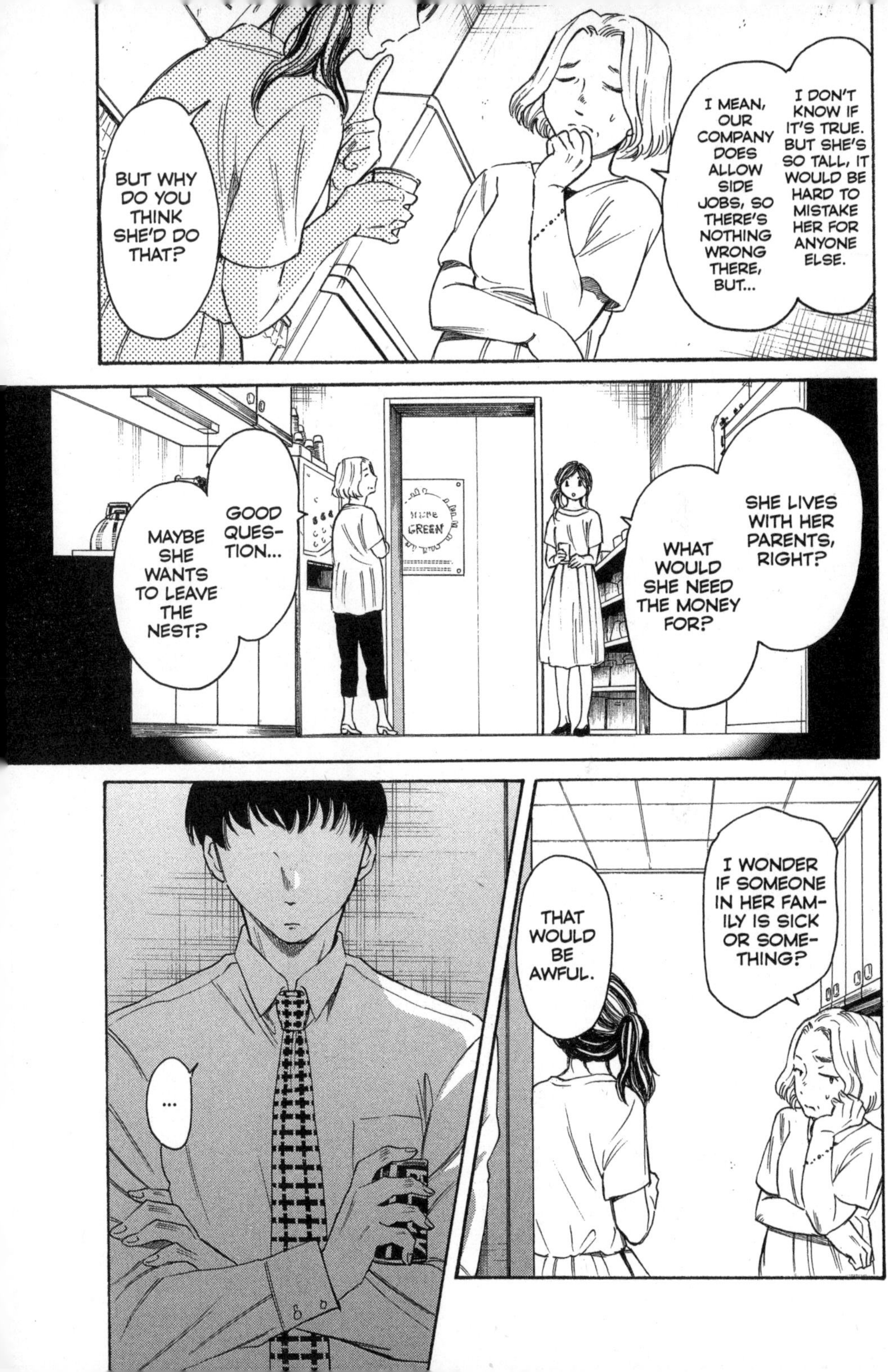
I DON'T KNOW IF IT'S TRUE. BUT SHE'S SO TALL, IT WOULD BE HARD TO MISTAKE HER FOR ANYONE ELSE.
I MEAN, OUR COMPANY DOES ALLOW SIDE JOBS, SO THERE'S NOTHING WRONG THERE, BUT...
BUT WHY DO YOU THINK SHE'D DO THAT?
SHE LIVES WITH HER PARENTS, RIGHT?
WHAT WOULD SHE NEED THE MONEY FOR?
GREEN
GOOD QUESTION...
MAYBE SHE WANTS TO LEAVE THE NEST?
I WONDER IF SOMEONE IN HER FAMILY IS SICK OR SOMETHING?
THAT WOULD BE AWFUL.
...

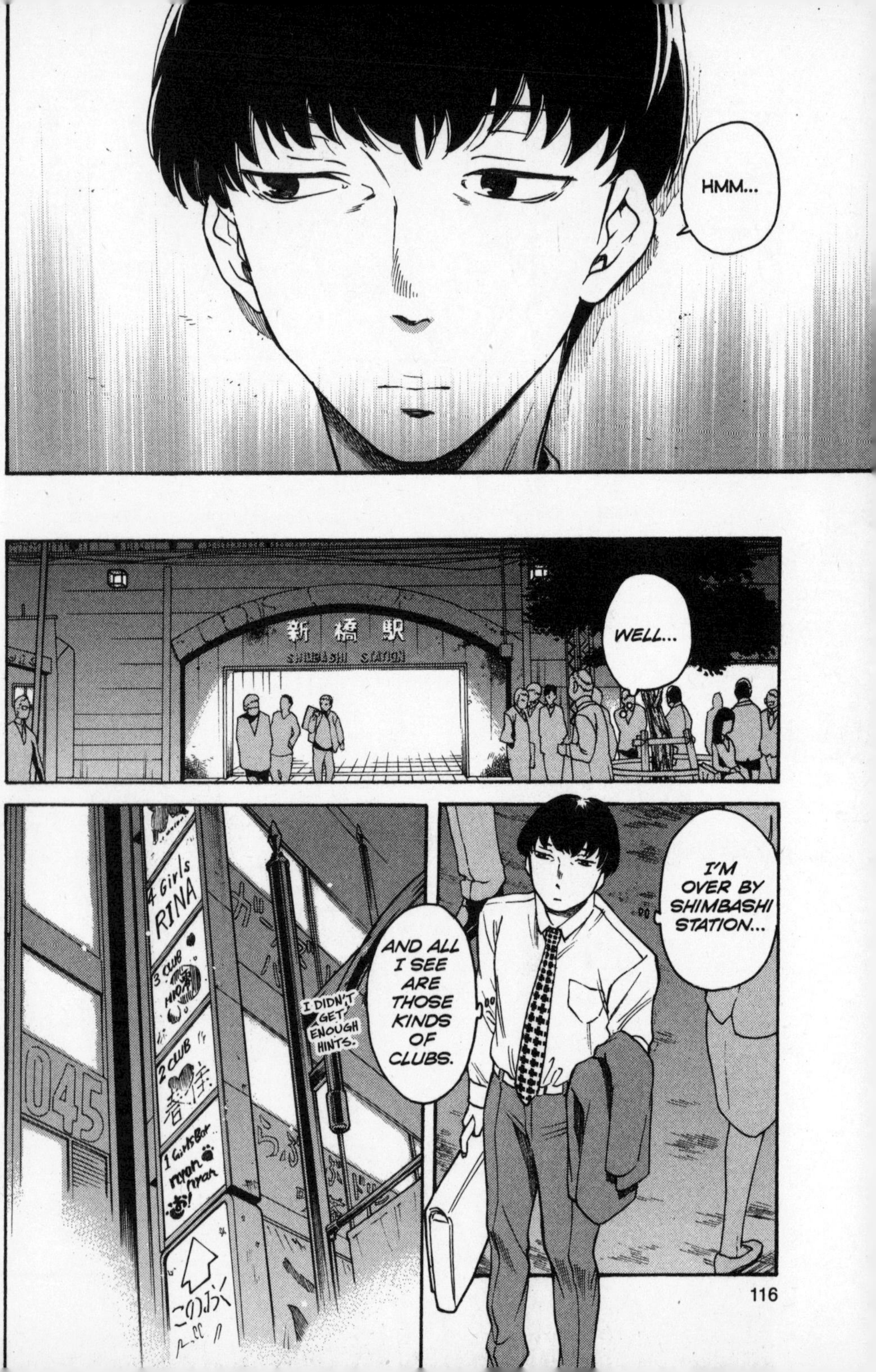
HMM...
新橋駅
SHIMBASHI STATION
WELL...
I'M OVER BY SHIMBASHI STATION...
AND ALL I SEE ARE THOSE KINDS OF CLUBS.
I DIDN'T GET ENOUGH HINTS.
4 Girls RINA
3 CLUB
2 CLUB
1 GirlsBar nyan nyan
045

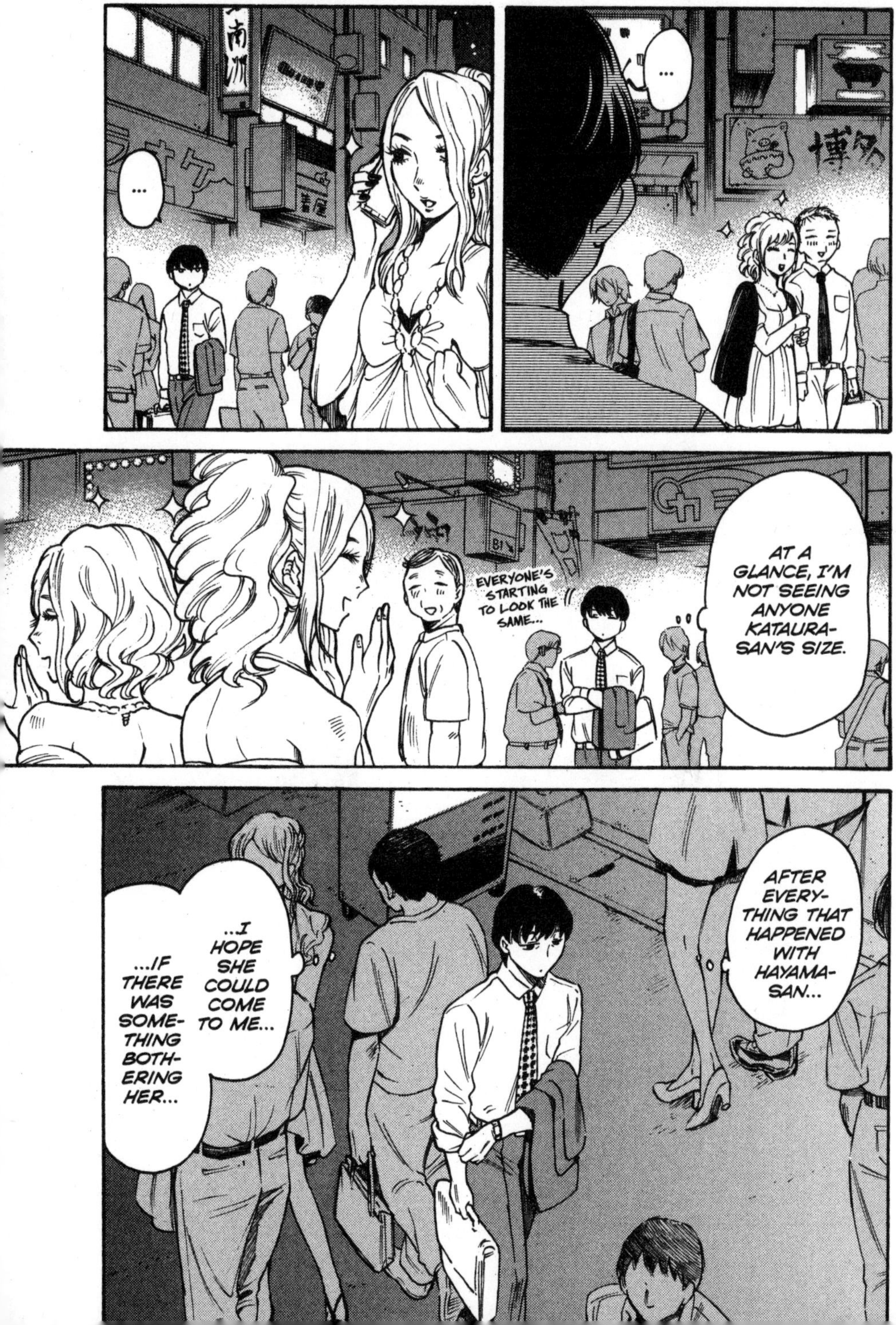
...
...
AT A GLANCE, I'M NOT SEEING ANYONE KATAURA-SAN'S SIZE.
EVERYONE'S STARTING TO LOOK THE SAME...
AFTER EVERY-THING THAT HAPPENED WITH HAYAMA-SAN...
...I HOPE SHE COULD COME TO ME...
...IF THERE WAS SOME-THING BOTH-ERING HER...

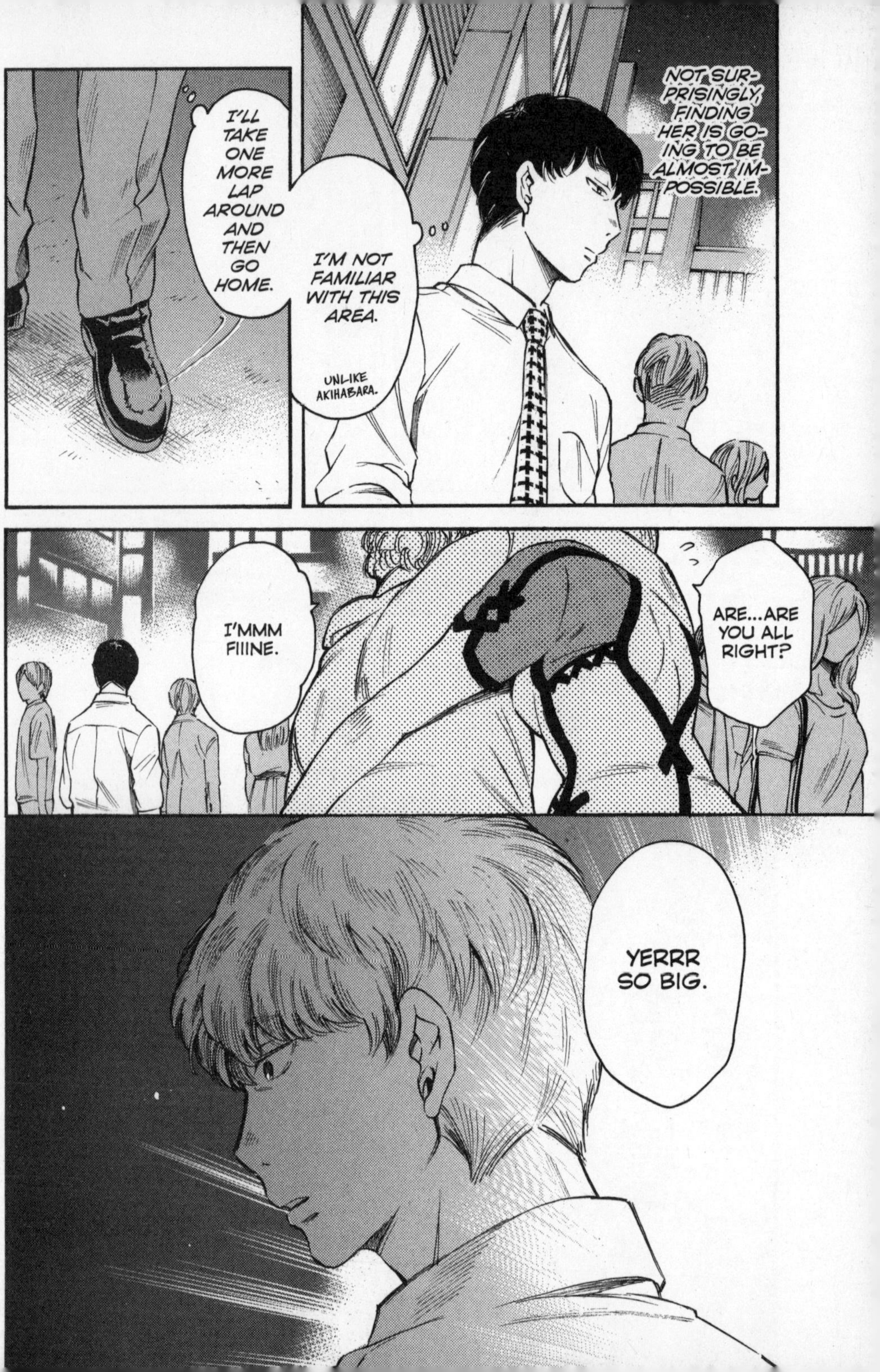
NOT SURPRISINGLY, FINDING HER IS GOING TO BE ALMOST IMPOSSIBLE.
I'M NOT FAMILIAR WITH THIS AREA.
UNLIKE AKIHABARA.
I'LL TAKE ONE MORE LAP AROUND AND THEN GO HOME.
ARE...ARE YOU ALL RIGHT?
I'MMM FIIINE.
YERRR SO BIG.

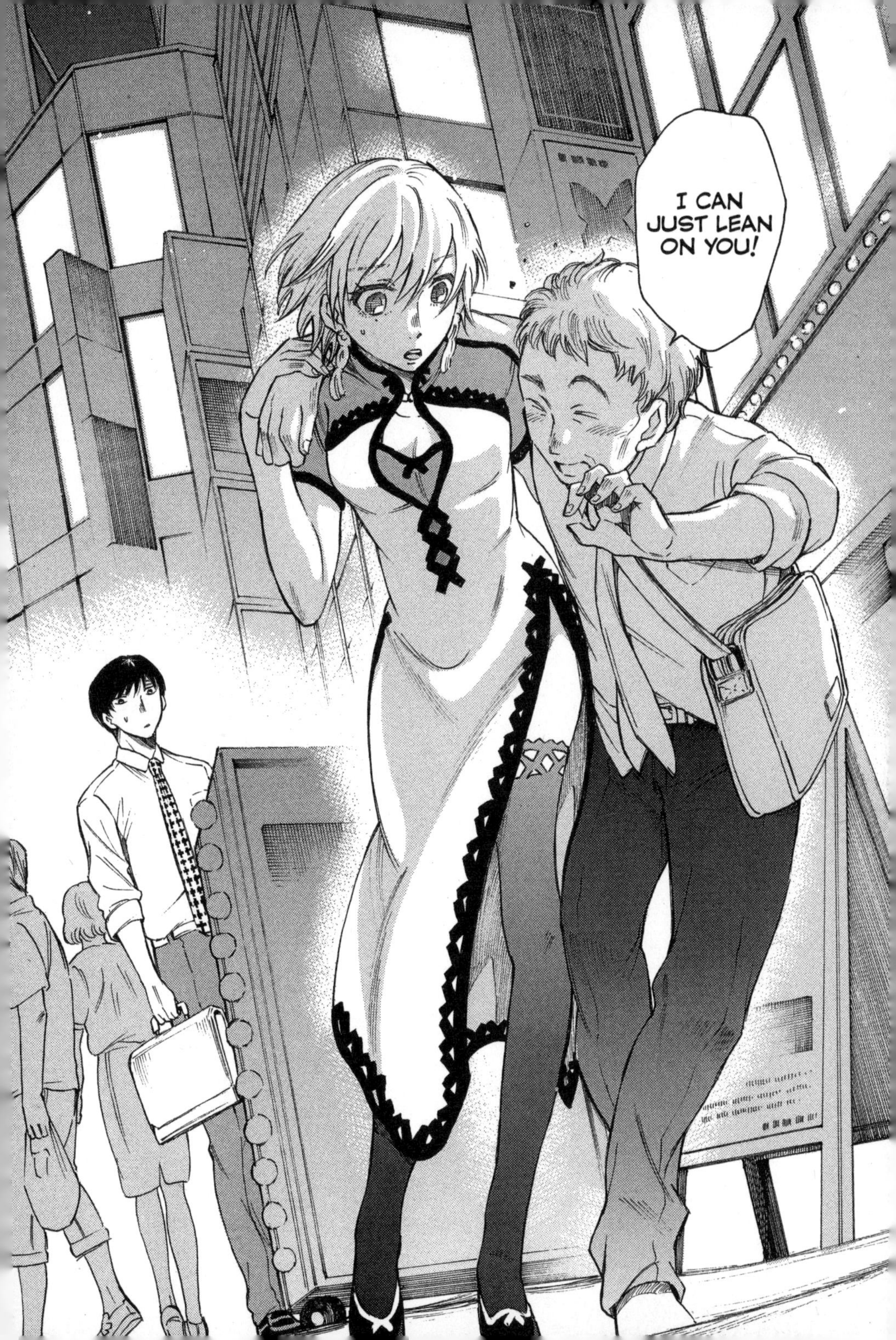
I CAN JUST LEAN ON YOU!

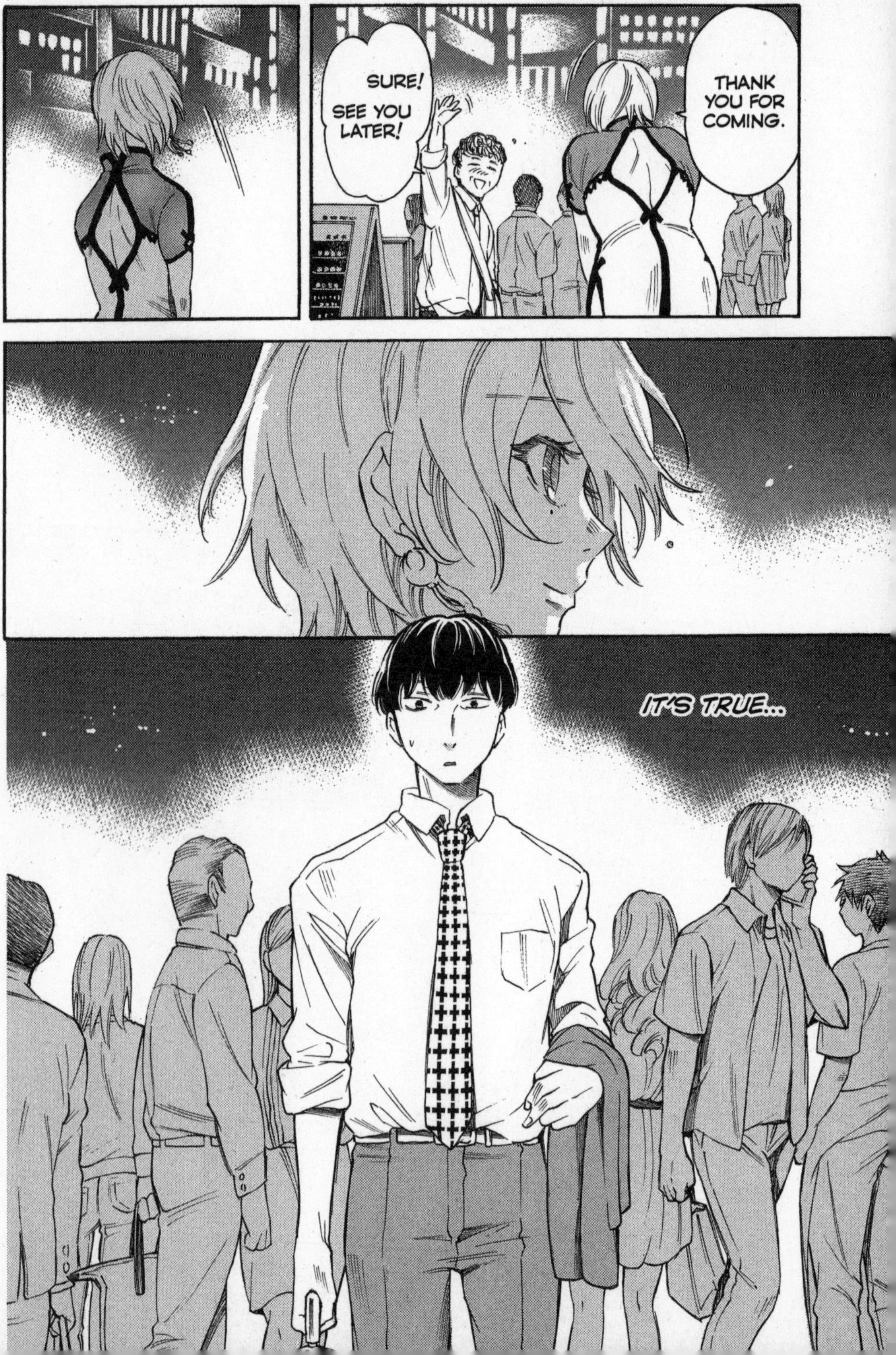
THANK YOU FOR COMING.
SURE! SEE YOU LATER!
IT'S TRUE...

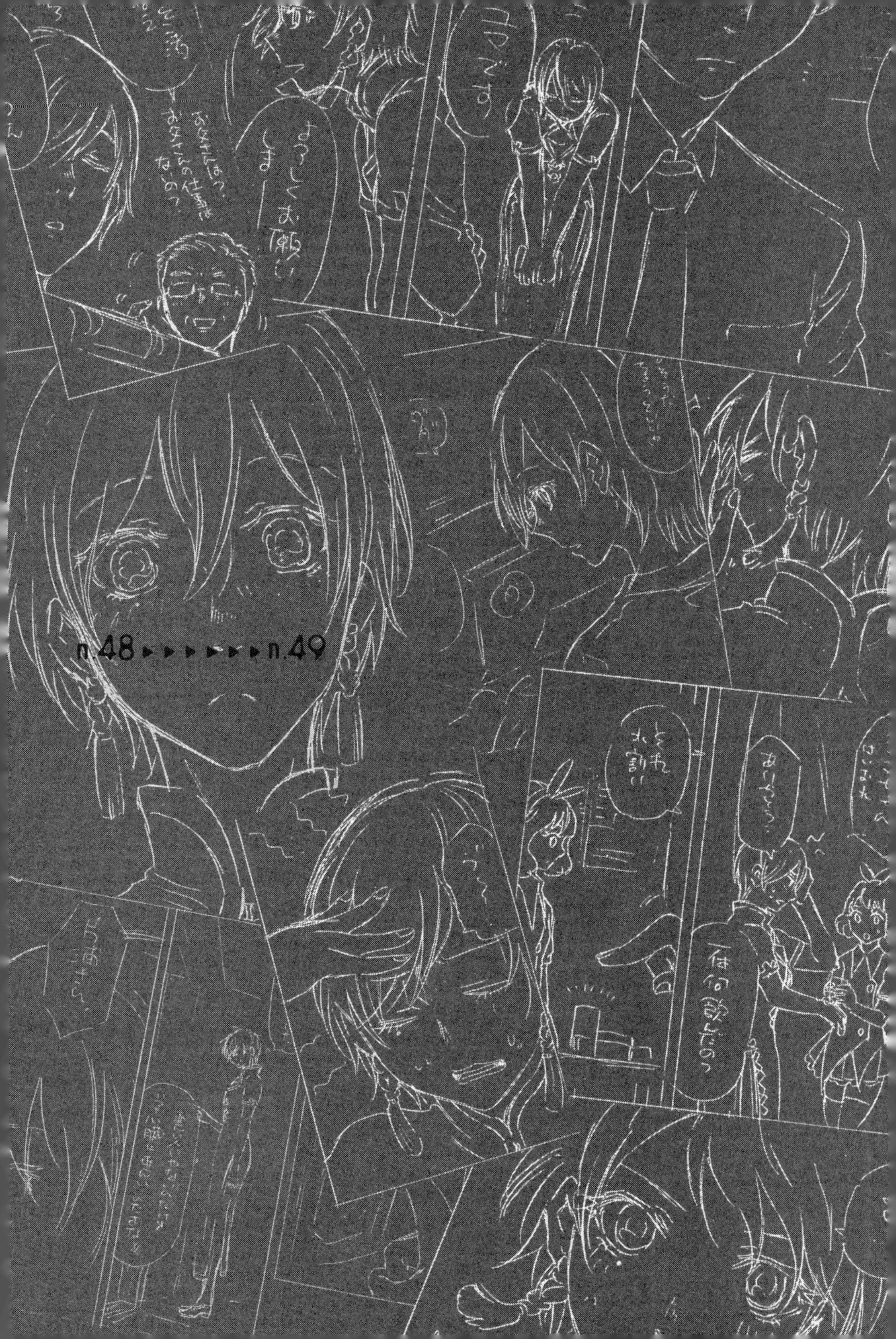
よろしくお願いします
n.48 ▶▶▶▶▶▶▶ n.49

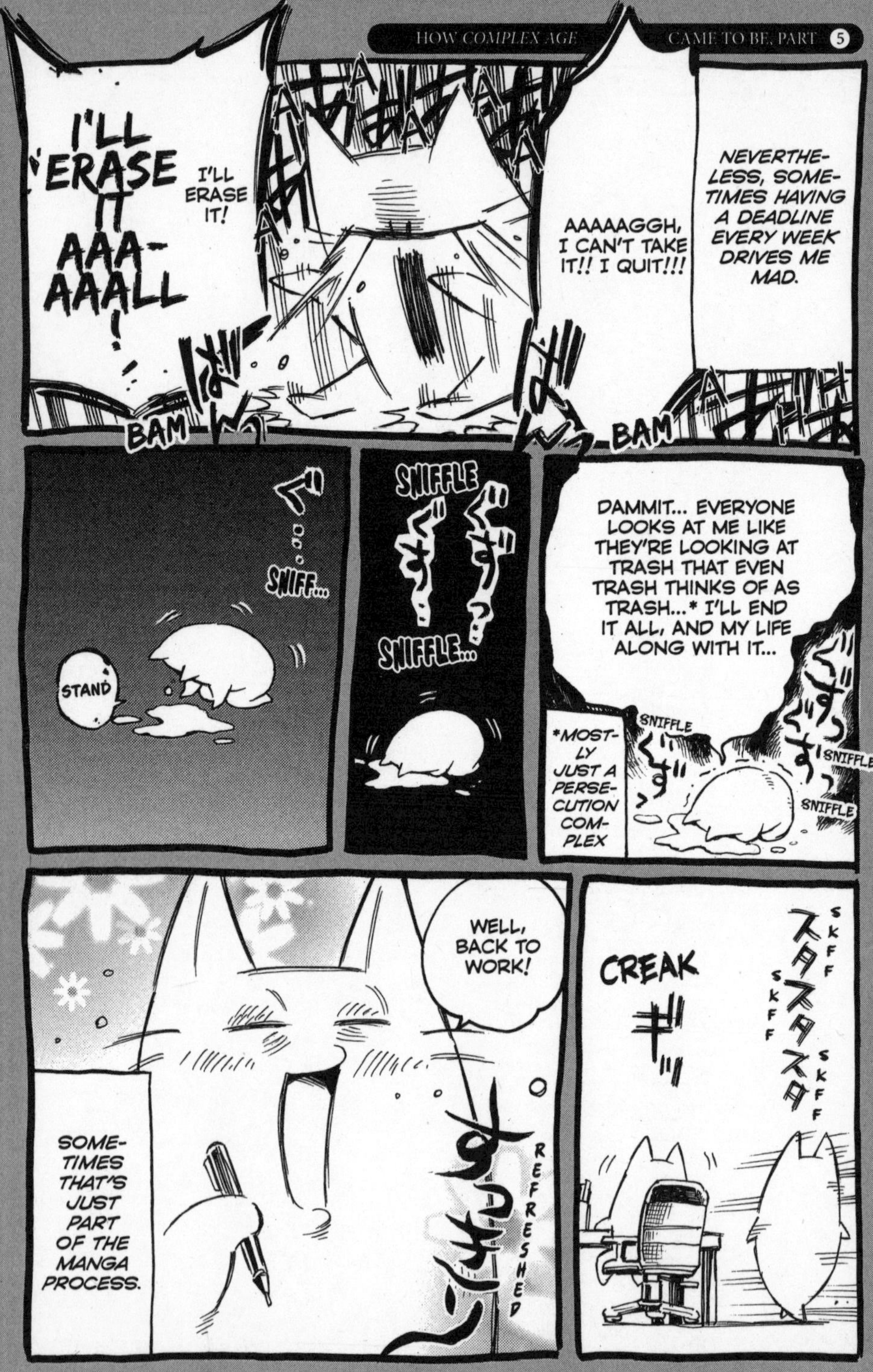
NEVERTHELESS, SOMETIMES HAVING A DEADLINE EVERY WEEK DRIVES ME MAD.
AAAAAGGH, I CAN'T TAKE IT!! I QUIT!!!
BAM
I'LL ERASE IT!
I'LL ERASE IT AAAAAALL!
BAM
DAMMIT... EVERYONE LOOKS AT ME LIKE THEY'RE LOOKING AT TRASH THAT EVEN TRASH THINKS OF AS TRASH...* I'LL END IT ALL, AND MY LIFE ALONG WITH IT...
SNIFFLE
SNIFFLE
SNIFFLE
*MOSTLY JUST A PERSECUTION COMPLEX
SNIFFLE
SNIFFLE...
SNIFF...
STAND
SKFF SKFF SKFF SKFF
CREAK
WELL, BACK TO WORK!
REFRESHED
SOMETIMES THAT'S JUST PART OF THE MANGA PROCESS.

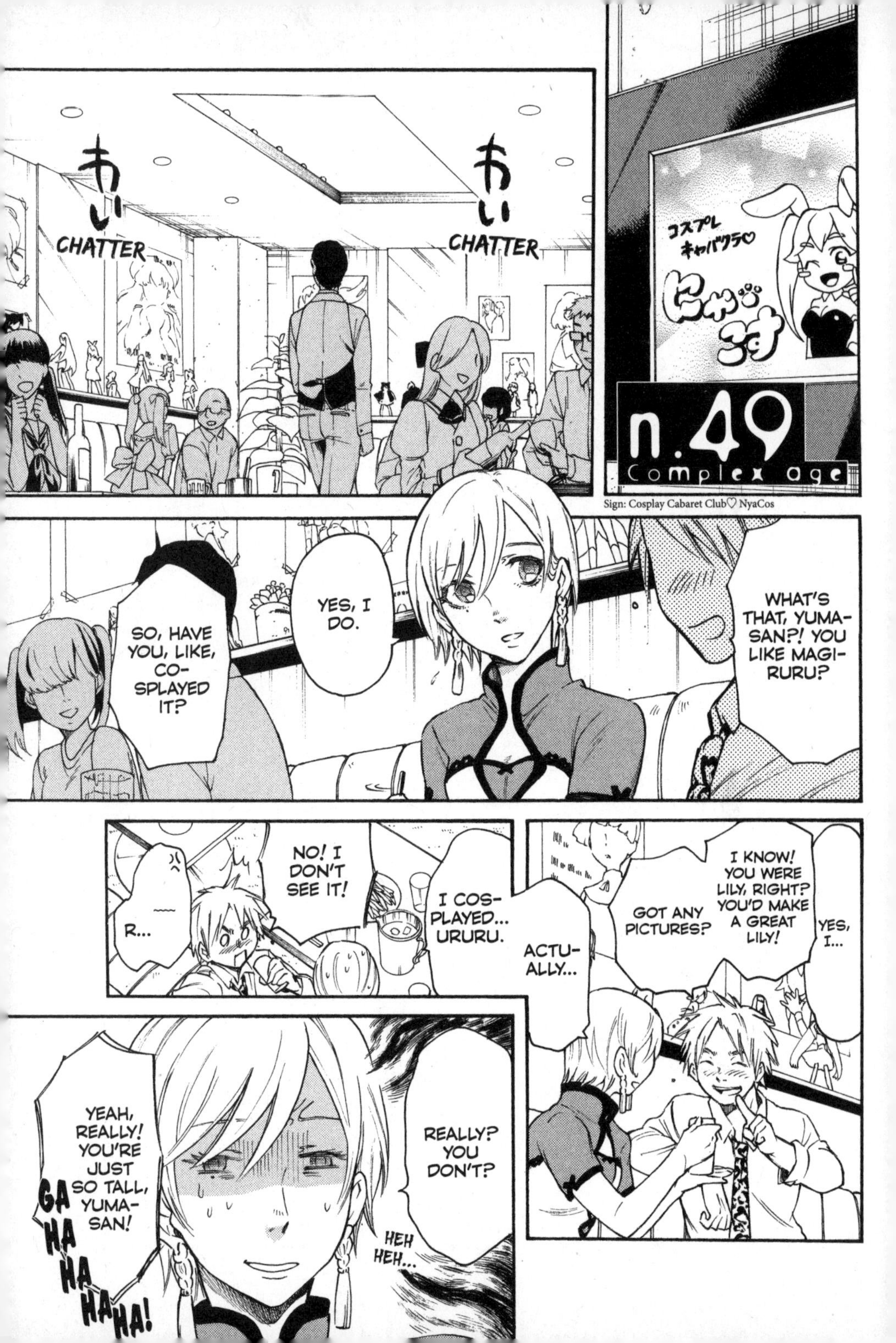

コスプレ キャバクラ♡
n.49
Complex age
Sign: Cosplay Cabaret Club♡ NyaCos
わい CHATTER
わい CHATTER
WHAT'S THAT, YUMA-SAN?! YOU LIKE MAGI-RURU?
YES, I DO.
SO, HAVE YOU, LIKE, CO-SPLAYED IT?
YES, I...
I KNOW! YOU WERE LILY, RIGHT? YOU'D MAKE A GREAT LILY!
GOT ANY PICTURES?
ACTU-ALLY...
I COS-PLAYED... URURU.
NO! I DON'T SEE IT!
R...
REALLY? YOU DON'T?
HEH HEH...
YEAH, REALLY! YOU'RE JUST SO TALL, YUMA-SAN!
GA HA HA HA HA!

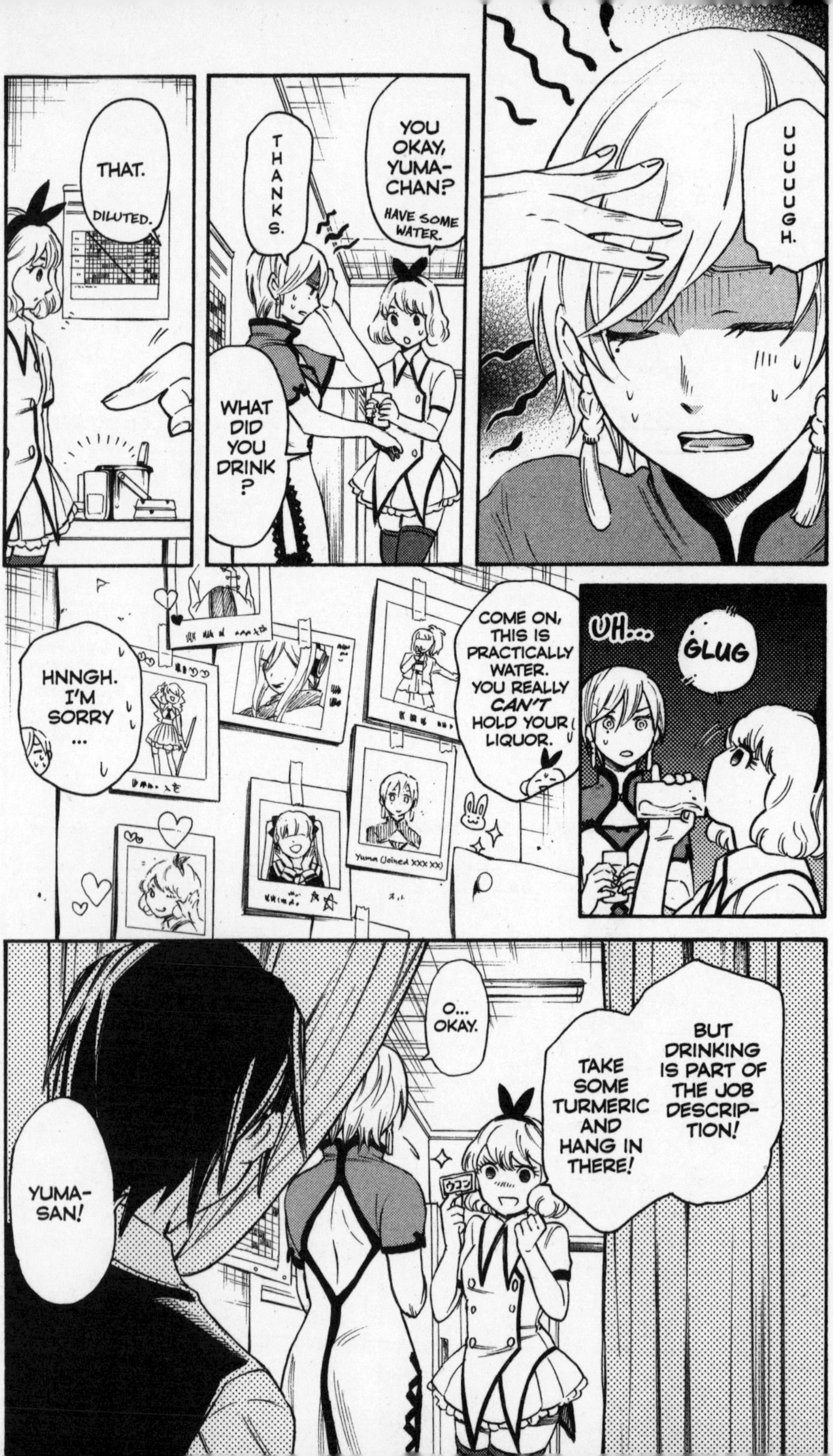
UUUUUGH.
YOU OKAY, YUMA-CHAN? HAVE SOME WATER.
THANKS.
WHAT DID YOU DRINK?
THAT.
DILUTED.
UH...
GLUG
COME ON, THIS IS PRACTICALLY WATER. YOU REALLY CAN'T HOLD YOUR LIQUOR.
HNNGH. I'M SORRY...
Yuma (Joined XXX XX)
BUT DRINKING IS PART OF THE JOB DESCRIPTION!
TAKE SOME TURMERIC AND HANG IN THERE!
ウコン
O... OKAY.
YUMA-SAN!

Label: Turmeric

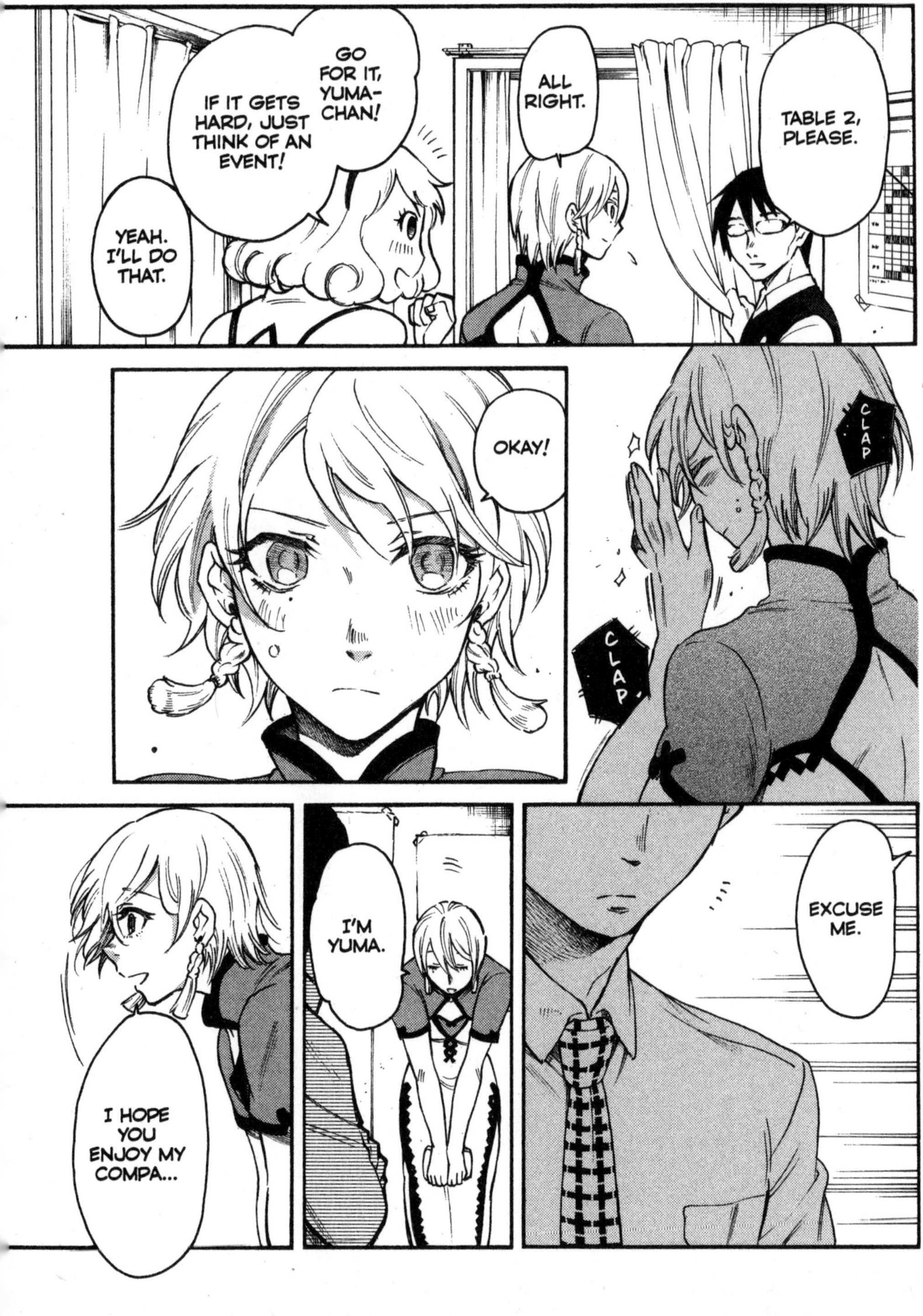
TABLE 2, PLEASE.
ALL RIGHT.
GO FOR IT, YUMA-CHAN!
IF IT GETS HARD, JUST THINK OF AN EVENT!
YEAH. I'LL DO THAT.
CLAP
CLAP
OKAY!
EXCUSE ME.
I'M YUMA.
I HOPE YOU ENJOY MY COMPA...

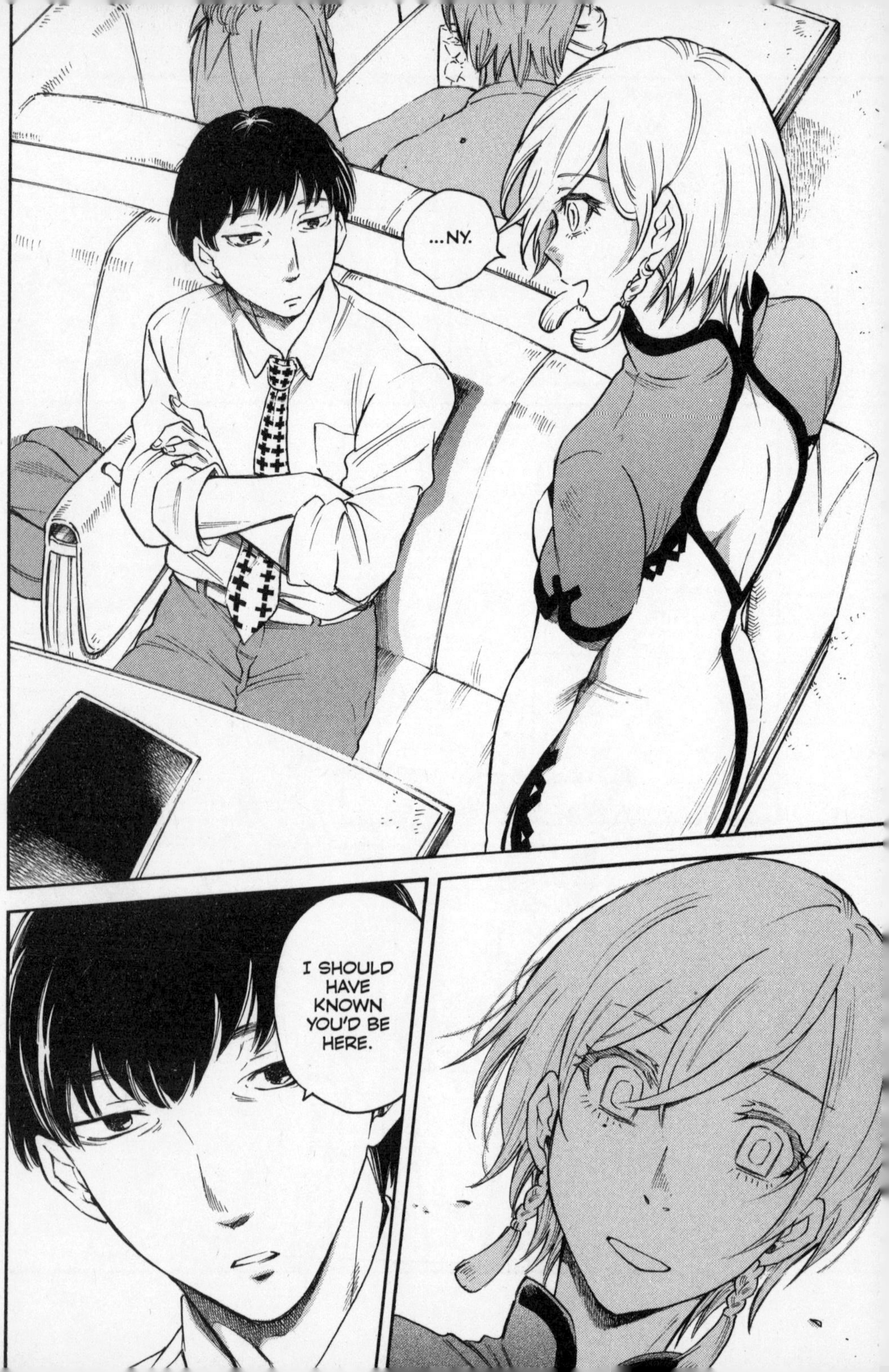
...NY.
I SHOULD HAVE KNOWN YOU'D BE HERE.

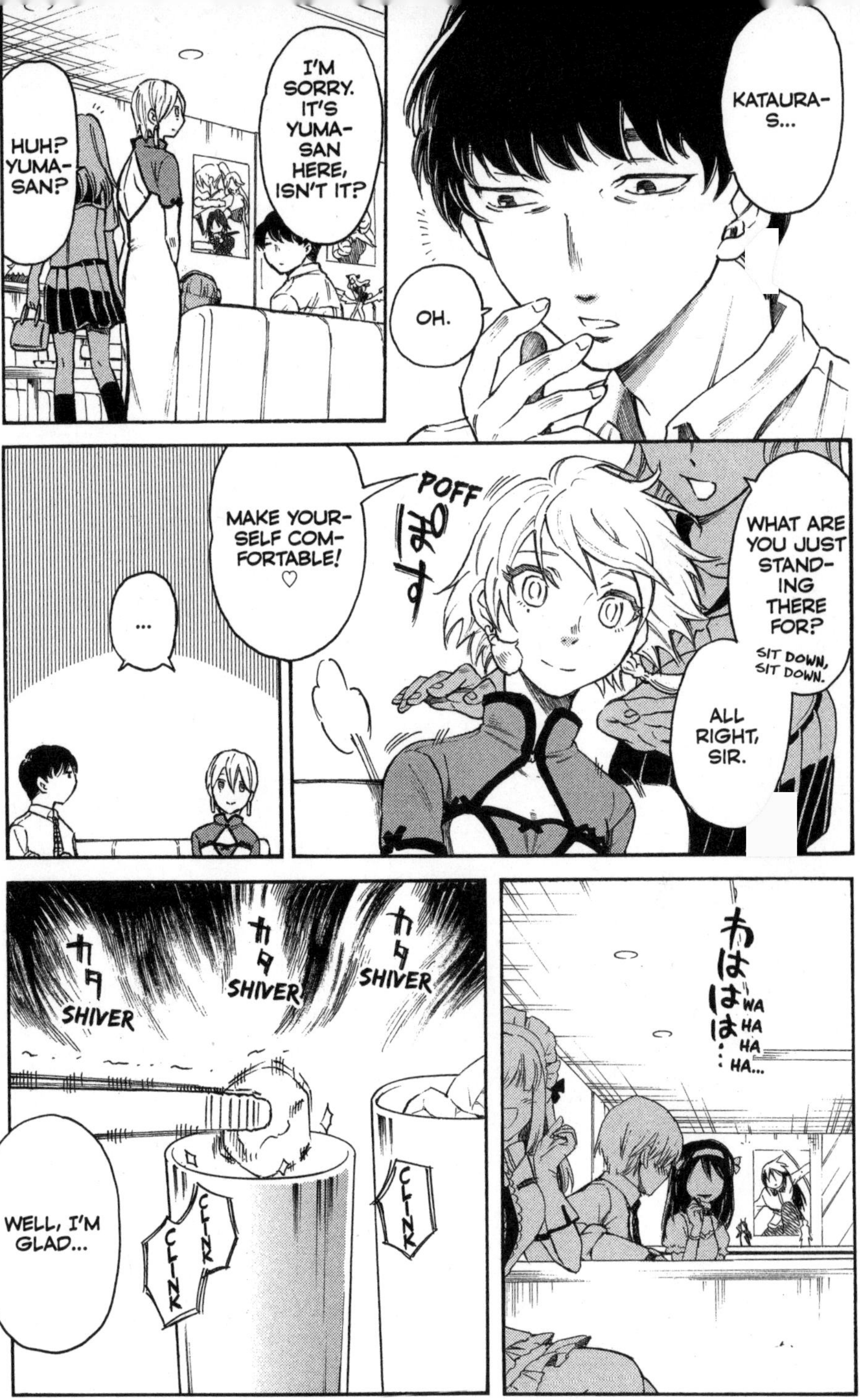
KATAURA-S...
OH.
I'M SORRY. IT'S YUMA-SAN HERE, ISN'T IT?
HUH? YUMA-SAN?
WHAT ARE YOU JUST STANDING THERE FOR?
SIT DOWN, SIT DOWN.
ALL RIGHT, SIR.
ぽす POFF
MAKE YOURSELF COMFORTABLE! ♡
...
わははは… WA HA HA HA...
カタ SHIVER
カタ SHIVER
カタ SHIVER
CLINK
CLINK CLINK
WELL, I'M GLAD...

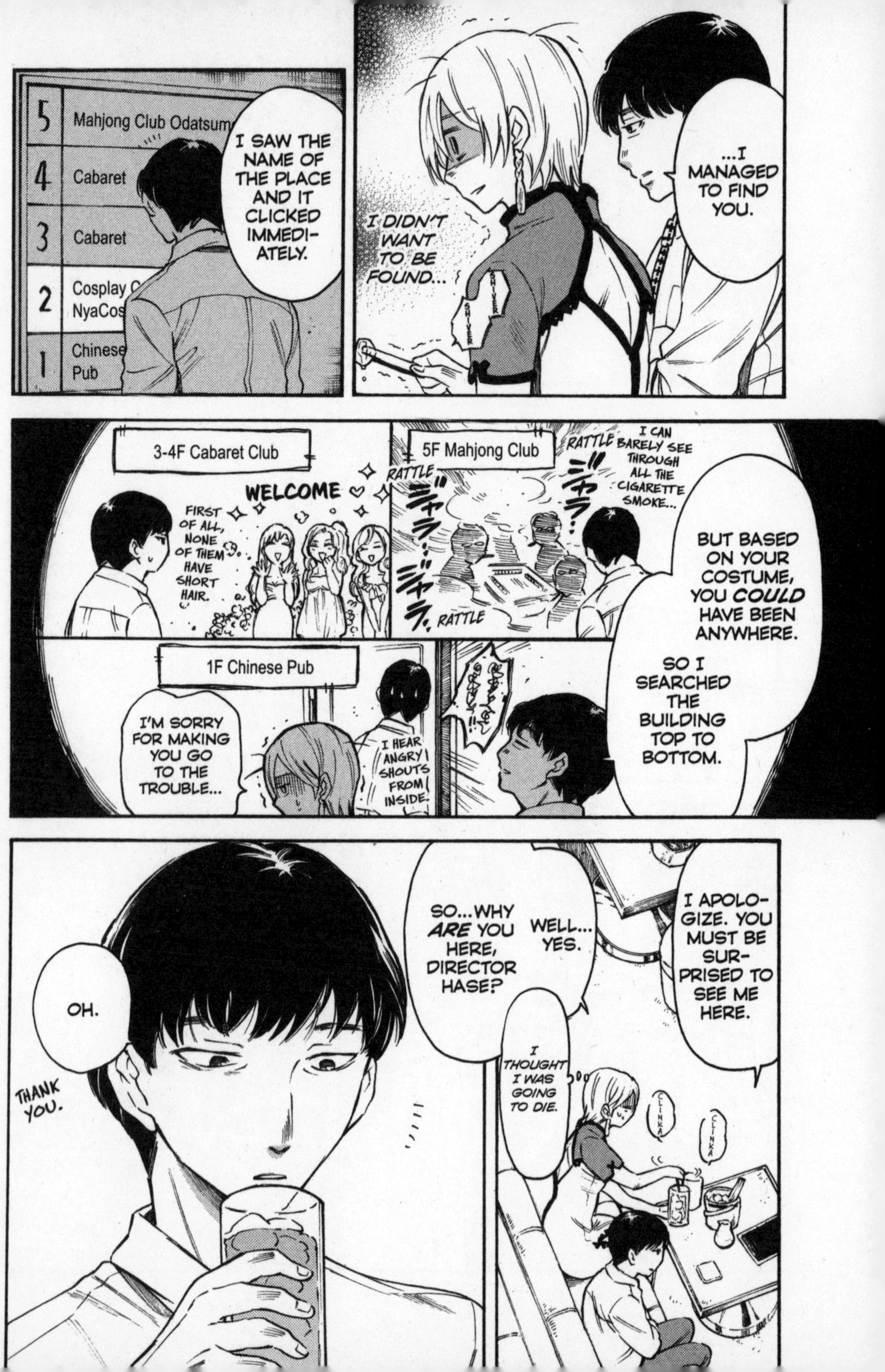
...I MANAGED TO FIND YOU.
I DIDN'T WANT TO BE FOUND...
SHIVER
SHIVER
5 Mahjong Club Odatsum
4 Cabaret
3 Cabaret
2 Cosplay C NyaCos
1 Chinese Pub
I SAW THE NAME OF THE PLACE AND IT CLICKED IMMEDIATELY.
BUT BASED ON YOUR COSTUME, YOU *COULD* HAVE BEEN ANYWHERE.
SO I SEARCHED THE BUILDING TOP TO BOTTOM.
5F Mahjong Club
RATTLE
I CAN BARELY SEE THROUGH ALL THE CIGARETTE SMOKE...
RATTLE
RATTLE
3-4F Cabaret Club
WELCOME
FIRST OF ALL, NONE OF THEM HAVE SHORT HAIR.
I HEAR ANGRY SHOUTS FROM INSIDE.
1F Chinese Pub
I'M SORRY FOR MAKING YOU GO TO THE TROUBLE...
I APOLOGIZE. YOU MUST BE SURPRISED TO SEE ME HERE.
WELL... YES.
SO...WHY *ARE* YOU HERE, DIRECTOR HASE?
I THOUGHT I WAS GOING TO DIE.
CLINKA
CLINKA
OH.
THANK YOU.

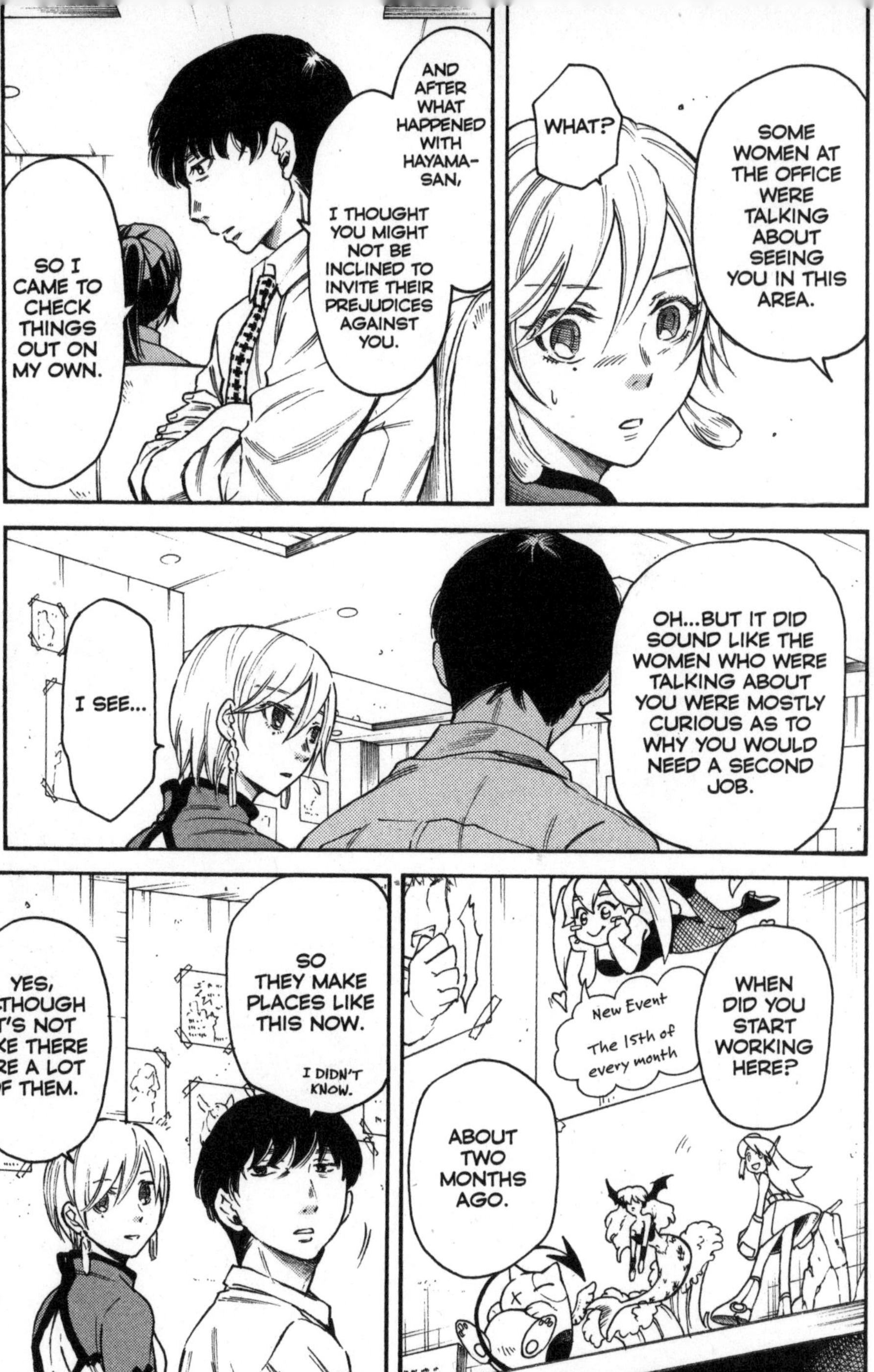
SOME WOMEN AT THE OFFICE WERE TALKING ABOUT SEEING YOU IN THIS AREA.
WHAT?
AND AFTER WHAT HAPPENED WITH HAYAMA-SAN,
I THOUGHT YOU MIGHT NOT BE INCLINED TO INVITE THEIR PREJUDICES AGAINST YOU.
SO I CAME TO CHECK THINGS OUT ON MY OWN.
OH...BUT IT DID SOUND LIKE THE WOMEN WHO WERE TALKING ABOUT YOU WERE MOSTLY CURIOUS AS TO WHY YOU WOULD NEED A SECOND JOB.
I SEE...
WHEN DID YOU START WORKING HERE?
New Event
The 15th of every month
ABOUT TWO MONTHS AGO.
SO THEY MAKE PLACES LIKE THIS NOW.
I DIDN'T KNOW.
YES, ALTHOUGH IT'S NOT LIKE THERE ARE A LOT OF THEM.

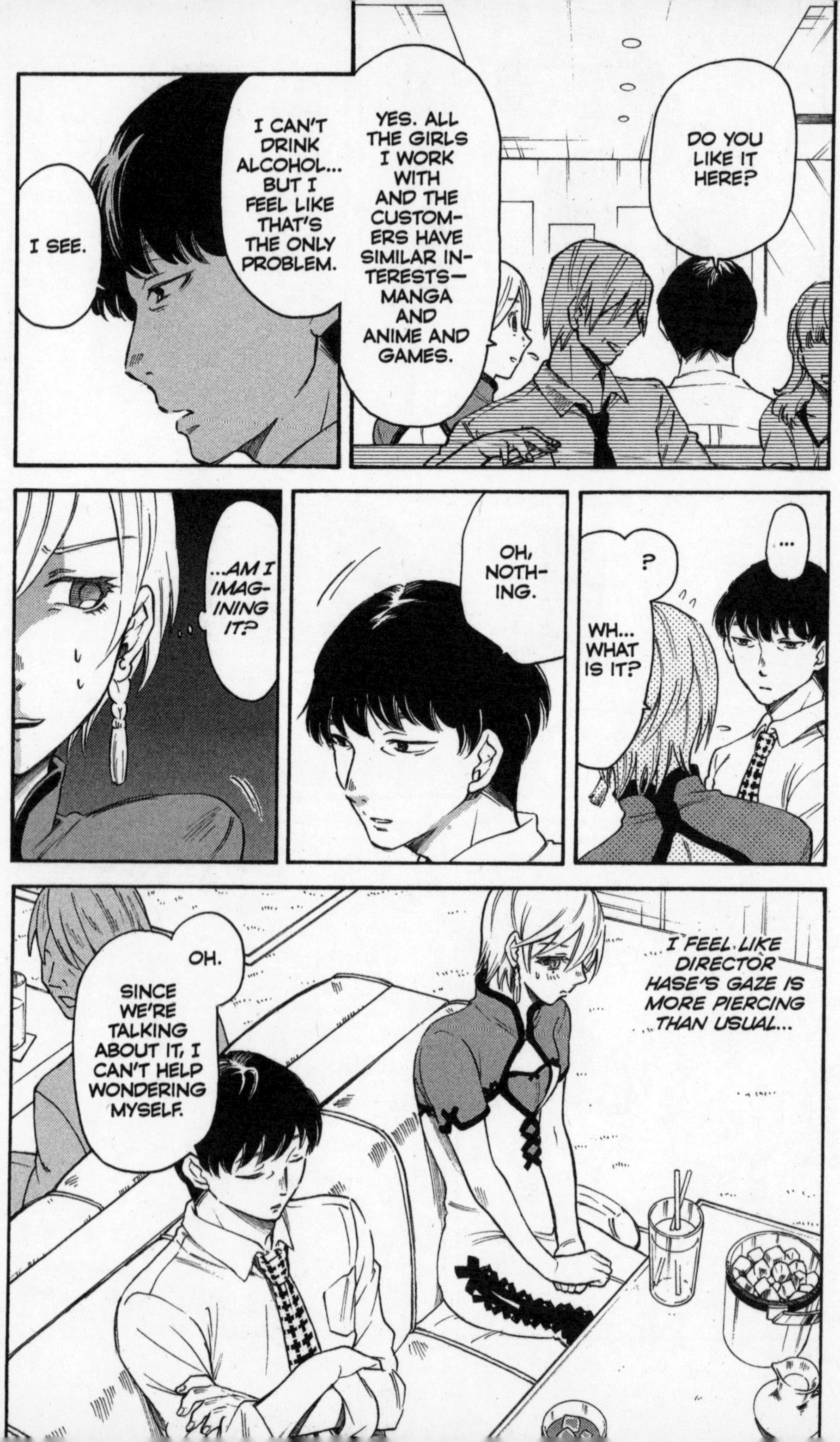
DO YOU LIKE IT HERE?
YES. ALL THE GIRLS I WORK WITH AND THE CUSTOMERS HAVE SIMILAR INTERESTS—MANGA AND ANIME AND GAMES.
I CAN'T DRINK ALCOHOL... BUT I FEEL LIKE THAT'S THE ONLY PROBLEM.
I SEE.
...
?
WH... WHAT IS IT?
OH, NOTHING.
...AM I IMAGINING IT?
I FEEL LIKE DIRECTOR HASE'S GAZE IS MORE PIERCING THAN USUAL...
OH.
SINCE WE'RE TALKING ABOUT IT, I CAN'T HELP WONDERING MYSELF.

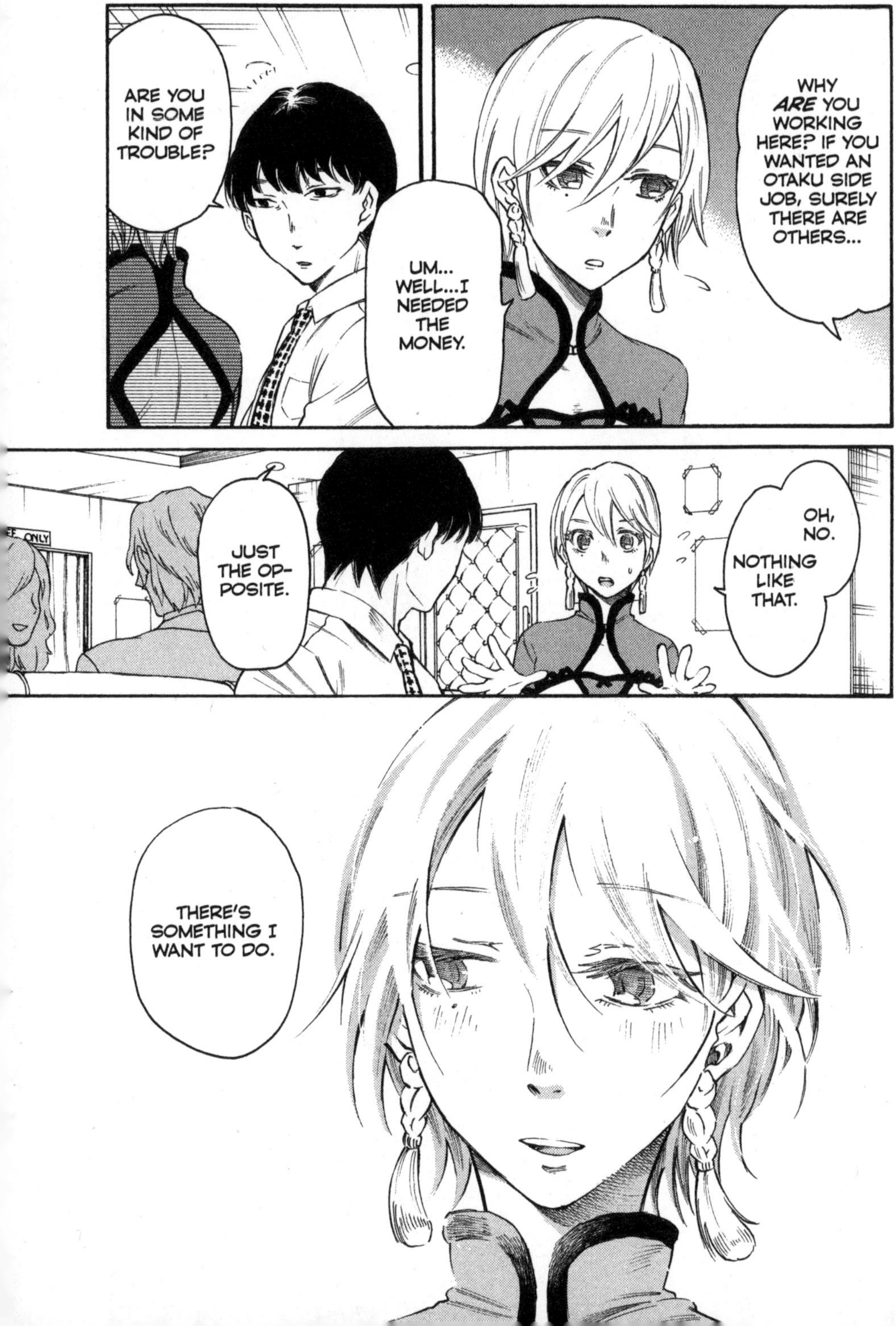
WHY *ARE* YOU WORKING HERE? IF YOU WANTED AN OTAKU SIDE JOB, SURELY THERE ARE OTHERS...
UM... WELL...I NEEDED THE MONEY.
ARE YOU IN SOME KIND OF TROUBLE?
OH, NO.
NOTHING LIKE THAT.
JUST THE OP-POSITE.
THERE'S SOMETHING I WANT TO DO.

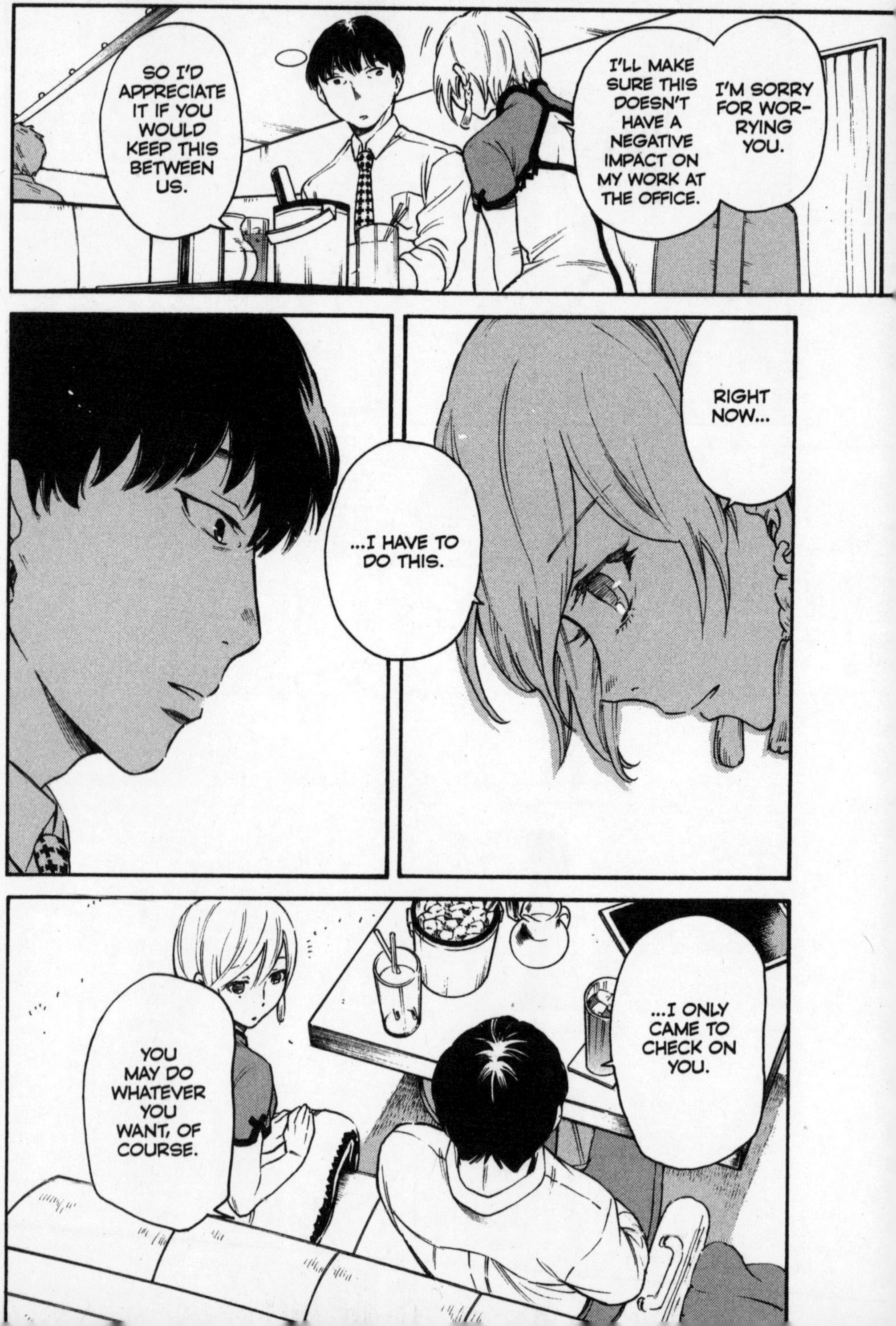
I'M SORRY FOR WOR-RYING YOU.
I'LL MAKE SURE THIS DOESN'T HAVE A NEGATIVE IMPACT ON MY WORK AT THE OFFICE.
SO I'D APPRECIATE IT IF YOU WOULD KEEP THIS BETWEEN US.
RIGHT NOW...
...I HAVE TO DO THIS.
...I ONLY CAME TO CHECK ON YOU.
YOU MAY DO WHATEVER YOU WANT, OF COURSE.

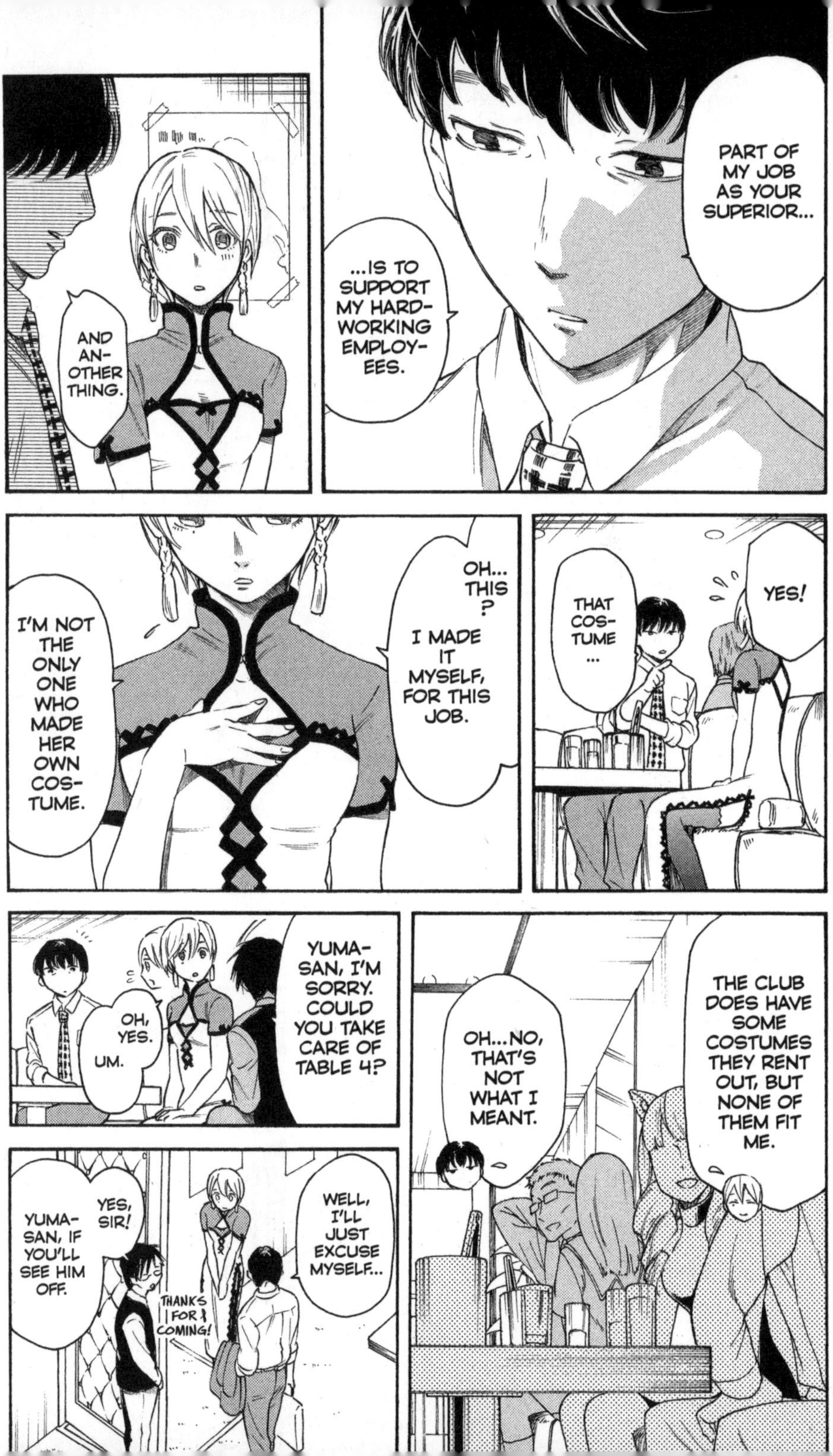
PART OF MY JOB AS YOUR SUPERIOR...
...IS TO SUPPORT MY HARD-WORKING EMPLOYEES.
AND ANOTHER THING.
YES!
THAT COSTUME...
OH... THIS?
I MADE IT MYSELF, FOR THIS JOB.
I'M NOT THE ONLY ONE WHO MADE HER OWN COSTUME.
THE CLUB DOES HAVE SOME COSTUMES THEY RENT OUT, BUT NONE OF THEM FIT ME.
OH...NO, THAT'S NOT WHAT I MEANT.
YUMA-SAN, I'M SORRY. COULD YOU TAKE CARE OF TABLE 4?
OH, YES.
UM.
WELL, I'LL JUST EXCUSE MYSELF...
THANKS FOR COMING!
YES, SIR!
YUMA-SAN, IF YOU'LL SEE HIM OFF.

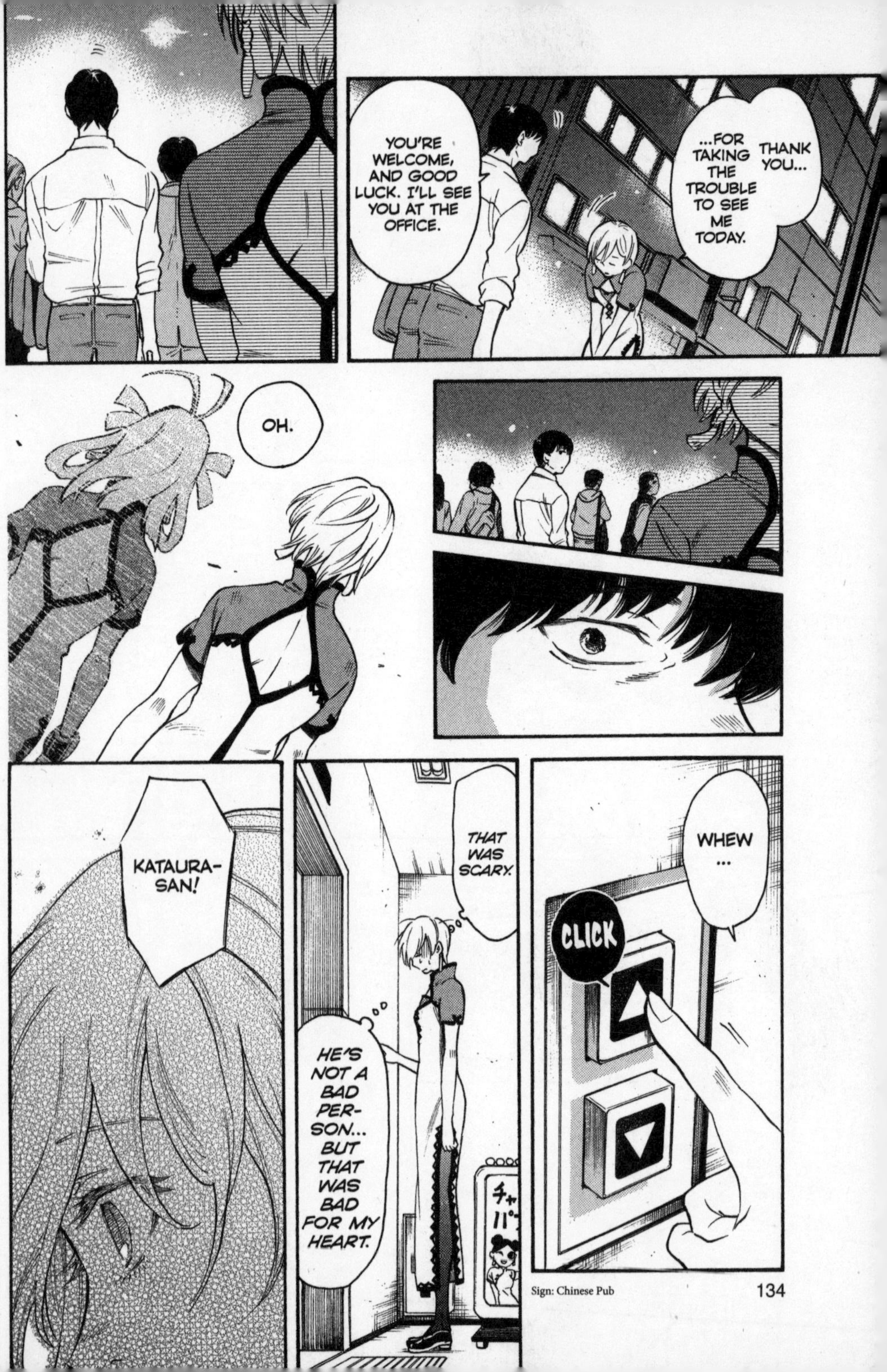
THANK YOU...
...FOR TAKING THE TROUBLE TO SEE ME TODAY.
YOU'RE WELCOME, AND GOOD LUCK. I'LL SEE YOU AT THE OFFICE.
OH.
WHEW ...
CLICK
THAT WAS SCARY.
HE'S NOT A BAD PER-SON... BUT THAT WAS BAD FOR MY HEART.
KATAURA-SAN!

Sign: Chinese Pub

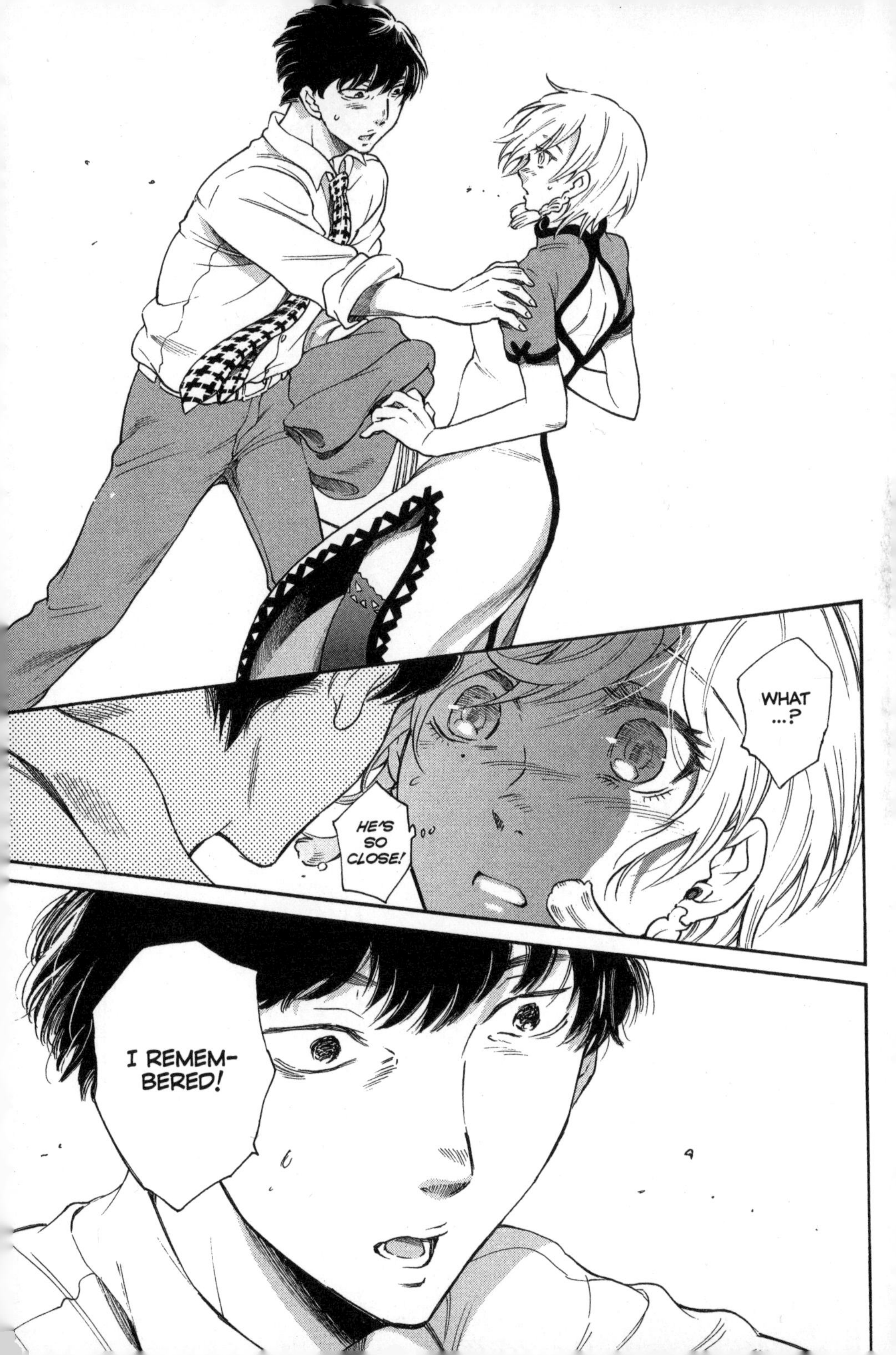
WHAT ...?
HE'S SO CLOSE!
I REMEMBERED!

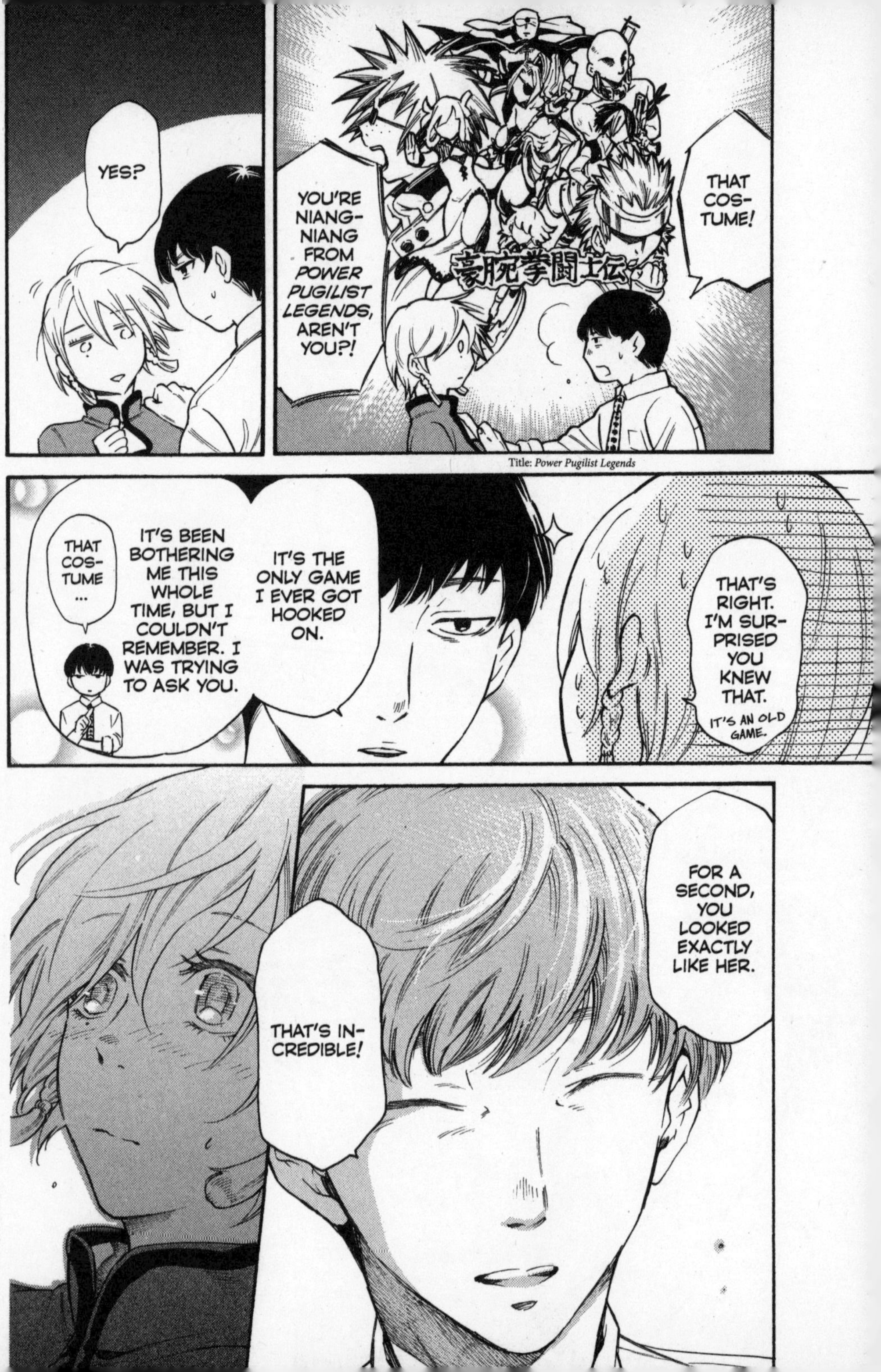
THAT COS-TUME!
YOU'RE NIANG-NIANG FROM *POWER PUGILIST LEGENDS*, AREN'T YOU?!
豪腕死拳闘士伝
YES?
Title: *Power Pugilist Legends*
THAT'S RIGHT. I'M SUR-PRISED YOU KNEW THAT.
IT'S AN OLD GAME.
IT'S THE ONLY GAME I EVER GOT HOOKED ON.
IT'S BEEN BOTHERING ME THIS WHOLE TIME, BUT I COULDN'T REMEMBER. I WAS TRYING TO ASK YOU.
THAT COS-TUME ...
FOR A SECOND, YOU LOOKED EXACTLY LIKE HER.
THAT'S IN-CREDIBLE!

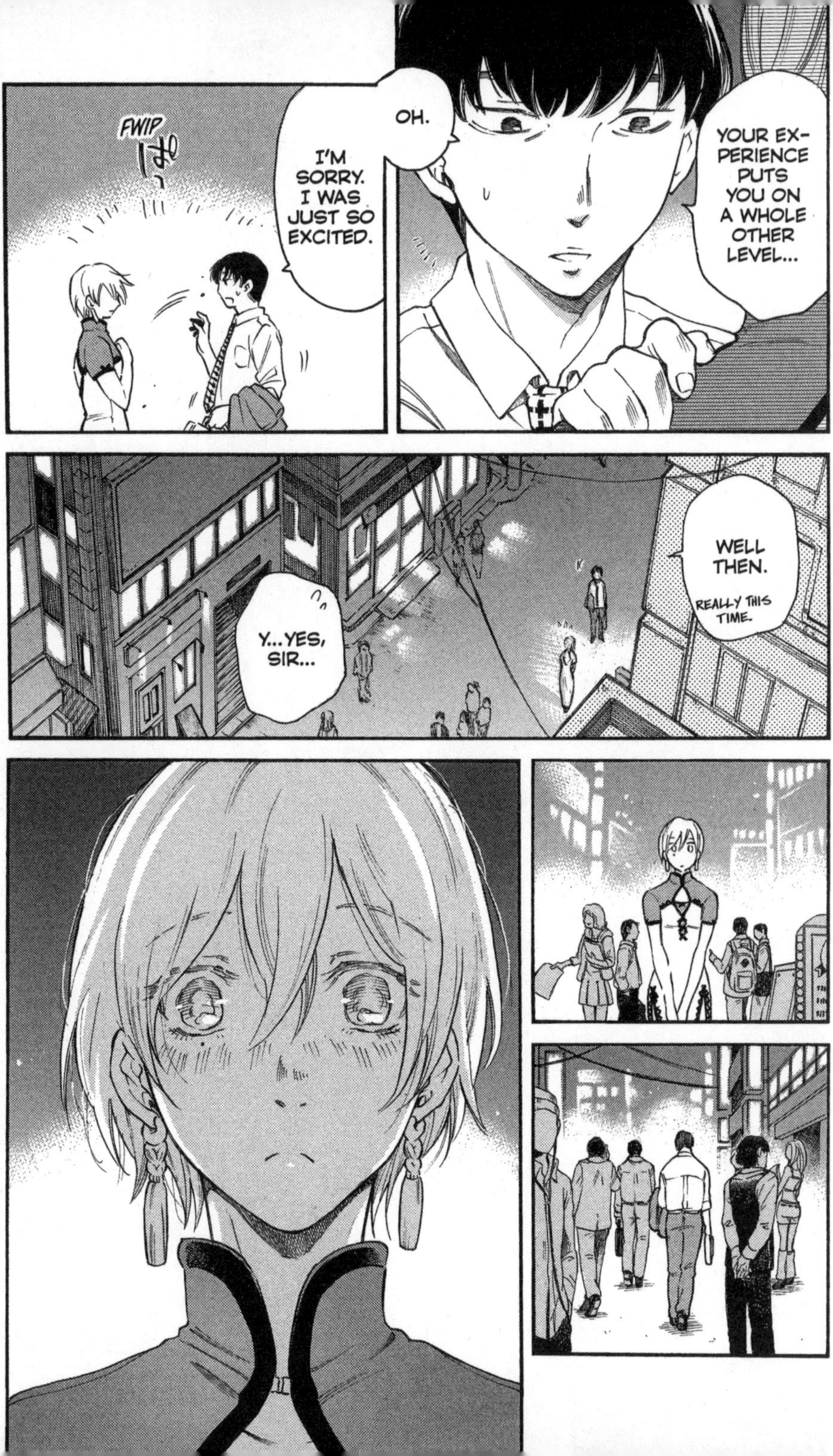
YOUR EX-PERIENCE PUTS YOU ON A WHOLE OTHER LEVEL...
OH.
FWIP ぱっ
I'M SORRY. I WAS JUST SO EXCITED.
WELL THEN.
REALLY THIS TIME.
Y...YES, SIR...

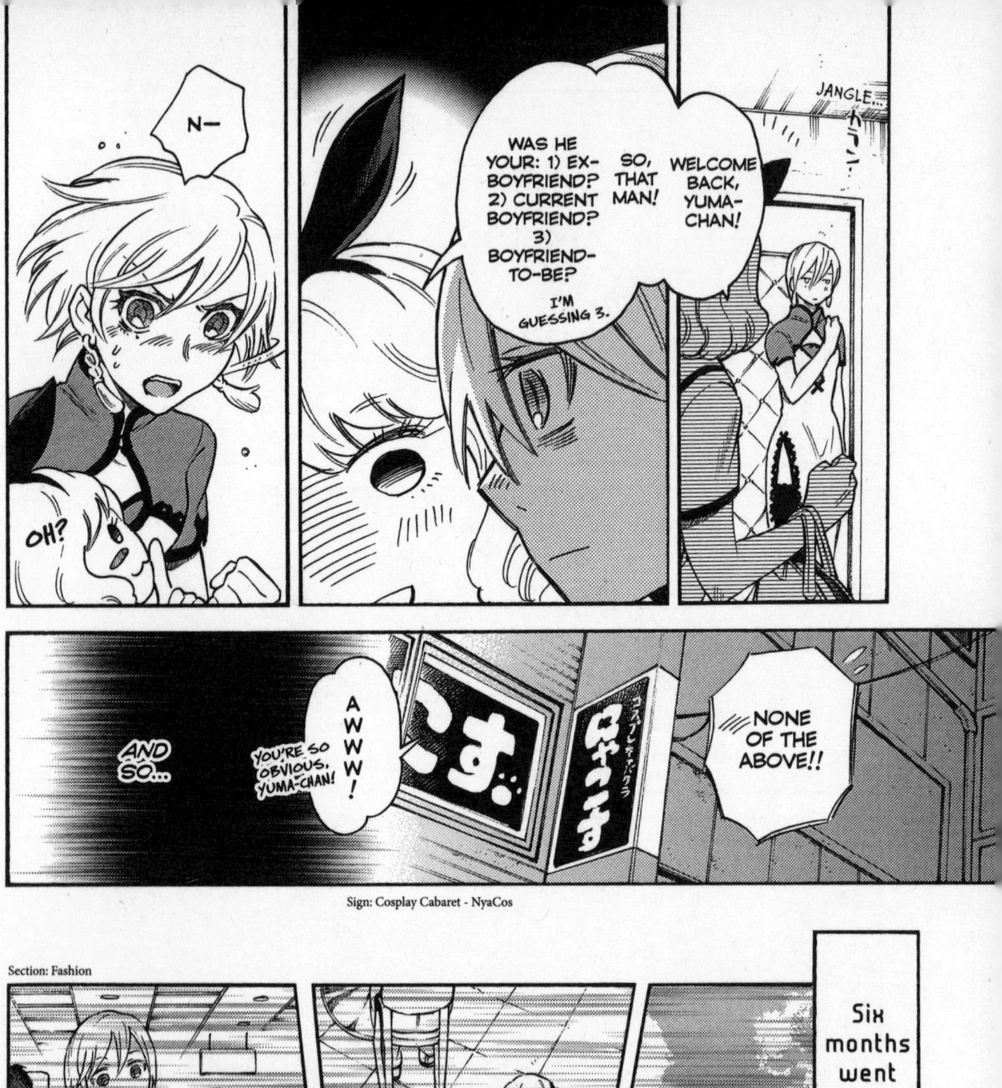
JANGLE...
WELCOME BACK, YUMA-CHAN!
SO, THAT MAN!
WAS HE YOUR: 1) EX-BOYFRIEND? 2) CURRENT BOYFRIEND? 3) BOYFRIEND-TO-BE?
I'M GUESSING 3.
N—
OH?
NONE OF THE ABOVE!!
AWWW!
YOU'RE SO OBVIOUS, YUMA-CHAN!
AND SO...

Sign: Cosplay Cabaret - NyaCos

Section: Fashion

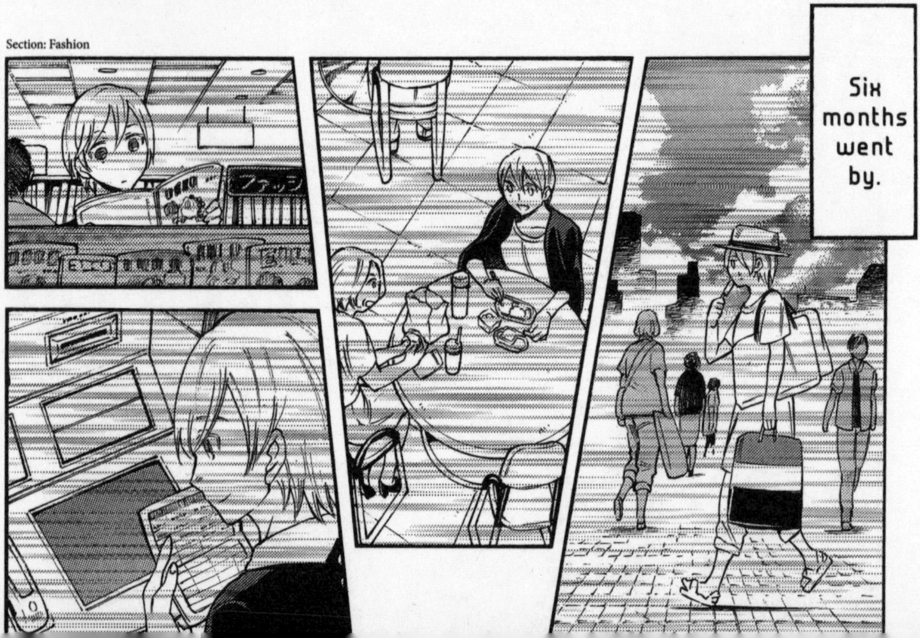
Six months went by.

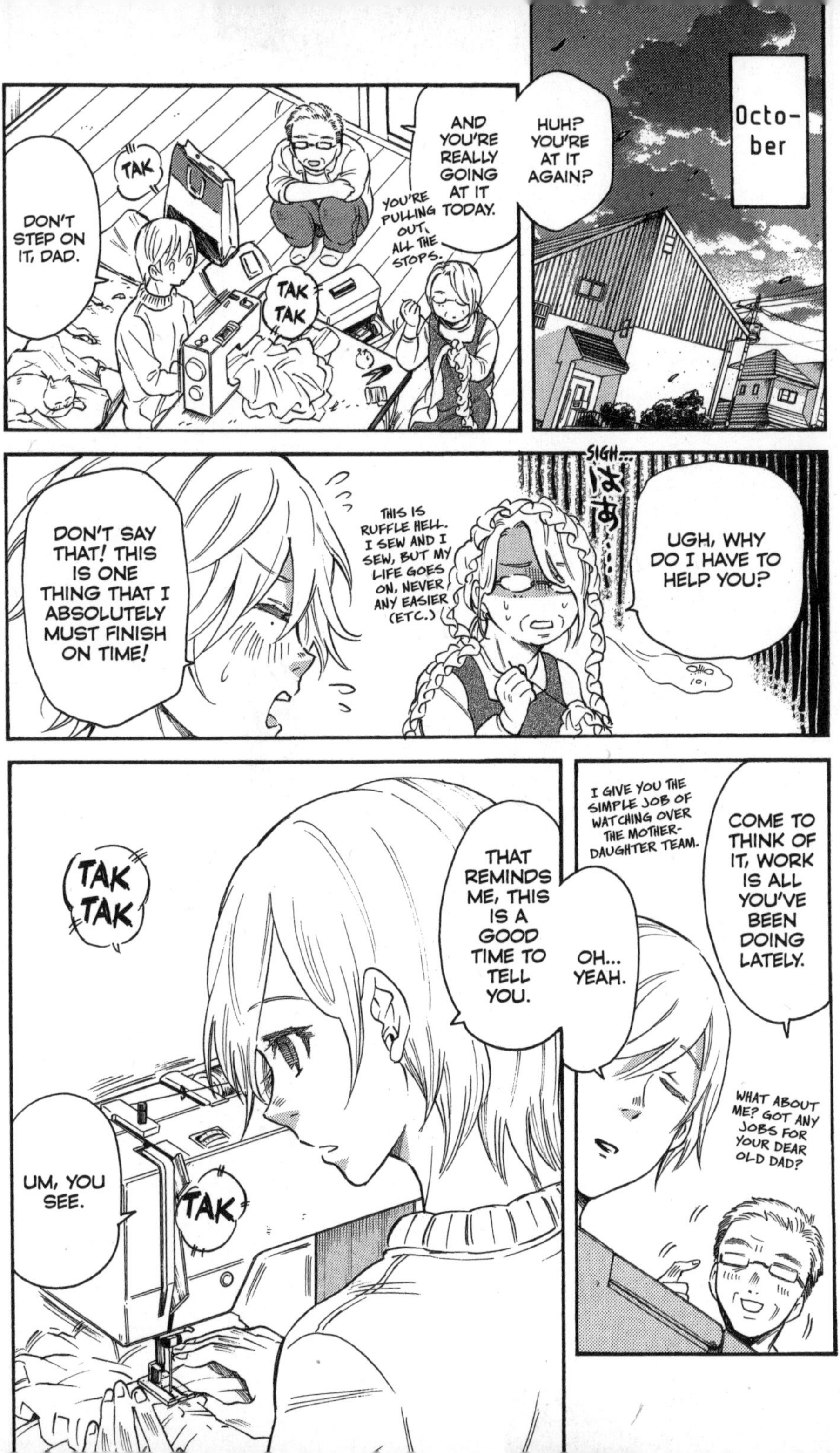
October
HUH? YOU'RE AT IT AGAIN?
AND YOU'RE REALLY GOING AT IT TODAY.
YOU'RE PULLING OUT, ALL THE STOPS.
TAK TAK
TAK
DON'T STEP ON IT, DAD.
SIGH... はあ・・・
UGH, WHY DO I HAVE TO HELP YOU?
THIS IS RUFFLE HELL. I SEW AND I SEW, BUT MY LIFE GOES ON, NEVER ANY EASIER (ETC.)
DON'T SAY THAT! THIS IS ONE THING THAT I ABSOLUTELY MUST FINISH ON TIME!
COME TO THINK OF IT, WORK IS ALL YOU'VE BEEN DOING LATELY.
I GIVE YOU THE SIMPLE JOB OF WATCHING OVER THE MOTHER-DAUGHTER TEAM.
OH... YEAH.
WHAT ABOUT ME? GOT ANY JOBS FOR YOUR DEAR OLD DAD?
THAT REMINDS ME, THIS IS A GOOD TIME TO TELL YOU.
TAK TAK
TAK
UM, YOU SEE.

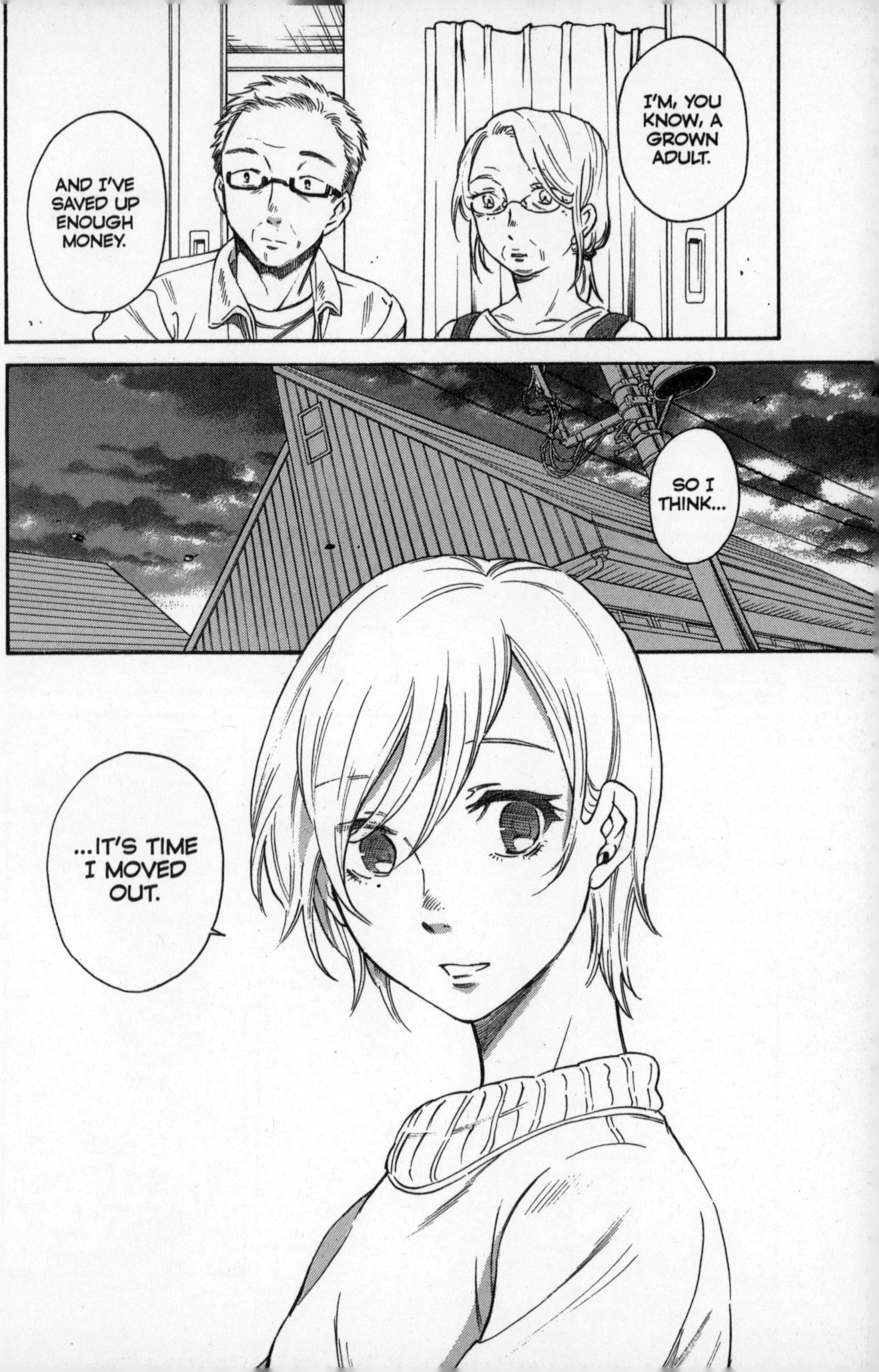
I'M, YOU KNOW, A GROWN ADULT.
AND I'VE SAVED UP ENOUGH MONEY.
SO I THINK...
...IT'S TIME I MOVED OUT.

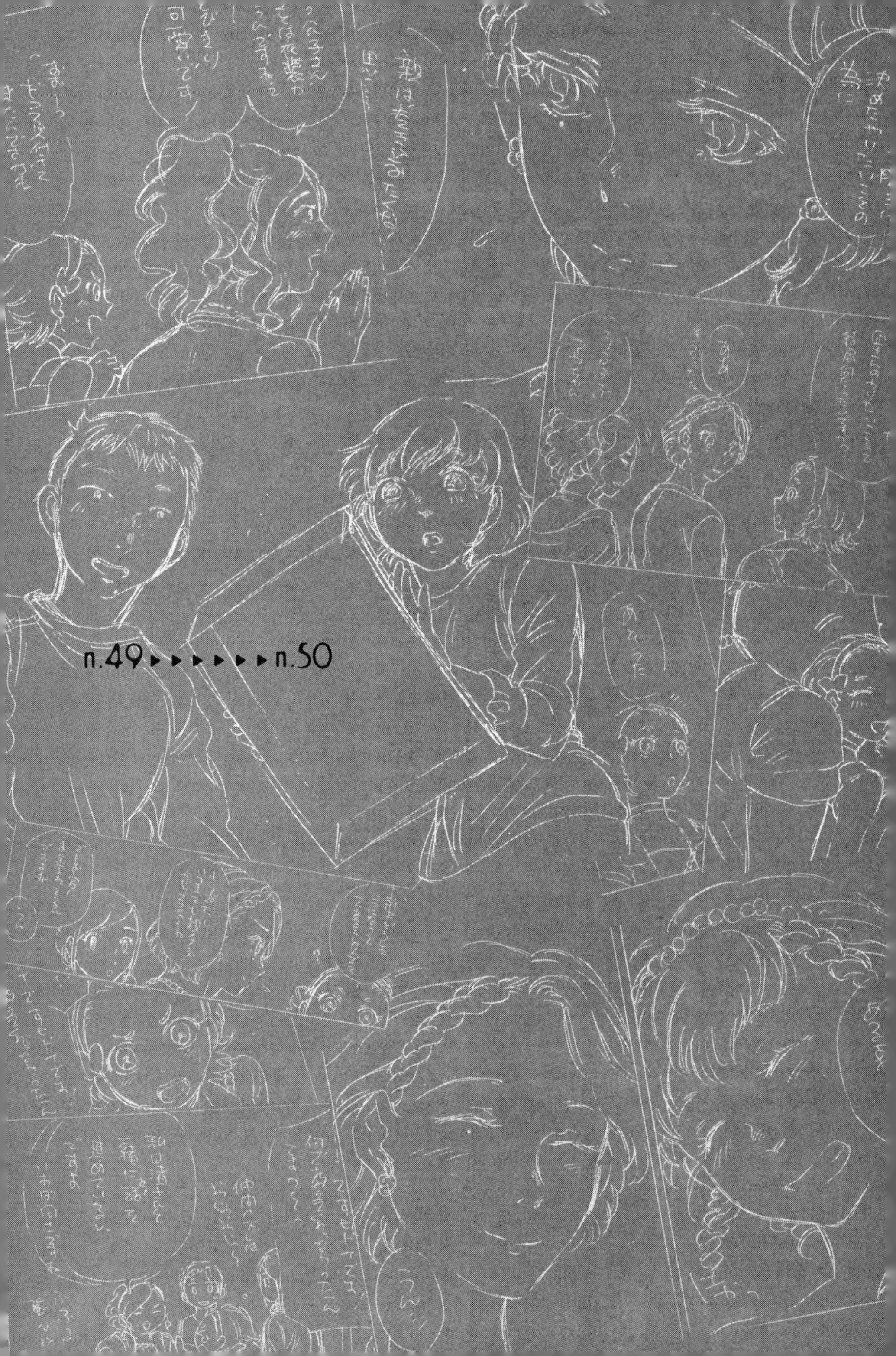
n.49▸▸▸▸▸▸▸n.50

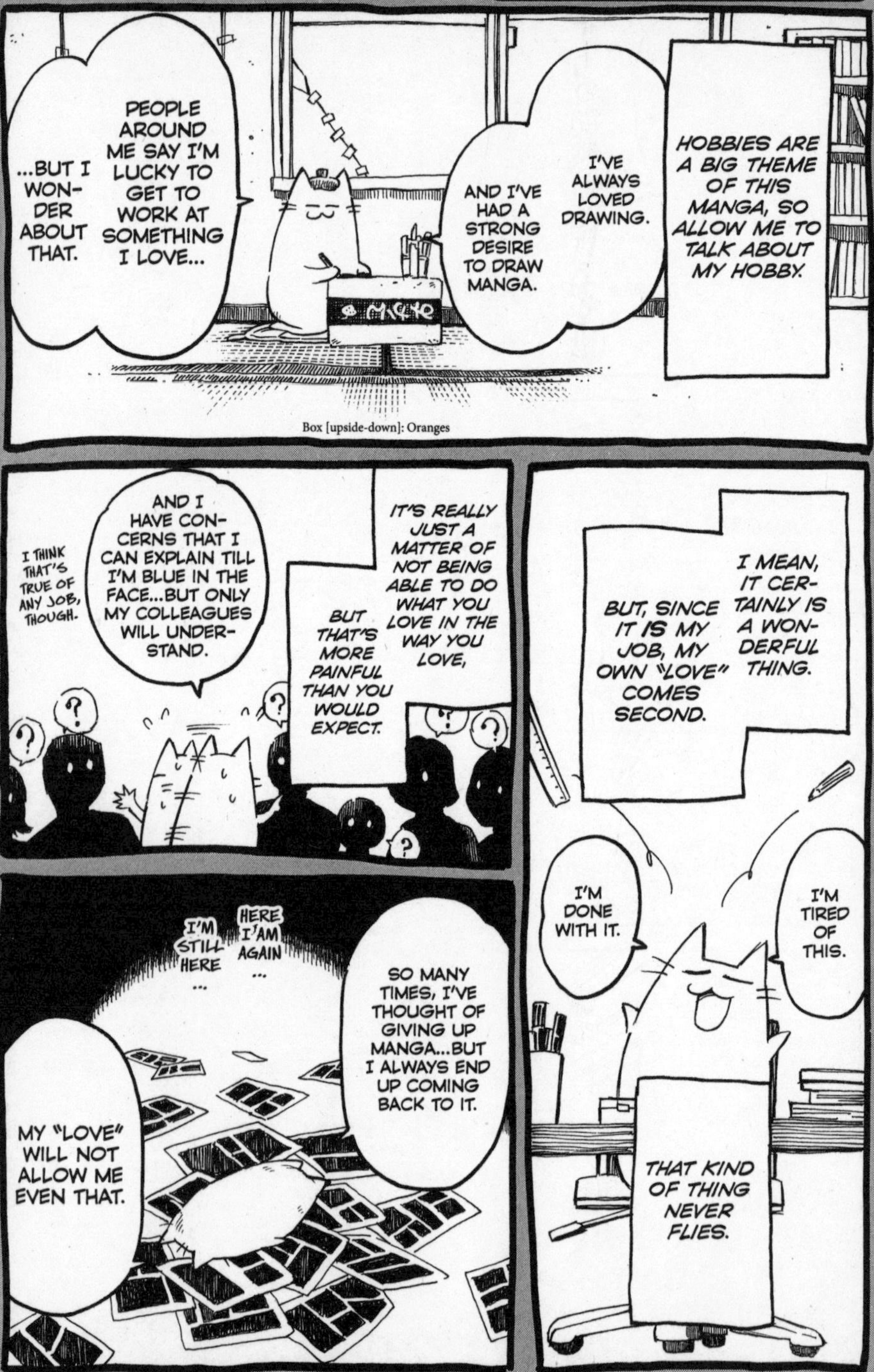
HOBBIES ARE A BIG THEME OF THIS MANGA, SO ALLOW ME TO TALK ABOUT MY HOBBY.
I'VE ALWAYS LOVED DRAWING.
AND I'VE HAD A STRONG DESIRE TO DRAW MANGA.
PEOPLE AROUND ME SAY I'M LUCKY TO GET TO WORK AT SOMETHING I LOVE...
...BUT I WONDER ABOUT THAT.
I MEAN, IT CERTAINLY IS A WONDERFUL THING.
BUT, SINCE IT *IS* MY JOB, MY OWN "LOVE" COMES SECOND.
I'M TIRED OF THIS.
I'M DONE WITH IT.
THAT KIND OF THING NEVER FLIES.
IT'S REALLY JUST A MATTER OF NOT BEING ABLE TO DO WHAT YOU LOVE IN THE WAY YOU LOVE,
BUT THAT'S MORE PAINFUL THAN YOU WOULD EXPECT.
AND I HAVE CONCERNS THAT I CAN EXPLAIN TILL I'M BLUE IN THE FACE...BUT ONLY MY COLLEAGUES WILL UNDERSTAND.
I THINK THAT'S TRUE OF ANY JOB, THOUGH.
SO MANY TIMES, I'VE THOUGHT OF GIVING UP MANGA...BUT I ALWAYS END UP COMING BACK TO IT.
HERE I AM AGAIN...
I'M STILL HERE...
MY "LOVE" WILL NOT ALLOW ME EVEN THAT.

Box [upside-down]: Oranges

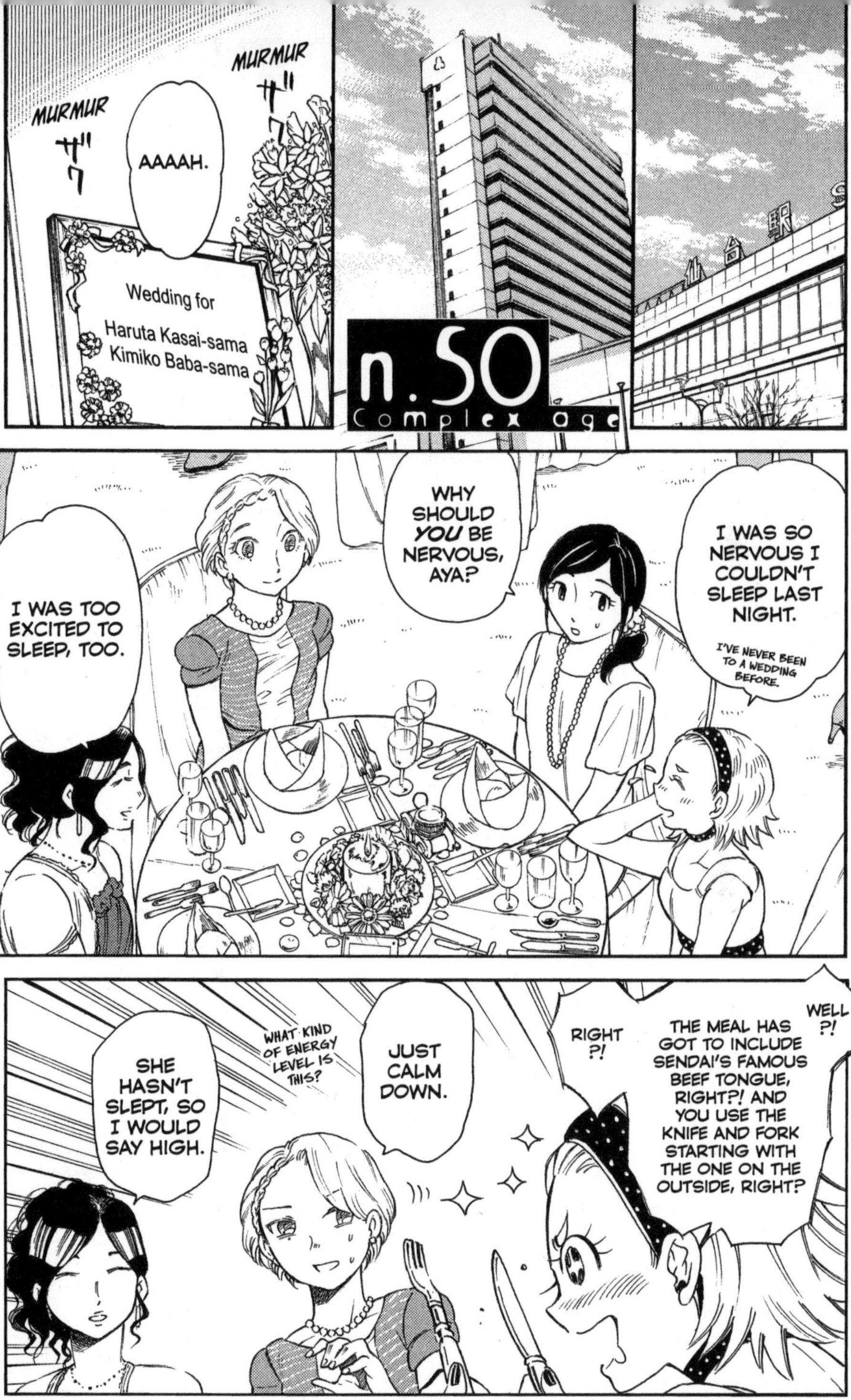
n.50
Complex age
MURMUR
AAAAH.
MURMUR
Wedding for
Haruta Kasai-sama
Kimiko Baba-sama
I WAS SO NERVOUS I COULDN'T SLEEP LAST NIGHT.
I'VE NEVER BEEN TO A WEDDING BEFORE.
WHY SHOULD *YOU* BE NERVOUS, AYA?
I WAS TOO EXCITED TO SLEEP, TOO.
WELL ?!
THE MEAL HAS GOT TO INCLUDE SENDAI'S FAMOUS BEEF TONGUE, RIGHT?! AND YOU USE THE KNIFE AND FORK STARTING WITH THE ONE ON THE OUTSIDE, RIGHT?
RIGHT ?!
JUST CALM DOWN.
WHAT KIND OF ENERGY LEVEL IS THIS?
SHE HASN'T SLEPT, SO I WOULD SAY HIGH.

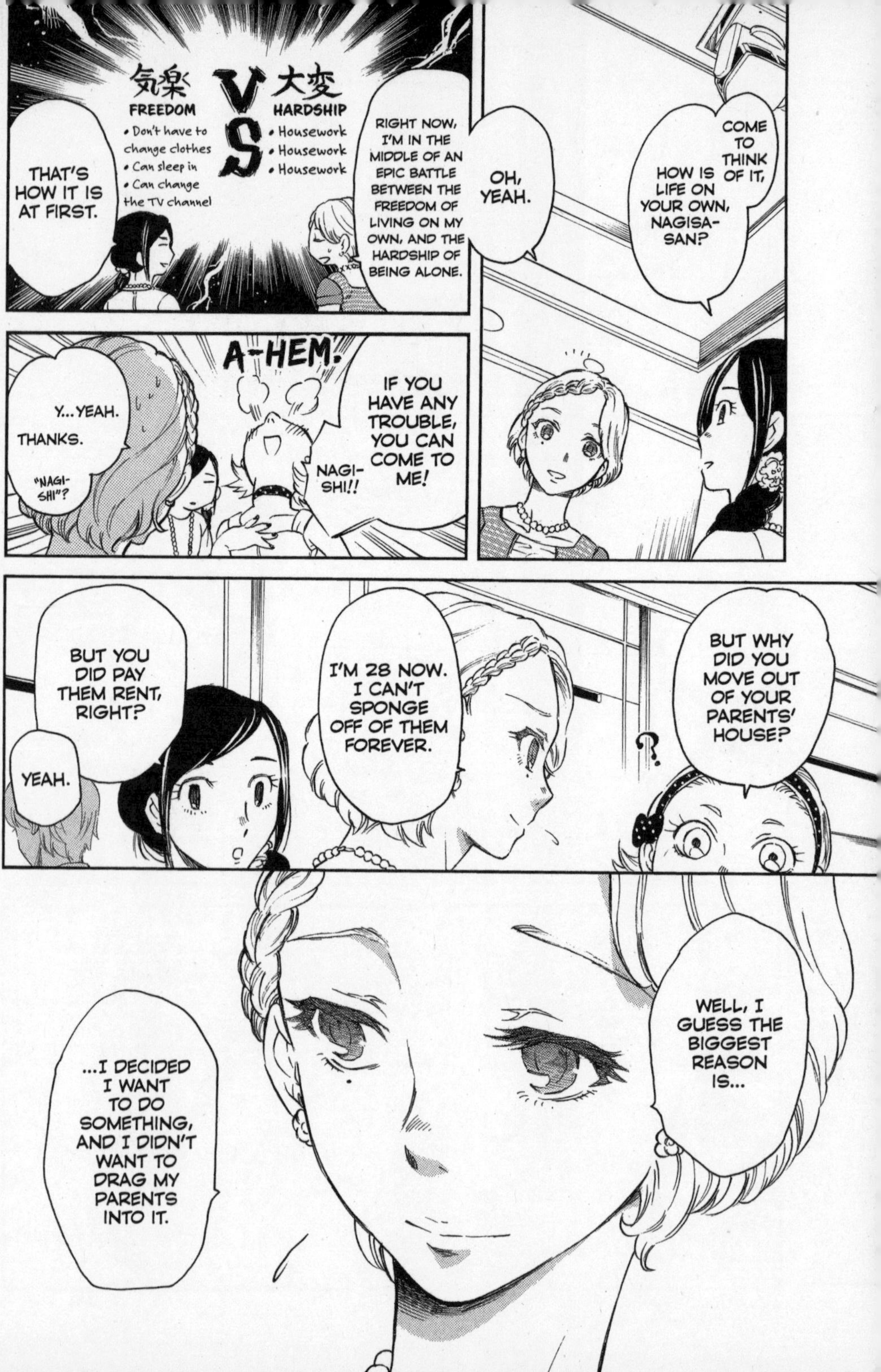
COME TO THINK OF IT,
HOW IS LIFE ON YOUR OWN, NAGISA-SAN?
OH, YEAH.
RIGHT NOW, I'M IN THE MIDDLE OF AN EPIC BATTLE BETWEEN THE FREEDOM OF LIVING ON MY OWN, AND THE HARDSHIP OF BEING ALONE.
大変 HARDSHIP
• Housework • Housework • Housework
VS
気楽 FREEDOM
• Don't have to change clothes • Can sleep in • Can change the TV channel
THAT'S HOW IT IS AT FIRST.
A-HEM!
IF YOU HAVE ANY TROUBLE, YOU CAN COME TO ME!
NAGI-SHI!!
Y...YEAH.
THANKS.
"NAGI-SHI"?
BUT WHY DID YOU MOVE OUT OF YOUR PARENTS' HOUSE?
?
I'M 28 NOW. I CAN'T SPONGE OFF OF THEM FOREVER.
BUT YOU DID PAY THEM RENT, RIGHT?
YEAH.
WELL, I GUESS THE BIGGEST REASON IS...
...I DECIDED I WANT TO DO SOMETHING, AND I DIDN'T WANT TO DRAG MY PARENTS INTO IT.

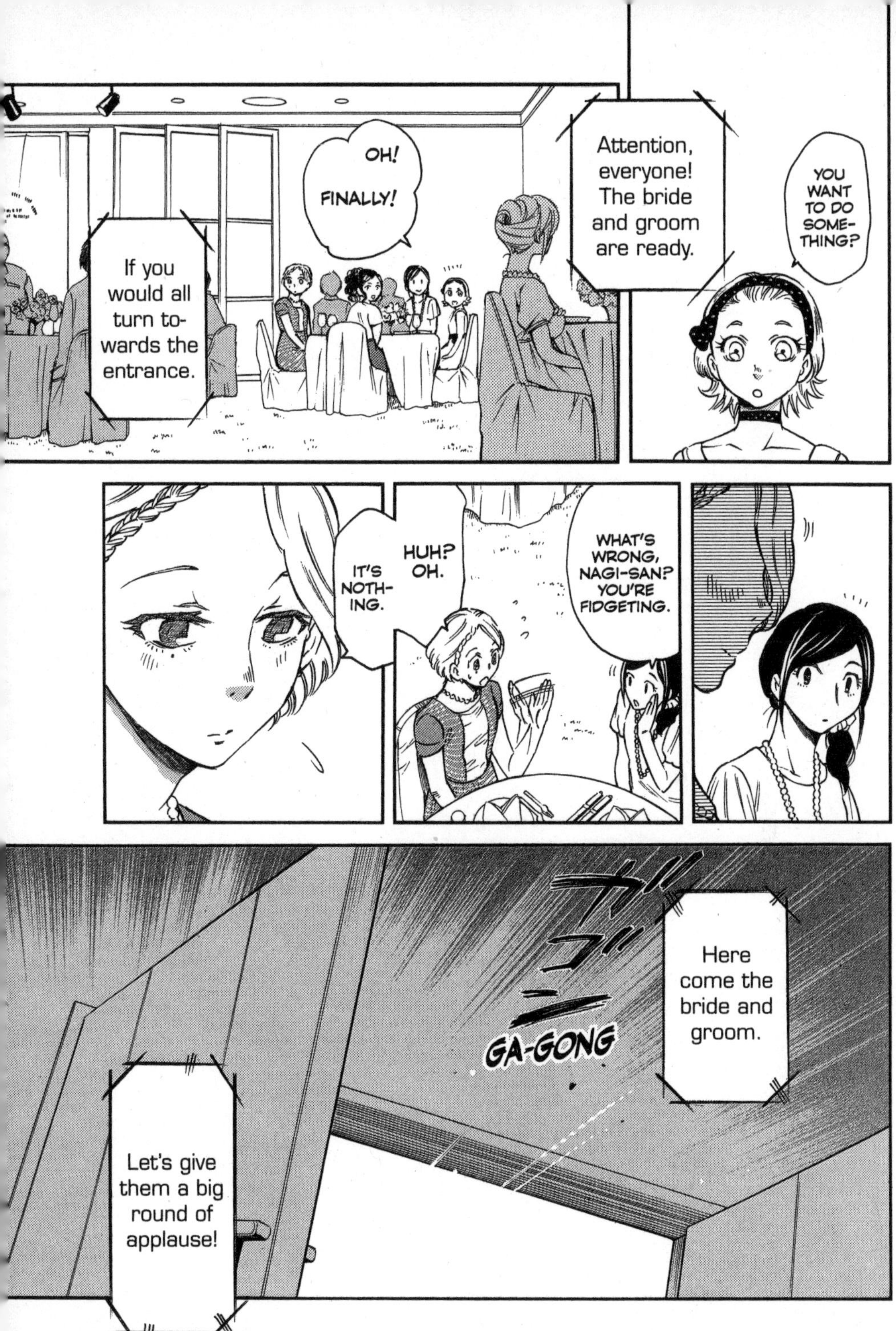
Attention, everyone! The bride and groom are ready.
YOU WANT TO DO SOME-THING?
OH!
FINALLY!
If you would all turn to-wards the entrance.
WHAT'S WRONG, NAGI-SAN? YOU'RE FIDGETING.
HUH? OH.
IT'S NOTH-ING.
Here come the bride and groom.
GA-GONG
Let's give them a big round of applause!

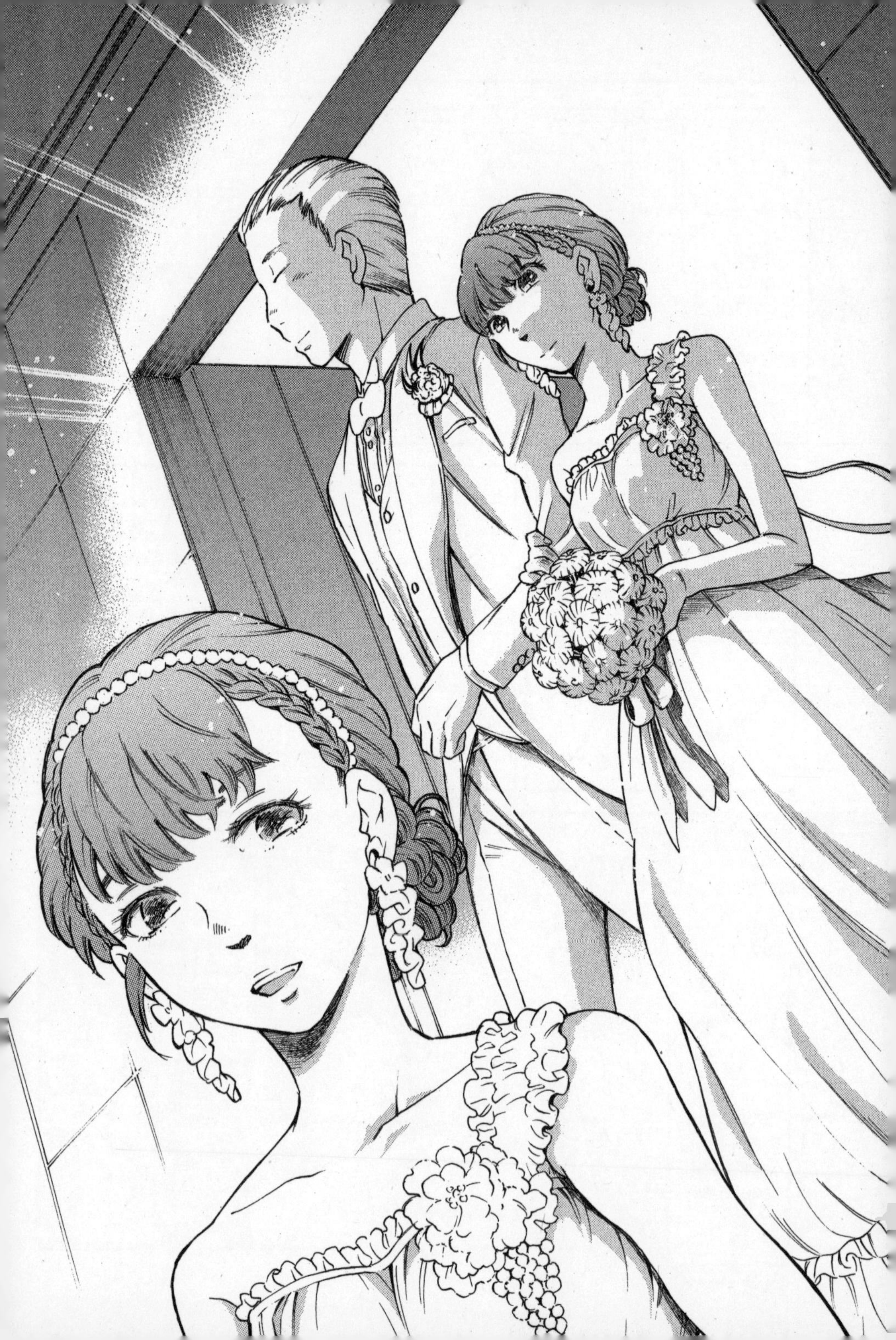

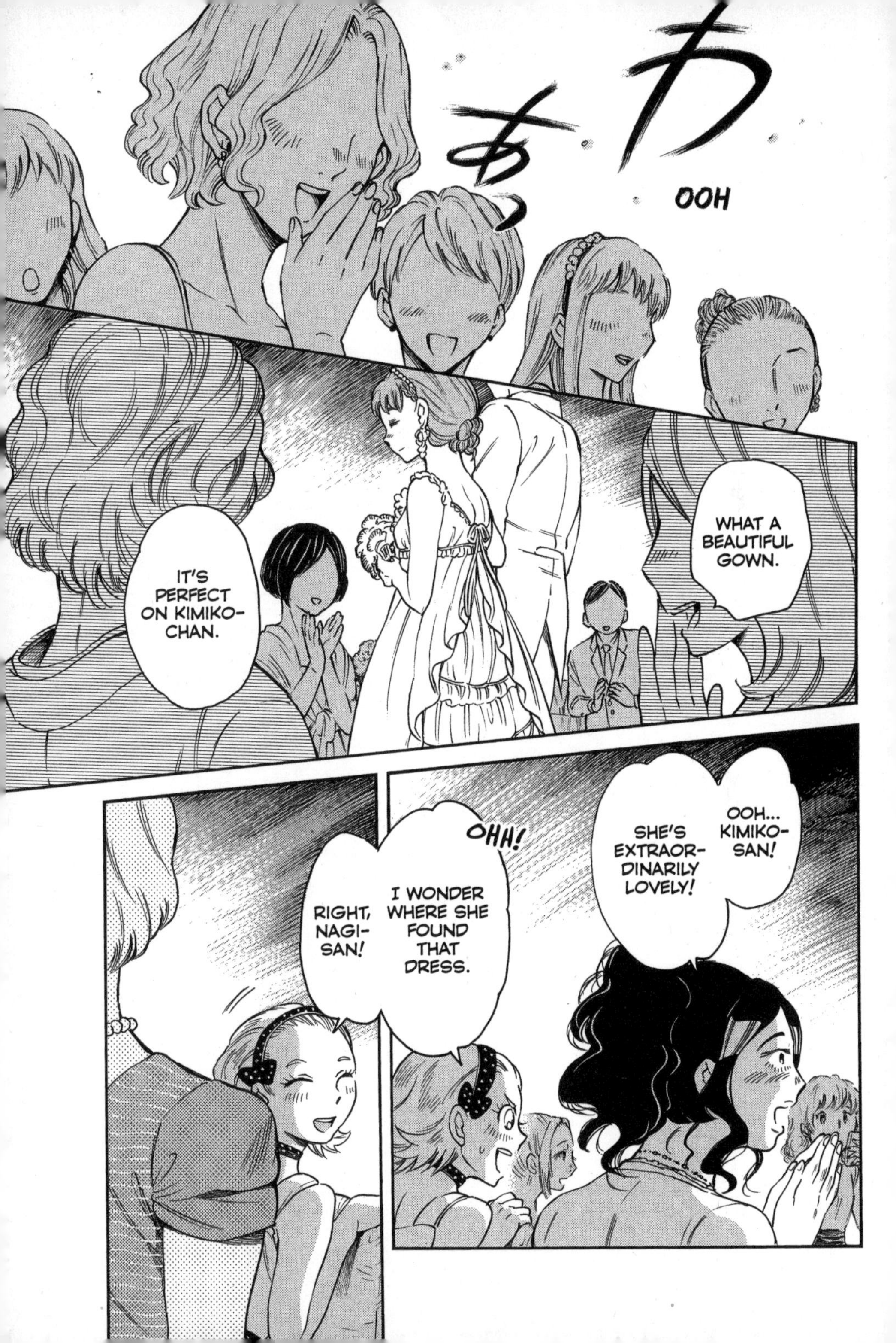
OOH
WHAT A BEAUTIFUL GOWN.
IT'S PERFECT ON KIMIKO-CHAN.
OOH... KIMIKO-SAN!
SHE'S EXTRAORDINARILY LOVELY!
OHH!
I WONDER WHERE SHE FOUND THAT DRESS.
RIGHT, NAGI-SAN!

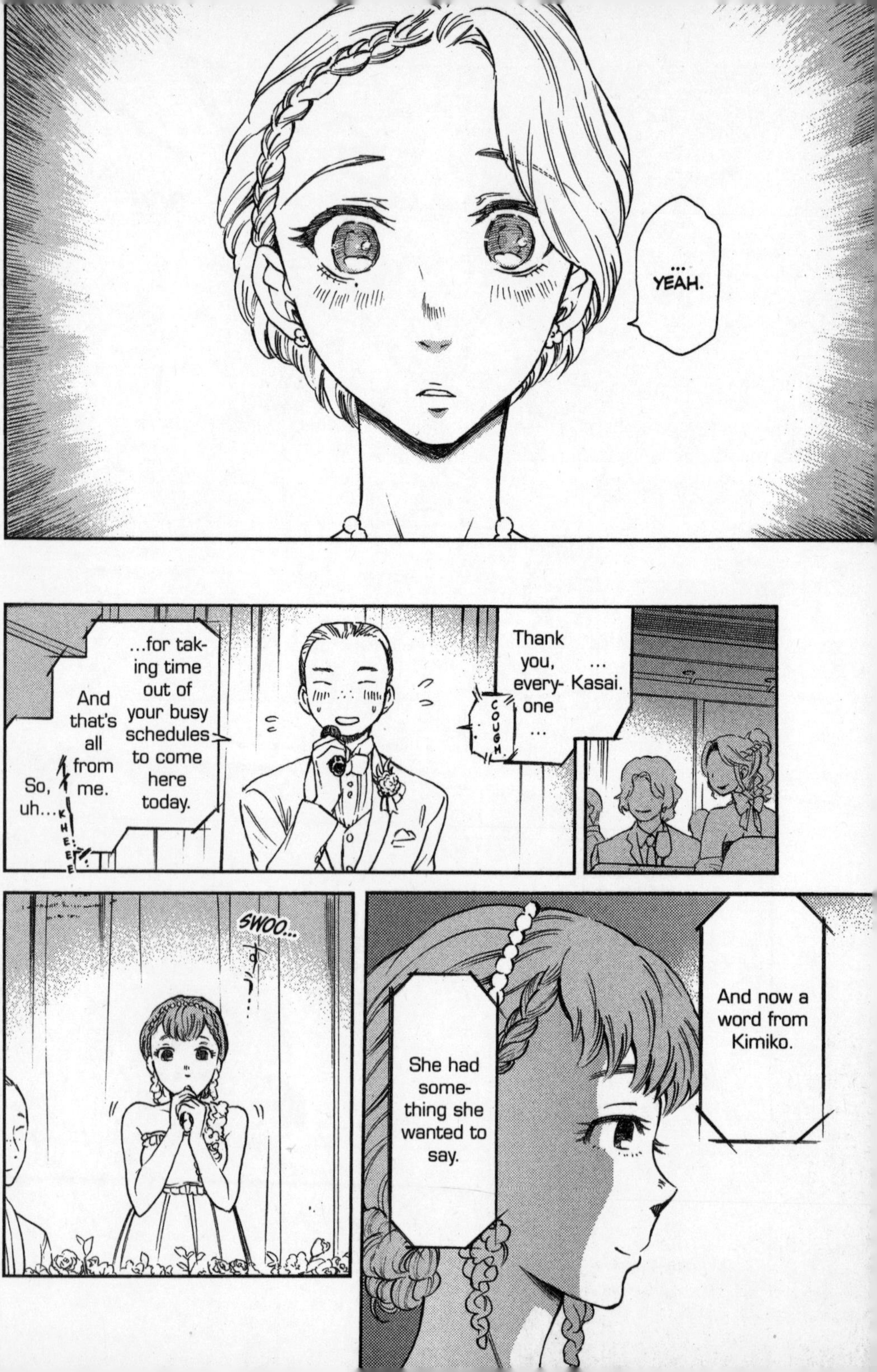
...YEAH.
Thank you, everyone...
...Kasai.
COUGH
...for taking time out of your busy schedules to come here today.
And that's all from me.
So, uh...
KHEEE
And now a word from Kimiko.
She had something she wanted to say.
SWOO...
すっ…

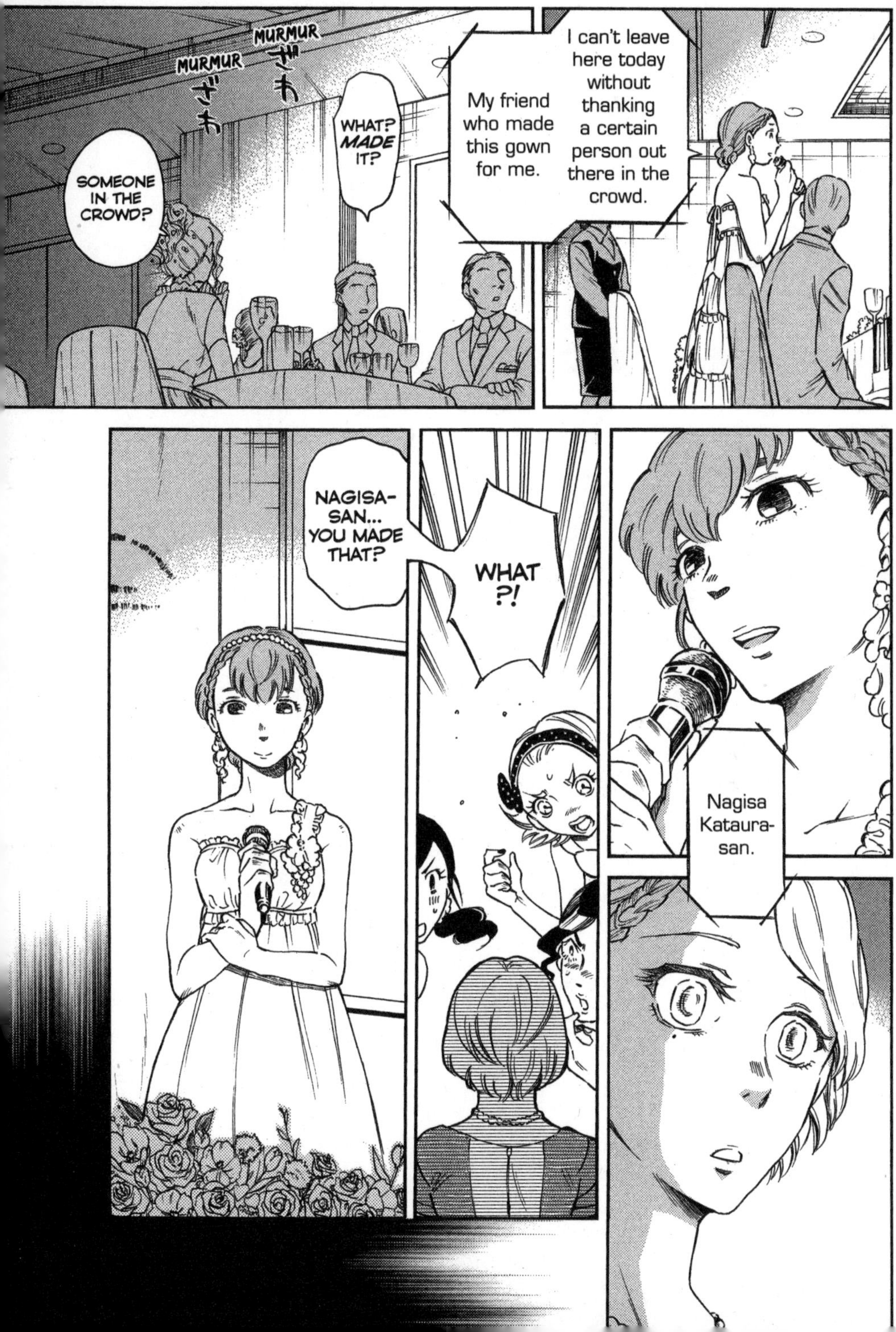
I can't leave here today without thanking a certain person out there in the crowd.
My friend who made this gown for me.
WHAT? MADE IT?
MURMUR
ざわ
MURMUR
ざわ
SOMEONE IN THE CROWD?
Nagisa Kataura-san.
WHAT?!
NAGISA-SAN... YOU MADE THAT?

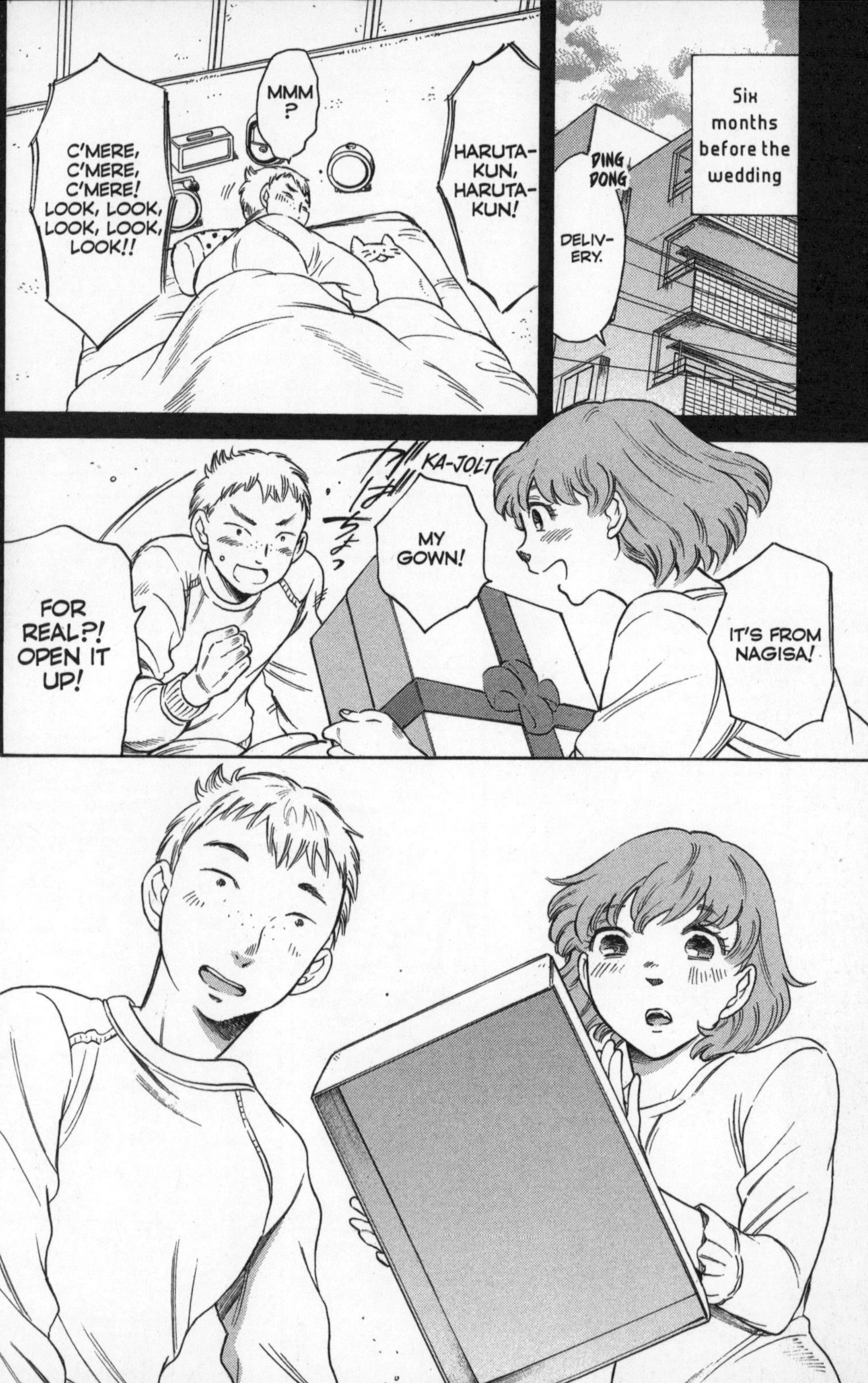
Six months before the wedding
DING DONG
DELIV-ERY.
HARUTA-KUN, HARUTA-KUN!
MMM?
C'MERE, C'MERE, C'MERE! LOOK, LOOK, LOOK, LOOK, LOOK!!
IT'S FROM NAGISA!
KA-JOLT
MY GOWN!
FOR REAL?! OPEN IT UP!

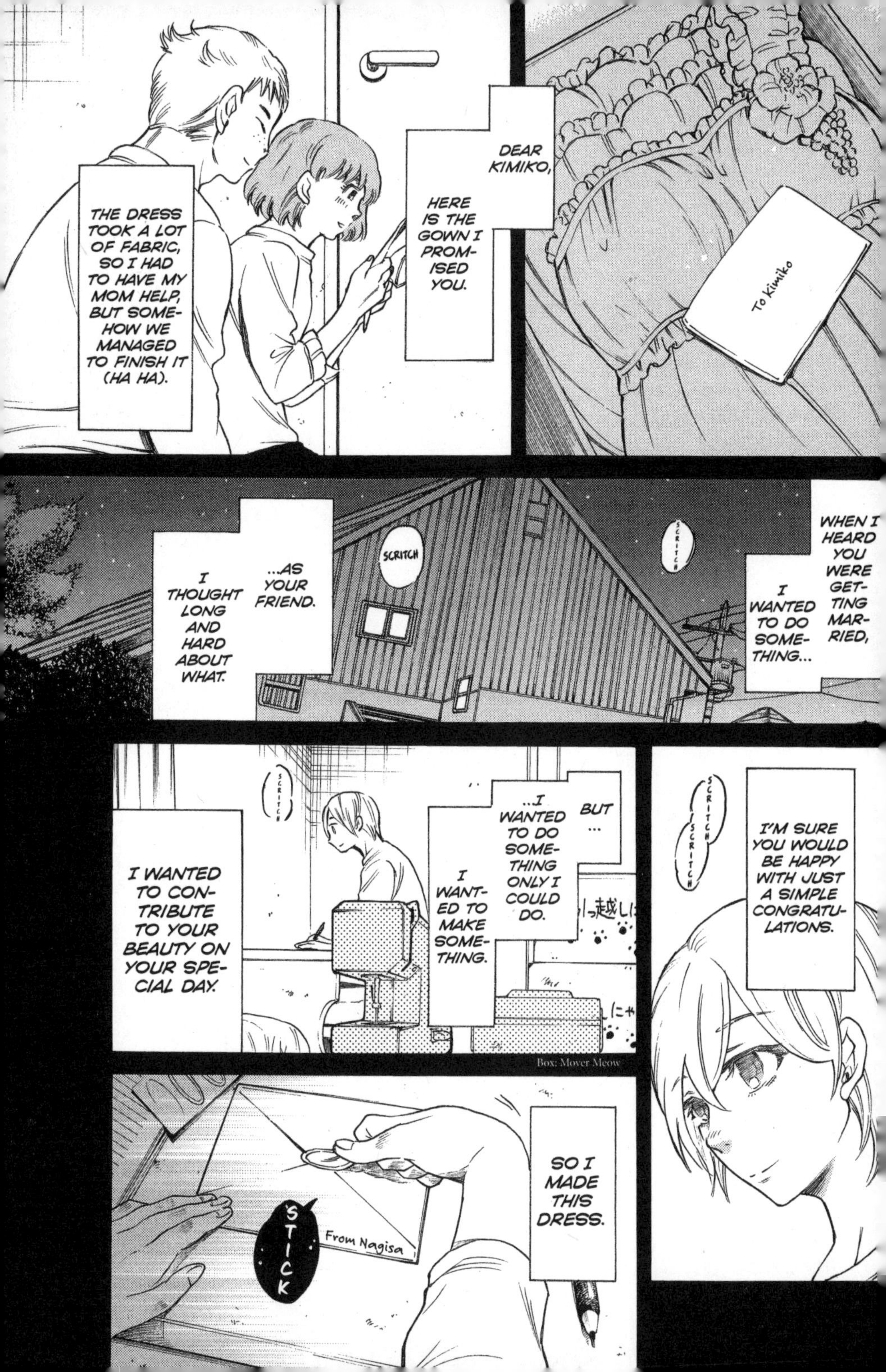
To Kimiko
DEAR KIMIKO,
HERE IS THE GOWN I PROMISED YOU.
THE DRESS TOOK A LOT OF FABRIC, SO I HAD TO HAVE MY MOM HELP, BUT SOMEHOW WE MANAGED TO FINISH IT (HA HA).
WHEN I HEARD YOU WERE GETTING MARRIED,
I WANTED TO DO SOMETHING...
SCRITCH
SCRITCH
...AS YOUR FRIEND.
I THOUGHT LONG AND HARD ABOUT WHAT.
SCRITCH SCRITCH
I'M SURE YOU WOULD BE HAPPY WITH JUST A SIMPLE CONGRATULATIONS.
BUT...
...I WANTED TO DO SOMETHING ONLY I COULD DO.
I WANTED TO MAKE SOMETHING.
SCRITCH
I WANTED TO CONTRIBUTE TO YOUR BEAUTY ON YOUR SPECIAL DAY.
Box: Mover Meow
SO I MADE THIS DRESS.
From Nagisa
STICK

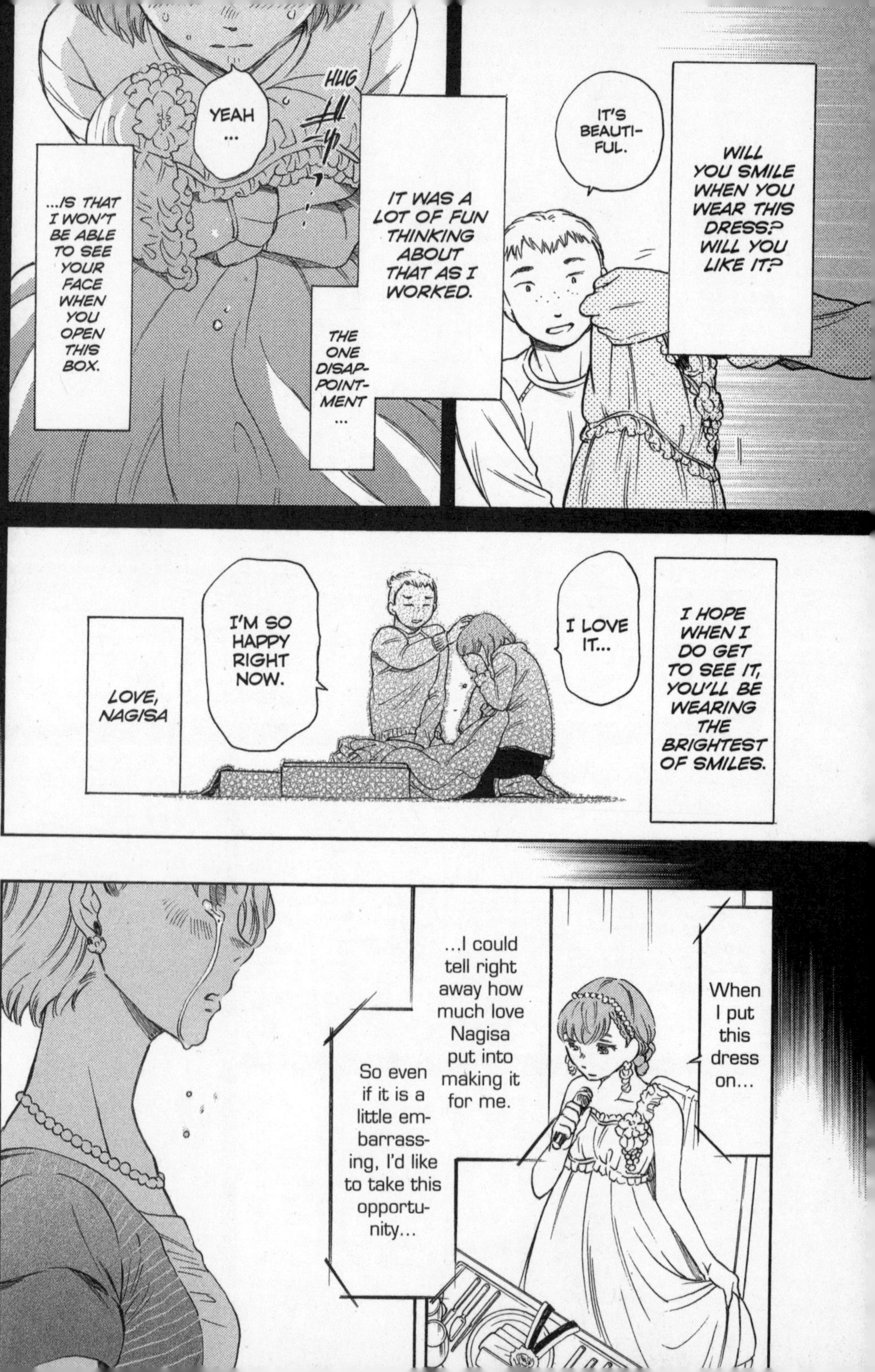
WILL YOU SMILE WHEN YOU WEAR THIS DRESS? WILL YOU LIKE IT?
IT'S BEAUTIFUL.
IT WAS A LOT OF FUN THINKING ABOUT THAT AS I WORKED.
THE ONE DISAPPOINTMENT...
HUG
YEAH...
...IS THAT I WON'T BE ABLE TO SEE YOUR FACE WHEN YOU OPEN THIS BOX.
I HOPE WHEN I DO GET TO SEE IT, YOU'LL BE WEARING THE BRIGHTEST OF SMILES.
I LOVE IT...
I'M SO HAPPY RIGHT NOW.
LOVE, NAGISA
When I put this dress on...
...I could tell right away how much love Nagisa put into making it for me.
So even if it is a little embarrassing, I'd like to take this opportunity...

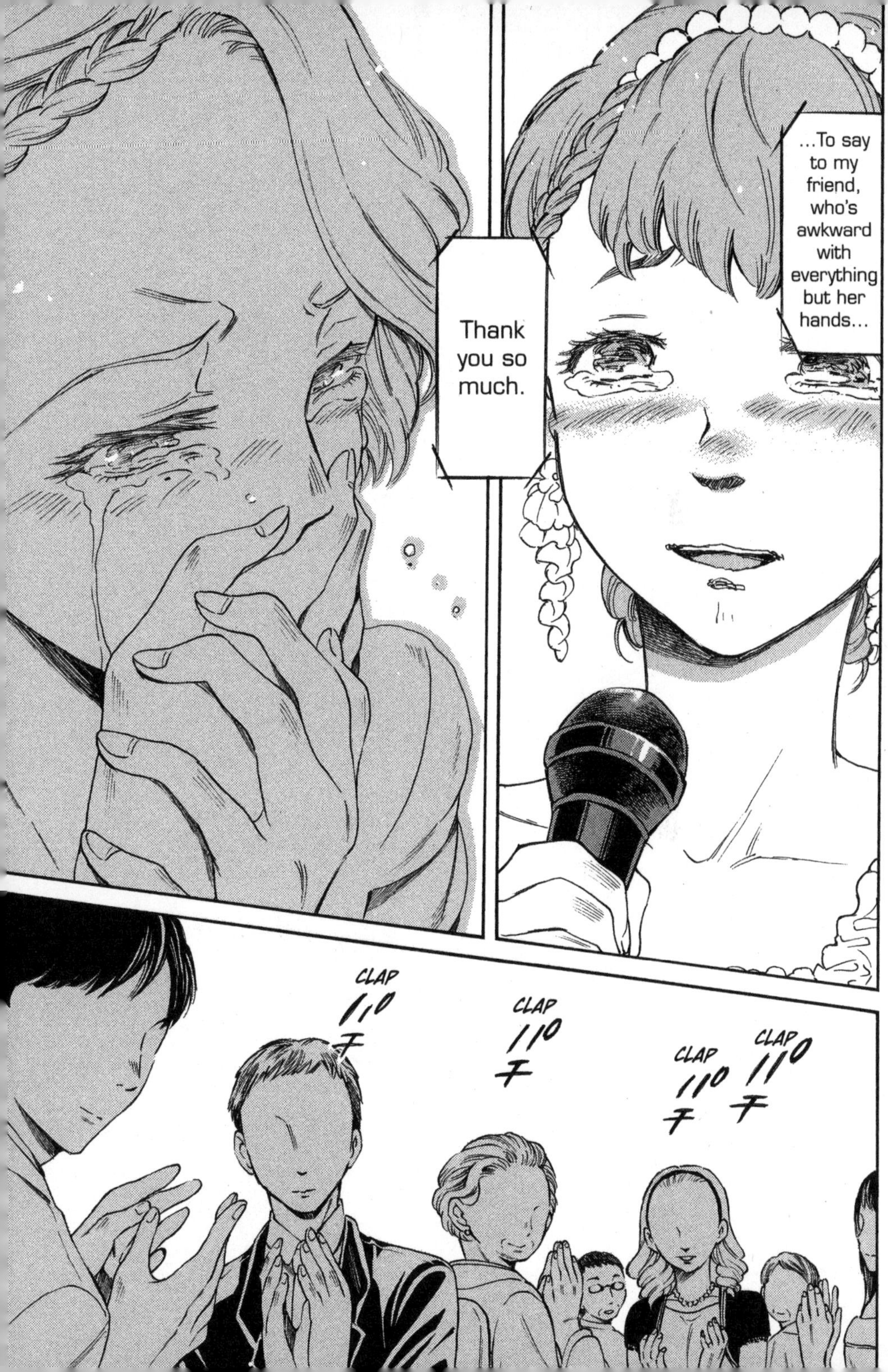
...To say to my friend, who's awkward with everything but her hands...
Thank you so much.
CLAP
CLAP
CLAP
CLAP

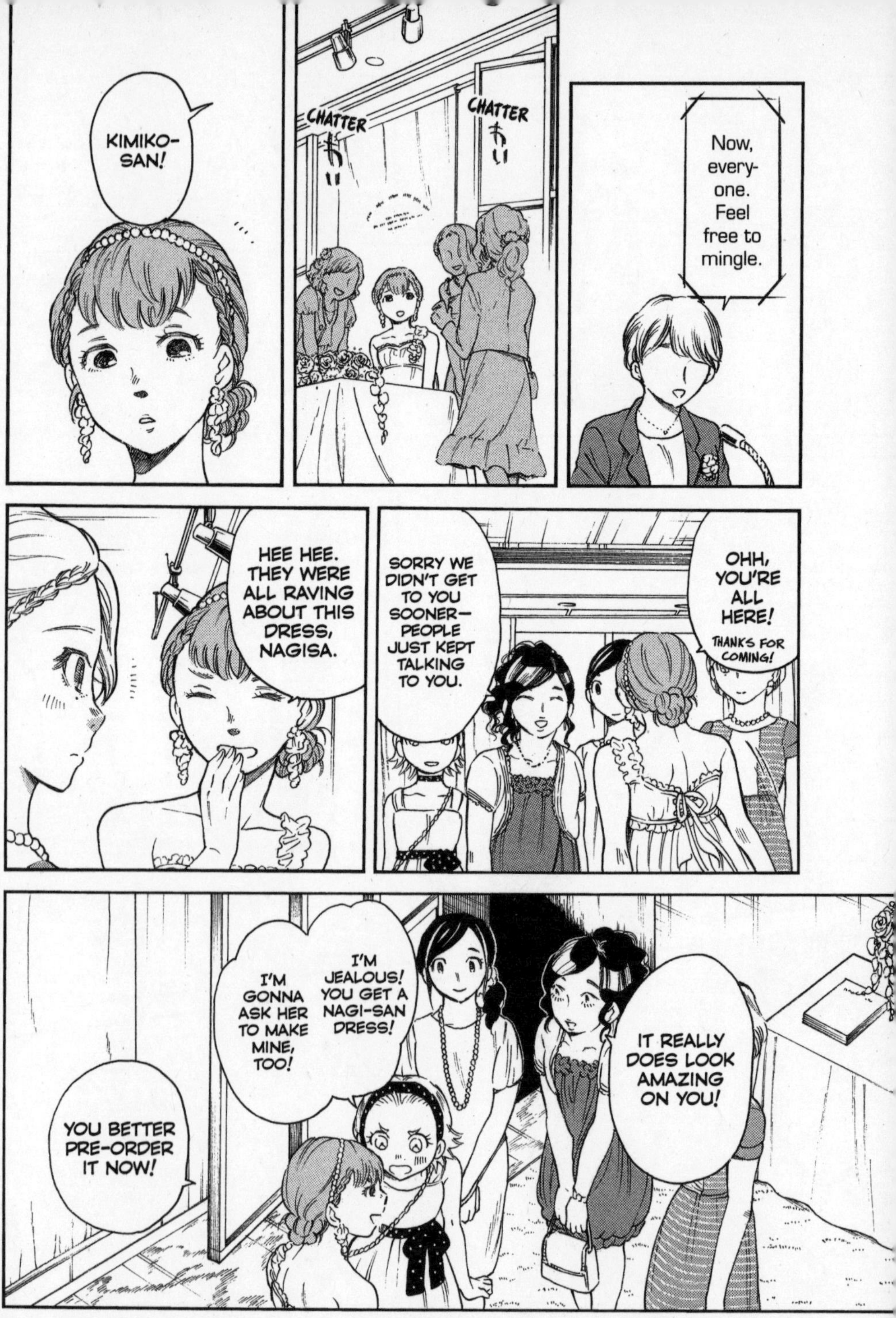
Now, every-one. Feel free to mingle.
CHATTER
CHATTER
KIMIKO-SAN!
OHH, YOU'RE ALL HERE!
THANKS FOR COMING!
SORRY WE DIDN'T GET TO YOU SOONER—PEOPLE JUST KEPT TALKING TO YOU.
HEE HEE. THEY WERE ALL RAVING ABOUT THIS DRESS, NAGISA.
IT REALLY DOES LOOK AMAZING ON YOU!
I'M JEALOUS! YOU GET A NAGI-SAN DRESS!
I'M GONNA ASK HER TO MAKE MINE, TOO!
YOU BETTER PRE-ORDER IT NOW!

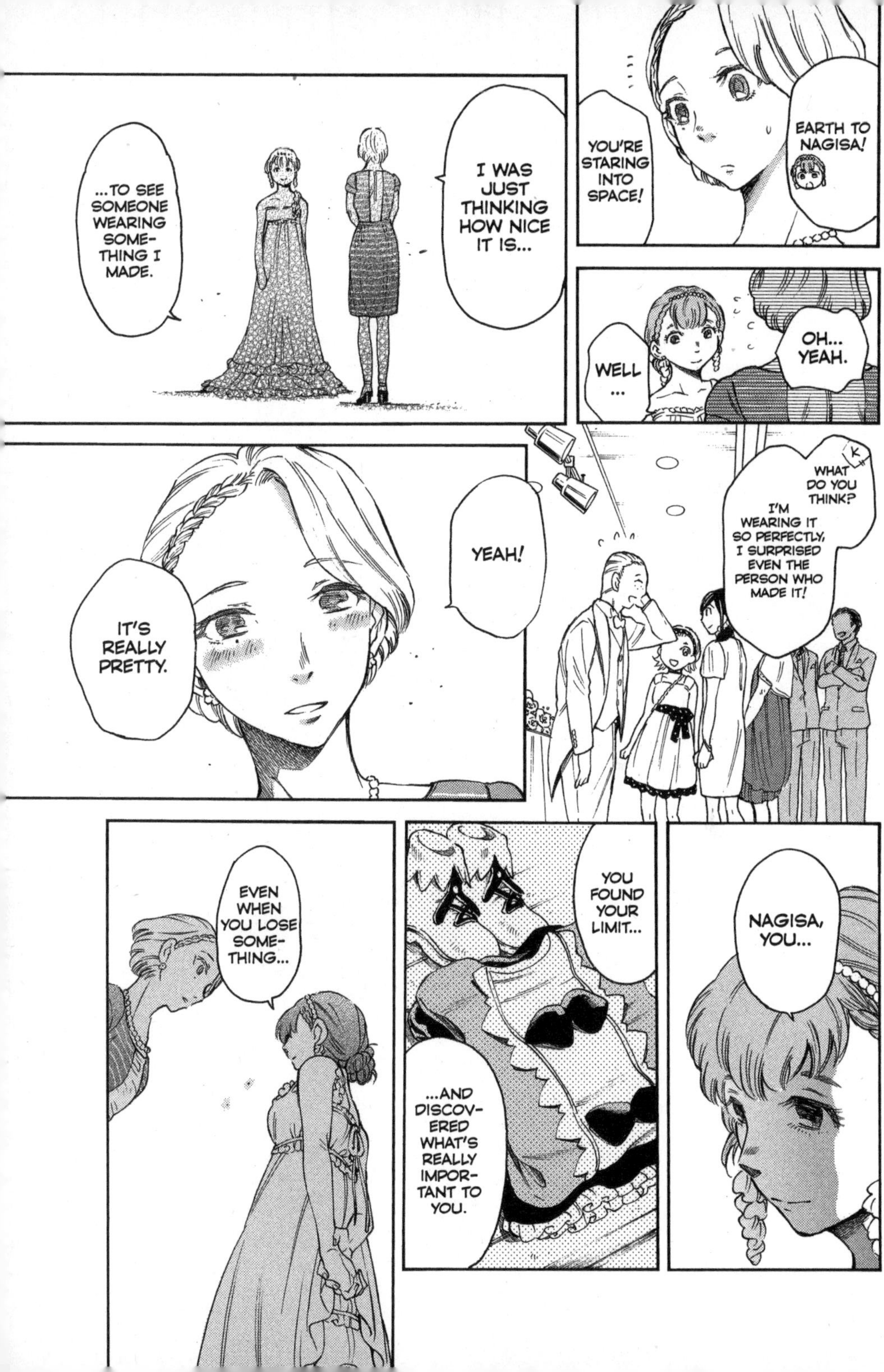
EARTH TO NAGISA!
YOU'RE STARING INTO SPACE!
OH... YEAH.
WELL...
I WAS JUST THINKING HOW NICE IT IS...
...TO SEE SOMEONE WEARING SOMETHING I MADE.
WHAT DO YOU THINK? I'M WEARING IT SO PERFECTLY, I SURPRISED EVEN THE PERSON WHO MADE IT!
YEAH!
IT'S REALLY PRETTY.
NAGISA, YOU...
YOU FOUND YOUR LIMIT...
...AND DISCOVERED WHAT'S REALLY IMPORTANT TO YOU.
EVEN WHEN YOU LOSE SOMETHING...

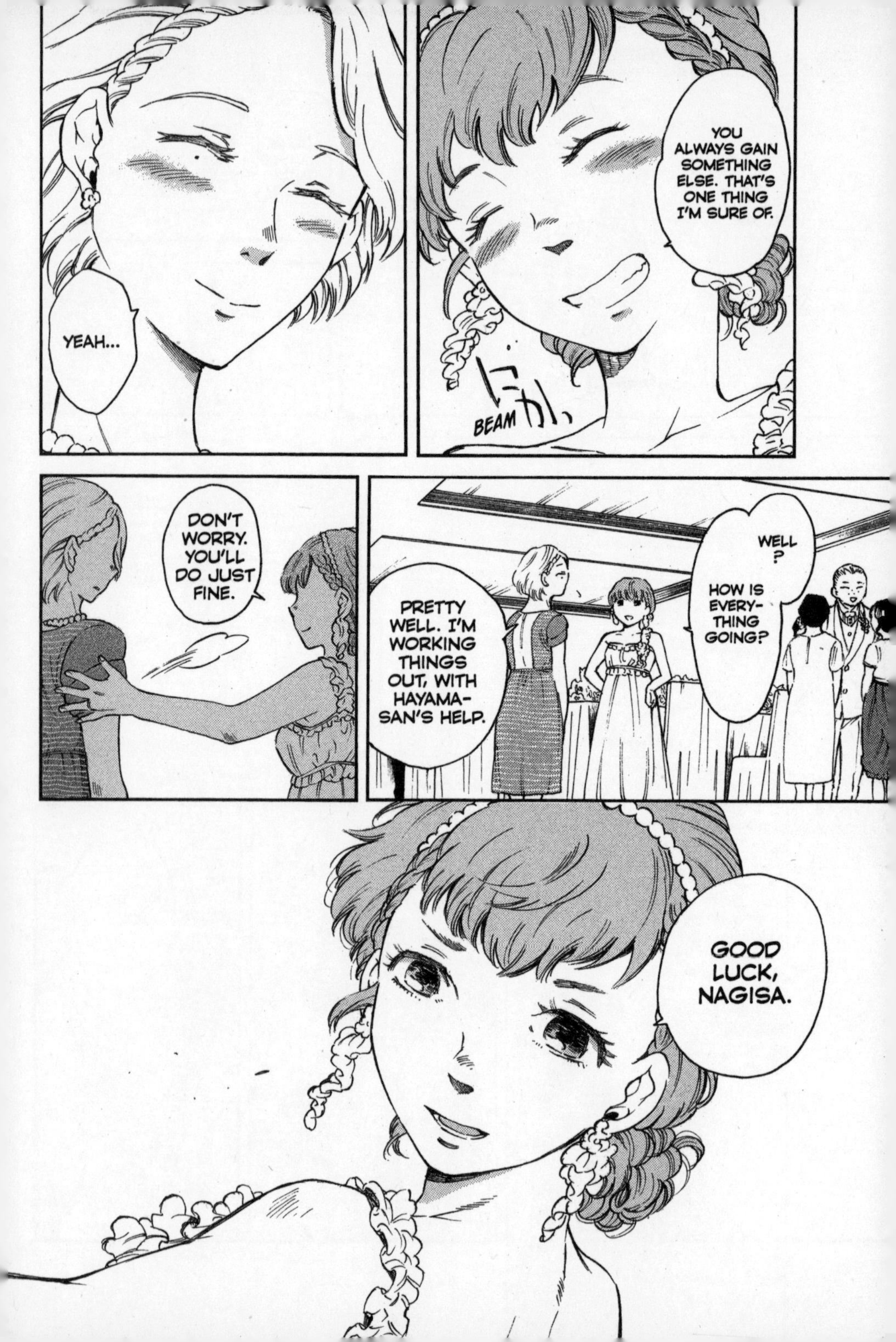
YOU ALWAYS GAIN SOMETHING ELSE. THAT'S ONE THING I'M SURE OF.
BEAM
YEAH...
WELL? HOW IS EVERYTHING GOING?
PRETTY WELL. I'M WORKING THINGS OUT, WITH HAYAMA-SAN'S HELP.
DON'T WORRY. YOU'LL DO JUST FINE.
GOOD LUCK, NAGISA.

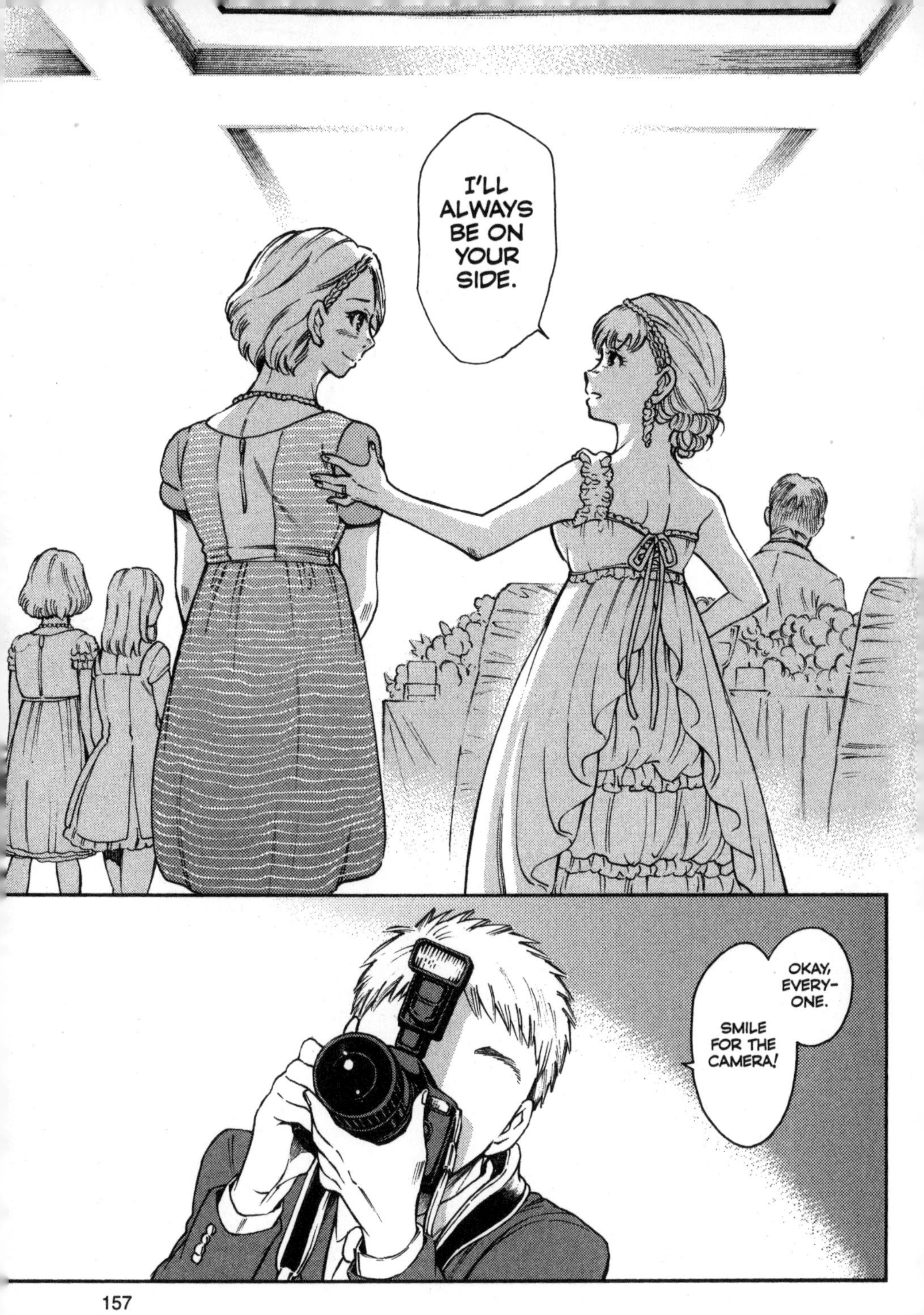
I'LL ALWAYS BE ON YOUR SIDE.
OKAY, EVERY-ONE.
SMILE FOR THE CAMERA!

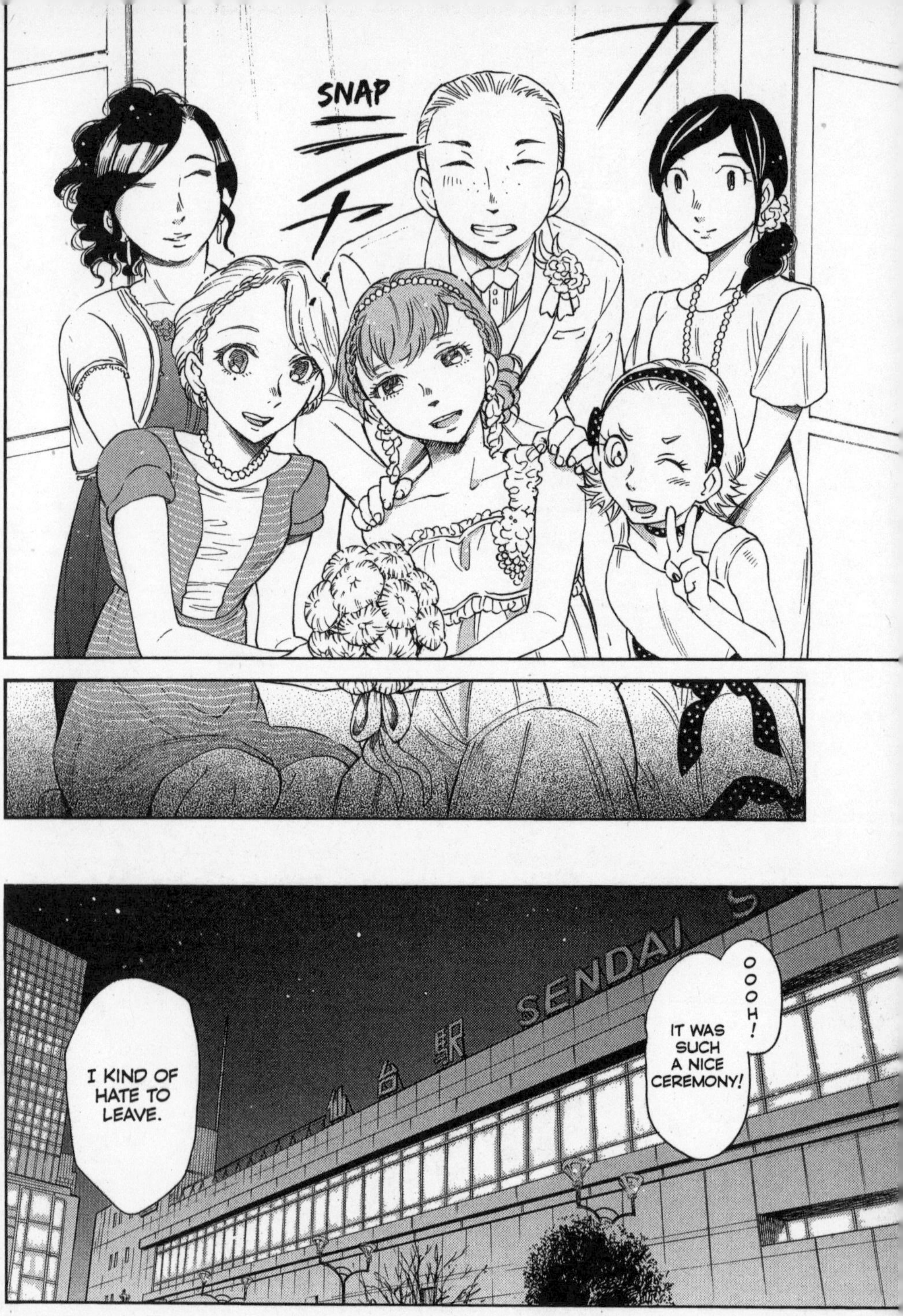
SNAP
SENDAI
仙台駅
OOOOH!
IT WAS SUCH A NICE CEREMONY!
I KIND OF HATE TO LEAVE.

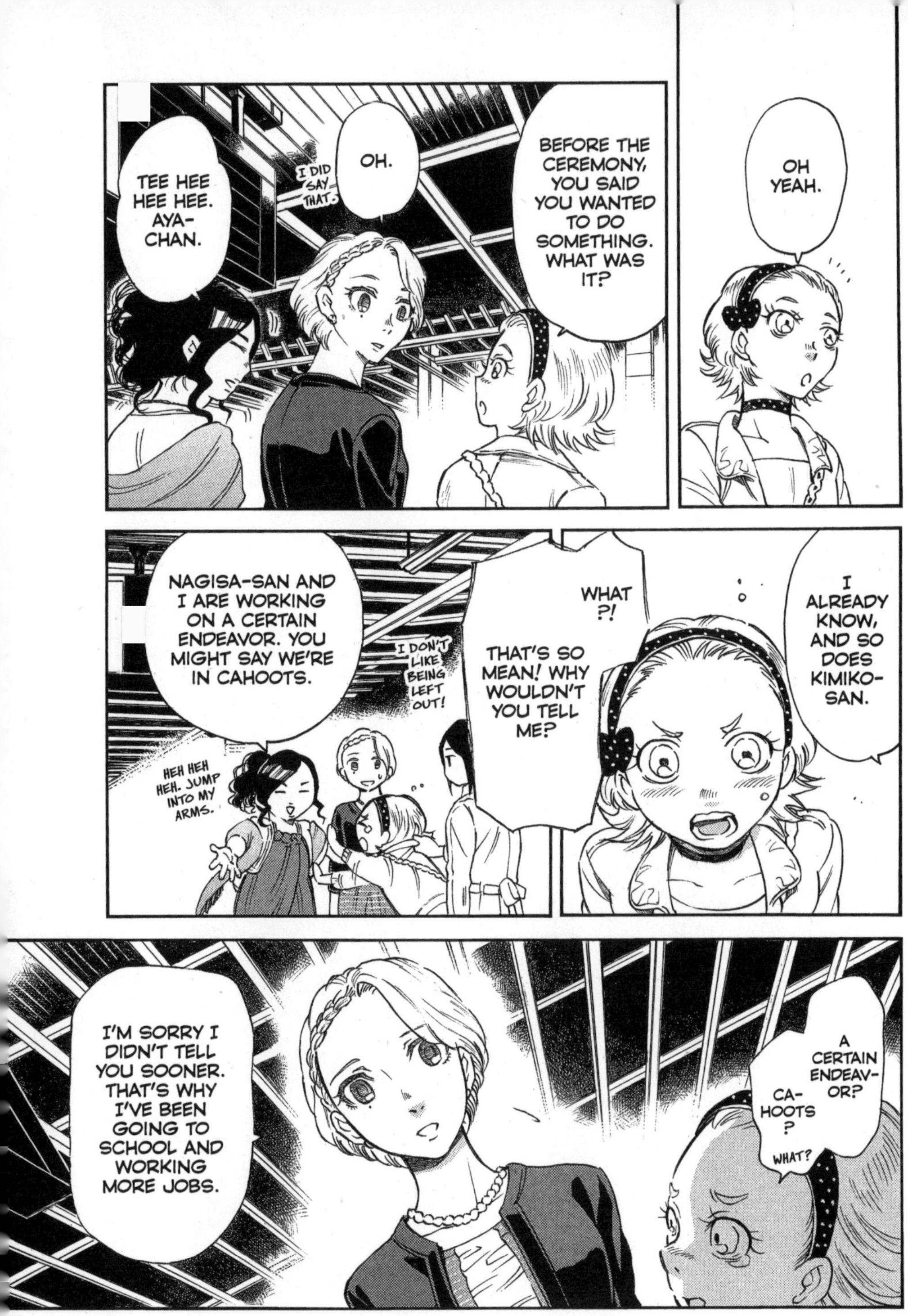
OH YEAH.
BEFORE THE CEREMONY, YOU SAID YOU WANTED TO DO SOMETHING. WHAT WAS IT?
OH.
I DID SAY THAT.
TEE HEE HEE HEE. AYA-CHAN.
I ALREADY KNOW, AND SO DOES KIMIKO-SAN.
WHAT ?!
THAT'S SO MEAN! WHY WOULDN'T YOU TELL ME?
I DON'T LIKE BEING LEFT OUT!
NAGISA-SAN AND I ARE WORKING ON A CERTAIN ENDEAVOR. YOU MIGHT SAY WE'RE IN CAHOOTS.
HEH HEH HEH. JUMP INTO MY ARMS.
A CERTAIN ENDEAVOR?
CA-HOOTS ?
WHAT?
I'M SORRY I DIDN'T TELL YOU SOONER. THAT'S WHY I'VE BEEN GOING TO SCHOOL AND WORKING MORE JOBS.

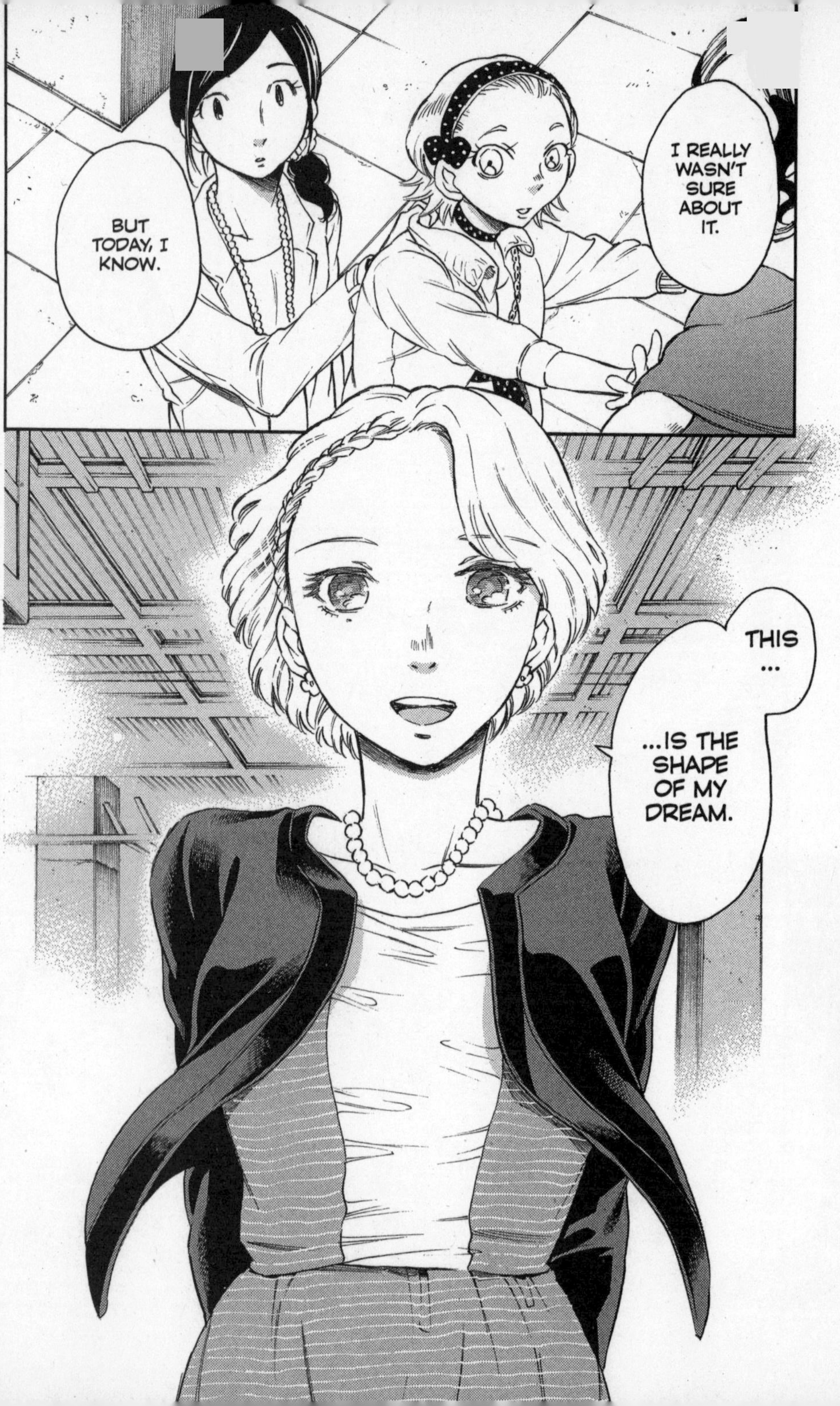
I REALLY WASN'T SURE ABOUT IT.
BUT TODAY, I KNOW.
THIS ...
...IS THE SHAPE OF MY DREAM.

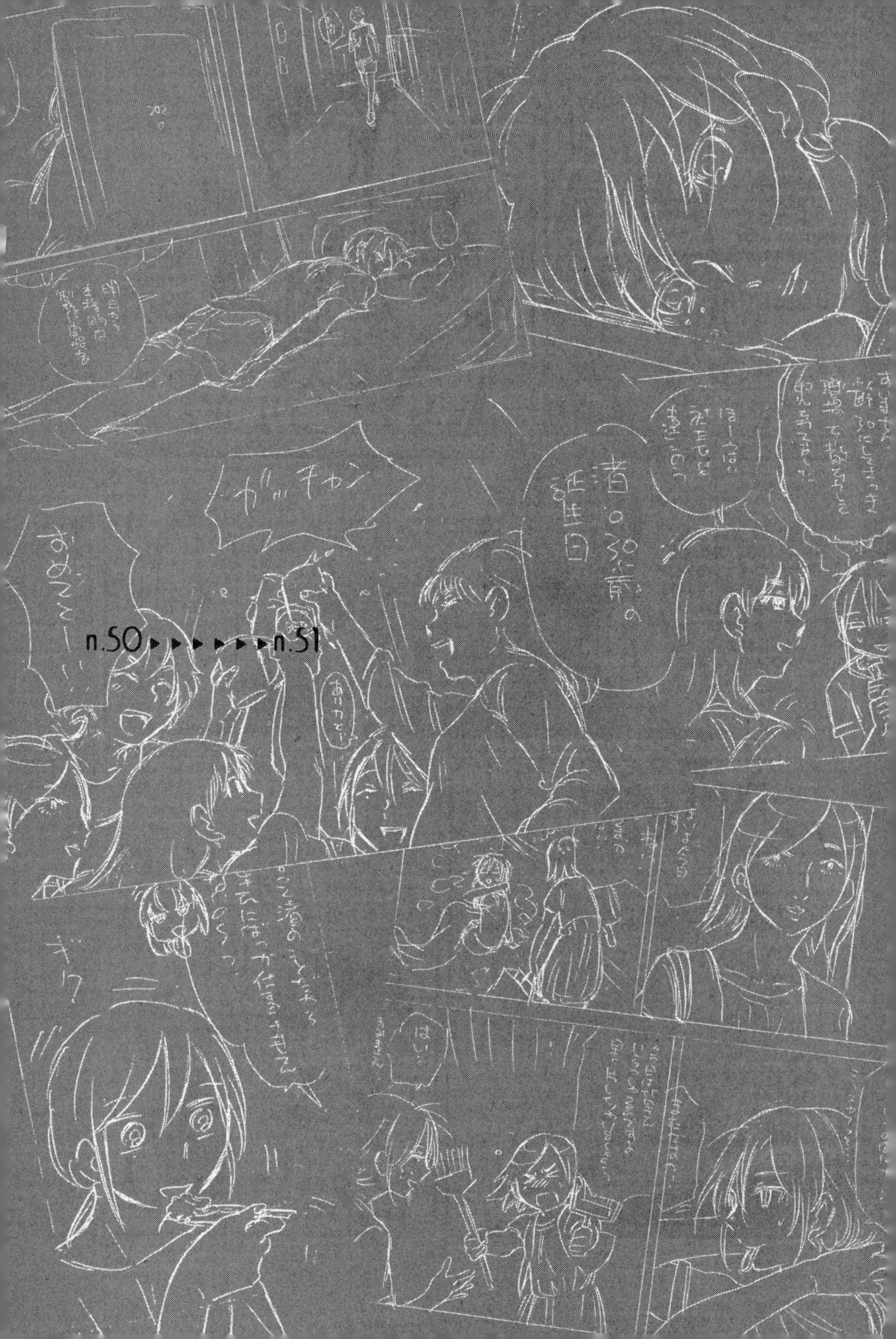

渚の30歳の誕生日
ガッチャン
n.50▸▸▸▸▸▸▸n.51
ありがとー

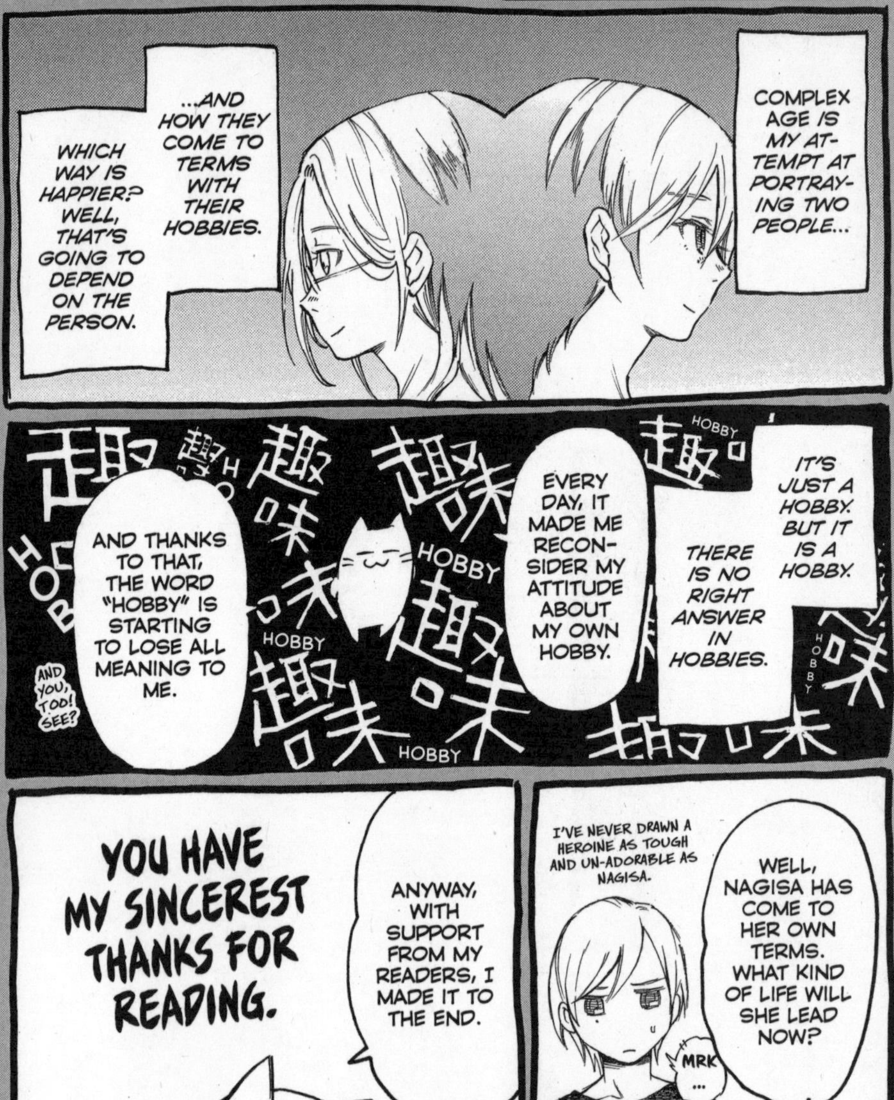
COMPLEX AGE IS MY ATTEMPT AT PORTRAYING TWO PEOPLE...
...AND HOW THEY COME TO TERMS WITH THEIR HOBBIES.
WHICH WAY IS HAPPIER? WELL, THAT'S GOING TO DEPEND ON THE PERSON.
IT'S JUST A HOBBY. BUT IT IS A HOBBY.
THERE IS NO RIGHT ANSWER IN HOBBIES.
EVERY DAY, IT MADE ME RECONSIDER MY ATTITUDE ABOUT MY OWN HOBBY.
AND THANKS TO THAT, THE WORD "HOBBY" IS STARTING TO LOSE ALL MEANING TO ME.
AND YOU, TOO! SEE?
趣味
HOBBY
I'VE NEVER DRAWN A HEROINE AS TOUGH AND UN-ADORABLE AS NAGISA.
WELL, NAGISA HAS COME TO HER OWN TERMS. WHAT KIND OF LIFE WILL SHE LEAD NOW?
MRK...
SHE WAS REALLY DIFFICULT TO HANDLE...
BUT WE MAINTAINED A GOOD DISTANCE.
ANYWAY, WITH SUPPORT FROM MY READERS, I MADE IT TO THE END.
YOU HAVE MY SINCEREST THANKS FOR READING.
LET US MEET AGAIN SOMEDAY.

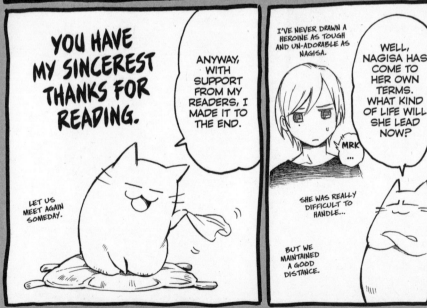

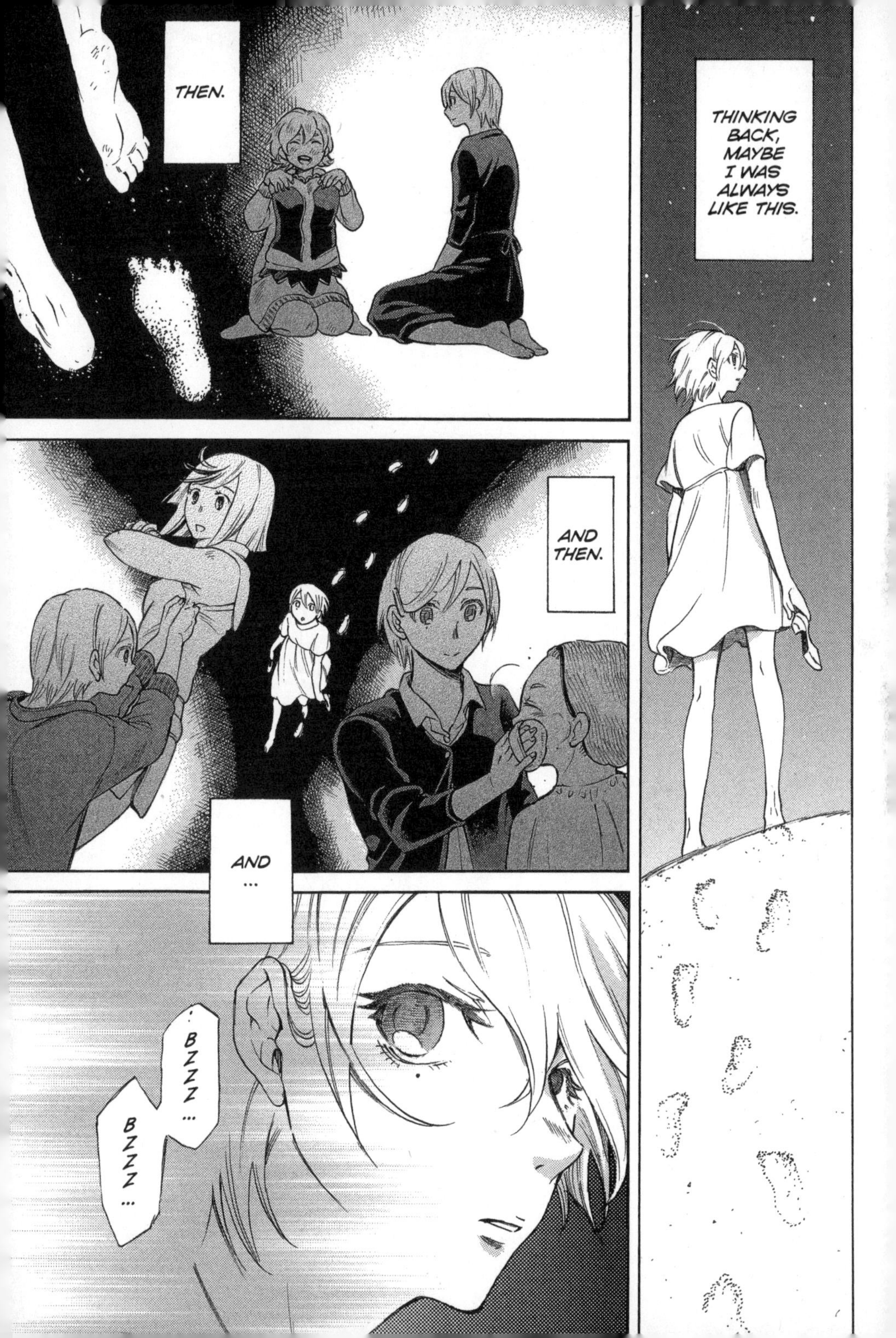
THINKING BACK, MAYBE I WAS ALWAYS LIKE THIS.
THEN.
AND THEN.
AND ...
... BZZZ ...
BZZZ ...

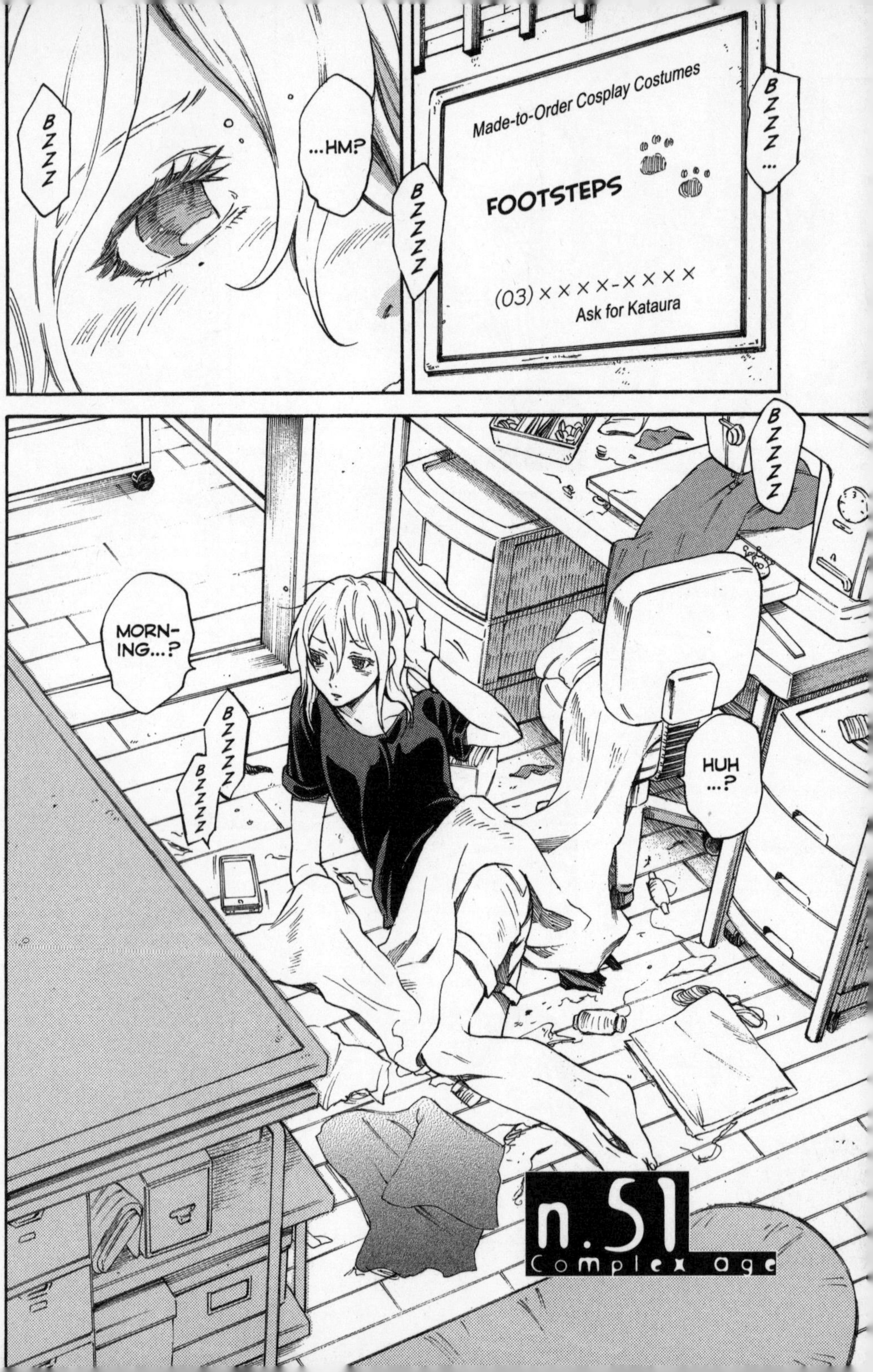
BZZZ...
Made-to-Order Cosplay Costumes
FOOTSTEPS
(03) ××××-××××
Ask for Kataura
BZZZZ
...HM?
BZZZ
BZZZZ
HUH ...?
MORN-ING...?
BZZZZ
BZZZZ
n.51
Complex age

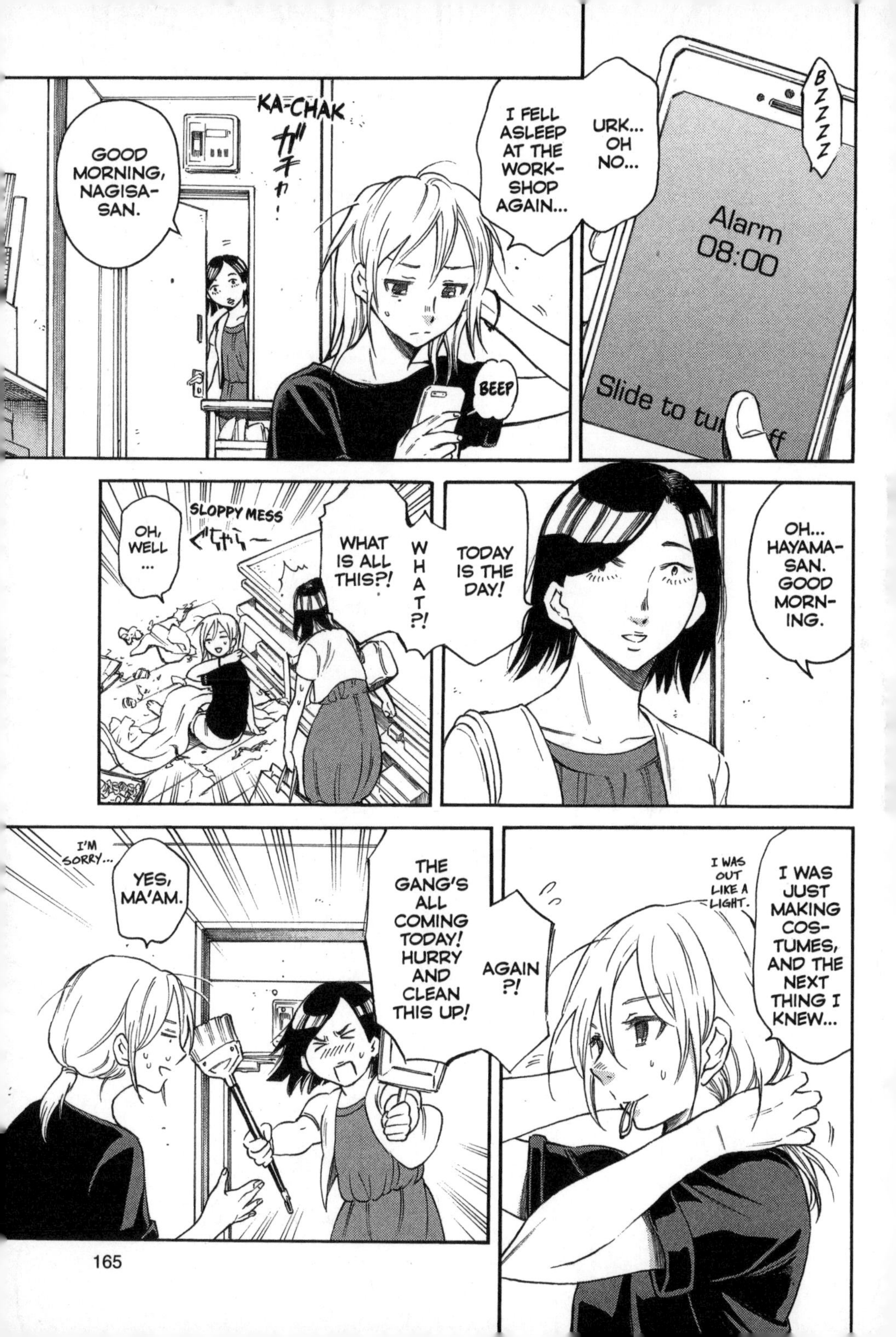
BZZZZ
Alarm 08:00
Slide to tu ff
URK... OH NO...
I FELL ASLEEP AT THE WORKSHOP AGAIN...
BEEP
KA-CHAK ガチャ
GOOD MORNING, NAGISA-SAN.
OH... HAYAMA-SAN. GOOD MORNING.
TODAY IS THE DAY!
WHAT?!
WHAT IS ALL THIS?!
SLOPPY MESS ぐちゃら〜
OH, WELL...
I WAS JUST MAKING COSTUMES, AND THE NEXT THING I KNEW...
I WAS OUT LIKE A LIGHT.
AGAIN?!
THE GANG'S ALL COMING TODAY! HURRY AND CLEAN THIS UP!
YES, MA'AM.
I'M SORRY...

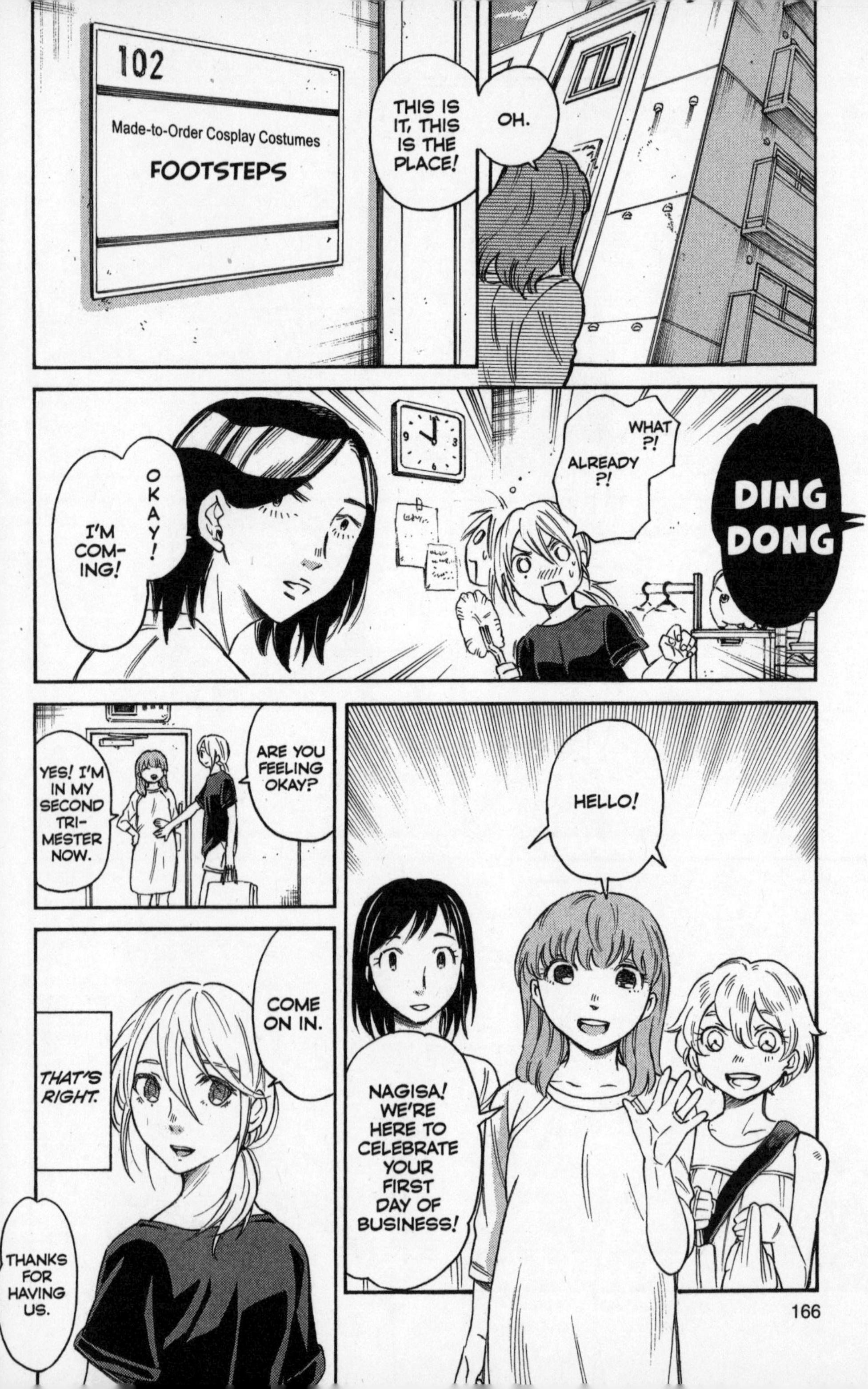
OH.
THIS IS IT, THIS IS THE PLACE!
102
Made-to-Order Cosplay Costumes
FOOTSTEPS
DING DONG
WHAT?! ALREADY?!
OKAY!
I'M COMING!
HELLO!
NAGISA! WE'RE HERE TO CELEBRATE YOUR FIRST DAY OF BUSINESS!
ARE YOU FEELING OKAY?
YES! I'M IN MY SECOND TRIMESTER NOW.
COME ON IN.
THAT'S RIGHT.
THANKS FOR HAVING US.

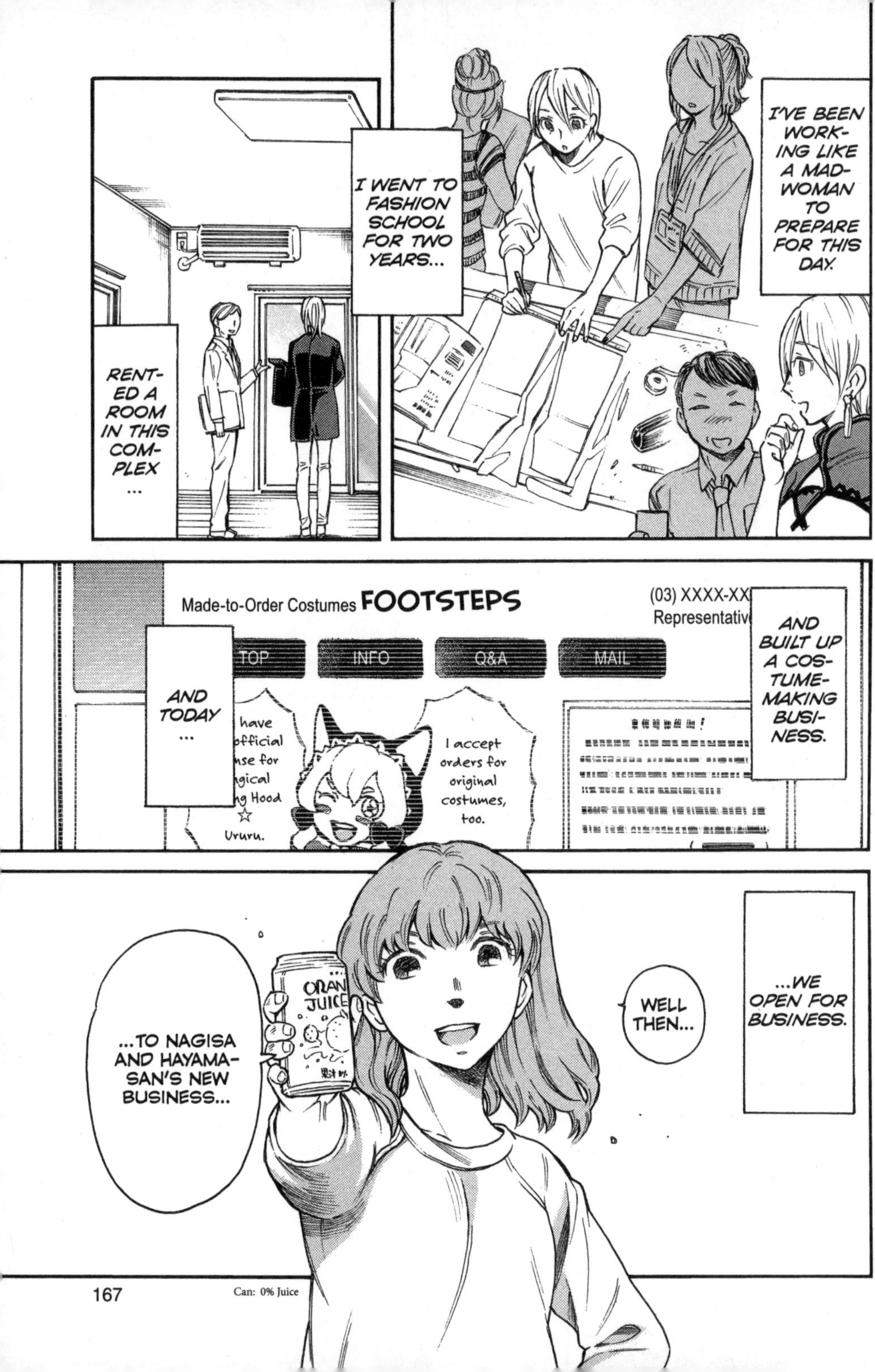
I'VE BEEN WORKING LIKE A MADWOMAN TO PREPARE FOR THIS DAY.
I WENT TO FASHION SCHOOL FOR TWO YEARS...
RENTED A ROOM IN THIS COMPLEX...
AND BUILT UP A COSTUME-MAKING BUSINESS.
Made-to-Order Costumes FOOTSTEPS
(03) XXXX-XX
Representative
TOP
INFO
Q&A
MAIL
I accept orders for original costumes, too.
AND TODAY...
...WE OPEN FOR BUSINESS.
WELL THEN...
...TO NAGISA AND HAYAMA-SAN'S NEW BUSINESS...

Can: 0% Juice

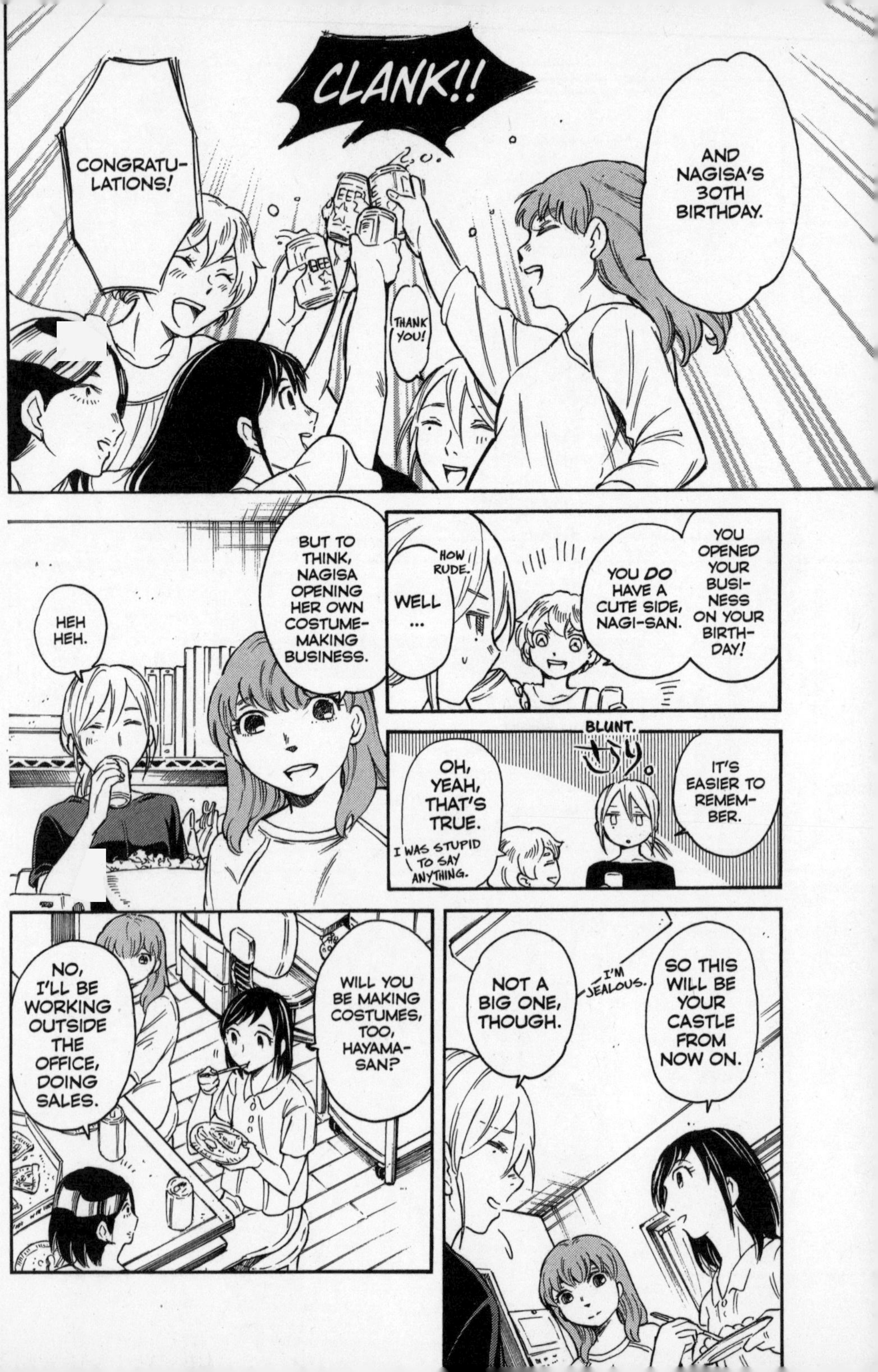
AND NAGISA'S 30TH BIRTHDAY.
CLANK!!
CONGRATULATIONS!
THANK YOU!
YOU OPENED YOUR BUSINESS ON YOUR BIRTHDAY!
YOU DO HAVE A CUTE SIDE, NAGI-SAN.
HOW RUDE.
WELL...
IT'S EASIER TO REMEMBER.
BLUNT.
OH, YEAH, THAT'S TRUE.
I WAS STUPID TO SAY ANYTHING.
BUT TO THINK, NAGISA OPENING HER OWN COSTUME-MAKING BUSINESS.
HEH HEH.
SO THIS WILL BE YOUR CASTLE FROM NOW ON.
I'M JEALOUS.
NOT A BIG ONE, THOUGH.
WILL YOU BE MAKING COSTUMES, TOO, HAYAMA-SAN?
NO, I'LL BE WORKING OUTSIDE THE OFFICE, DOING SALES.

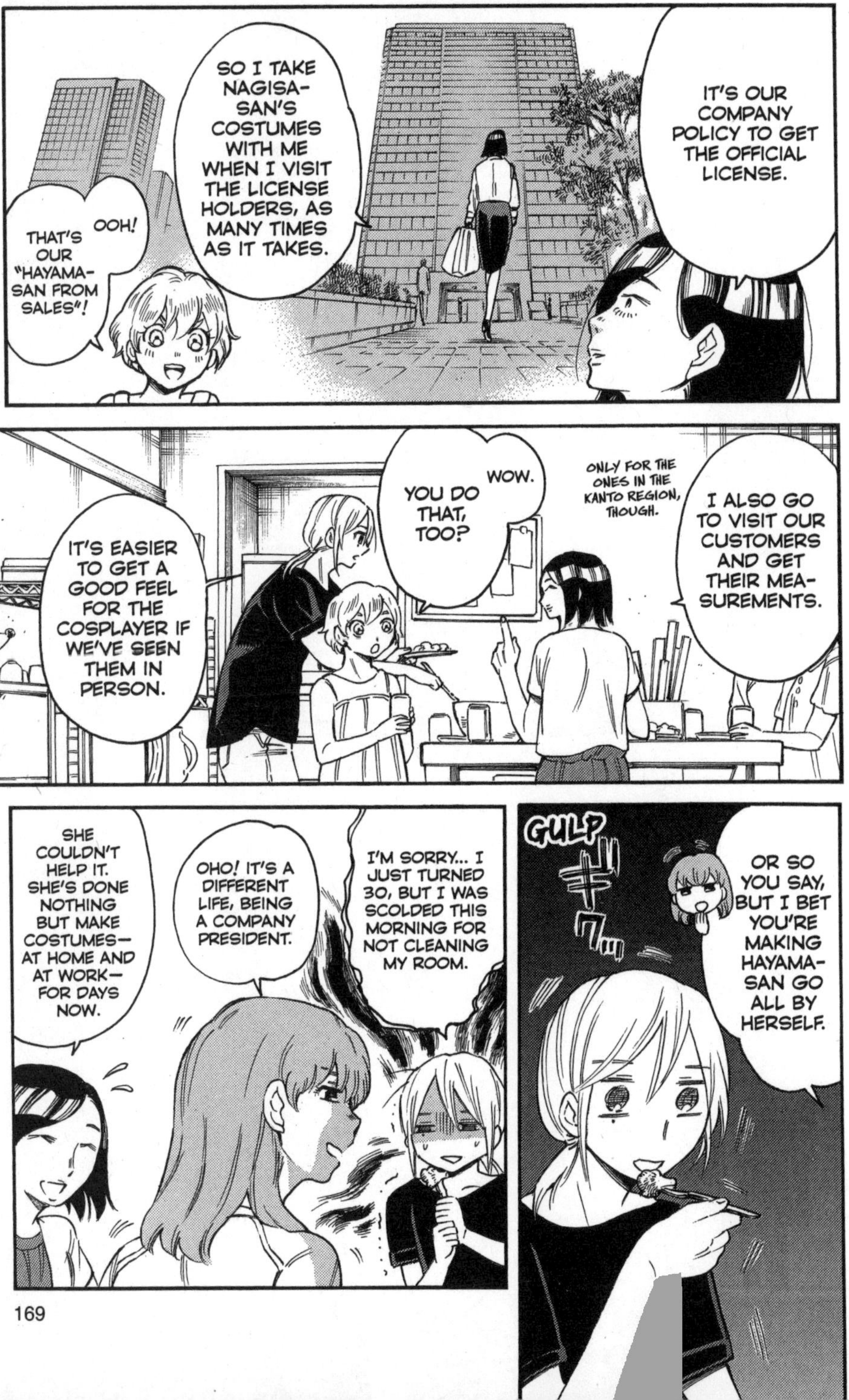
IT'S OUR COMPANY POLICY TO GET THE OFFICIAL LICENSE.
SO I TAKE NAGISA-SAN'S COSTUMES WITH ME WHEN I VISIT THE LICENSE HOLDERS, AS MANY TIMES AS IT TAKES.
OOH!
THAT'S OUR "HAYAMA-SAN FROM SALES"!
I ALSO GO TO VISIT OUR CUSTOMERS AND GET THEIR MEA-SUREMENTS.
ONLY FOR THE ONES IN THE KANTO REGION, THOUGH.
WOW.
YOU DO THAT, TOO?
IT'S EASIER TO GET A GOOD FEEL FOR THE COSPLAYER IF WE'VE SEEN THEM IN PERSON.
GULP
OR SO YOU SAY, BUT I BET YOU'RE MAKING HAYAMA-SAN GO ALL BY HERSELF.
I'M SORRY... I JUST TURNED 30, BUT I WAS SCOLDED THIS MORNING FOR NOT CLEANING MY ROOM.
OHO! IT'S A DIFFERENT LIFE, BEING A COMPANY PRESIDENT.
SHE COULDN'T HELP IT. SHE'S DONE NOTHING BUT MAKE COSTUMES—AT HOME AND AT WORK—FOR DAYS NOW.

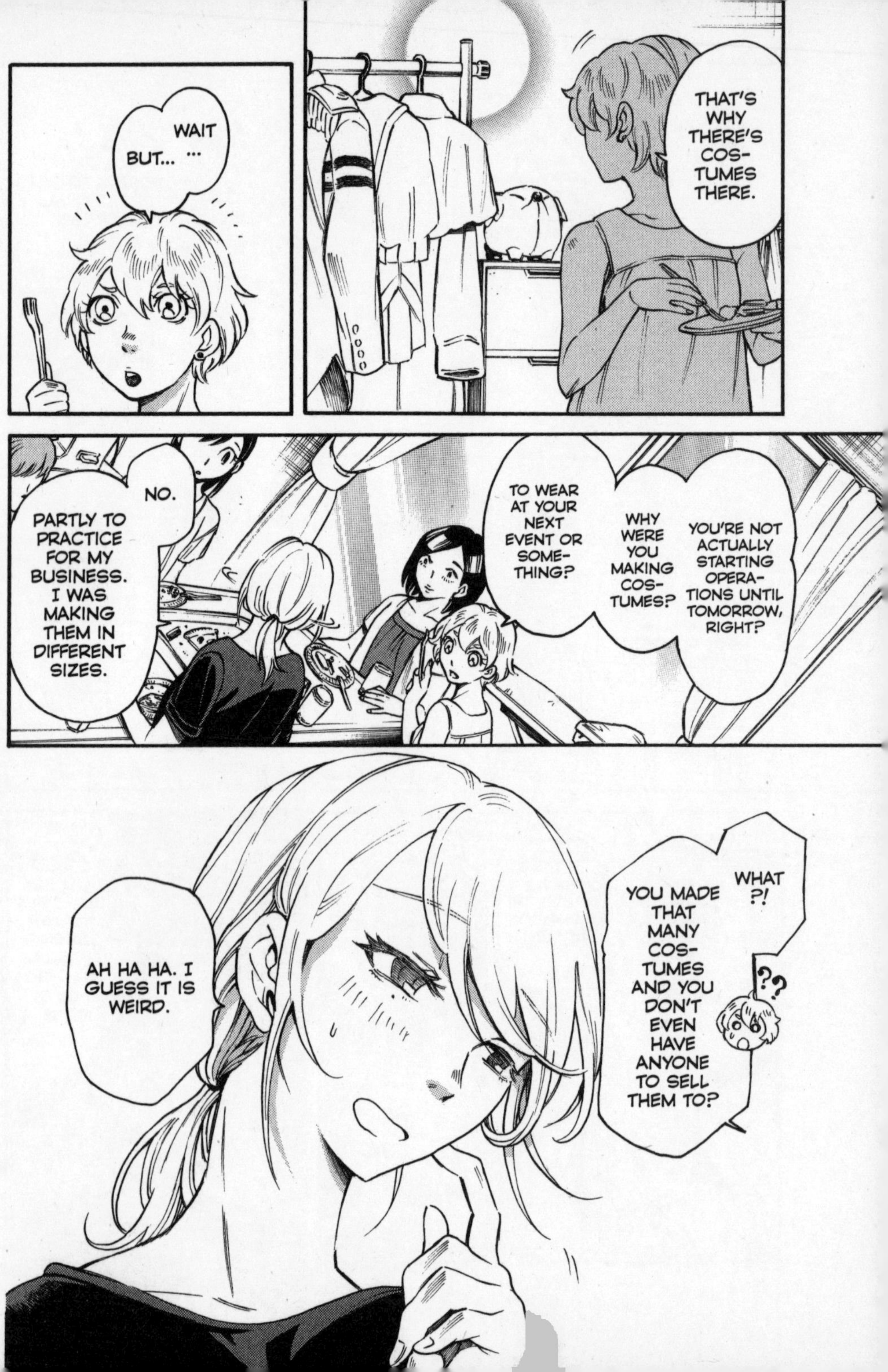
THAT'S WHY THERE'S COSTUMES THERE.
WAIT ... BUT...
YOU'RE NOT ACTUALLY STARTING OPERATIONS UNTIL TOMORROW, RIGHT?
WHY WERE YOU MAKING COSTUMES?
TO WEAR AT YOUR NEXT EVENT OR SOMETHING?
NO.
PARTLY TO PRACTICE FOR MY BUSINESS. I WAS MAKING THEM IN DIFFERENT SIZES.
WHAT?!
YOU MADE THAT MANY COSTUMES AND YOU DON'T EVEN HAVE ANYONE TO SELL THEM TO?
??
AH HA HA. I GUESS IT IS WEIRD.

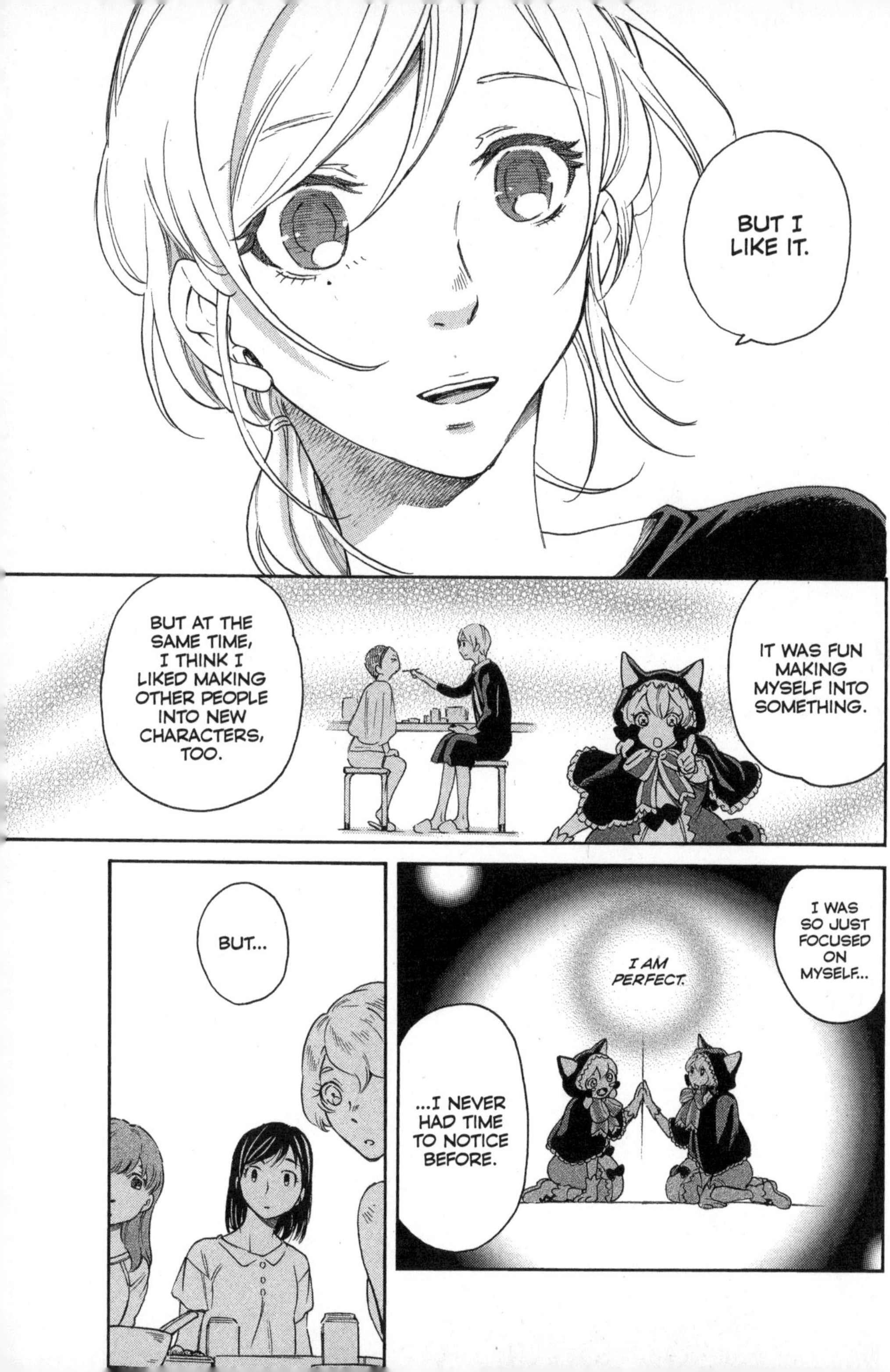
BUT I LIKE IT.
IT WAS FUN MAKING MYSELF INTO SOMETHING.
BUT AT THE SAME TIME, I THINK I LIKED MAKING OTHER PEOPLE INTO NEW CHARACTERS, TOO.
I WAS SO JUST FOCUSED ON MYSELF...
I AM PERFECT.
...I NEVER HAD TIME TO NOTICE BEFORE.
BUT...

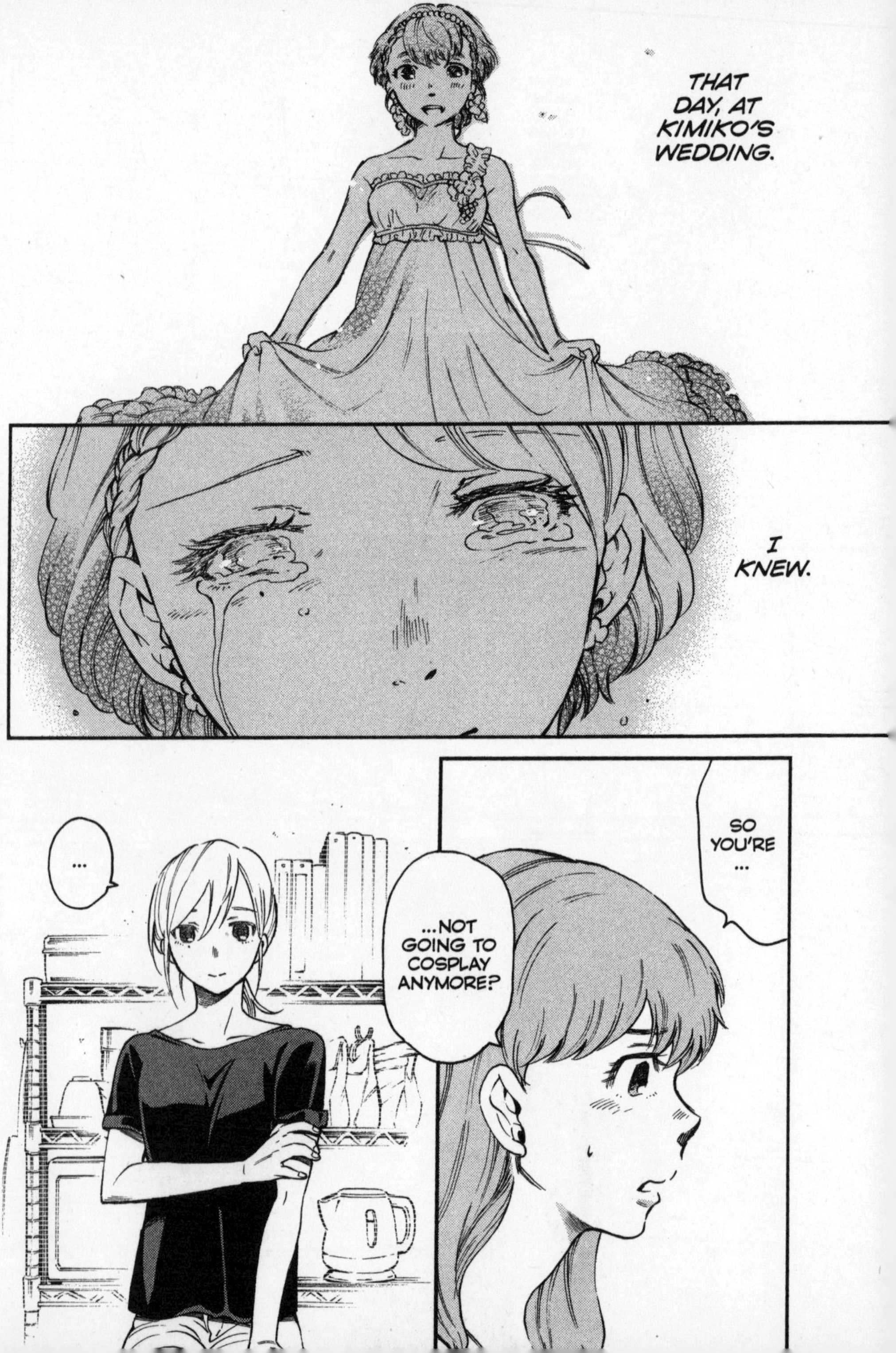
THAT DAY, AT KIMIKO'S WEDDING.
I KNEW.
SO YOU'RE ...
...NOT GOING TO COSPLAY ANYMORE?
...

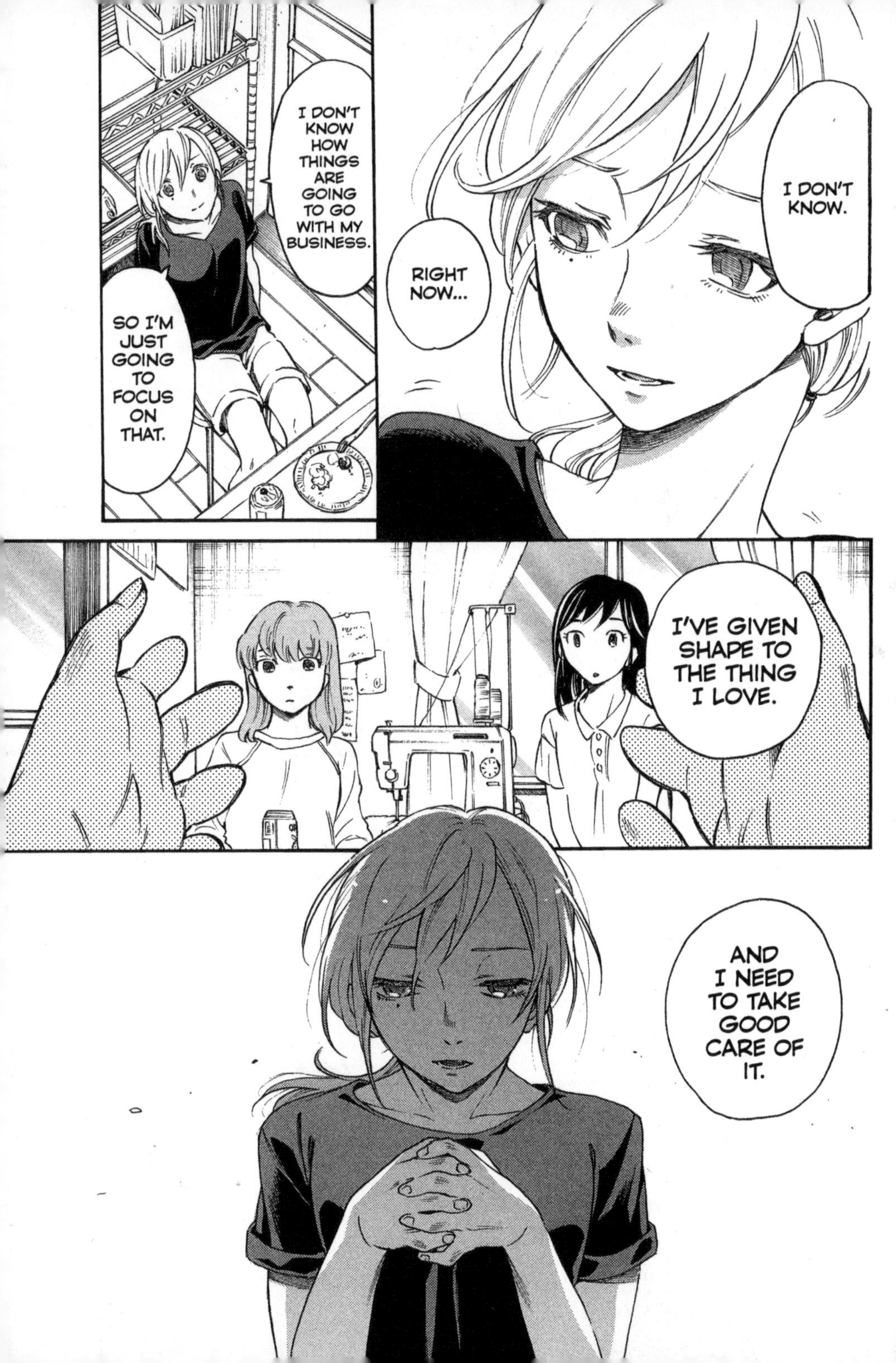
I DON'T KNOW.
RIGHT NOW...
I DON'T KNOW HOW THINGS ARE GOING TO GO WITH MY BUSINESS.
SO I'M JUST GOING TO FOCUS ON THAT.
I'VE GIVEN SHAPE TO THE THING I LOVE.
AND I NEED TO TAKE GOOD CARE OF IT.

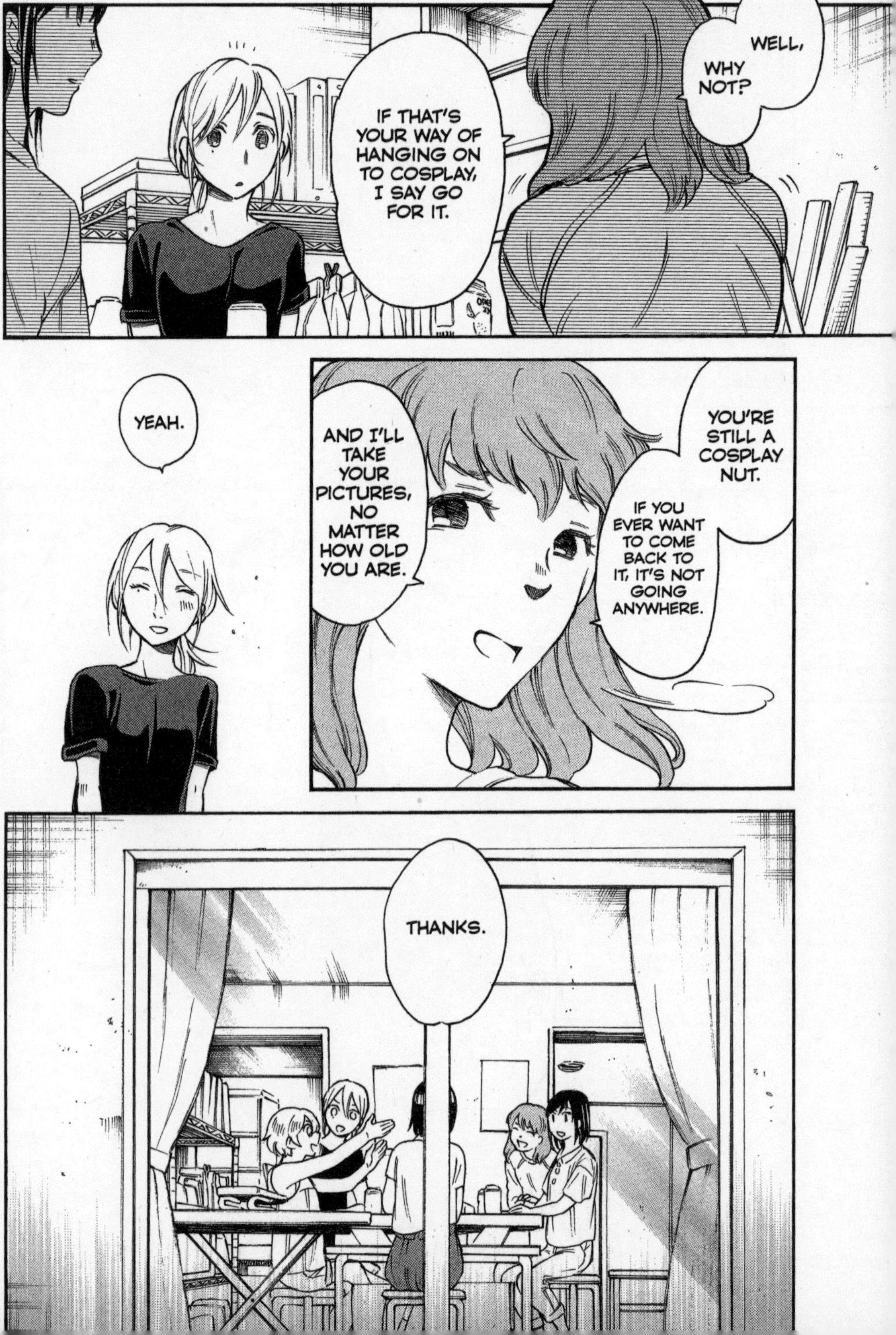
WELL, WHY NOT?
IF THAT'S YOUR WAY OF HANGING ON TO COSPLAY, I SAY GO FOR IT.
YOU'RE STILL A COSPLAY NUT.
IF YOU EVER WANT TO COME BACK TO IT, IT'S NOT GOING ANYWHERE.
AND I'LL TAKE YOUR PICTURES, NO MATTER HOW OLD YOU ARE.
YEAH.
THANKS.

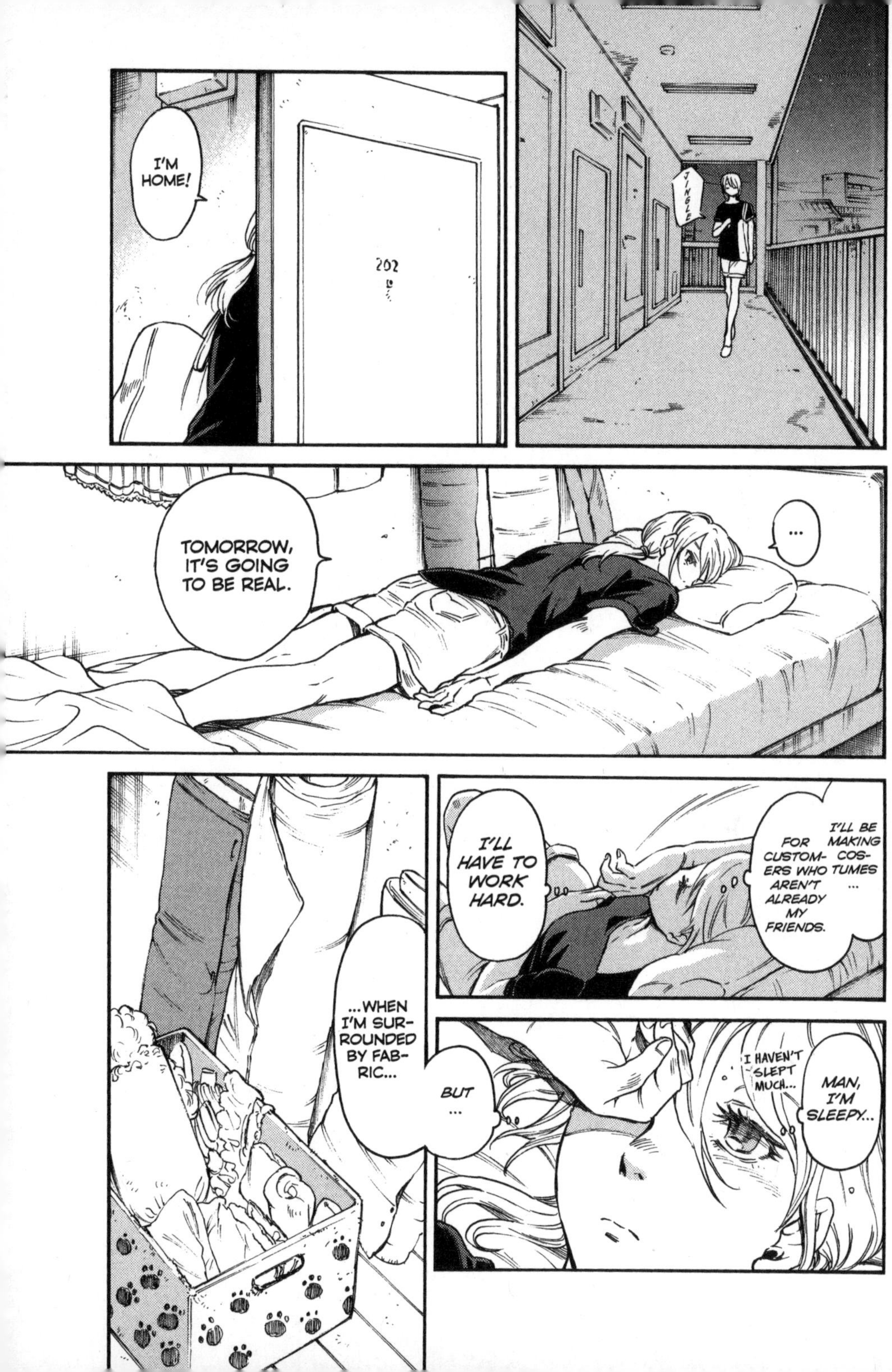
JINGLE
I'M HOME!
...
TOMORROW, IT'S GOING TO BE REAL.
I'LL BE MAKING COSTUMES... FOR CUSTOMERS WHO AREN'T ALREADY MY FRIENDS.
I'LL HAVE TO WORK HARD.
MAN, I'M SLEEPY...
I HAVEN'T SLEPT MUCH...
BUT...
...WHEN I'M SURROUNDED BY FABRIC...
202

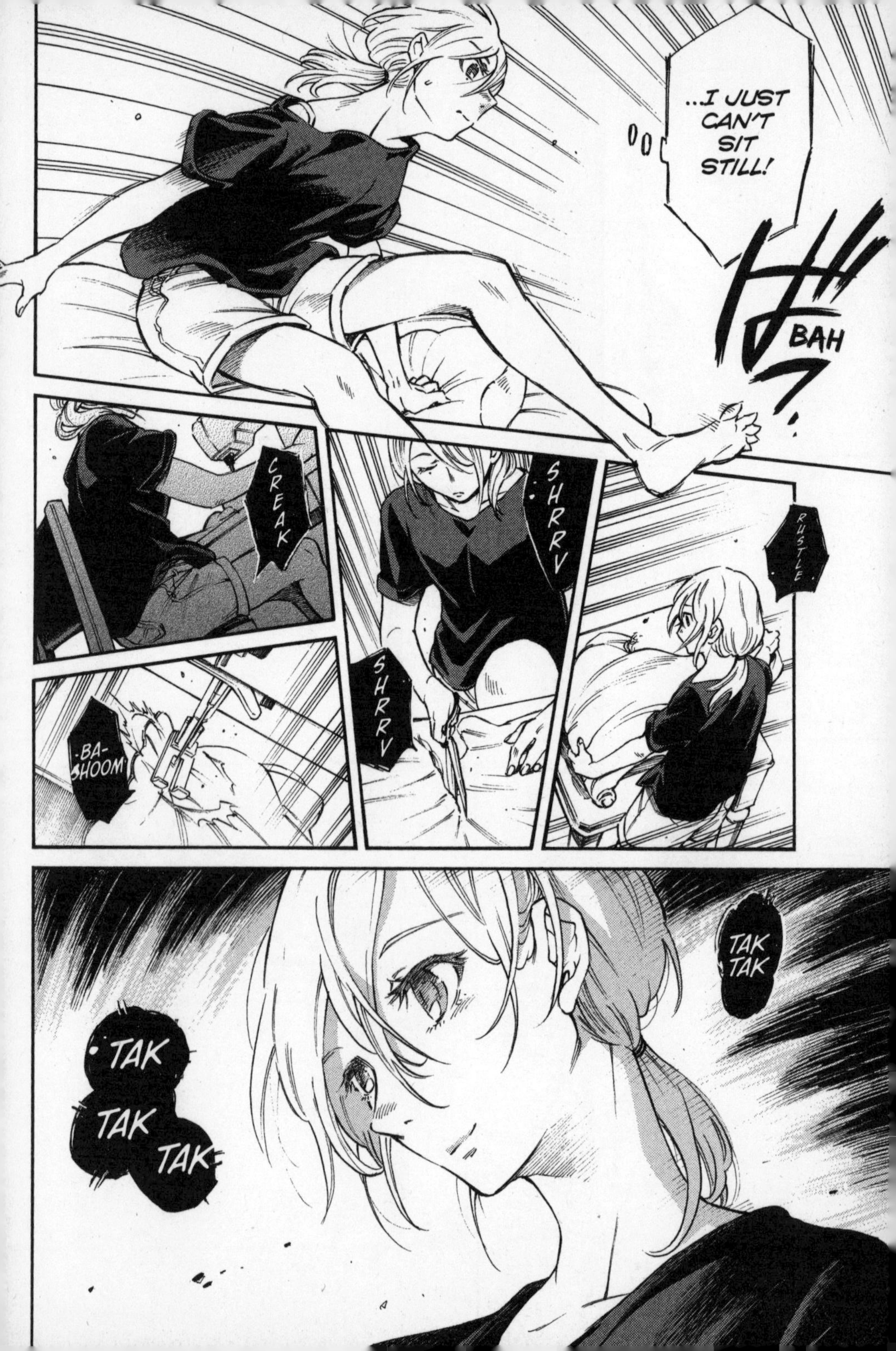
...I JUST CAN'T SIT STILL!
BAH
RUSTLE
SHRRV
SHRRV
CREAK
BA-SHOOM
TAK TAK
TAK
TAK
TAK

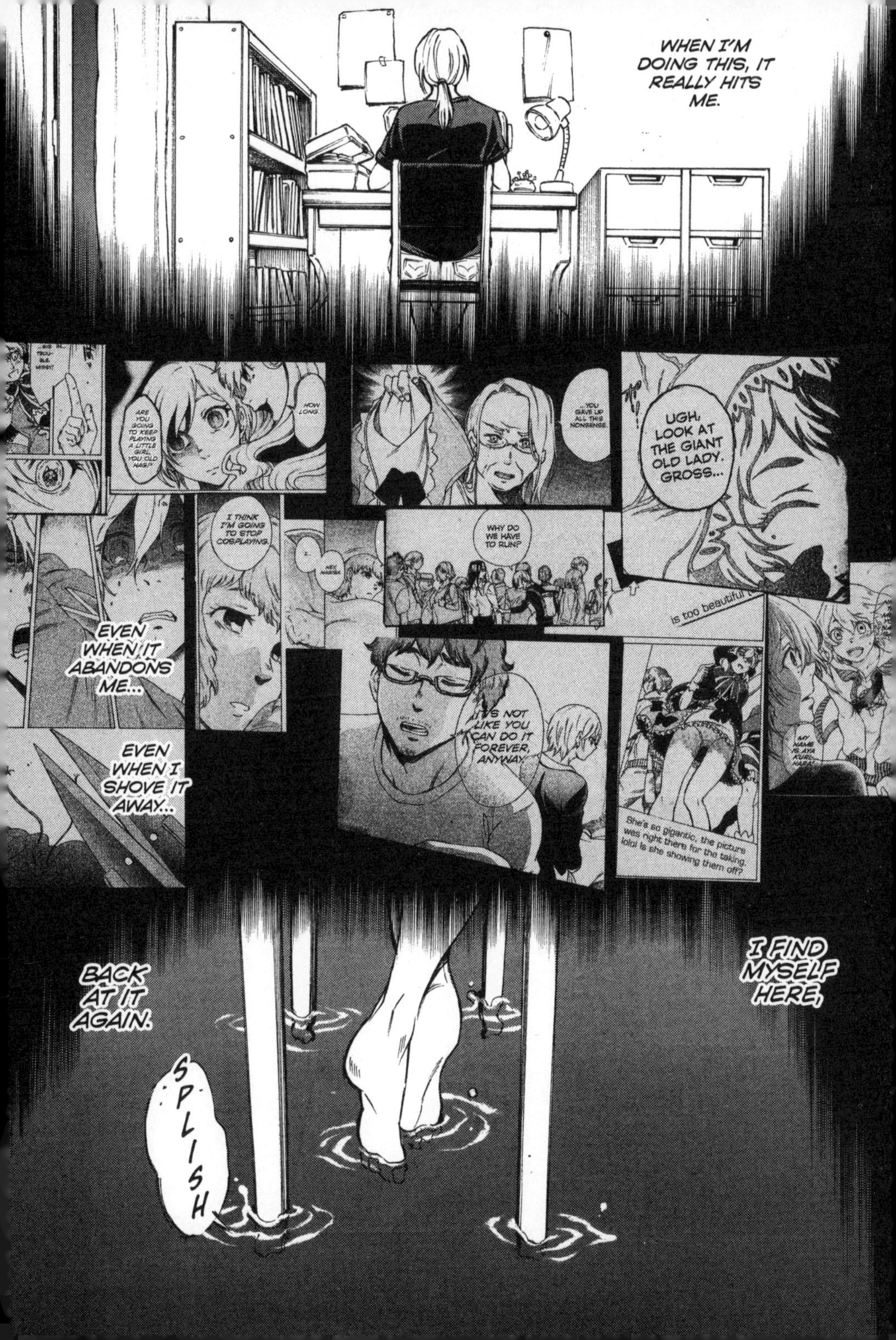
WHEN I'M DOING THIS, IT REALLY HITS ME.
UGH, LOOK AT THE GIANT OLD LADY. GROSS...
...YOU GAVE UP ALL THIS NONSENSE.
HOW LONG...
ARE YOU GOING TO KEEP PLAYING A LITTLE GIRL, YOU OLD HAG?
MY NAME IS AYA KURIHARA!
is too beautiful
She's so gigantic, the picture was right there for the taking. lolol Is she showing them off?
WHY DO WE HAVE TO RUN?
I...
I THINK I'M GOING TO STOP COSPLAYING.
IT'S NOT LIKE YOU CAN DO IT FOREVER, ANYWAY.
EVEN WHEN IT ABANDONS ME...
EVEN WHEN I SHOVE IT AWAY...
I FIND MYSELF HERE,
BACK AT IT AGAIN.
SPLISH

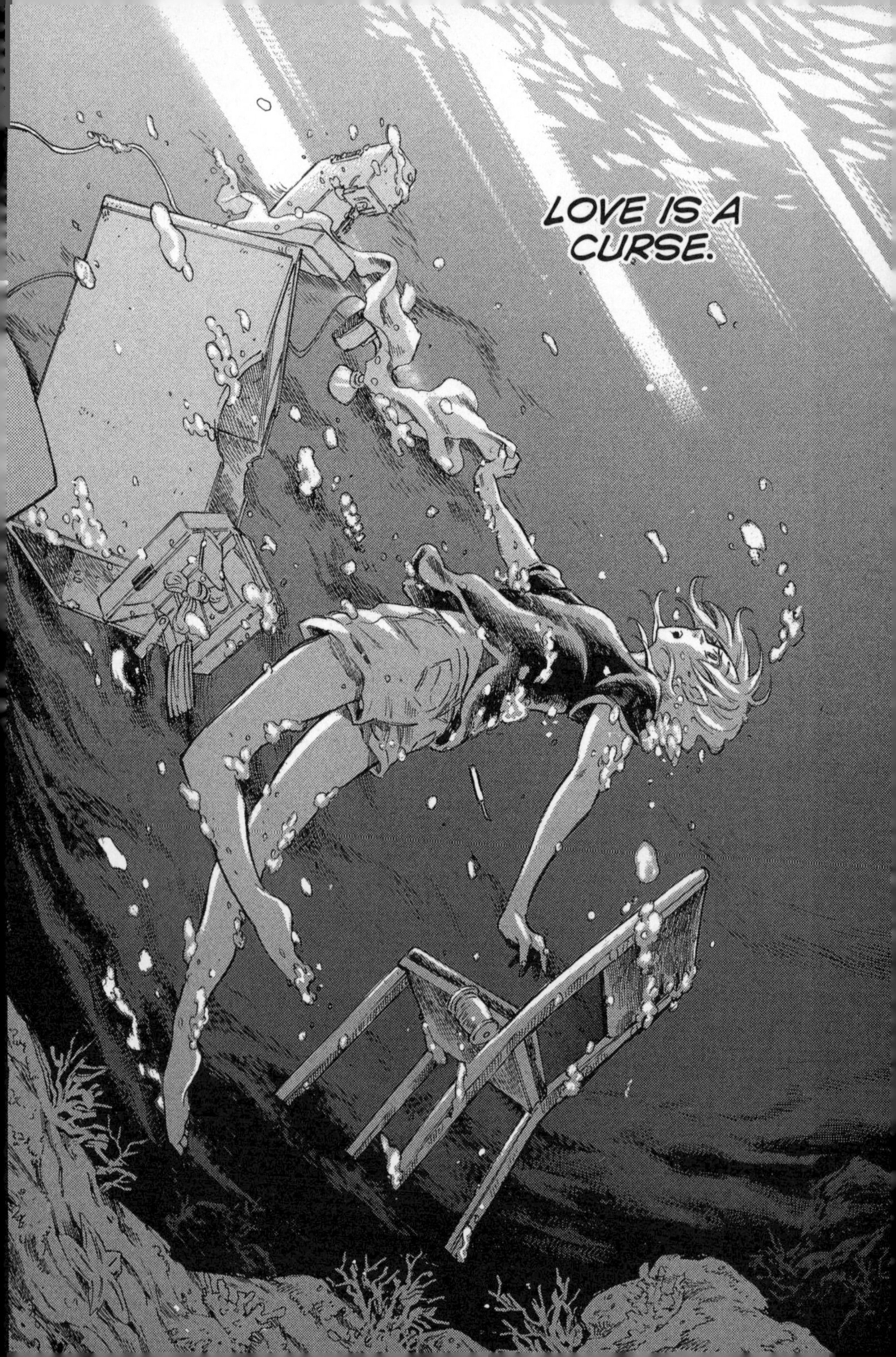
LOVE IS A CURSE.

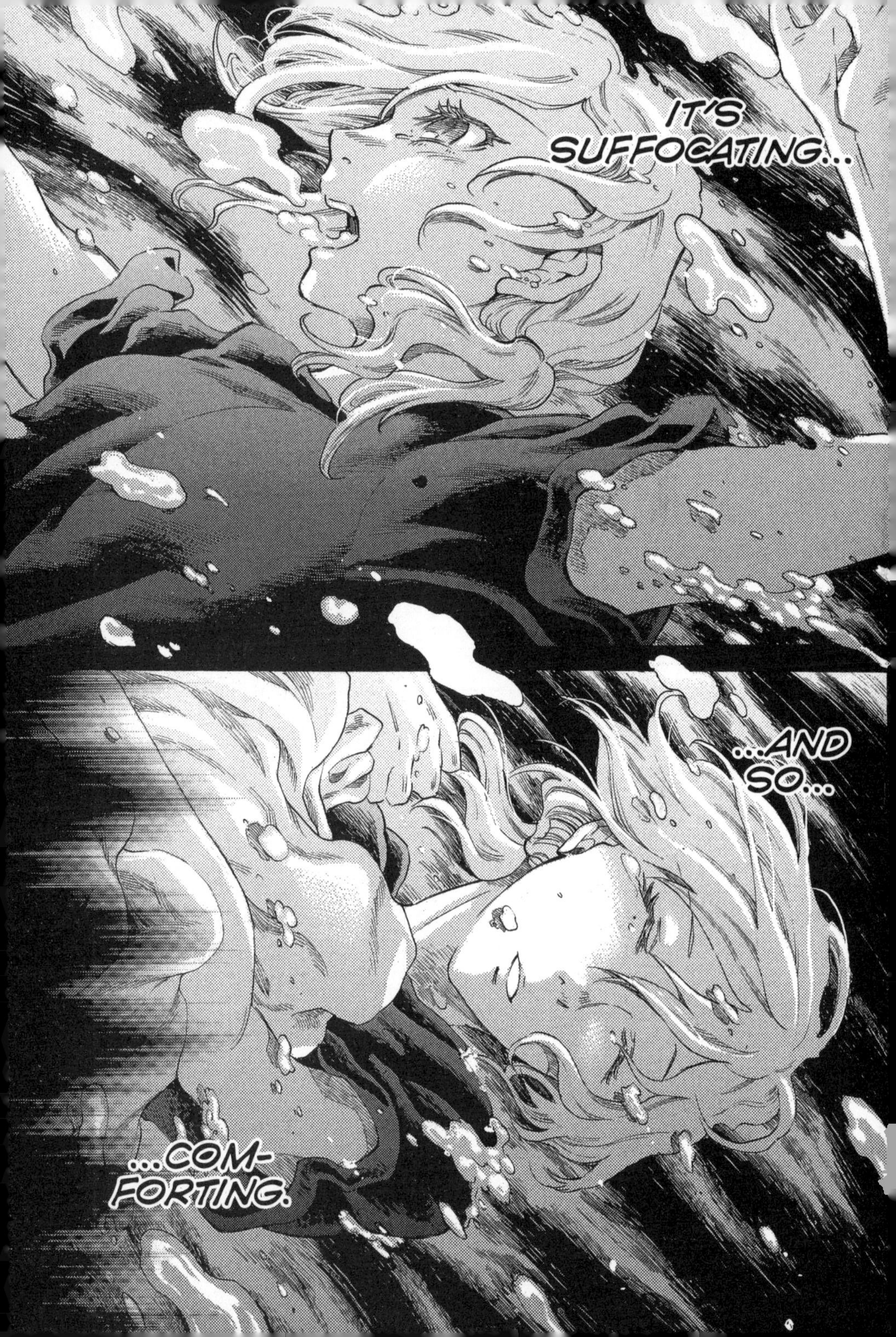
IT'S SUFFOCATING...
...AND SO...
...COM-FORTING.

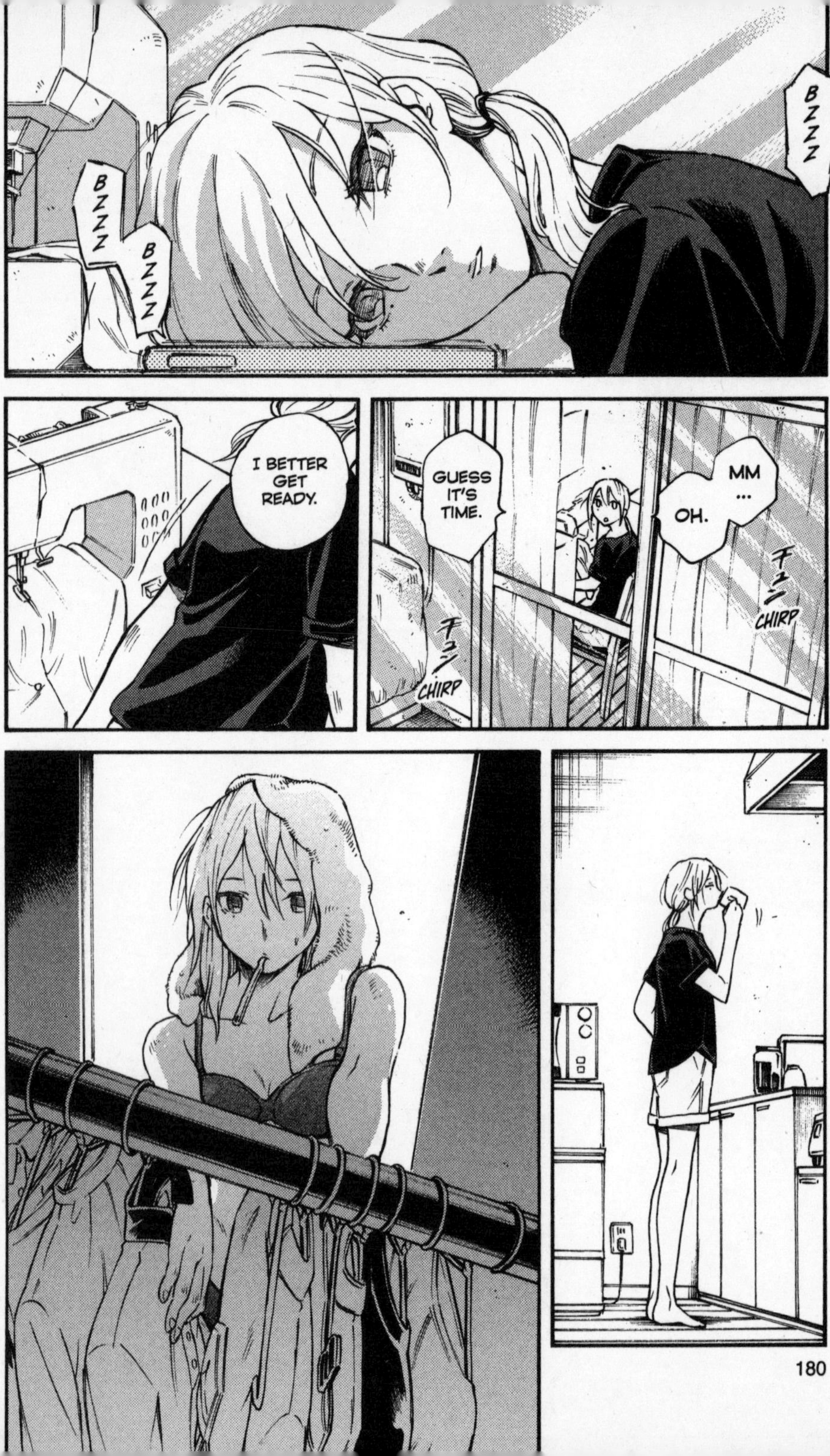
BZZZ
BZZZ
BZZZ
MM...
OH.
GUESS IT'S TIME.
チュン
CHIRP
チュン
CHIRP
I BETTER GET READY.

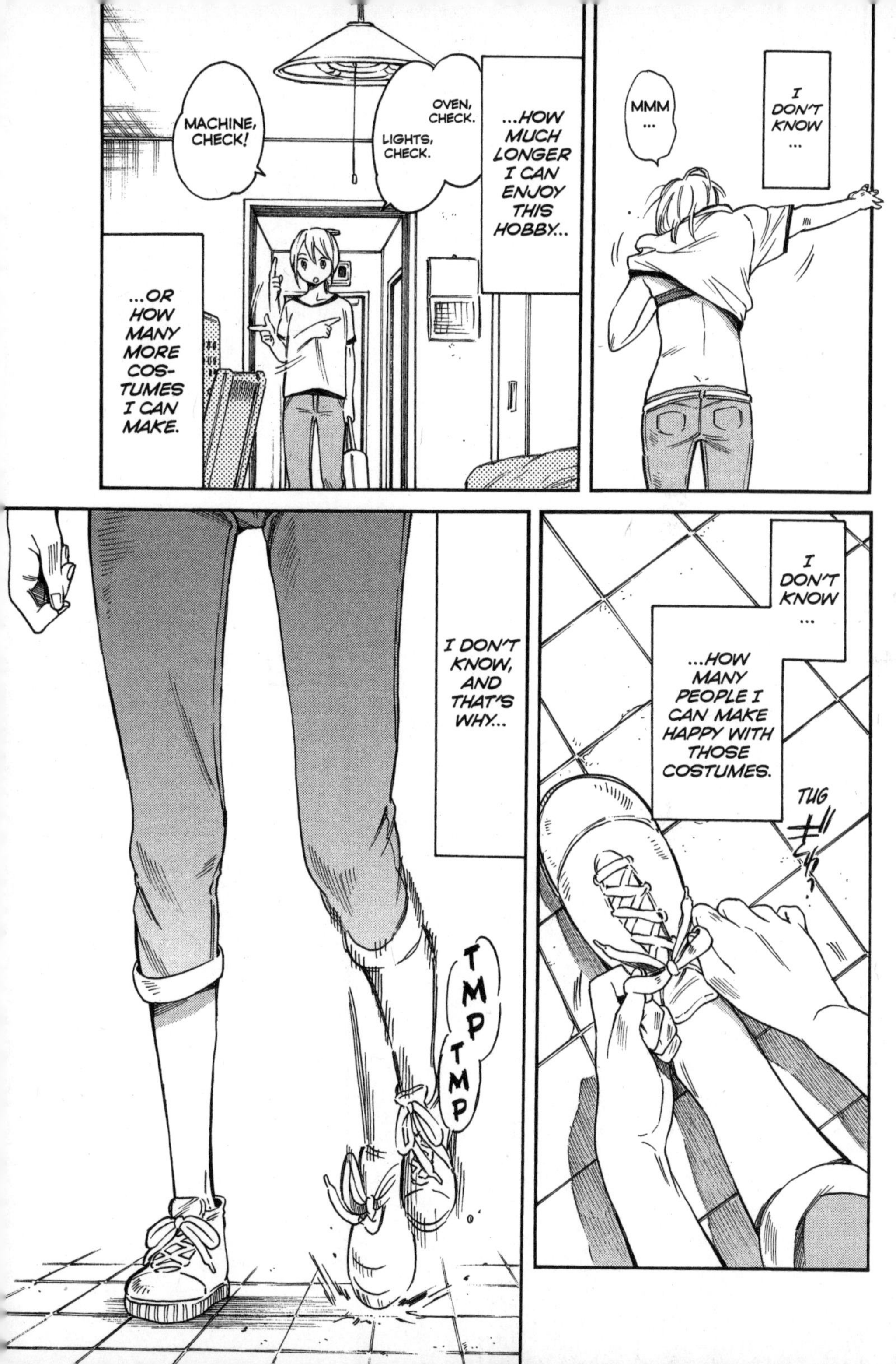
I DON'T KNOW...
MMM...
...HOW MUCH LONGER I CAN ENJOY THIS HOBBY...
OVEN, CHECK.
LIGHTS, CHECK.
MACHINE, CHECK!
...OR HOW MANY MORE COSTUMES I CAN MAKE.
I DON'T KNOW...
...HOW MANY PEOPLE I CAN MAKE HAPPY WITH THOSE COSTUMES.
TUG
I DON'T KNOW, AND THAT'S WHY...
TMP TMP

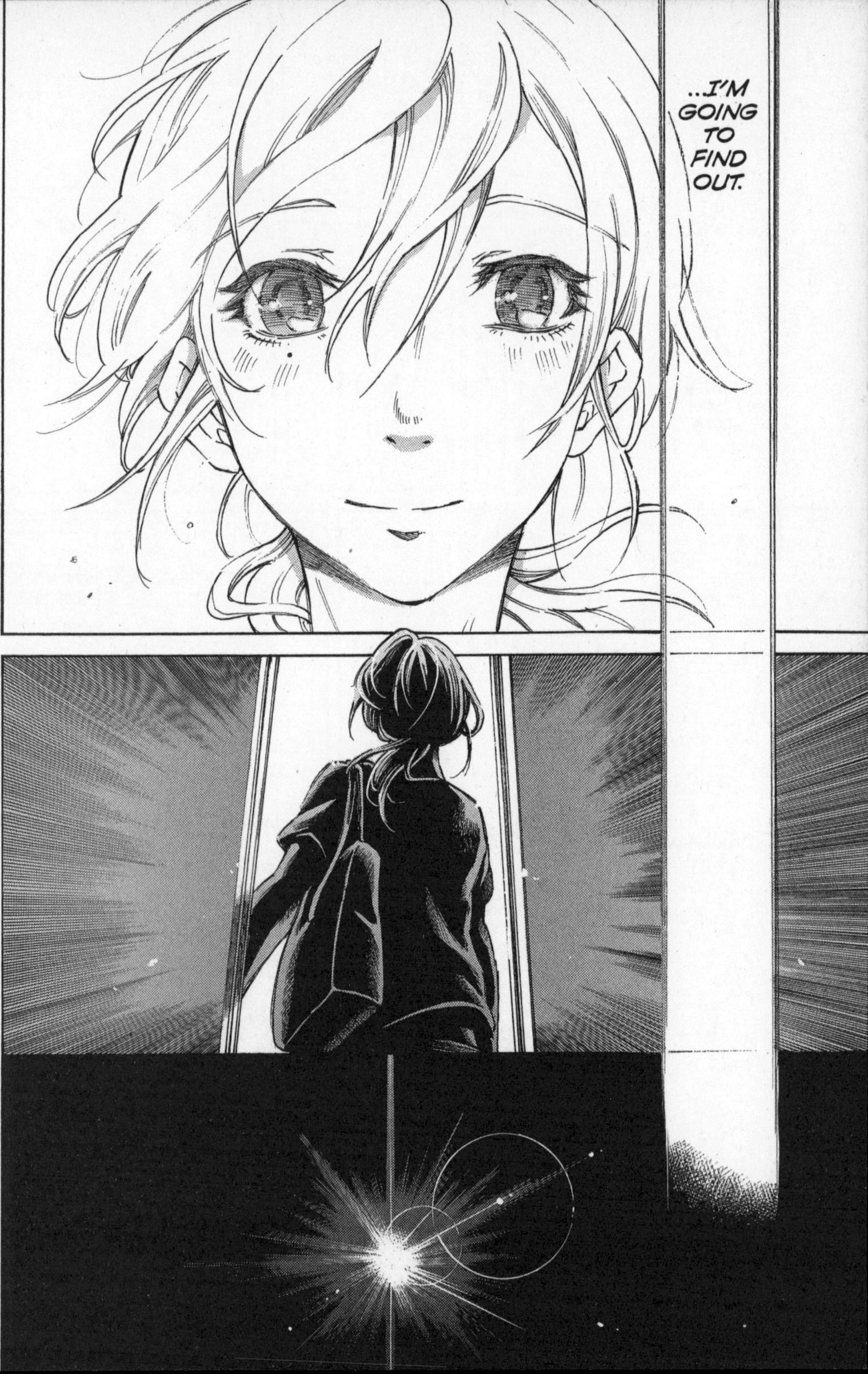
...I'M GOING TO FIND OUT.

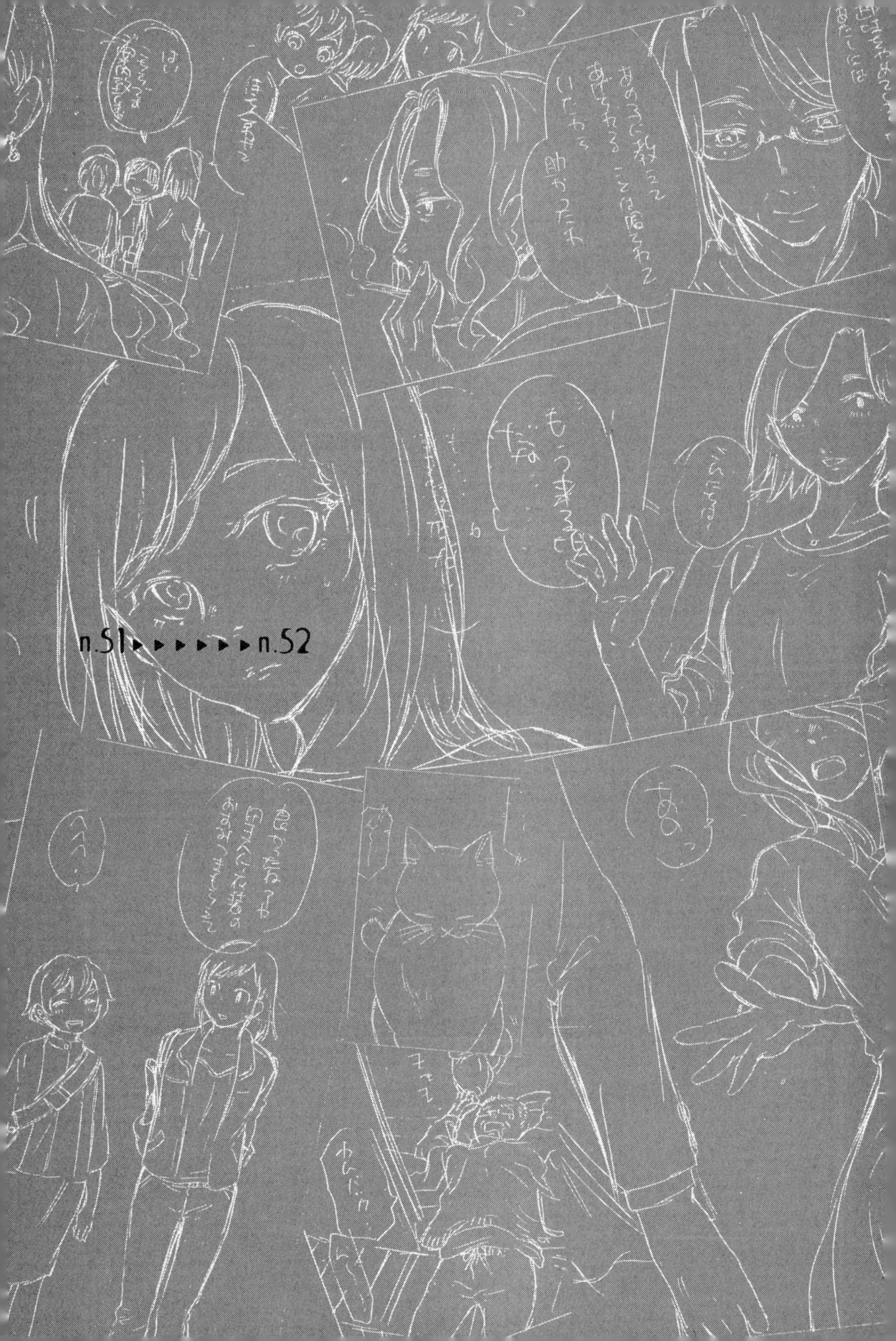

n.51▸▸▸▸▸▸▸n.52

FINALE.

ONE YEAR. THIS SERIES WAS ONLY ONE YEAR LONG, BUT THERE WERE SO MANY TIMES MY FEET DRAGGED AS I HEADED TOWARD MY DESK.

WHAT SUPPORTED ME IN THOSE TIMES WAS, OF COURSE, MY READERS, AND MY ASSISTANTS, MY EDITORS, MY FRIENDS, AND MANGA, ANIME, AND GAMES!!

IF EVEN ONE OF THOSE THINGS HAD BEEN MISSING, I DON'T THINK I COULD HAVE MADE IT THROUGH THE YEAR.

TRULY, THANK YOU.

SEE YOU AGAIN.

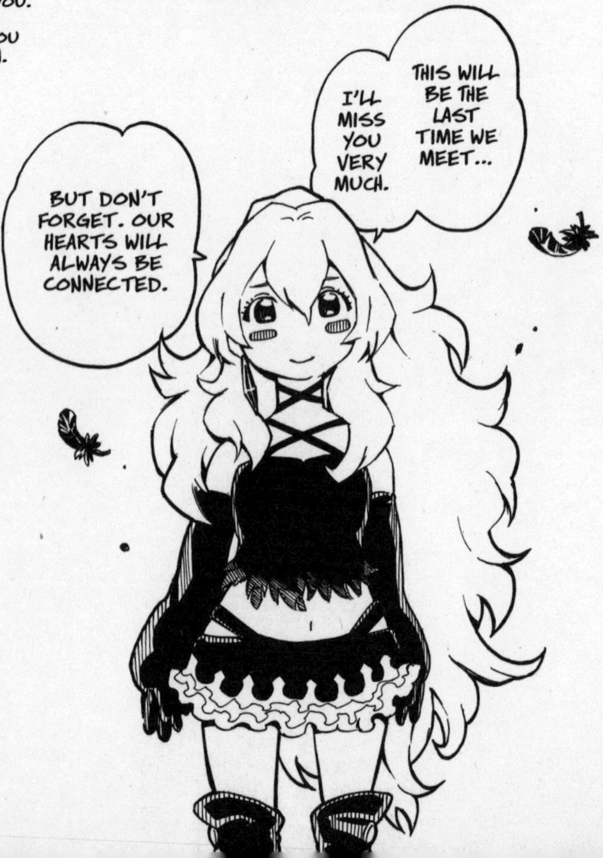
THIS WILL BE THE LAST TIME WE MEET...
I'LL MISS YOU VERY MUCH.
BUT DON'T FORGET. OUR HEARTS WILL ALWAYS BE CONNECTED.

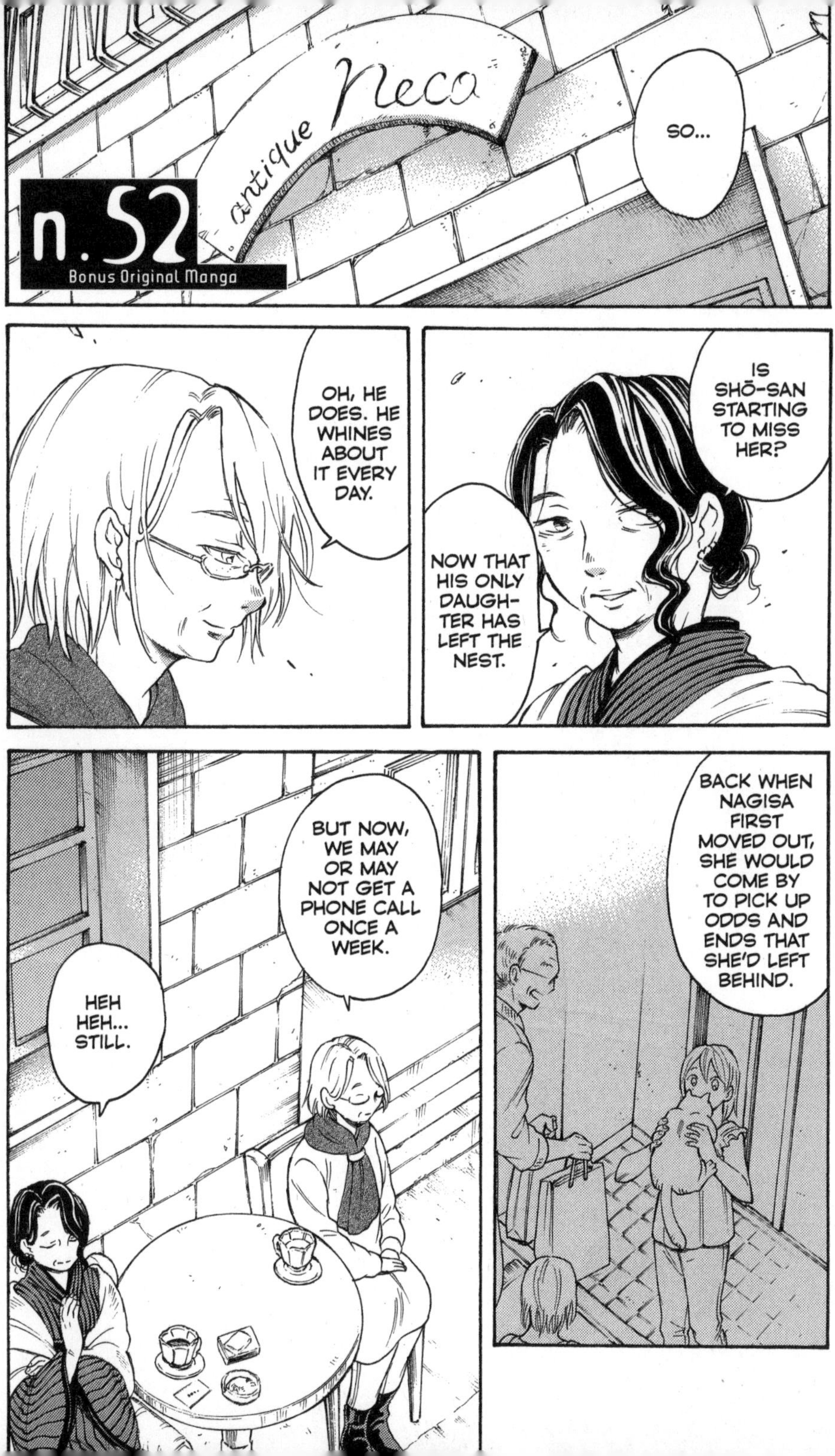
antique neco
n. 52
Bonus Original Manga
SO...
IS SHŌ-SAN STARTING TO MISS HER?
NOW THAT HIS ONLY DAUGHTER HAS LEFT THE NEST.
OH, HE DOES. HE WHINES ABOUT IT EVERY DAY.
BACK WHEN NAGISA FIRST MOVED OUT, SHE WOULD COME BY TO PICK UP ODDS AND ENDS THAT SHE'D LEFT BEHIND.
BUT NOW, WE MAY OR MAY NOT GET A PHONE CALL ONCE A WEEK.
HEH HEH... STILL.

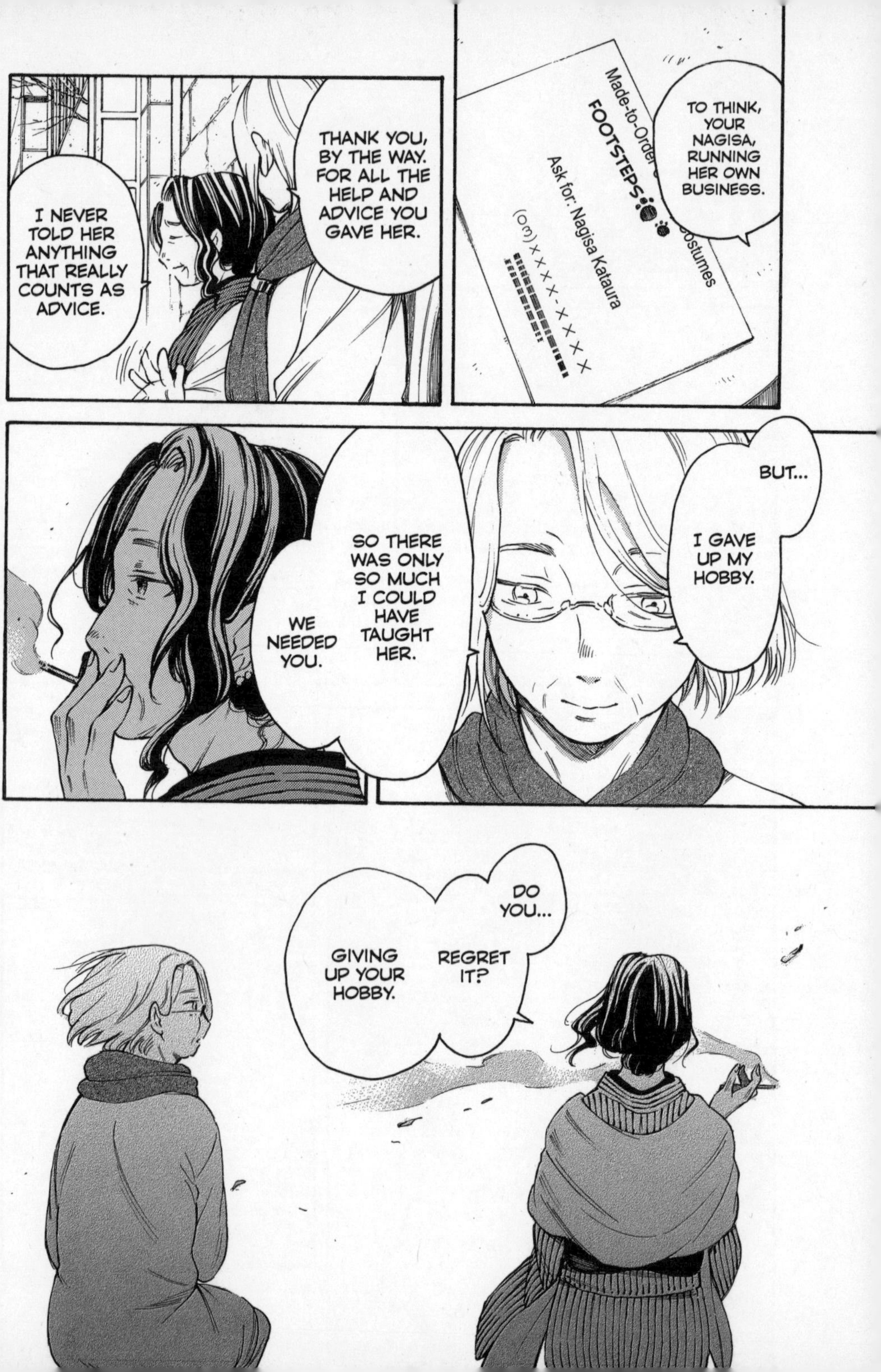
Made-to-Order
Costumes
FOOTSTEPS
Ask for: Nagisa Kataura
(○○)××××-××××
TO THINK, YOUR NAGISA, RUNNING HER OWN BUSINESS.
THANK YOU, BY THE WAY. FOR ALL THE HELP AND ADVICE YOU GAVE HER.
I NEVER TOLD HER ANYTHING THAT REALLY COUNTS AS ADVICE.
BUT...
I GAVE UP MY HOBBY.
SO THERE WAS ONLY SO MUCH I COULD HAVE TAUGHT HER.
WE NEEDED YOU.
DO YOU...
REGRET IT?
GIVING UP YOUR HOBBY.

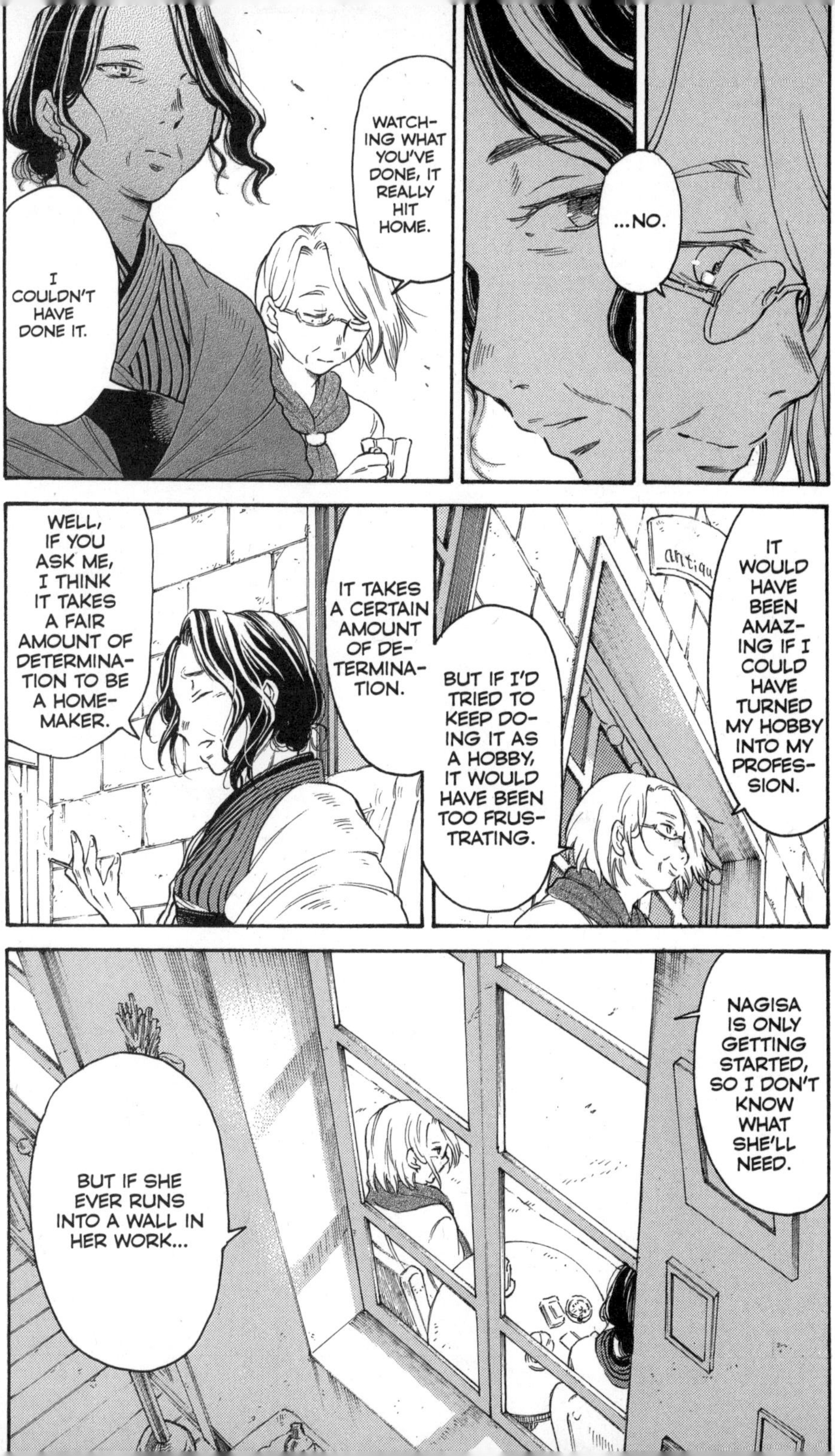
...NO.
WATCHING WHAT YOU'VE DONE, IT REALLY HIT HOME.
I COULDN'T HAVE DONE IT.
IT WOULD HAVE BEEN AMAZING IF I COULD HAVE TURNED MY HOBBY INTO MY PROFESSION.
BUT IF I'D TRIED TO KEEP DOING IT AS A HOBBY, IT WOULD HAVE BEEN TOO FRUSTRATING.
IT TAKES A CERTAIN AMOUNT OF DETERMINATION.
WELL, IF YOU ASK ME, I THINK IT TAKES A FAIR AMOUNT OF DETERMINATION TO BE A HOMEMAKER.
NAGISA IS ONLY GETTING STARTED, SO I DON'T KNOW WHAT SHE'LL NEED.
BUT IF SHE EVER RUNS INTO A WALL IN HER WORK...

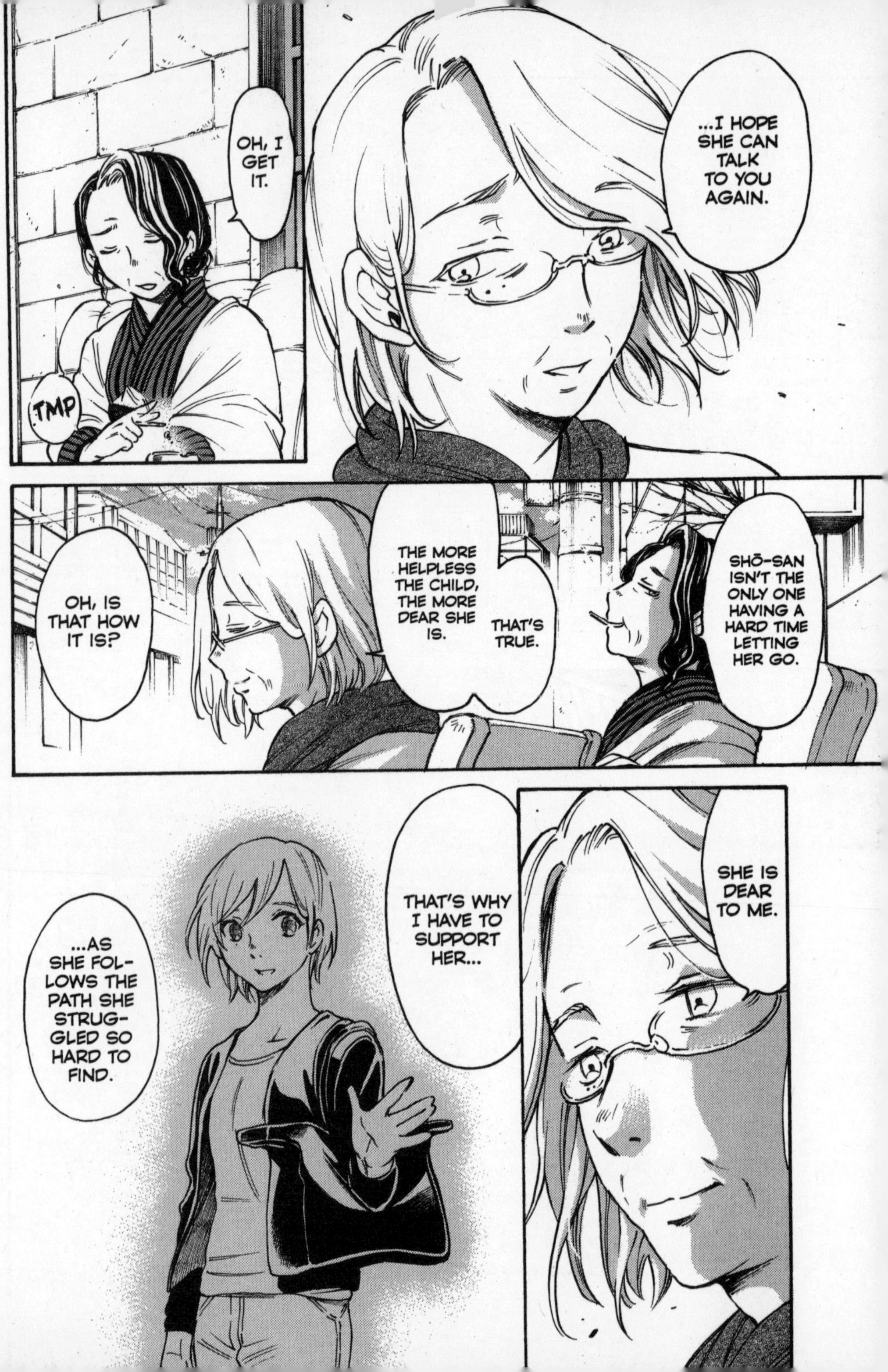
...I HOPE SHE CAN TALK TO YOU AGAIN.
OH, I GET IT.
TMP
SHŌ-SAN ISN'T THE ONLY ONE HAVING A HARD TIME LETTING HER GO.
THAT'S TRUE.
THE MORE HELPLESS THE CHILD, THE MORE DEAR SHE IS.
OH, IS THAT HOW IT IS?
SHE IS DEAR TO ME.
THAT'S WHY I HAVE TO SUPPORT HER...
...AS SHE FOLLOWS THE PATH SHE STRUGGLED SO HARD TO FIND.

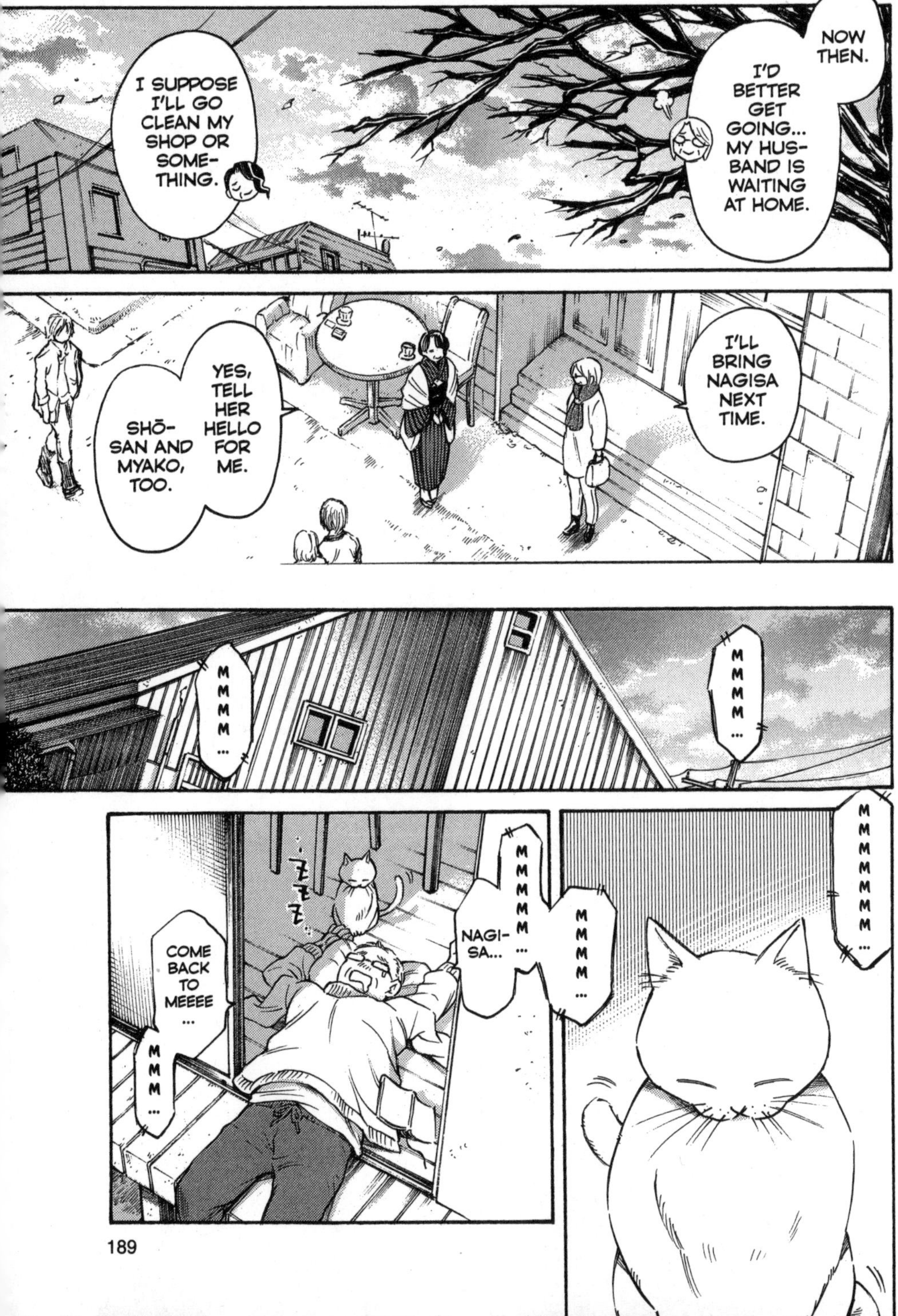
NOW THEN.
I'D BETTER GET GOING... MY HUSBAND IS WAITING AT HOME.
I SUPPOSE I'LL GO CLEAN MY SHOP OR SOMETHING.
I'LL BRING NAGISA NEXT TIME.
YES, TELL HER HELLO FOR ME.
SHŌ-SAN AND MYAKO, TOO.
MMMM...
MMMM...
MMMMMMM...
MMMMM...
NAGI-SA...
MMMM...
COME BACK TO MEEEE...
MMM...

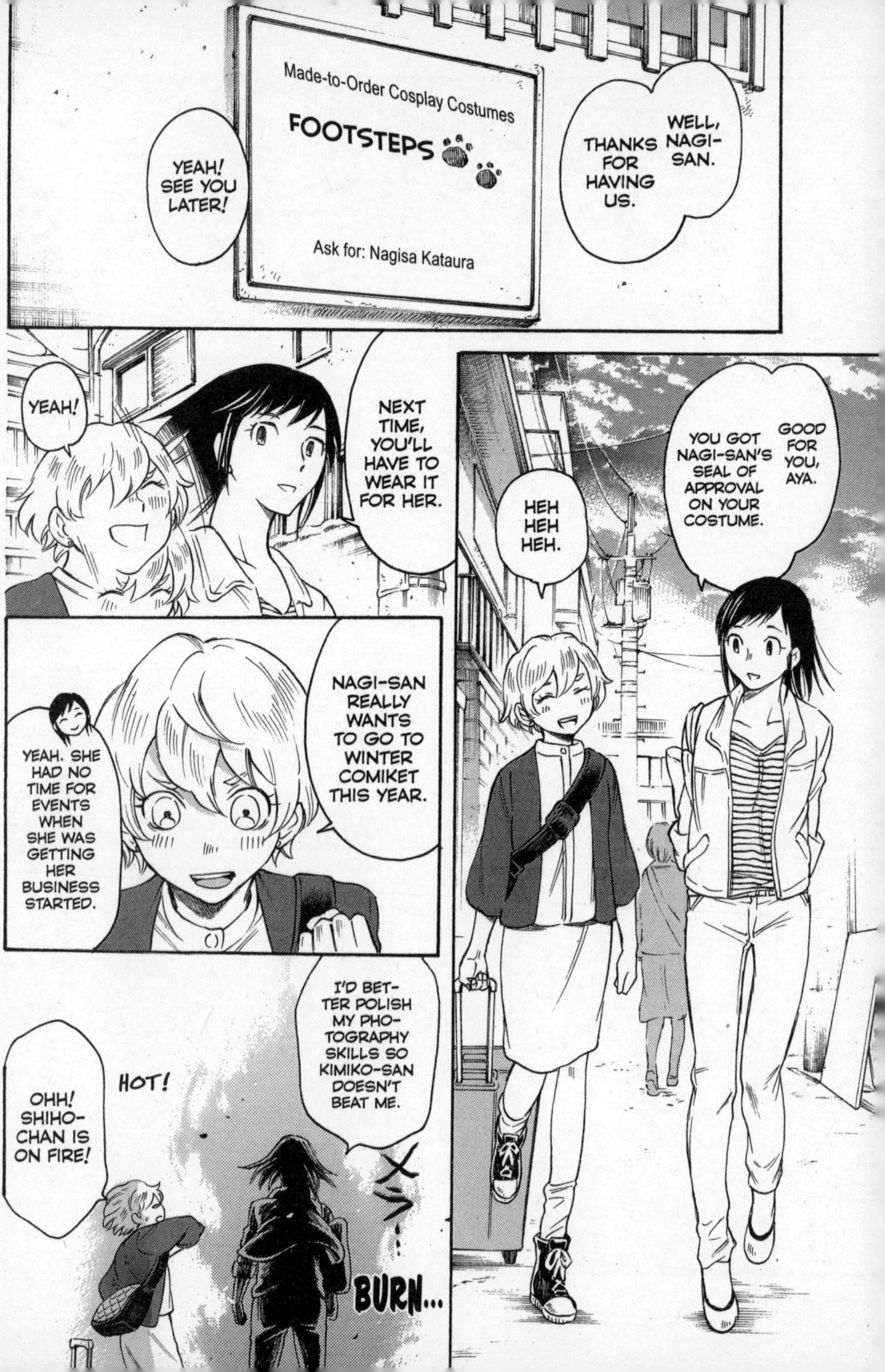
WELL, NAGI-SAN.
THANKS FOR HAVING US.
Made-to-Order Cosplay Costumes
FOOTSTEPS
Ask for: Nagisa Kataura
YEAH! SEE YOU LATER!
GOOD FOR YOU, AYA.
YOU GOT NAGI-SAN'S SEAL OF APPROVAL ON YOUR COSTUME.
HEH HEH HEH.
NEXT TIME, YOU'LL HAVE TO WEAR IT FOR HER.
YEAH!
NAGI-SAN REALLY WANTS TO GO TO WINTER COMIKET THIS YEAR.
YEAH. SHE HAD NO TIME FOR EVENTS WHEN SHE WAS GETTING HER BUSINESS STARTED.
I'D BETTER POLISH MY PHOTOGRAPHY SKILLS SO KIMIKO-SAN DOESN'T BEAT ME.
BURN...
HOT!
OHH! SHIHO-CHAN IS ON FIRE!

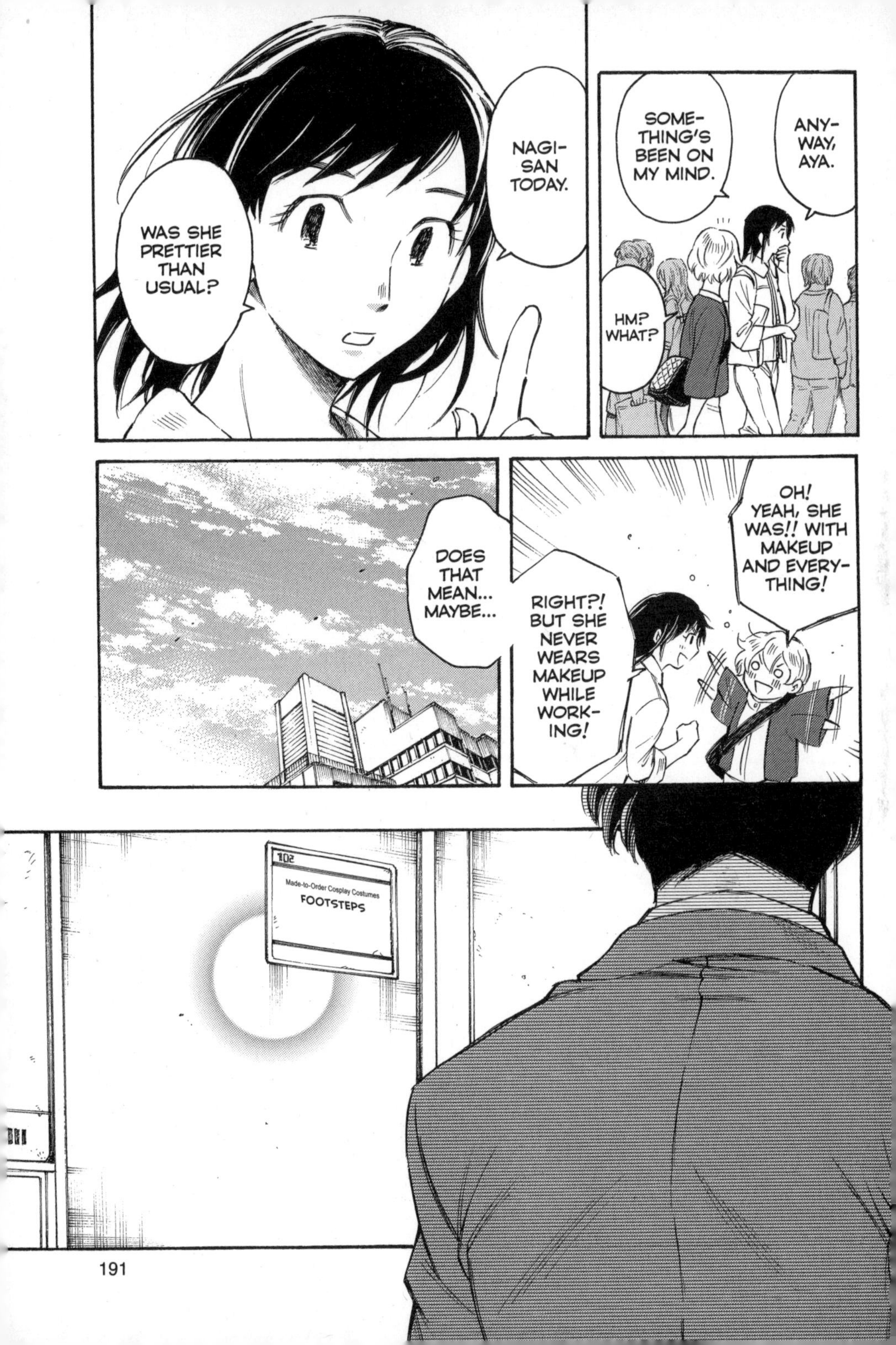
ANYWAY, AYA.
SOMETHING'S BEEN ON MY MIND.
HM? WHAT?
NAGI-SAN TODAY.
WAS SHE PRETTIER THAN USUAL?
OH! YEAH, SHE WAS!! WITH MAKEUP AND EVERYTHING!
RIGHT?! BUT SHE NEVER WEARS MAKEUP WHILE WORKING!
DOES THAT MEAN... MAYBE...
102
Made-to-Order Cosplay Costumes
FOOTSTEPS

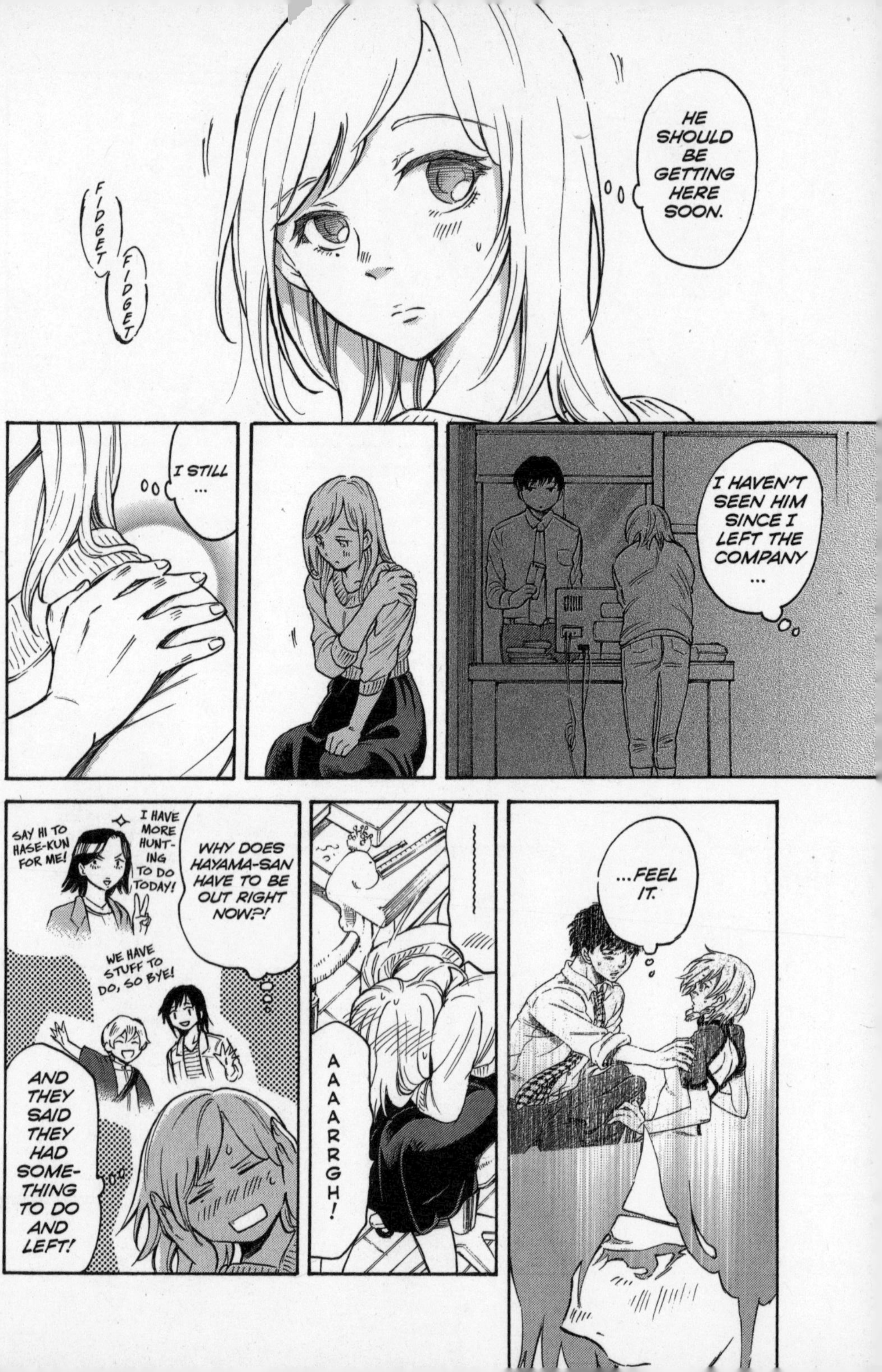
HE SHOULD BE GETTING HERE SOON.
FIDGET FIDGET
I HAVEN'T SEEN HIM SINCE I LEFT THE COMPANY ...
I STILL ...
...FEEL IT.
......
AAAARRGH!
WHY DOES HAYAMA-SAN HAVE TO BE OUT RIGHT NOW?!
I HAVE MORE HUNT-ING TO DO TODAY!
SAY HI TO HASE-KUN FOR ME!
WE HAVE STUFF TO DO, SO BYE!
AND THEY SAID THEY HAD SOME-THING TO DO AND LEFT!

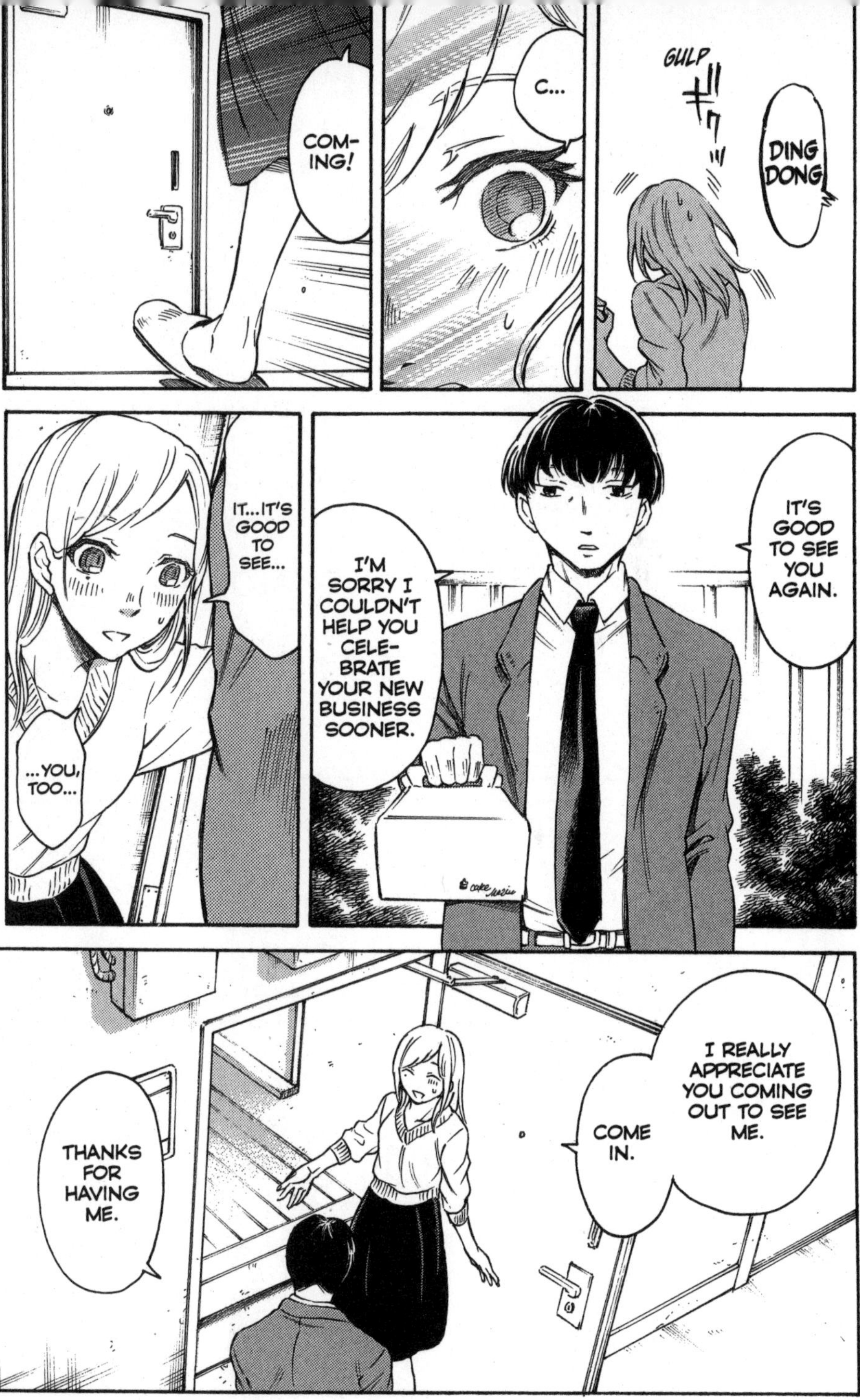
GULP
DING DONG
C...
COMING!
IT'S GOOD TO SEE YOU AGAIN.
I'M SORRY I COULDN'T HELP YOU CELEBRATE YOUR NEW BUSINESS SOONER.
IT...IT'S GOOD TO SEE...
...YOU, TOO...
I REALLY APPRECIATE YOU COMING OUT TO SEE ME.
COME IN.
THANKS FOR HAVING ME.

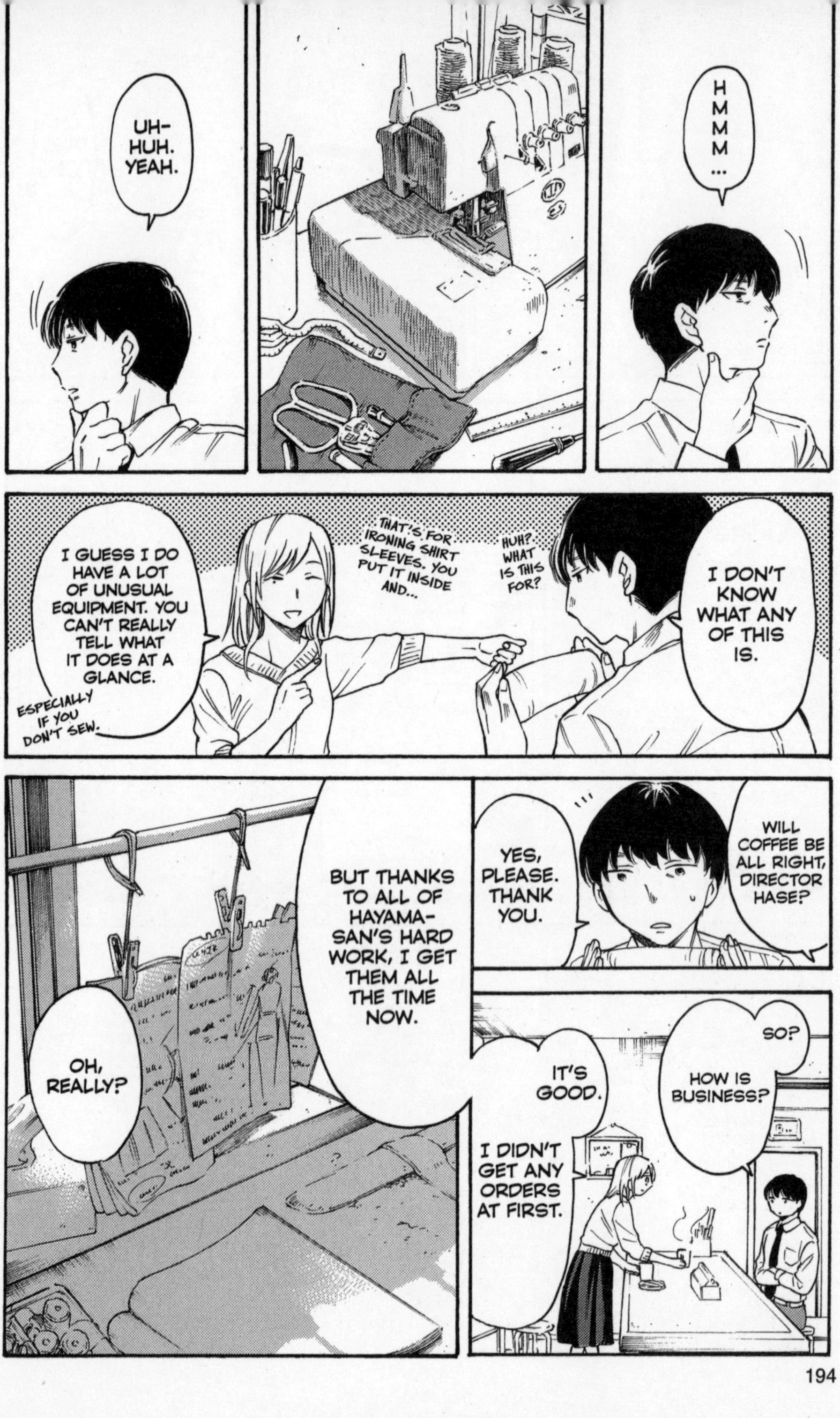
HMMM...
UH-HUH. YEAH.
I DON'T KNOW WHAT ANY OF THIS IS.
HUH? WHAT IS THIS FOR?
THAT'S FOR IRONING SHIRT SLEEVES. YOU PUT IT INSIDE AND...
I GUESS I DO HAVE A LOT OF UNUSUAL EQUIPMENT. YOU CAN'T REALLY TELL WHAT IT DOES AT A GLANCE.
ESPECIALLY IF YOU DON'T SEW.
WILL COFFEE BE ALL RIGHT, DIRECTOR HASE?
YES, PLEASE. THANK YOU.
SO?
HOW IS BUSINESS?
IT'S GOOD.
I DIDN'T GET ANY ORDERS AT FIRST.
BUT THANKS TO ALL OF HAYAMA-SAN'S HARD WORK, I GET THEM ALL THE TIME NOW.
OH, REALLY?

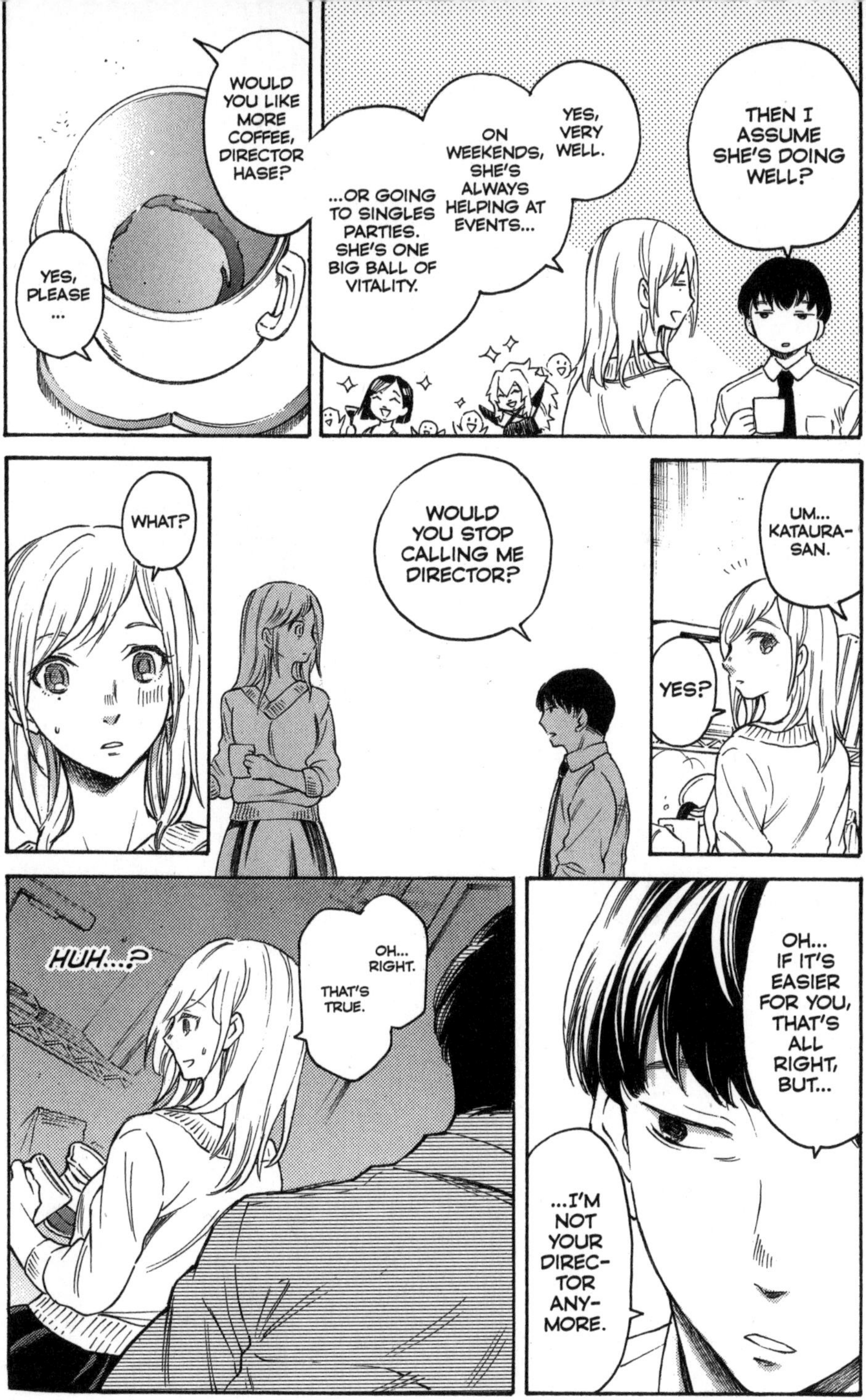
THEN I ASSUME SHE'S DOING WELL?
YES, VERY WELL.
ON WEEKENDS, SHE'S ALWAYS HELPING AT EVENTS...
...OR GOING TO SINGLES PARTIES. SHE'S ONE BIG BALL OF VITALITY.
WOULD YOU LIKE MORE COFFEE, DIRECTOR HASE?
YES, PLEASE ...
UM... KATAURA-SAN.
YES?
WOULD YOU STOP CALLING ME DIRECTOR?
WHAT?
OH... IF IT'S EASIER FOR YOU, THAT'S ALL RIGHT, BUT...
...I'M NOT YOUR DIREC-TOR ANY-MORE.
OH... RIGHT.
THAT'S TRUE.
HUH...?

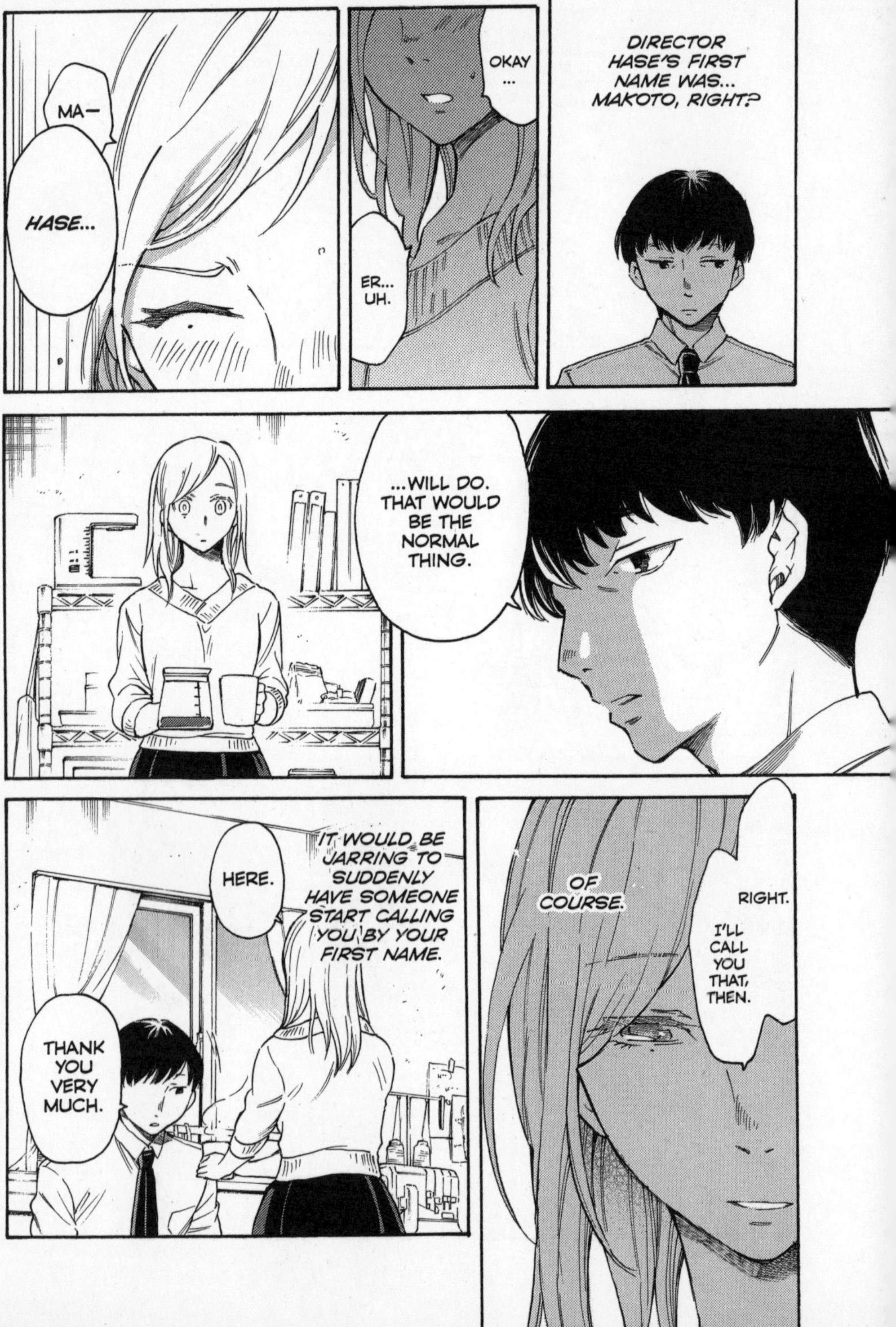
DIRECTOR HASE'S FIRST NAME WAS... MAKOTO, RIGHT?
OKAY ...
ER... UH.
MA—
HASE...
...WILL DO. THAT WOULD BE THE NORMAL THING.
RIGHT.
I'LL CALL YOU THAT, THEN.
OF COURSE.
IT WOULD BE JARRING TO SUDDENLY HAVE SOMEONE START CALLING YOU BY YOUR FIRST NAME.
HERE.
THANK YOU VERY MUCH.

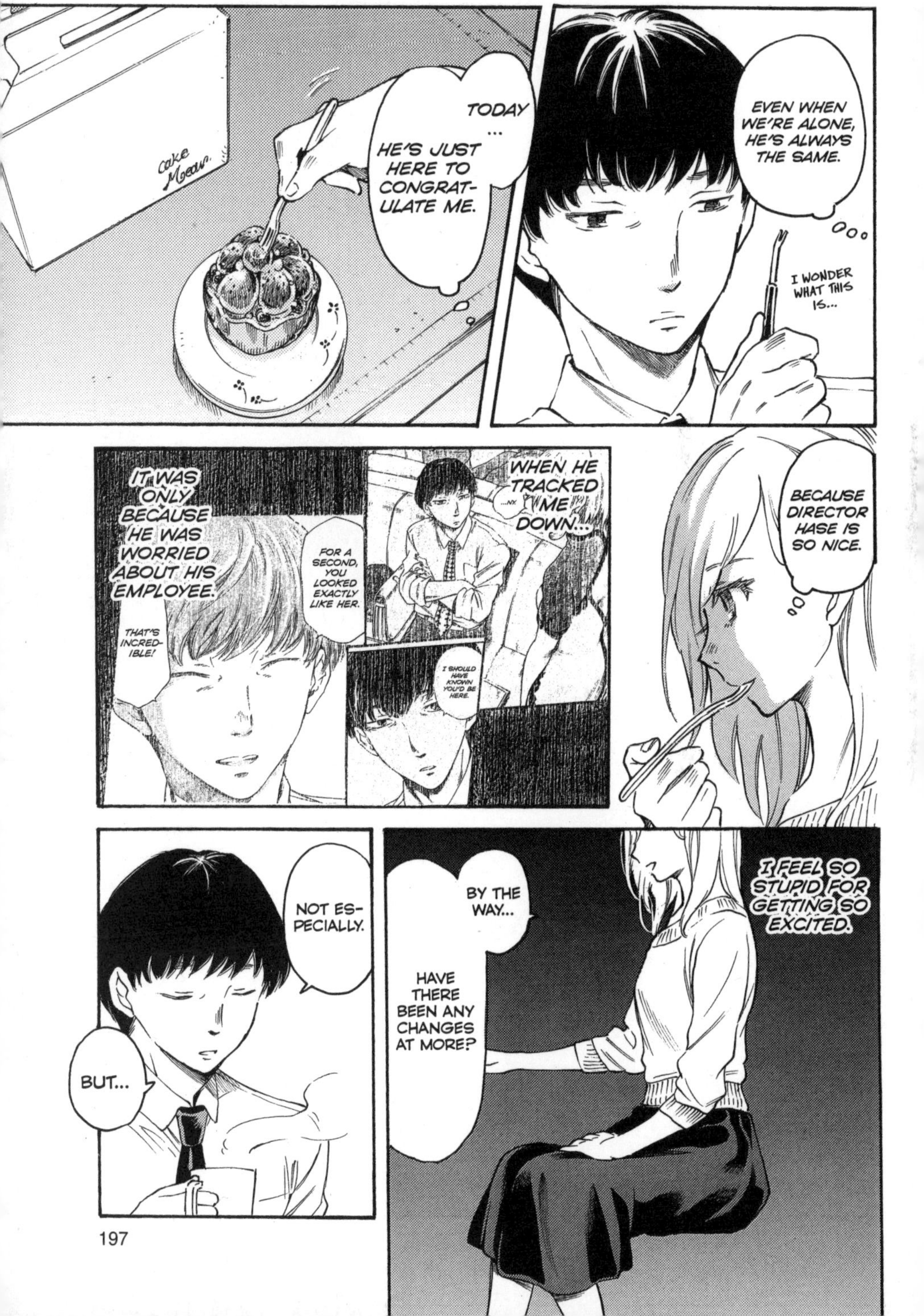
EVEN WHEN WE'RE ALONE, HE'S ALWAYS THE SAME.
I WONDER WHAT THIS IS...
TODAY...
HE'S JUST HERE TO CONGRAT-ULATE ME.
BECAUSE DIRECTOR HASE IS SO NICE.
WHEN HE TRACKED ME DOWN...
IT WAS ONLY BECAUSE HE WAS WORRIED ABOUT HIS EMPLOYEE.
FOR A SECOND, YOU LOOKED EXACTLY LIKE HER.
THAT'S INCRED-IBLE!
I SHOULD HAVE KNOWN YOU'D BE HERE.
I FEEL SO STUPID FOR GETTING SO EXCITED.
BY THE WAY...
HAVE THERE BEEN ANY CHANGES AT MORE?
NOT ES-PECIALLY.
BUT...

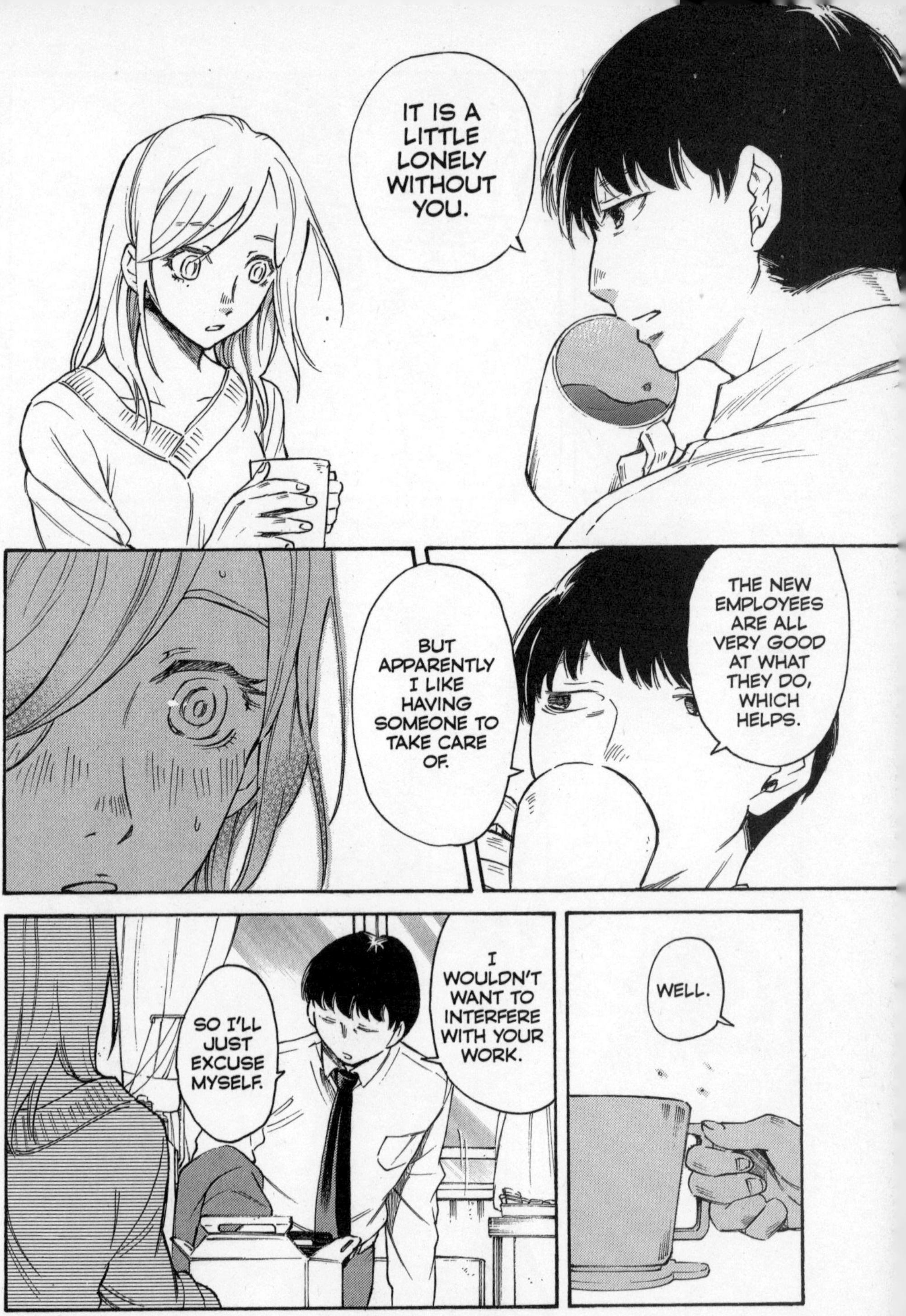
IT IS A LITTLE LONELY WITHOUT YOU.
THE NEW EMPLOYEES ARE ALL VERY GOOD AT WHAT THEY DO, WHICH HELPS.
BUT APPARENTLY I LIKE HAVING SOMEONE TO TAKE CARE OF.
WELL.
I WOULDN'T WANT TO INTERFERE WITH YOUR WORK.
SO I'LL JUST EXCUSE MYSELF.

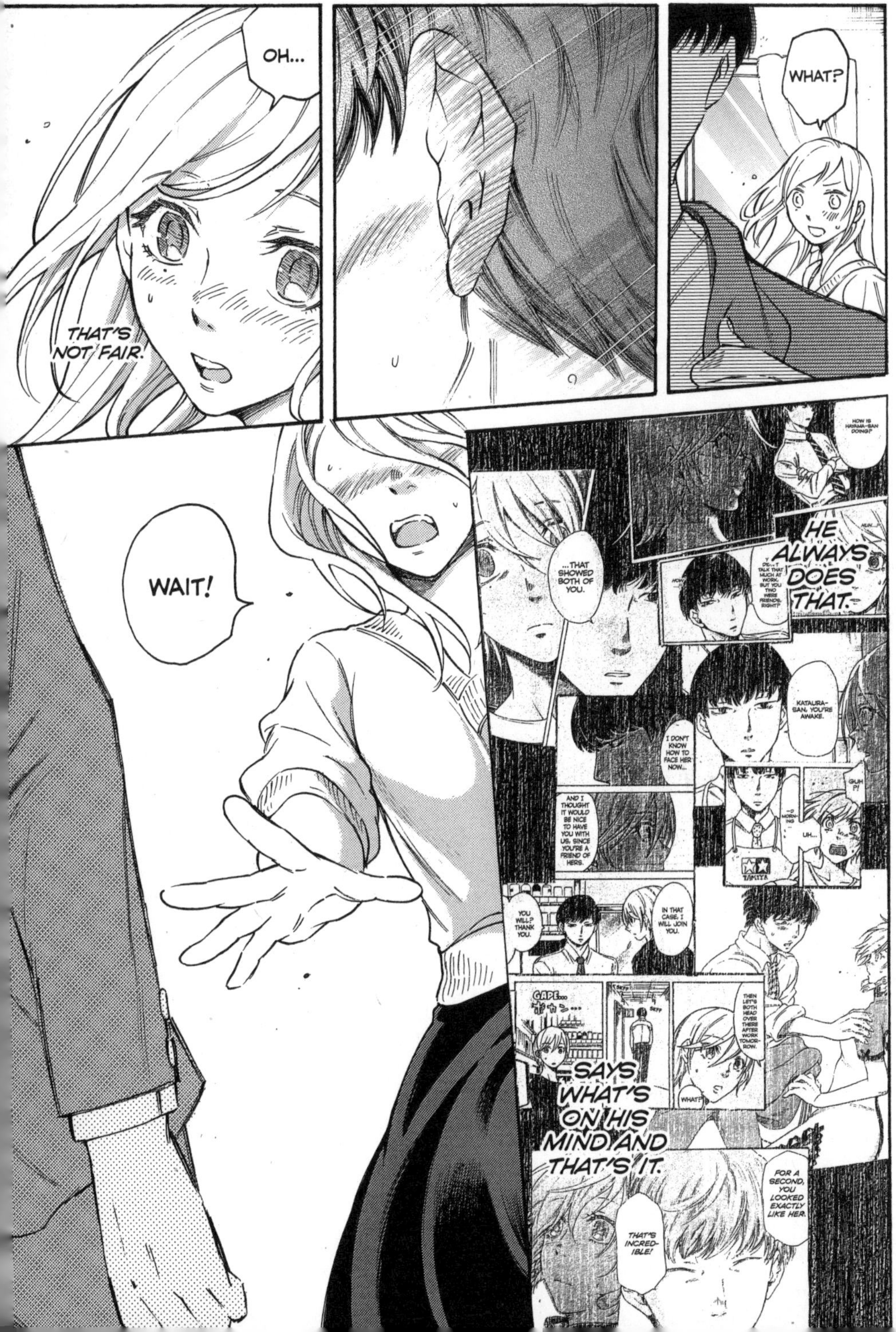
WHAT?
OH...
THAT'S NOT FAIR.
HOW IS HAYAMA-SAN DOING?
HUH...?
HE ALWAYS DOES THAT.
TALK THAT MUCH AT WORK, BUT YOU TWO WERE FRIENDS, RIGHT?
...THAT SHOWED BOTH OF YOU.
KATAURA-SAN, YOU'RE AWAKE.
I DON'T KNOW HOW TO FACE HER NOW...
GUH ?!
--G MORNING...
UH...
AND I THOUGHT IT WOULD BE NICE TO HAVE YOU WITH US, SINCE YOU'RE A FRIEND OF HERS.
IN THAT CASE, I WILL JOIN YOU.
YOU WILL? THANK YOU.
THEN LET'S BOTH HEAD OVER THERE AFTER WORK TOMORROW.
WHAT?
SKFF
SKFF
GAPE...
ポカン...
--SAYS WHAT'S ON HIS MIND AND THAT'S IT.
FOR A SECOND, YOU LOOKED EXACTLY LIKE HER.
THAT'S INCREDIBLE!
WAIT!

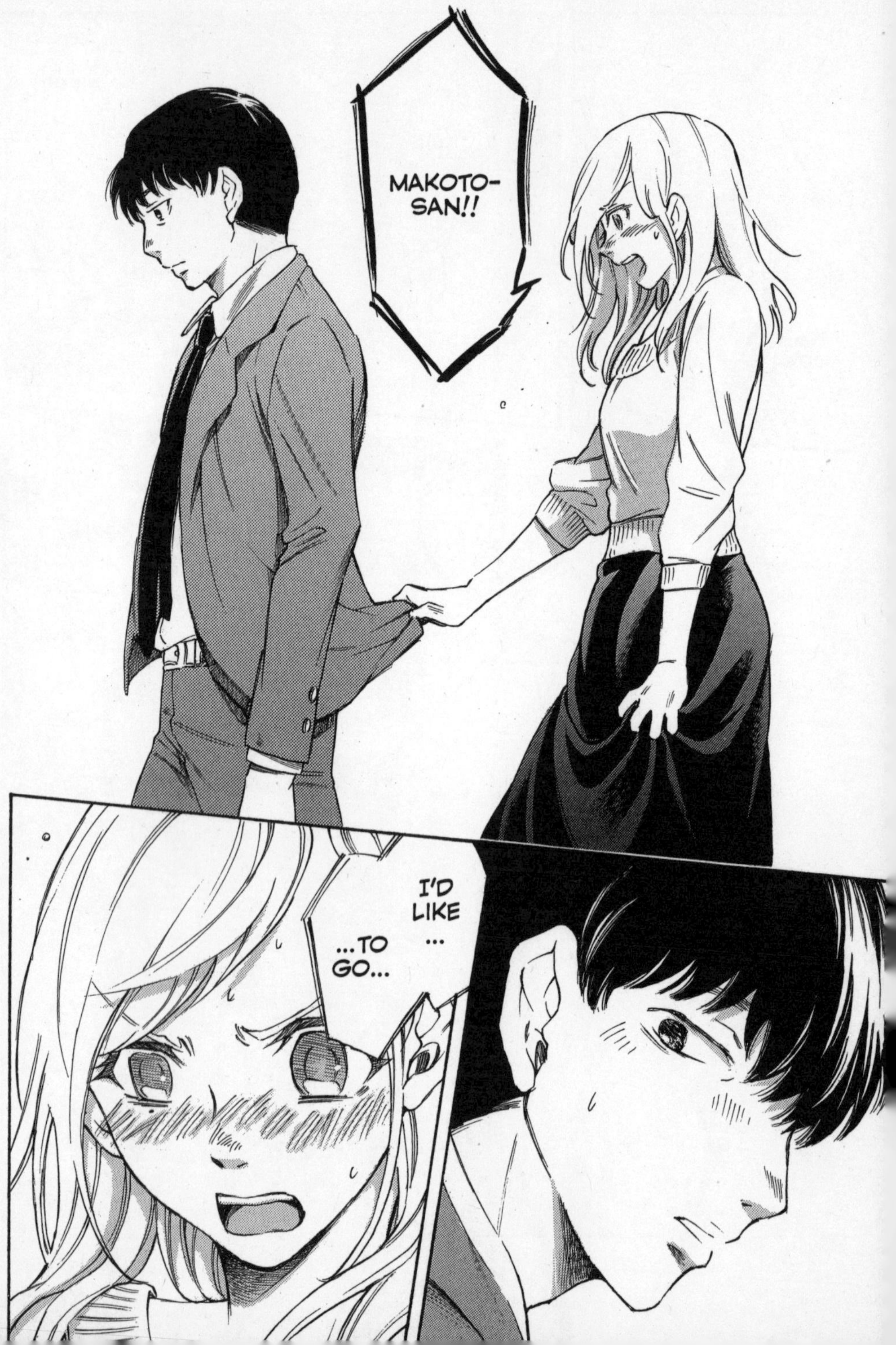
MAKOTO-SAN!!
I'D LIKE ...
...TO GO...

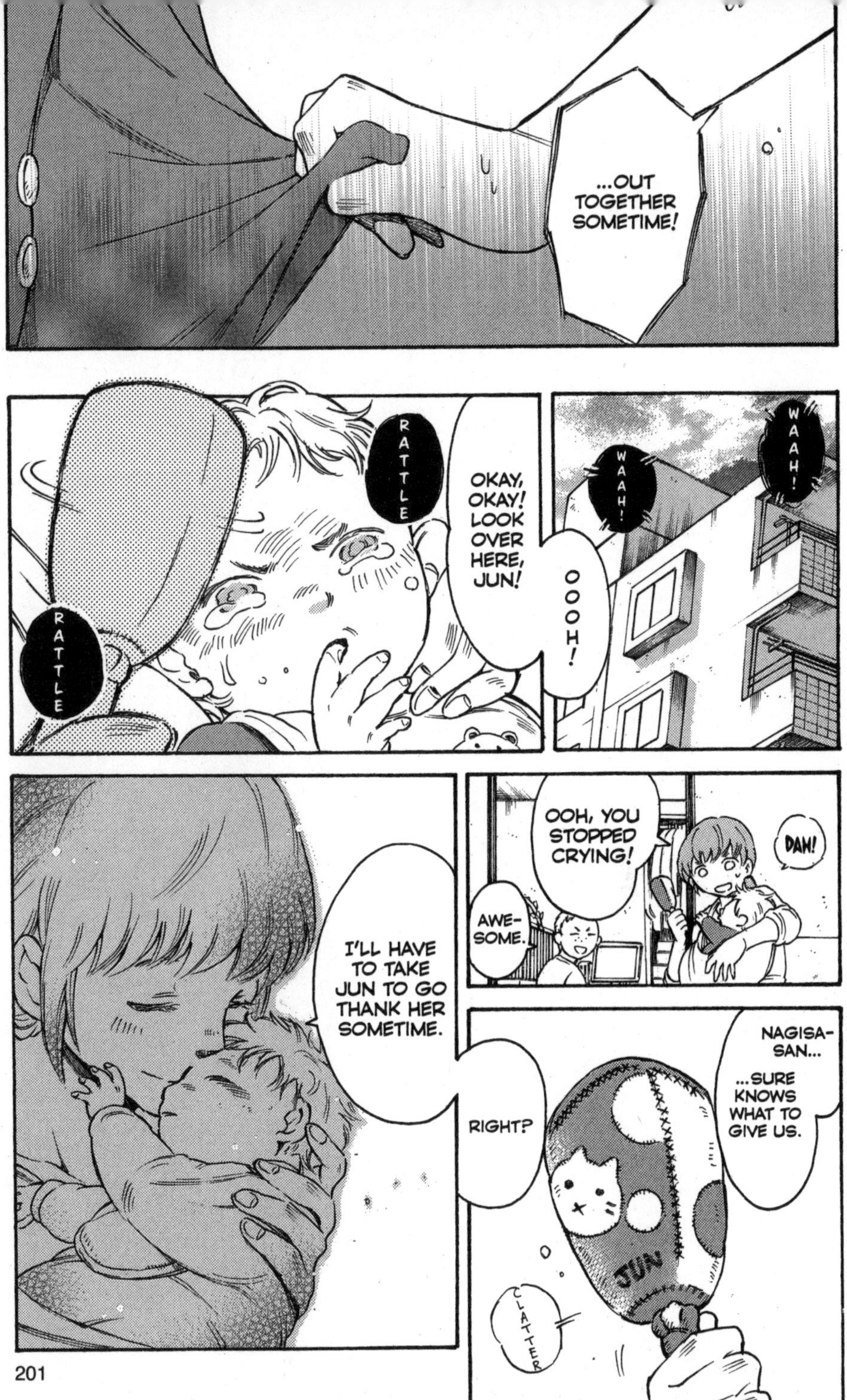

...OUT TOGETHER SOMETIME!
WAAH!
WAAH!
OOOH!
OKAY, OKAY! LOOK OVER HERE, JUN!
RATTLE
RATTLE
DAH!
OOH, YOU STOPPED CRYING!
AWE-SOME.
NAGISA-SAN...
...SURE KNOWS WHAT TO GIVE US.
RIGHT?
JUN
CLATTER
I'LL HAVE TO TAKE JUN TO GO THANK HER SOMETIME.

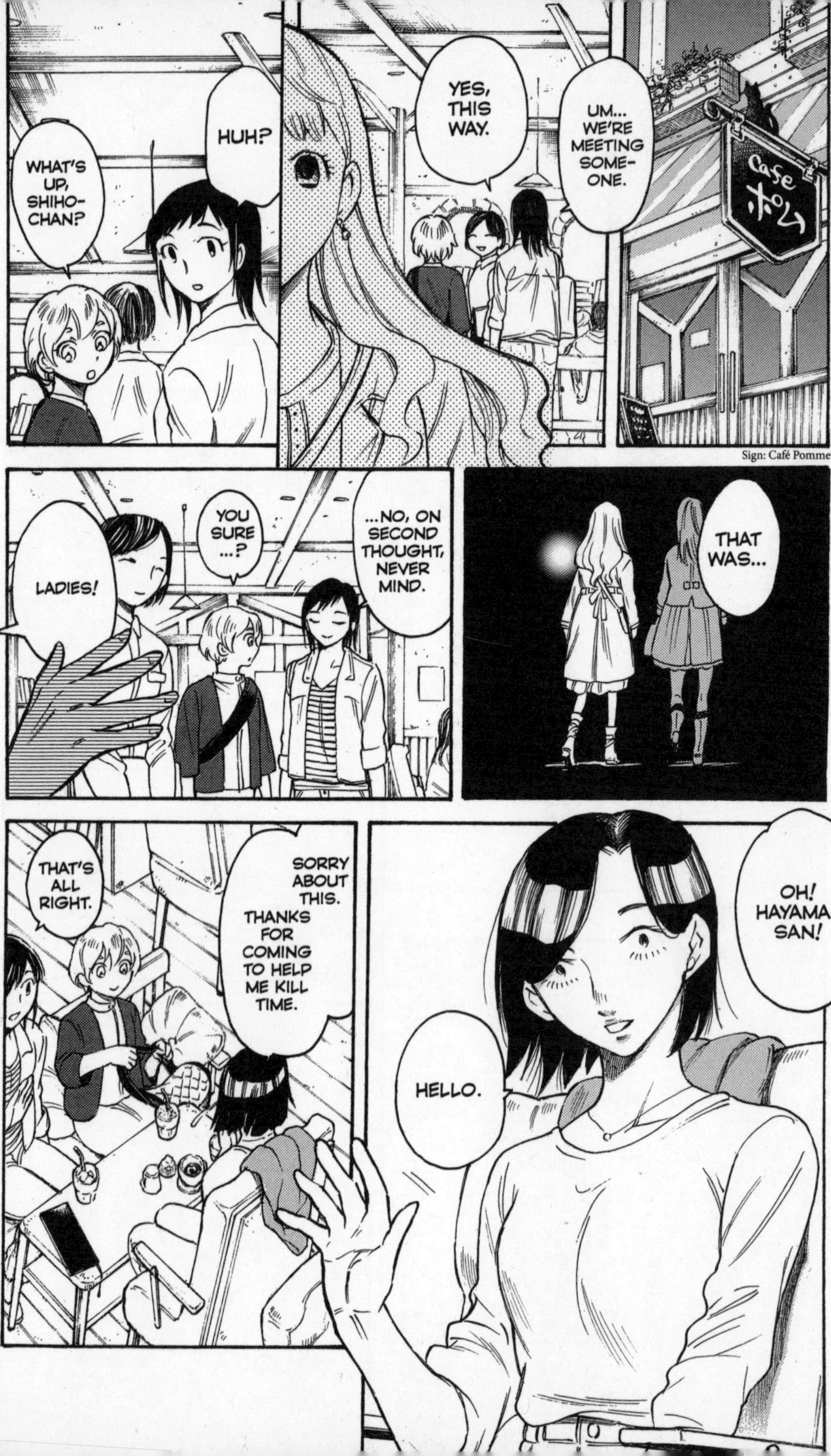
cafe ポム
UM... WE'RE MEETING SOME-ONE.
YES, THIS WAY.
HUH?
WHAT'S UP, SHIHO-CHAN?
THAT WAS...
...NO, ON SECOND THOUGHT, NEVER MIND.
YOU SURE ...?
LADIES!
OH! HAYAMA-SAN!
HELLO.
SORRY ABOUT THIS. THANKS FOR COMING TO HELP ME KILL TIME.
THAT'S ALL RIGHT.
Sign: Café Pomme

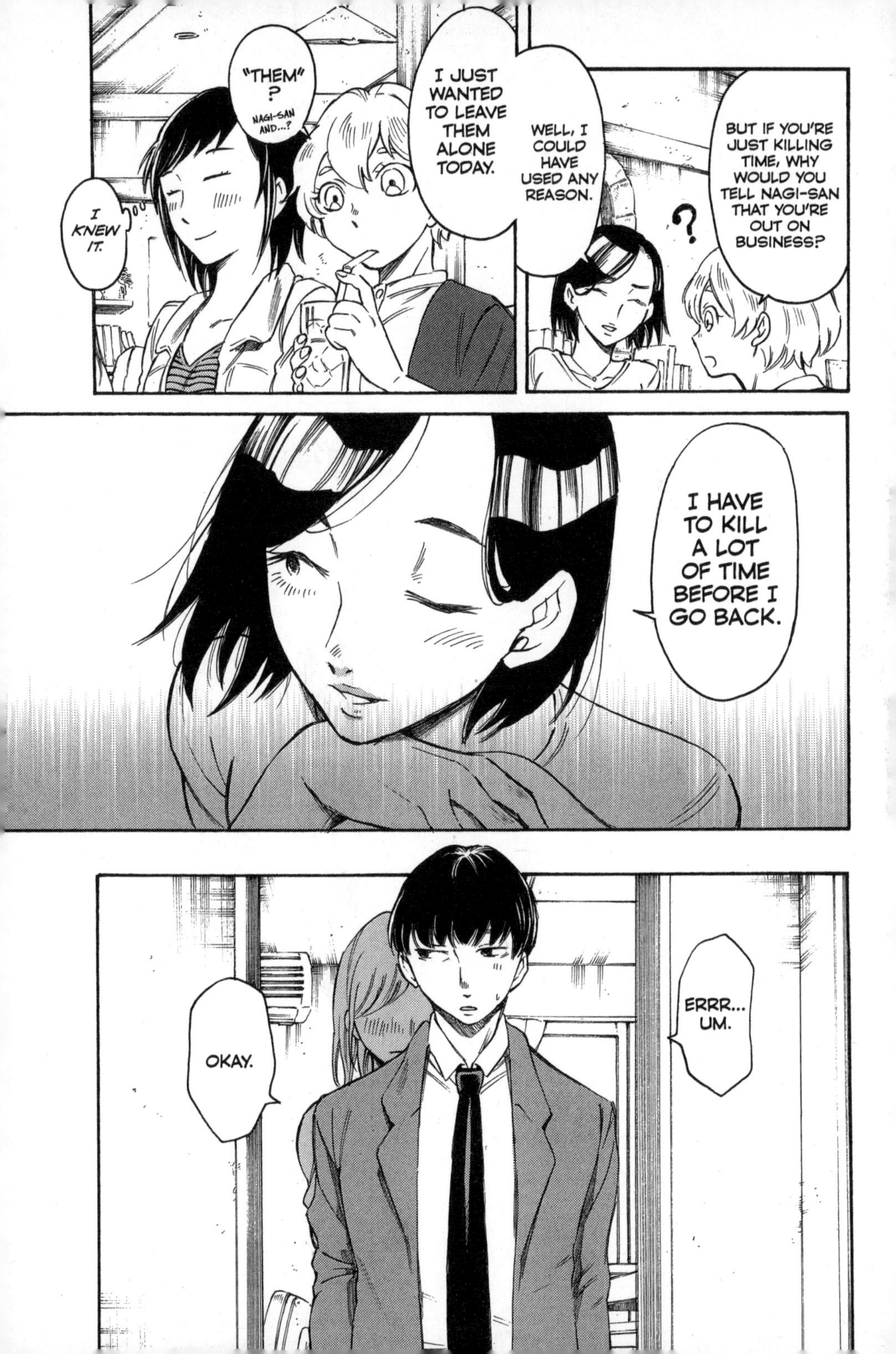
BUT IF YOU'RE JUST KILLING TIME, WHY WOULD YOU TELL NAGI-SAN THAT YOU'RE OUT ON BUSINESS?
?
WELL, I COULD HAVE USED ANY REASON.
I JUST WANTED TO LEAVE THEM ALONE TODAY.
"THEM"?
NAGI-SAN AND...?
I KNEW IT.
I HAVE TO KILL A LOT OF TIME BEFORE I GO BACK.
ERRR... UM.
OKAY.

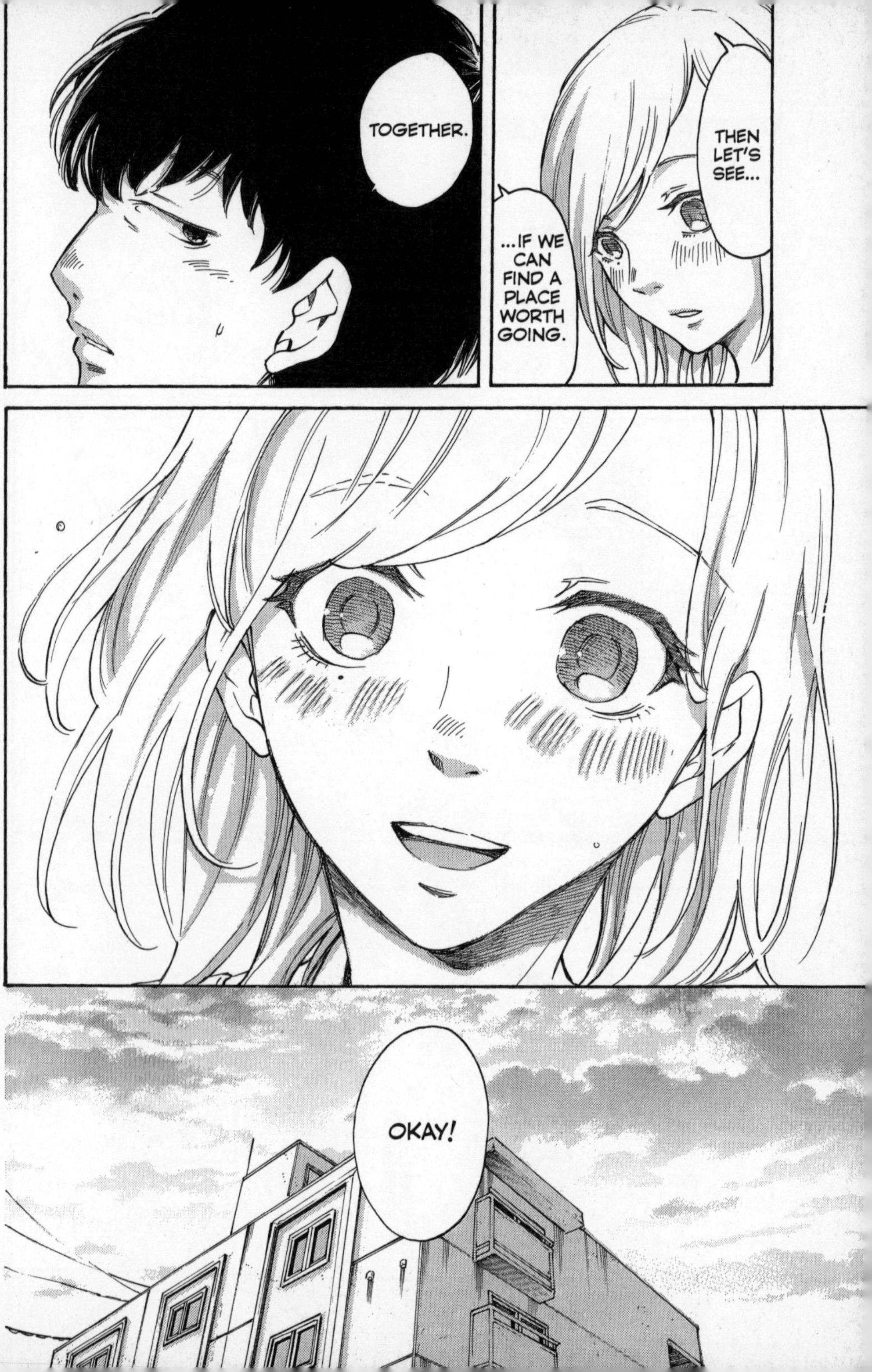
THEN LET'S SEE...
...IF WE CAN FIND A PLACE WORTH GOING.
TOGETHER.
OKAY!

Complex age.

REGULAR STAFF

RANA SATŌ
NAGOMU HARAGUCHI
AENA MIYASATO
YŌKO

EDITOR

KŌJI TERAYAMA
NATSUMI ŌMICHI

DESIGNER

KŌHEI
NAWATA

MIZUKI
NAKASHIMA

SPECIAL THANKS

TSUMA
SAKABA-SAN

LET'S
MEET AGAIN
SOMEWHERE.

WITH MANY,
MANY
THANKS.

fin.

Cospedia

[GLOSSARY OF COSPLAY TERMS]

Supervisor: コスプレイモード COSPLAY MODE

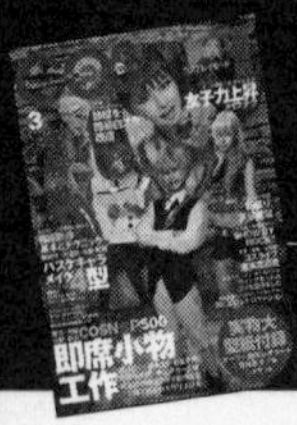
即席小物
工作

The cosplay magazine that has taken over the reins of Cosmode magazine, which ran until spring 2014. It publishes everything related to cosplay, including pinup photos, fan-submitted cosplay photos, and information on costumes, makeup, photography, armor and prop building, and cosplay culture. Released on the 3rd of every even-numbered month. (Published by Famima.com)

n.43

▶ Page 10
"A lot of enthusiasts my age wear kimono."
Japanese goth is coming into its own as a subgenre of gothic lolita (see Volume 2: Gothic Lolita), combining traditional Japanese style with gothic lolita. There's also the combination of Japanese style clothing and standard lolita, Japanese Loli. In March 2013, there was a Kaga-Loli fashion show, featuring traditional Japanese crafts by artisans such as Yūzen Kaga.

▶ Page 19
Antique Shop
A shop that deals in old furniture, old artwork, etc. A United States tariff act from 1934 defines an antique as "crafts, handicrafts, and works of art which were produced 100 or more years ago," and this definition has been adopted by the WTO (World Trade Organization). Incidentally, items that are fewer than 100 years old are referred to as "vintage" or "junk."

n.44

▶ Page 23
Shimokitazawa
There are numerous store-lined streets in

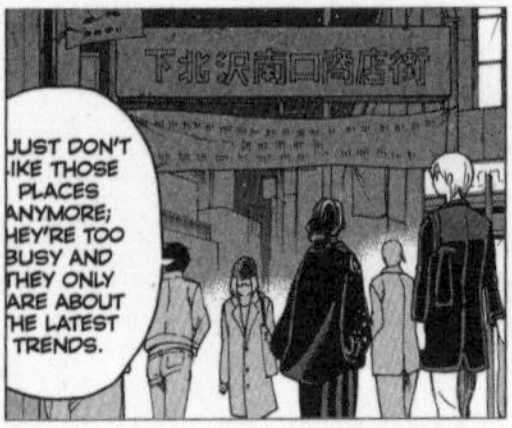
下北沢南口商店街
JUST DON'T IKE THOSE PLACES ANYMORE; HEY'RE TOO BUSY AND THEY ONLY ARE ABOUT HE LATEST TRENDS.

the neighborhood surrounding Shimokitazawa Station. Each street has its own unique features, and contains many variety shops and secondhand clothing stores. The district at the south exit has an especially high concentration of fashion and accessory stores. There are also several theaters and music clubs, so it is also known as Tokyo's theater town. Every year in February, several theaters get together to hold the Shimokitazawa theater festival.

▶ Page 28
Buyer
The person who buys all the products that are on display in the store fronts of retail stores, department stores, etc. The job doesn't require any special qualifications, but very few people jump into it with no experience. To use the apparel industry as an example, generally someone will get a job at a department store or shop, then, after gaining experience as a salesperson, they will become a buyer.

▶ Page 29
"I'm renting the space out to other people."
For those who want to perform retail on a small scale, there is great merit in renting a part of a store. Many people rent places through personal connections, but there are also stores that will rent out a few square decimeters, and internet services such as Nokisaki.com that will match renters and leasers.

n.45

▶ Page 46
"That's amazing, Aya-chan! You're in a magazine!"
Appearing in cosplay magazines, game magazines, anime magazines, etc. is a type of status symbol among cosplayers, and many layers have been known to improve their skills with that goal in mind. When a layer's picture is published in a magazine, some will post a picture of the page on their Twitter accounts or blogs.

▶ Page 50
Vacuum storage bags
A product that allows for compact storage of blankets and clothes by removing air from the bag. Some have a valve that lets the user suck the air out with a vacuum cleaner, while others have a check valve so the user can push the air out by hand. But a layer must be careful, because compressing fabric too much will cause it to wrinkle.

▶ Page 51
Wig stand
A product for storing wigs without flattening them. They are used to prevent tangles during storage, as well as for styling the hair. They come in a variety of styles, ranging from the 1,000-yen variety to the Styrofoam heads that can be found at the 100-yen shops. It is also possible to make simple ones at home using plastic bottles, etc.

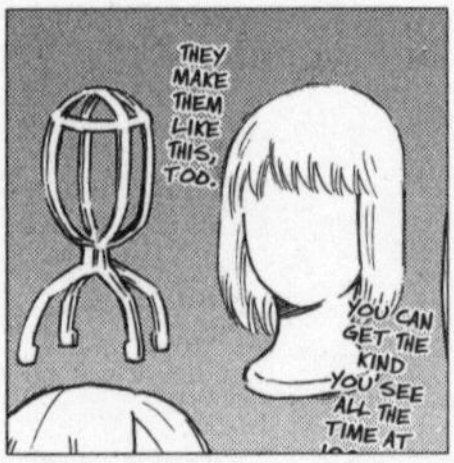
THEY MAKE THEM LIKE THIS, TOO.
YOU CAN GET THE KIND YOU SEE ALL THE TIME AT

n.46

▶ Page 74
Yuzawaya
A store chain that deals in craft and art supplies, established in Kamata, Tokyo in October 1955. Not only

The common practice is to include a photography ticket as an extra to go with purchases. When an attendee uses the photography ticket, he or she can take a picture of the layer at the event.

n.47

▶ Page 84
Circle
Short for *dōjin* circle. A group of like-minded fans. Almost all circles are formed among close friends and acquaintances. Once a

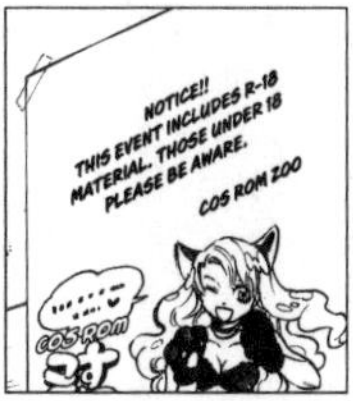
NOTICE!!
THIS EVENT INCLUDES R-18 MATERIAL. THOSE UNDER 18 PLEASE BE AWARE.
COS ROM ZOO

buying and selling handmade products, and opening the Yuzawaya Art School for people who wish to take their crafting to the highest level.

▶ Page 79
Cos Rom Market
Events for selling CD(DVD)-ROM discs of cosplay photos and videos. The many events are divided into the target age groups of all ages, R-15, and R-18. As the target age goes up, the amount of fabric in the costumes has a tendency to go down, but if taken too far, sales will be prohibited.

do they sell merchandise, but they also perform a wide range of business services involving handicrafts, including running the Yuzawaya Market web service for

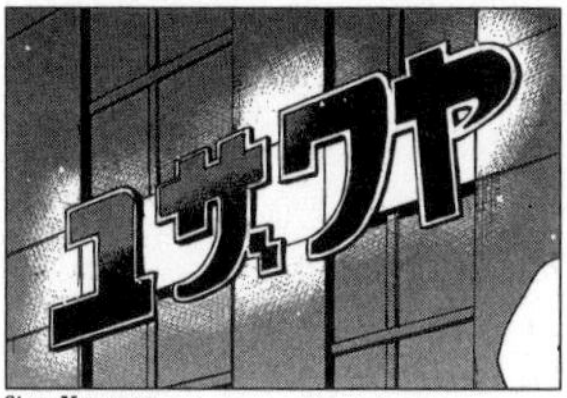
ユザワヤ

Sign: Yuzawaya

are these costumes lacking in durability, they come with other problems, such as the inability to go through the wash. Generally it is considered uncool to have visible tape on a costume, but when a layer's main goal is a studio photo shoot, the tape can be erased using Photoshop (see Volume 4: Photoshop).

n.49

▶ Page 123
Cosplay Cabaret Club
An establishment whose employees wear maid uniforms or character cosplay outfits while offering the same services as at ordinary cabaret clubs. Many of

talents who started out as cosplay models and went on to become celebrities. On the other side of the spectrum, there has been a dramatic increase in cases where students or otherwise employed people will be appointed as cosplay staff for a company as a part-time job.

▶ Page 90
"I see your tape."
By using packing tape, double-stick tape, staplers, etc., it is possible to construct a costume without a sewing machine, and in a shorter period of time. However, not only

group decides on a circle name, cosplay names (see Volume 1: Nagi-san!), and genre, they can make books and other goods to sell and participate in cosplay events as a circle.

▶ Page 87
Layer Model
Commonly known as a cosplay model. A professional cosplayer that works for a talent agency, and is expected to get as close to *kan-cos* ("perfect cosplay," see Volume 1: I am perfect) as possible for any character. There are also cosplay

▶ Page 151
"The dress took a lot of fabric."
Because many wedding dresses have very long skirts with two or more layers, they require a substantial amount of fabric. Incidentally, the gown that appears in this manga has what is called an Empire waist. Because the skirt falls from just under the bust, it easily hides the contours of the wearer's lower body to produce a natural look.

grilled beef
tongue was first served in Japan in Sendai in 1948, when Keishirō Sano, the founder of the Tasuke, was inspired by the beef tongue in Western cuisine and served it in his own restaurant.

▶ Page 144
"Nagi-shi!!"
The honorific -*shi* is mainly used for men, and is attached to a name as a term of respect. It is basically used only in writing, but there are people who use it in speech. It often appears in anime and manga as a very "otaku" way of addressing people.

them will sing karaoke anime or idol songs, and at some clubs, the employees and customers will dance along with the song.

n.50

▶ Page 143
Sendai beef tongue
Grilled *gyūtan*, or beef tongue, a Sendai delicacy. It is believed that

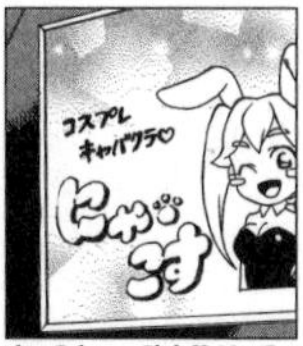

Sign: Cosplay Cabaret Club♡ NyaCos

▶ Page 169
Official License
Obtaining official legal permission to use characters from an anime or manga. In many cases, the licensing fee (royalties) is 3-5% of the sales price.

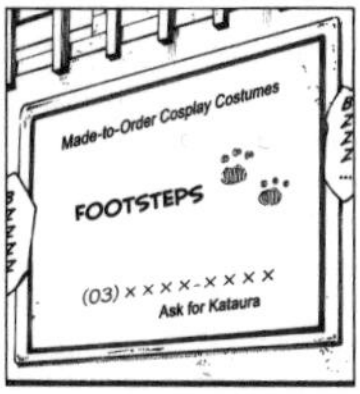
Made-to-Order Cosplay Costumes
FOOTSTEPS
(03) ××××-××××
Ask for Kataura

▶ Page 167
Fashion School
A school that specializes in fashion. Not only do students learn basic design concepts such as the production process, materials, color coordination, and sewing, but depending on the course, they can learn a wide range of other subjects, including makeup techniques, how to design accessories such as bags and hats, and how to be a buyer.

n.51

▶ Page 164
Made-to-Order Cosplay Costumes
Cosplay costumes that are made to order using anime, manga, etc. as reference. They are more expensive than store-bought costumes, but feature the abilities to choose size and fabric, and to obtain costumes for minor or original characters. In many cases, in addition to communicating with the seamstress via email and telephone, the customer can meet her in person to discuss the order.

Translation Notes

PAGE 15

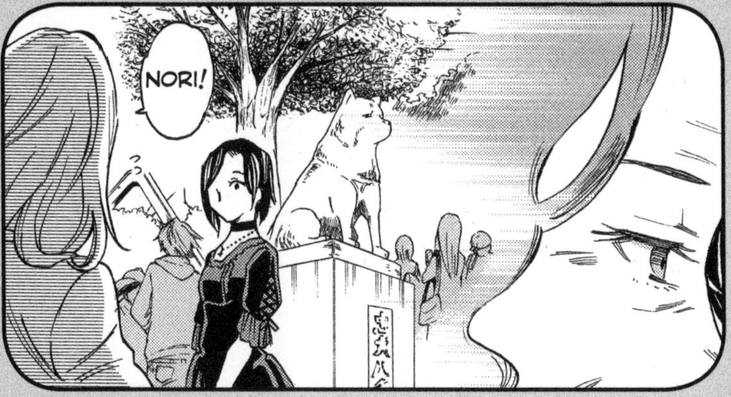
NORI!

LOYAL HACHIKO

This famous statue in Shibuya is dedicated to the loyal dog Hachiko, who came to the train station to wait for his master's arrival every day. When his master passed away while at work, and failed to arrive at the station, Hachiko waited, and returned to the station every day at the same time for nine years until his own death. In honor of his faithfulness, he has been immortalized as a bronze statue, which has become a popular spot to meet up with friends for a day in Shibuya.

PAGE 23

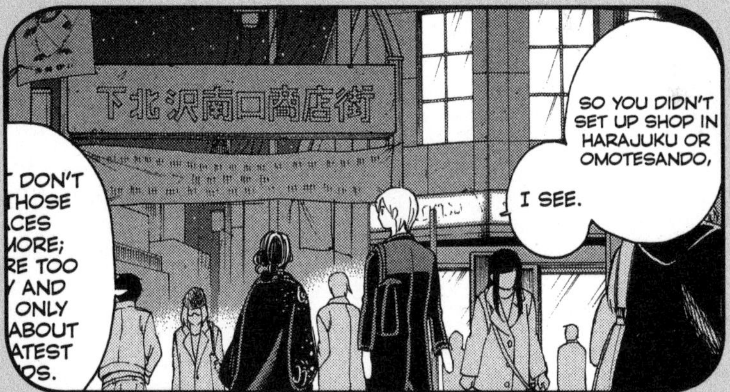
SO YOU DIDN'T SET UP SHOP IN HARAJUKU OR OMOTESANDO,
I SEE.
下北沢南口商店街

HARAJUKU AND OMOTESANDO

Both of the places Nagisa mentions are districts in Tokyo that are known for attracting the fashion-conscious. They are home to several big brand-name stores, as opposed to Shimokitazawa, which features mostly small, independent shops.

PAGE 44

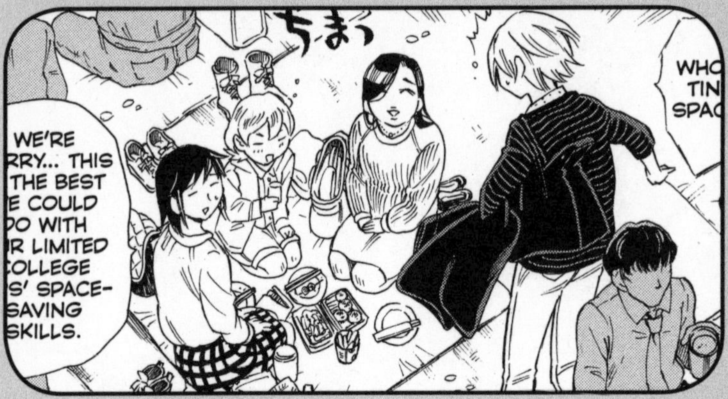
WHO
TIN
SPAC
ちまっ
WE'RE
RRY... THIS
THE BEST
E COULD
DO WITH
R LIMITED
COLLEGE
S' SPACE-
SAVING
SKILLS.

SAVING SPACE

Early spring is cherry blossom season in Japan, and everyone goes outside for a picnic to enjoy their beauty. So many people, in fact, that the parks are packed, and finding a place to lay out one's picnic can be quite a challenge. Aya and Shiho apologize for their lack of experience, which allowed them to find only a very small space.

PAGE 124

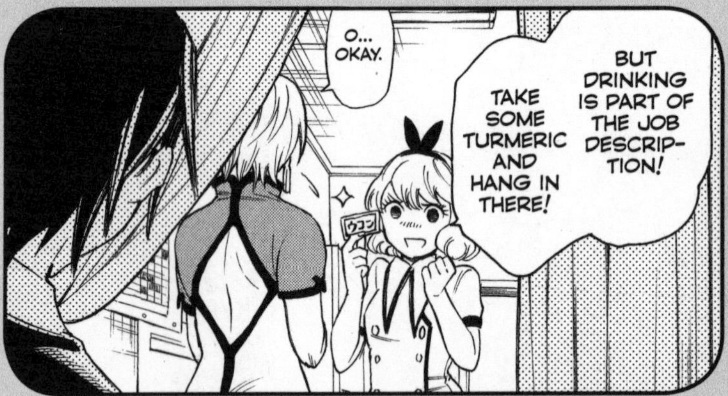
BUT DRINKING IS PART OF THE JOB DESCRIP-TION!
TAKE SOME TURMERIC AND HANG IN THERE!
O... OKAY.
ウコン

TAKE SOME TURMERIC

Turmeric is believed to be effective in preventing hangovers because it improves liver function. In fact, there is even a drink called *Ukon no Chikara* (the power of turmeric) which is specially designed for this purpose. However, Nagisa's coworker doesn't appear to be holding a drink, so she may be referring to simple turmeric.

PAGE 139

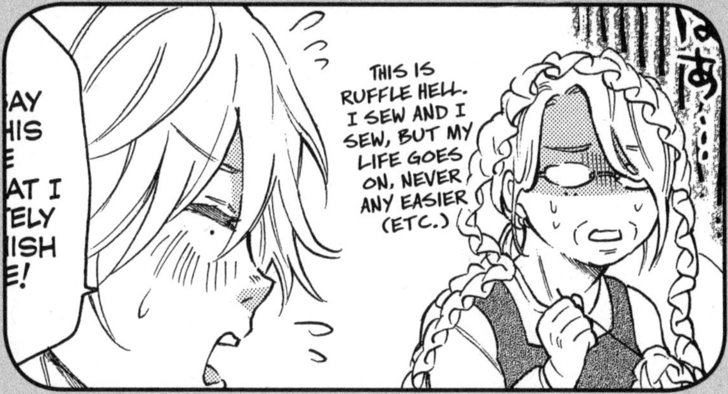
THIS IS RUFFLE HELL. I SEW AND I SEW, BUT MY LIFE GOES ON, NEVER ANY EASIER (ETC.)

LIFE GOES ON

This is a reference to a poem by Takuboku Ishikawa, which translates roughly to:

> I work and I work,
> And then I work even more, but my life goes on, never any easier.
> I merely stare at my hands.

The poem is the lament of a man who, although he works all the time, never manages to earn enough money to improve his situation.

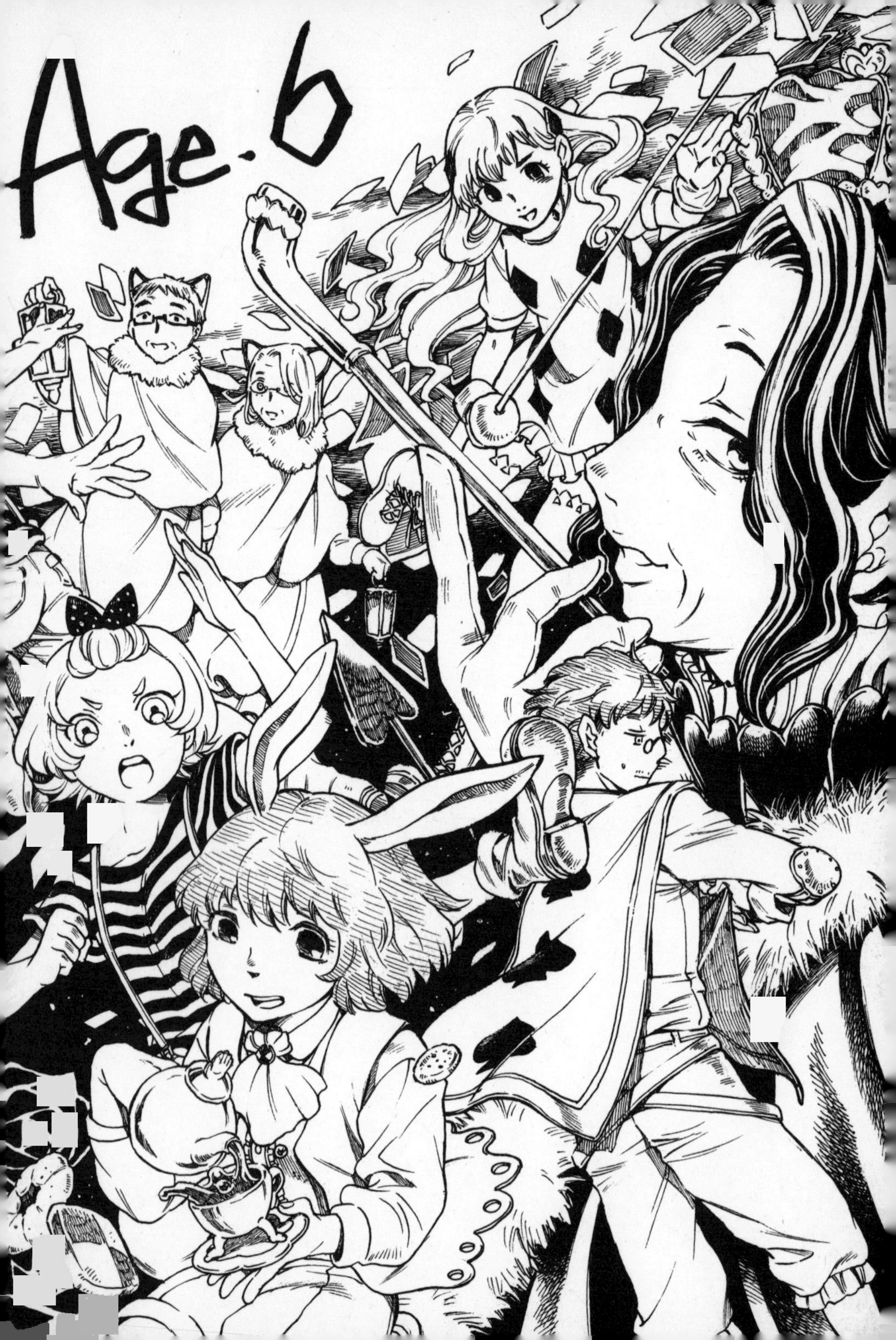
Age.6

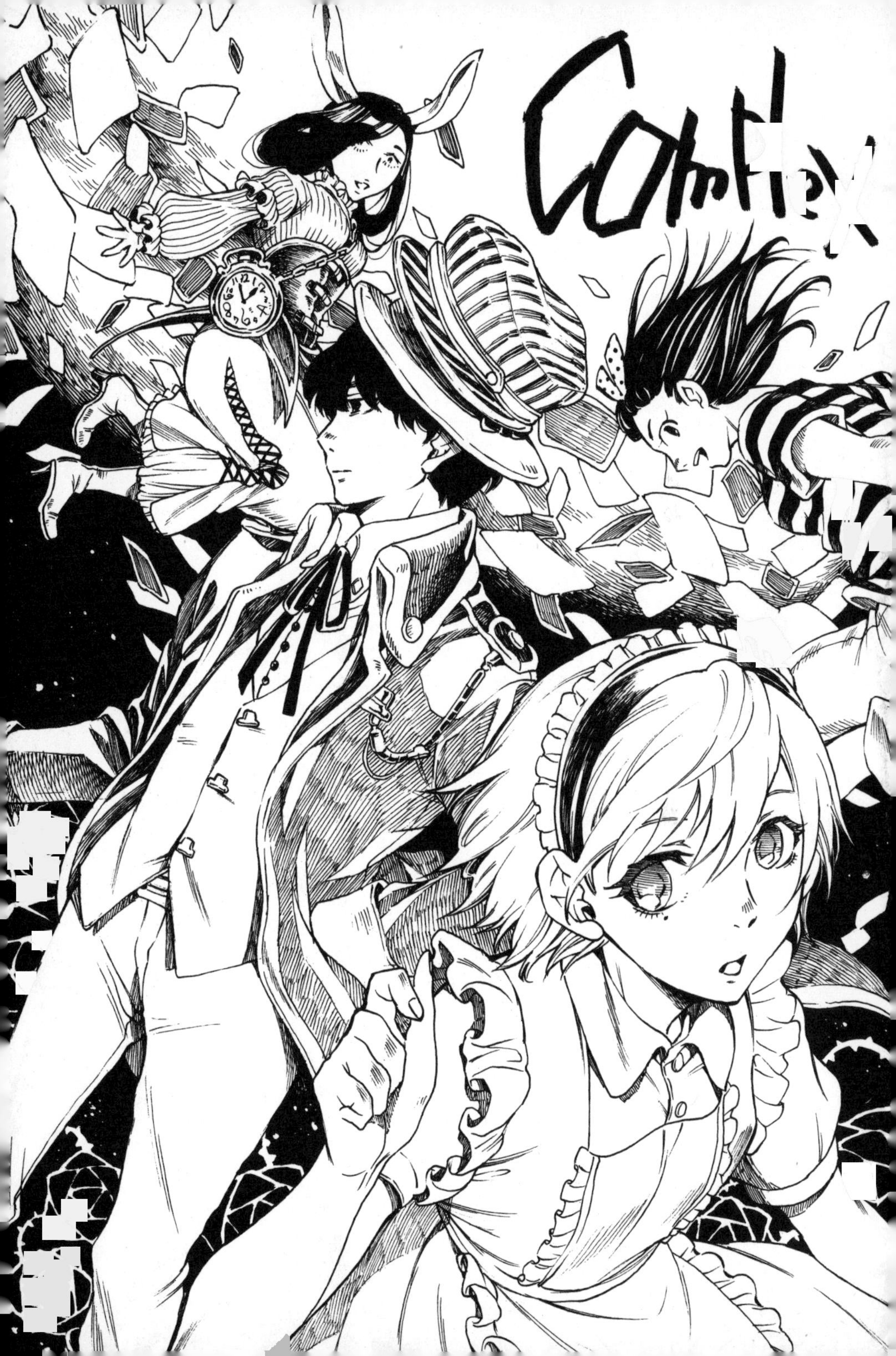

Japan's most powerful spirit medium delves into the ghost world's greatest mysteries!

Story by Kyo Shirodaira, famed author of mystery fiction and creator of *Spiral*, *Blast of Tempest*, and *The Record of a Fallen Vampire*.

Both touched by spirits called yôkai, Kotoko and Kurô have gained unique superhuman powers. But to gain her powers Kotoko has given up an eye and a leg, and Kurô's personal life is in shambles. So when Kotoko suggests they team up to deal with renegades from the spirit world, Kurô doesn't have many other choices, but Kotoko might just have a few ulterior motives...

IN/SPECTRE

STORY BY **KYO SHIRODAIRA**
ART BY **CHASHIBA KATASE**

KODANSHA COMICS

"I'm pleasantly surprised to find modern shojo using cross-dressing as a dramatic device to deliver social commentary... Recommended."

-Otaku USA Magazine

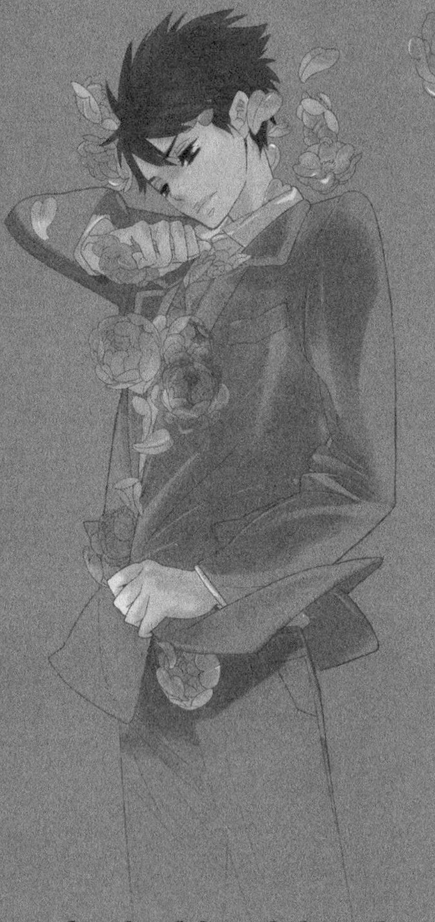

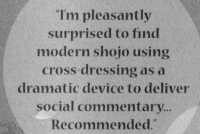

The prince in his dark days

By Hico Yamanaka

A drunkard for a father, a household of poverty... For 17-year-old Atsuko, misfortune is all she knows and believes in. Until one day, a chance encounter with Itaru–the wealthy heir of a huge corporation–changes everything. The two look identical, uncannily so. When Itaru curiously goes missing, Atsuko is roped into being his stand-in. There, in his shoes, Atsuko must parade like a prince in a palace. She encounters many new experiences, but at what cost...?

Based on the critically acclaimed classic horror manga

The first new *Parasyte* manga in over 20 years!

NEO ParaSyte f

BY ASUMIKO NAKAMURA, EMA TOYAMA, MIKI RINNO, LALAKO KOJIMA, KAORI YUKI, BANKO KUZE, YUUKI OBATA, KASHIO, YUI KUROE, ASIA WATANABE, MIKIMAKI, HIKARU SURUGA, HAJIME SHINJO, RENJURO KINDAICHI, AND YURI NARUSHIMA

A collection of chilling new *Parasyte* stories from Japan's top shojo artists!

Parasites: shape-shifting aliens whose only purpose is to assimilate with and consume the human race... but do these monsters have a different side? A parasite becomes a prince to save his romance-obsessed female host from a dangerous stalker. Another hosts a cooking show, in which the real monsters are revealed. These and 13 more stories, from some of the greatest shojo manga artists alive today, together make up a chilling, funny, and entertaining tribute to one of manga's horror classics!

KC
KODANSHA
COMICS

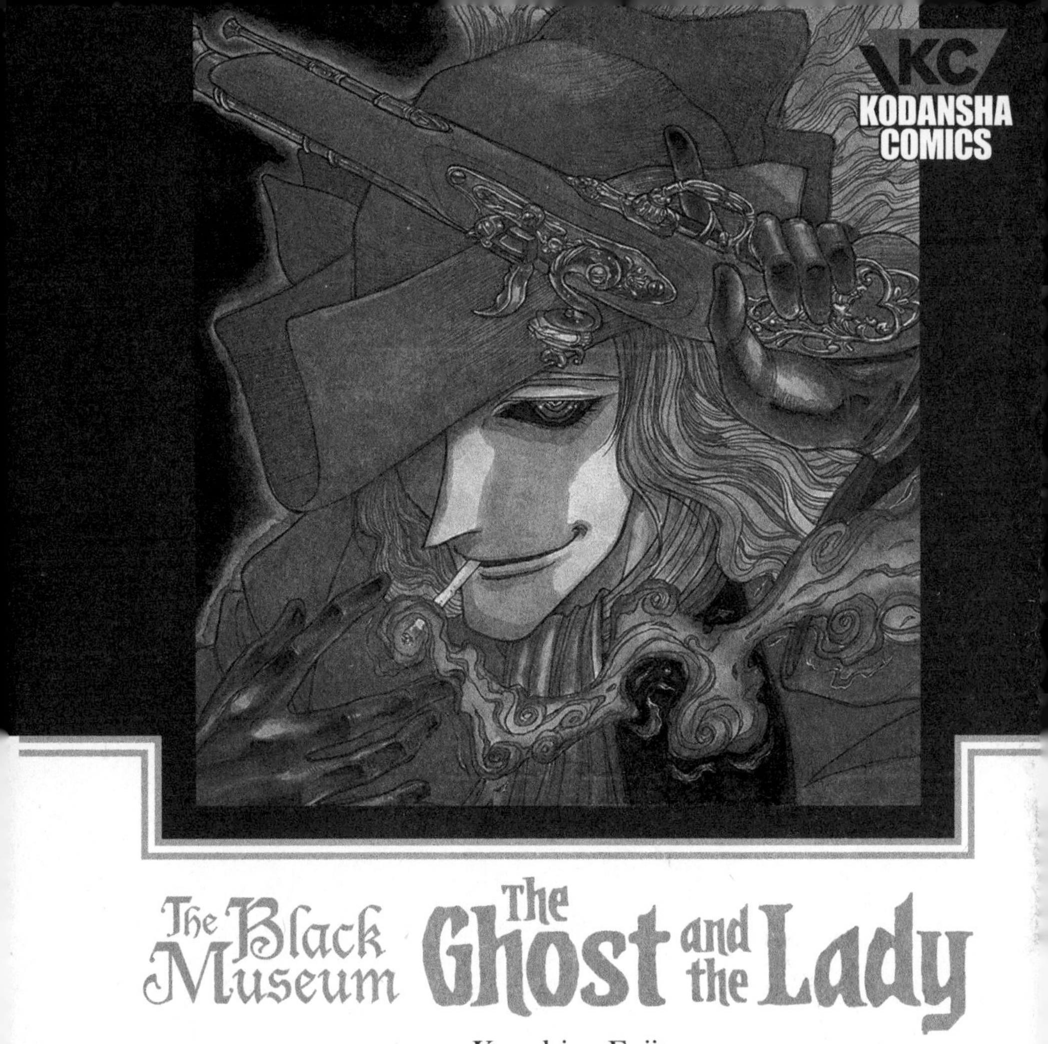

KODANSHA COMICS

The Black Museum: The Ghost and the Lady

By Kazuhiro Fujita

Deep in Scotland Yard in London sits an evidence room dedicated to the greatest mysteries of British history. In this "Black Museum" sits a misshapen hunk of lead—two bullets fused together—the key to a wartime encounter between Florence Nightingale, the mother of modern nursing, and a supernatural Man in Grey. This story is unknown to most scholars of history, but a special guest of the museum will tell the tale of The Ghost and the Lady...

Praise for Kazuhiro Fujita's *Ushio and Tora*

"A charming revival that combines a classic look with modern depth and pacing... **Essential viewing both for curmudgeons and new fans alike.**" — Anime News Network

"**GREAT!** The first episode of Ushio and Tora captures the essence of '90s anime." — IGN

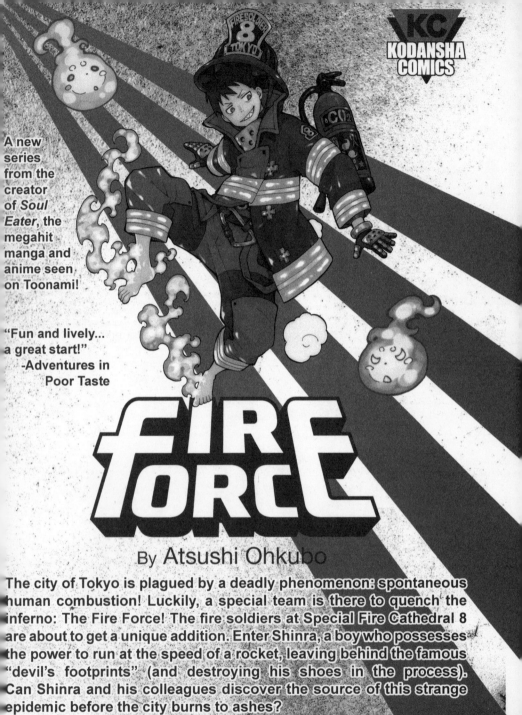

A new
series
from the
creator
of *Soul
Eater*, the
megahit
manga and
anime seen
on Toonami!

"Fun and lively...
a great start!"
-Adventures in
Poor Taste

FIRE FORCE

By Atsushi Ohkubo

The city of Tokyo is plagued by a deadly phenomenon: spontaneous human combustion! Luckily, a special team is there to quench the inferno: The Fire Force! The fire soldiers at Special Fire Cathedral 8 are about to get a unique addition. Enter Shinra, a boy who possesses the power to run at the speed of a rocket, leaving behind the famous "devil's footprints" (and destroying his shoes in the process). Can Shinra and his colleagues discover the source of this strange epidemic before the city burns to ashes?

HAPPINESS

—ハピネス—

By Shuzo Oshimi

From the creator of *The Flowers of Evil*

Nothing interesting is happening in Makoto Ozaki's first year of high school. His life is a series of quiet humiliations: low-grade bullies, unreliable friends, and the constant frustration of his adolescent lust. But one night, a pale, thin girl knocks him to the ground in an alley and offers him a choice. Now everything is different. Daylight is searingly bright. Food tastes awful. And worse than anything is the terrible, consuming thirst...

Praise for Shuzo Oshimi's *The Flowers of Evil*

"A shockingly readable story that vividly—one might even say queasily—evokes the fear and confusion of discovering one's own sexuality. Recommended." —The Manga Critic

"A page-turning tale of sordid middle school blackmail." —Otaku USA Magazine

"A stunning new horror manga." —Third Eye Comics

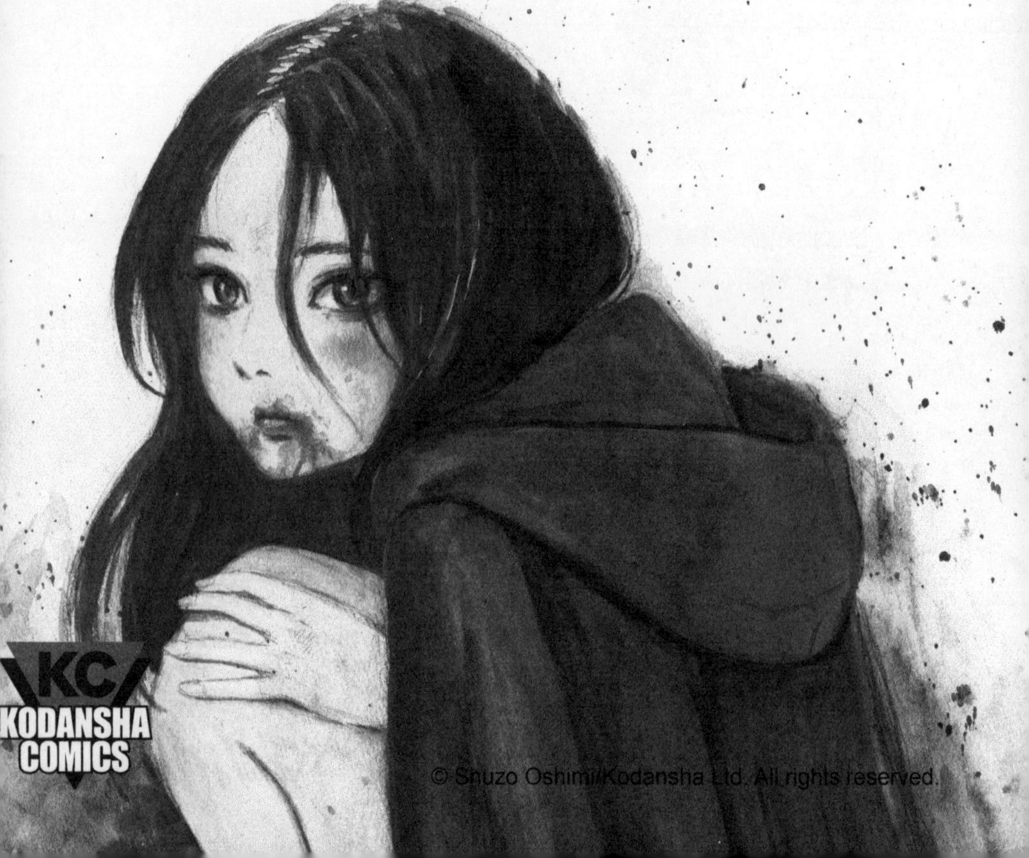

KODANSHA COMICS

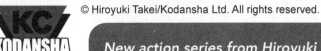

New action series from Hiroyuki Takei, creator of the classic shonen franchise Shaman King!

In medieval Japan, a bell hanging on the collar is a sign that a cat has a master. Norachiyo's bell hangs from his katana sheath, but he is nonetheless a stray — a ronin. This one-eyed cat samurai travels across a dishonest world, cutting through pretense and deception with his blade.

NEKOGAHARA

STRAY CAT SAMURAI

By
Hiroyuki Takei

Having lost his wife, high school teacher Kōhei Inuzuka is doing his best to raise his young daughter Tsumugi as a single father. He's pretty bad at cooking and doesn't have a huge appetite to begin with, but chance brings his little family together with one of his students, the lonely Kotori. The three of them are anything but comfortable in the kitchen, but the healing power of home cooking might just work on their grieving hearts.

"This season's number-one feel-good anime!" —Anime News Network

"A beautifully-drawn story about comfort food and family and grief. Recommended." —Otaku USA Magazine

sweetness & lightning

By Gido Amagakure

KC
KODANSHA
COMICS

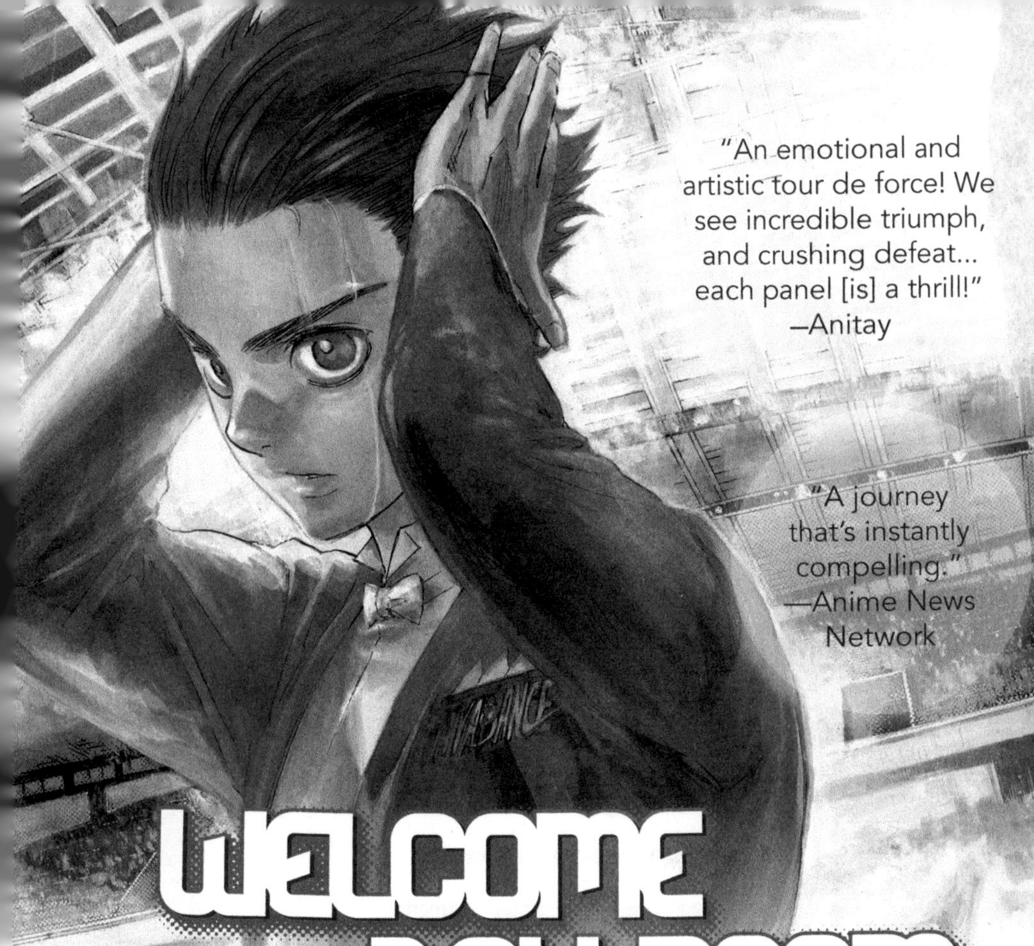
"An emotional and artistic tour de force! We see incredible triumph, and crushing defeat... each panel [is] a thrill!"
–Anitay
"A journey that's instantly compelling."
—Anime News Network

WELCOME TO THE BALLROOM

By Tomo Takeuchi

Feckless high school student Tatara Fujita wants to be good at something—anything. Unfortunately, he's about as average as a slouchy teen can be. The local bullies know this, and make it a habit to hit him up for cash, but all that changes when the debonair Kaname Sengoku sends them packing. Sengoku's not the neighborhood watch, though. He's a professional ballroom dancer. And once Tatara Fujita gets pulled into the world of ballroom, his life will never be the same.

KC KODANSHA COMICS

Complex Age volume 6 is a work of fiction. Names, characters, places, and incidents are the products of the author's imagination or are used fictitiously. Any resemblance to actual events, locales, or persons, living or dead, is entirely coincidental.

A Kodansha Comics Trade Paperback Original.

Published in the United States by Kodansha Comics, an imprint of Kodansha USA Publishing, LLC, New York.

Publication rights for this English edition arranged through Kodansha Ltd., Tokyo.

First published in Japan in 2015 by Kodansha Ltd., Tokyo, as *Complex*